Sports Betting

by Swain Scheps

Sports Betting For Dummies®

Published by: **John Wiley & Sons, Inc.**, 111 River Street, Hoboken, NJ 07030-5774, www.wiley.com

Copyright © 2020 by John Wiley & Sons, Inc., Hoboken, New Jersey

Published simultaneously in Canada

For general information on our other products and services, please contact our Customer Care Department within the U.S. at 877-762-2974, outside the U.S. at 317-572-3993, or fax 317-572-4002. For technical support, please visit https://hub.wiley.com/community/support/dummies.

Wiley publishes in a variety of print and electronic formats and by print-on-demand. Some material included with standard print versions of this book may not be included in e-books or in print-on-demand. If this book refers to media such as a CD or DVD that is not included in the version you purchased, you may download this material at http://booksupport.wiley.com. For more information about Wiley products, visit www.wiley.com.

Library of Congress Control Number: 2020904219

ISBN 978-1-119-65438-4 (pbk); ISBN 978-1-119-65441-4 (ebk); ISBN 978-1-119-65442-1 (ebk)

Manufactured in the United States of America

VFE9DA882-9AD1-423F-AB39-9E4C2EE27E0C_031220

Contents at a Glance

Table of Contents

CHAPTER 6: **Full Frontal Nudity (and Some Statistics and Probability)**

Foreword

By Norm Hitzges

Betting on sports is about looking forward, hoping to find clues or insights that will lead you to betting on the right side of a game. But good bettors also spend time looking *backward*, trying to figure out what clues they missed in yesterday's lost bet. When you spot those missed clues, your brain will whisper, "You're a dummy!" Try not to listen to that pesky brain.

If you're about to step tentatively into the sometime mystifying world of sports wagering, you must first understand one truism: No matter how long you work at it, sports betting will *always* provide moments where you'll feel like a dummy. Being wrong — sometimes badly, terribly, even *embarrassingly* wrong — is part of the deal.

And sometimes your luck will be so bad, you won't even be granted the dignity of merely being wrong! Often the bettor is done in by factors he or she has no control over, like injuries, weather, or — in the case of football — yellow handkerchiefs thrown by your fellow human beings at the worst possible times. Suffering *bad beats* (when the team you bet on gets an unlucky break, or somehow snatches defeat from the jaws of victory) is also a part of this hobby. You must accept them and move on as quickly as possible hoping that it all "evens out in the end." (That sentiment, while true, has never made anyone feel one bit better.)

Sports betting also involves work. Are you ready for it? Anybody can make a bet on a "hunch" and win a few bucks and have some laughs, but this isn't something you can dabble at if you expect to be consistently good at it. You'll need to study the sports betting marketplace, get comfortable with betting strategies and odds, find ways to research teams and players, and learn to keep good records. It takes time, patience, and no small amount of courage. (Did I mention those bad beats?)

So why do so many of us participate? Sports betting is *fun*. Not just game-of-Parcheesi-fun or go-to-the-movies fun. I'm talking about genuine *exhilaration*. Betting takes what you already love about sports to the next level. When you pick a winner, it can feel like you've solved a seemingly impossible riddle or uncovered a secret that nobody else knows. When you win a bet that all of your friends said you were crazy to make, it's a flavor of elation you won't soon forget.

So put aside your fear of being a dummy and start reading! Good luck, and I'll see you at the betting window. . . .

Norm Hitzges is a Texas Radio Hall of Fame member in his 45th straight year on the air in the Dallas/Fort Worth area. Norm is a veteran horse and sports handicapper and industry insider whose picks are offered every Friday as his acclaimed "Picks of the Pole" segment on KTCK (1310 AM / 96.7 FM, "SportsRadio 1310 The Ticket"). Norm also donates considerable time and energy to charitable work for many organizations, including the Austin Street Center and Texans Can Academy.

Introduction

L et's get one thing straight: Sports betting is an intellectual challenge with a tangible life-affirming, pocket-book-enhancing result at the end of each event (if all goes well). It's a test of your puzzle-solving skills. Can *you* find the hidden angle or discover some insight about the two teams on the field that the rest of the world missed?

In the old days, you'd have to travel to Nevada or have "a guy" if you wanted to bet on a sporting event. As the internet evolved, those with enough patience and tolerance for risk could pursue bets through offshore casinos. Thankfully, in this modern age, there are now a handful of states and Canadian provinces that permit sports betting. So if you're traveling to one of those regions, or if you're like me and you maintain an account with an online bookmaker, this is the book for you.

About This Book

If you've ever placed a friendly wager on a sporting event, then you understand the potential for fun. This book is going to explain the how the gambling market evolved for sports. I'll talk about the most common bets, the point spreads, the over/unders, the moneylines, the props, and the futures. I'll discuss how the sports betting market is constituted, and how you can participate.

In addition to the structure of the bet, I'll show you the step-by-step process for opening an account with an online bookmaker, and I'll show you how to read the menu of bets available at a casino or online bookmaker. I'll then show you how to recognize good bets and walk you through the process of placing a wager. My goal is to help you understand what you're up against, how you lose, and hopefully, how you win. Then I'll go sport by sport and talk about what it means to handicap a game, pick a winner, and bring home the bacon over the long run.

Las Vegas sports books have had one losing month over the last decade (July 2013, if you must know). Don't expect to stack money up by just throwing bets down on your favorite teams and players. Betting on sports is a process. Hobbyists are lucky if they break even. Professionals quit their day job if they can win 57 or 58 percent of their bets. I'll talk about why that's the case in this book, and I'll show you how you can emulate good bet-selection practices and payroll management.

But most of all, in *Sports Betting For Dummies*, I'm interested in putting you in a position to have fun. This is a hobby that can make you sing a song of joy and weep uncontrollably in the same day. Does that happen in your book club? Does stamp collecting invoke such highs and lows? Does golf? (Okay, maybe golf does.)

Many gambling books are built on assertions and platitudes, with little backing data. The point of this book is to not only provide you actionable strategies but to also build a foundation for you to find your own. I will help you learn how to interpret the betting market and how to assess betting propositions logically and quantitatively. I'll help you recognize when a tout is giving you a line of b.s. (can't curse in *Dummies* books), of which there is far too much of in this arena. I'll talk about the difference between something that's been asserted and something that has numbers behind it.

Sure, this book has "principles" and "rules of thumb" in spades. You'll learn lots of lessons and can be proud of yourself for that. But I also want to provide you with actionable intelligence. I'm holding nothing back: If I know a profitable approach to betting (like betting the home favorite the day after a double-header), I'm going to tell you about it. If I've learned bets to avoid, I'm going to tell you about them. I'm not only going to teach you to fish; I'm going to serve you some delicious sushi.

Gambling has its own private language, and sports betting has a sub-species of gamble-speak. This, more than the underlying concepts, can often be the biggest barrier to transitioning from a fan to a financially interested fan. So first and foremost, I'm going to demystify the language and basic concepts around sports betting.

Just so you know in advance, I'll set certain things apart in this book in specific ways so you know just what to do with the content:

>> When there's a new word, important phrase, or a term of art you should remember, I'll *italicize* it and define it.

>> There will be a chapter devoted to statistics and probability, and where a stand-alone equation is necessary, I'll explain each part to you.

>> Although it's not a requirement, there will also be references to Microsoft Excel functions and Excel VBA code. Most of it is in Chapter 16.

>> Different parts of the world have different ways of presenting odds to gamblers. I plan on using American odds notation.

Before You Go Any Further

The goal of the book is to instill you with the most useful 400 (or so) pages of information on sports betting. I'm going to promote beginners into functional sports betting dabblers. And I'm going to make knowledgeable gamblers out of dabblers. And if you think you're already more than just a dabbler, the book will introduce you to the full variety of popular sports and handicapping methodologies.

Having said that, it's not possible to cover every single opportunity to risk money on the outcome of a sporting event. There are so many sports and so many different kinds of bets out there. My goal is to focus on the sports you love, on the most accessible analysis methods, and on topics that I believe are the most underserved in libraries and bookstores today. If your "thing" is water polo or frog-jumping, or a sport or bet not covered in this book, I wish you much success, and I admit I won't have much to add.

So here are the topics that will either be lightly covered or downright ignored:

» Pari-mutuel betting (horse and dog racing, jai alai)

» Season-long fantasy sports

» Prediction markets (like betting on the Oscars or election results)

» Office pools (I will talk about placing bets on the Super Bowl and March Madness, but the focus will be on wagering, not winning goofy office contests.)

» E-sports

» Daily fantasy sports

The sports I've selected for this book are the ones most appealing to American and fans and bettors. If you're not a resident of North America, there is plenty in this book to help grow your understanding of sports betting in general and your approach to assessing and placing bets. But beware that if you have a specific sport you want to see addressed and it's not a sport that's terribly popular in North America, do yourself a favor and check the table of contents before embarking on this journey. I have no doubt that soccer, hockey, cricket, darts, handball, billiards, and bicycle racing are enthralling sports to watch and bet on, and I believe there are applicable lessons herein, but I'm sorry to say that I will not be specifically addressing those endeavors.

Foolish Assumptions

I can picture you, dear reader, reading this book. It was actually quite easy: When you ordered the book, your Alexa contacted my Alexa and told me everything about you. Here's what she told me, and here's the starting point for the book:

>> You're probably a dude. Research says when it comes to gambling activities, women prefer games based on luck, and men prefer games where skill is involved. It's a control thing. Given how much luck is involved in winning sports bets, you ladies should really give this hobby another look-see. This is a fun hobby, and if you're a person of the female persuasion, I'd like to offer a non-threatening platonic high-five welcoming you aboard. We could use more gender equality in terms of the bettors and so-called celebrity experts.

>> There's a distinct possibility that you are an avid fan of at least one major team sport; you might own a jersey with a spoiled millionaire's name on the back. If the team's any good, when their games are on TV, you cancel all plans, turn on your email "out of office" notification, and ask your significant other to find something else to do.

>> Let's not kid each other. If you're a North American, you love either college or pro football. You might gripe about somebody taking a knee during the anthem, but you're not gonna stop watching. And you likely have a secondary sport like baseball or golf that you'll watch as well. This book will devote a lot of pages to winning football bets because, well, do we have to keep talking about it?

>> You're a fantasy sports player. That makes you not only a fan but also a stat connoisseur. That's a good skill set to bring to the table. My guess is you get a little frustrated with the over-random nature of fantasy sports, which makes sports betting appealing to you.

>> I'd be willing to, er, bet, that you don't have a moral objection to gambling. You might even have a friend who regularly places bets, and you'd like to be able to converse intelligently about sports betting with him or her.

>> For sports you're less enthusiastic about, maybe it's tennis or baseball, you know, or at least suspect, that your level of fan intensity will rise exponentially if you have a dollar riding on the outcome. You've discovered the secret joy of sports betting (which is that a $1 wager can turn basket-weaving into the last episode of *The Sopranos*).

>> If you have some familiarity with the art and science of sports betting, you know there's more to learn, and you want to learn enough to keep your head above water. You don't mind losing a few bucks, but you'd rather win a few bucks.

>> If you are a regular sports bettor, you are looking for ways to bump up your winning percentage, or maybe you just want to expand your horizons and dig into more detail about sports you might not normally watch or bet on.

Icons Used in This Book

The icons are like little signposts to help readers recognize when critical information is about to come their way.

TIP

If you see this icon, I'm giving you some advice that's so on-point and important, you'll want to take note of it.

WARNING

There are all kinds of pitfalls when it comes to gambling in general and with sports betting in particular. If they can be summarized neatly and succinctly, I'll put this icon next to them so that you can avoid having something explode in your face.

REMEMBER

This book is full of facts and concepts that you'll want to commit to memory, so you'll see this icon next to those paragraphs.

Beyond the Book

This book comes with a free online Cheat Sheet that gives you some simple reminders of sports betting tenets, definitions, and even some standard odds you should keep in mind when you bet.

To get this Cheat Sheet, simply go to www.dummies.com and enter "Sports Betting For Dummies Cheat Sheet" in the Search box.

Where to Go from Here

If you're starting from scratch, and you don't know how sports betting markets work, what a bookmaker is, or how they make money, I suggest you start at the start and work through the chapters of Part 1.

If you know the basics but need a little refresher on some of the more advanced concepts related to sports betting, skip ahead to Part 2.

If you're a more experienced gambler and are interested in my approach to betting football, basketball, and/or baseball, you can head straight for Part 3 and beyond, where I'll discuss specific sports and ways to master the craft.

1

Sports Betting Basics

Get off to a fast start with sports betting by learning the essentials: how it works, why it's so popular, and what the law says about it.

Get a feel for the mechanics of a sports bet and learn some key terminology you'll need to know to move forward.

Assess yourself as a sports bettor and set some realistic goals for yourself.

If you need a refresher, read up on the most popular bet types so you can bet like a pro in no time.

Dip your toe into the basics of betting math and probability.

Get to know the organizations that post the odds and take your bets, and discover how to make your first sports bet.

Chapter **1**

Betting Sports for Fun and Profit

In some ways, sports betting is quite simple. You think one team is better than the other team, and you're willing to stake money on it.

But hidden beneath that easy-to-understand crust is the mantle of harder-to-grasp unpleasant truths. Lots of people lose lots of money at this endeavor. There are a million ways to bet. Your brain can sometimes be your worst enemy when it comes to betting. Once you start betting, it's hard to tell if you're any good at it. And there's the one undeniable truth that is so easy to forget: Teams do wacky, unpredictable things to confound every sensible prediction and make bettors pull their hair out.

That last truth is the first one I want to discuss. Because teams behaving in strange, unpredictable ways is something I experienced personally many years ago, and one game in particular started a fascination with this hobby that hasn't abated. It took place in October 1989. While the world was busy watching the Berlin Wall fall on CNN, I was doing something far more important: I was an end-of-the-depth-chart player on a football team about to have a slow-motion epiphany.

Eight Days in October

Naturally it was Friday the 13th. I looked it up recently: Friday, October 13, 1989.

I was a senior in high school and a proud member of the Grapevine High School varsity football team in Texas. I was the complete package: slow, weak, undersized, with almost a complete lack of athletic talent. Lucky for everyone involved, the coaches were wise enough to keep me far from the field on gameday. But that gave me a great vantage point for what was about to happen.

A surprise win

Memory is tricky, but here's my version of the events: The Grapevine Mustangs were 3–3 with 4 games left in the season and an outside chance at a playoff berth. Coach Snead, who would go on to win two state championships, had been telling us all week that we were better than our record indicated. We needed the confidence boost because we were about to face the 800-pound gorilla of the district, the Euless Trinity Tigers. Gorilla is an understatement. These guys were King Kong. They kicked our asses every year. In 1989, they were undefeated, well coached, confident, and clearly outmatched us at every position. Their quarterback was even dating the homecoming queen from our high school. Our goal was to avoid complete embarrassment. Winning wasn't a thought in our minds.

But it was Friday the 13th, after all. Strange things happened. On the opening drive of the game, the Trinity quarterback faked a handoff to the dive back, reverse-pivoted on the bootleg and ran smack into not one of our players but the *referee*, fumbling away the football. That lucky break was followed by another, and before we knew it, we were ahead. Then the guys actually started to play well — really well. We uncharacteristically caught every ball and made every tackle. We got every lucky bounce and every lucky call. It was like Bishop Pickering's miracle golf round in the rain in *Caddyshack*. And when the final whistle blew, we had beaten the gorilla by a gaudy 53–7 score.

53–7? The team, the fans, and even coach Snead were in shock.

Victory's revenge

So we did what teenagers do: We celebrated. Starting with the dogpile on the field at the end of the game, to the bus ride home, into the weekend. We just finally figured it out, right? We must be way better than we thought we were all along. There were so many broken arms from patting ourselves on the back that the training staff had to order more slings.

You can probably tell where this is going.

Our midseason celebration ended about three seconds after the opening whistle of the following week's game, played at home against the worst team in the district. In our 53-to-7 euphoria, we forgot we had to, you know, show up and play in the last three games of the season. The cliché fairy summarily revoked our "David Beats Goliath" status and put us into "Chickens Coming Home to Roost" mode. We looked like the Bad News Bears (from the early part of the movie, not later on when they went to the Astrodome and Walter Mathau starting believing in them). We were lazy and sloppy in every aspect of the game, just as we had been in practice all week, and lost that game to an "inferior" opponent. Playoff dream: dashed.

But in retrospect, there was something totally inevitable about that eight-day roller-coaster that ended in that ignominious crash-and-burn. We "overlearned" from the positive outcome of one week and formed a collective illusion that we could beat anybody without trying. It wasn't the fault of any single player or a coach; it was something that emanated from within every member of the team. We had just a little less focus in practice than normal. We were late getting to our spots. We ran a little slower; we cadillacked our way through the toughest drills. We held each other less accountable in practice as if we all had a tattoo that said "It's all good . . . we beat Trinity 53–7."

My acne-splotched, mullet-topped team in 1989 could have won the state championship if we played every game like we did the night of October 13, and with the same level of measurable talent and the same coaches, ten repeats of our October 20 performance would have led to a winless season.

Finding profit in the roller coaster

In college, I got interested in sports betting, and I did so with the lessons of October 1989 firmly in my mind: Not the lesson where freedom triumphs over tyranny in Eastern Europe, but that talent and measurable attributes only determine part of what happens on the field of play.

A team's personality can vary wildly from one week to the next because athletes are not robots (*not yet*, at least). They have memories. They have biases. They're superstitious. They react to things that happen to them. And while none of those things are easily measurable, they can show up at game time, in the same way that the 1989 Grapevine Mustangs reacted to their big win, and lay an egg.

And so for three decades, I've looked for, and sometimes found, those patterns across sports. My approach to sports betting is based on the essential premise that people and teams react predictably to events like winning, losing, surprise, disappointment, travel, breaks, and so on. From that basic proposition, I've added a little bit of mathematical rigor, some knowledge about the forces that push and pull betting markets, and an appreciation for the value of other approaches to the craft, whether it's information-based, stats-based, or something in between.

Today more than ever, the truth is out there and only a click or two away. I spent countless hours creating a database of sports scores and statistics from scratch on my ancient computer. That same information that I painstakingly collected is available today from dozens of web resources. Today's bettor can take advantage of astonishing quantities of detailed, esoteric historical sports data. And for the more enthusiastic gamblers, tools are out there to study and bet on any pattern they can dream up.

If you're a fan of a given sport and can match team patterns with analyses of personnel and schemes, all the better. There are two basic approaches to picking winners: numbers driven, or technical analysis, and information driven, or fundamental analysis. There is no one formula for success. What makes it fun and challenging is that you'll mix cold, hard facts with touchy-feely interpretations of human behavior. You'll need computer power as much as you'll need the coach's chalkboard and the psychiatrist's couch. You'll want to read Turing, Lombardi, *and* Freud.

Do Sports Bettors Win?

Is this a trick question? If not, the answer is: Some do; some don't. Cool?

If you're familiar with betting on table games at the casino, you know in the long run, you'll lose. Period. The probabilities associated with cards, dice, and the little bouncing ball on the roulette wheel mean the aggregate outcome is not in doubt. Narrow your focus to a single lucky person, or a single weekend in Las Vegas, or a crazy craps table, and it seems like there are winners everywhere. But the math makes it a physical certainty that the more people play, the longer they play, the more certain it is the gamblers are going down.

But sports betting is different. The sports bettor reads a menu of available bets at the bookmaker and decides whether or not to risk some of his bankroll on a certain outcome. The bookmaker makes predictions on games too, but they can't read the future.

Short of doing something the casinos would frown upon, the greatest blackjack, craps, and roulette players in the world will lose money at those games if they played forever. Sports betting is under no such stricture. Unlike table games at the casino, there is no physical or mathematical law that says, without a doubt, you will lose money gambling on sports. You just might be that unicorn who can spot those Grapevine-beats-Trinity moments better than anyone else in the world. The fact that you're not destined to lose is a start! It's something that should give you hope — just not too much.

REMEMBER

The conventional wisdom you'll inevitably hear is that most people lose betting sports. And when I say "most," I don't mean half the world wins and half the world loses. I mean many, many more lose than win. But since there are no mathematical certainties here as there are with cards and dice, we have to get *empirical.* That is, let's see what evidence and experience can teach us.

First off, I want to make it clear. If you asked 50 people in line at a sports book if they were ahead or behind in their lifetime of sports bets, all 50 would say they were ahead. As I'll discuss in Chapter 15, it's easy to lose track, and our brain tends to play tricks on us in terms of calculating wins and losses. So simply asking people to self-report results is a nonstarter when it comes to sports books.

Research on data pulled from a prominent European sports book a few years ago showed that only 10 to 15 percent of bettors were ahead a year after making their first deposit. A big swathe of people had lost a little, and there was a long tail of people who had lost their initial deposit plus money from subsequent deposits. But this data isn't satisfying to me; it's not clear that these gamblers didn't lose their money some other way besides sports betting. I don't think it follows that a given bettor only has a 15 percent chance of winning.

Another source of data is tightly controlled sports betting contests, where entrants must make regular picks on sports events as if they were bets. When gamblers can't shade the odds or misreport, you get a much better glimpse of the possibilities.

Have you ever tracked sports writers in a newspaper picking weekly games? There's a sports picks contest in nearly every (remaining) major newspaper. My own hometown rag is *The Dallas Morning News,* and in the last few years, they've asked local sports media to make virtual bets on football games throughout each week of the season. In spite of being plugged into sports news, of the eight pickers in *The Dallas Morning News,* only a few were above 50 percent, and only a single sports writer was in profitable territory (north of 52.38 percent, a number I'll discuss in later chapters). Maybe 15 percent is accurate after all.

Another example is the world-famous Station Casinos SuperContest Gold. Every football season, sports bettors flock to this exclusive winner-take-all contest for a $10,000 entry fee. Each contestant has to make five NFL picks every week against a menu of standard odds. These are folks so confident in their abilities to pick winners that they're putting up 10 grand to prove it. In the 2019–2020 contest, there were 42 contestants who would have showed a profit if they had been betting an even amount on each game. And there were 74 who weren't.

These contest results should tell you a few things: First, the contest winner picked games at a seemingly modest 61 percent. Believer it or not, that's an exceptional win/loss rate for sports betting. So set aside your delusions of grandeur. The luckiest, most talented pickers barely sniff the 60s. Second, the combined average of these 100-plus bettors was about 48 percent winners. We could interpret this outcome to mean there are a lot of skill-free sports-betting hobbyists with $10,000 to spare, or it could mean that it's just really difficult to pick winners over the course of a season. So you might take heart in the fact that one-third of these contestants were able to pick profitably. Or you might despair at the two-thirds who couldn't. Either way, my goal is to implant you with a simple idea: This is not easy, but it's also not impossible. Winning is within the grasp of a bettor who is willing and able to put the time in.

TIP

Pro gamblers will tell you that 55 percent wins is the day-job line. If you can beat 55 percent on a year-in, year-out basis, you can quit your day job in favor of sports betting. Sounds great right? Unfortunately, the odds are against you. It takes dedication to the craft and special talent to get to that level. That's why there aren't many people who can claim to make a living off of sports betting today. The sweet spot between 52.5 percent and 54 percent is a much more realistic goal for readers of this book. It might not sound sexy, and you won't be able to quit your day job, but maybe you can have some fun and make a little money along the way.

The Wagers of Sin

In a landmark decision in 2018, the U.S. Supreme Court finally released Americans from the shackles of earlier legal decisions that prevented them *legally* from doing something that is so common and comfortable that millions of us were already doing it. I'm not exaggerating about that number. If you count fantasy sports and office pools, there are tens of millions of people who have money riding on the outcome of an athletic event. It's a multi-billion dollar market, and it's growing.

Table 1-1 shows what UNLV Center of Gaming Research says the sportsbooks in Nevada have been doing for the last 25 years (while the other 49 states were looking on in envy) . . . and that's just the *legal* bookmakers.

TABLE 1-1   ## Sports Betting Revenue in Nevada

Total Bet on Sports in Nevada (1984-2018)	$87 billion
Football	$31 billion
Basketball	$21 billion
Baseball	$16 billion
Other Sports/Multi-sport Wagers	The rest

Betting on sports has its dark side, which I'll discuss later in this chapter. There's the possibility of corruption, and there's the addictive nature of gambling, and more. But for the majority of people who partake, betting on sports is not only fun and entertaining, but it borders on the sublime. Why? Athletic competition and gambling are practically written into our DNA.

For students of American history, the banning and subsequent unbanning of sports betting has echoes of the Volstead Act and the Prohibition Era. Nobody would claim alcohol consumption is good for your health, but to suddenly disallow a habit already so, er, engrained, in so many millions of people looks in retrospect to be ludicrous. With all of the undeniable problems that came along with alcohol consumption in early 20th-century America, its blanket prohibition not only didn't provide a solution, but it introduced its own set of problems.

Fans and Bettors: Better Fans

It's been proven by sociologists that it doesn't take more than a few dollars to increase the intensity of interest and emotional investment while you're watching a game. At the same time, that instinctive drive to bet as an enjoyment multiplier leads many people to bet from the hip. Betting instinctively certainly has its place. You might win; you might not. But if you care whether you win or not, you'll take some time to learn about the dynamics of the betting markets. You'll probably find that your prognostications get more accurate, and your wallet gets fatter (or at least less thin).

Chances are, you're not going to be able to quit your job based on your sports betting winnings. That's not the goal of this book. But if you treat sports betting as a *hobby* with a *chance* for monetary reward, you'll find a small investment of time and knowledge can pay you back over and over in terms of enjoyment . . . and maybe profit!

Sharps and squares

A vocabulary of convenience has grown up around sports betting that I'll use in this book repeatedly. You know how it works: As with any hobby, the vocabulary you use is a passport to respectability. There's a lingo with computer programmers, stand-up comics, golfers, yoga instructors, and every other hobby, sport, craft, and profession.

REMEMBER

Your first lesson in lingo is a pair of terms: *sharp* and *square*. Both words serve as both nouns and adjectives. A sharp is an experienced, discriminating sports bettor who wins money in the long run. And no, a square is not the only person at the high school party who refuses to break the rules for fear of getting caught. In this world, a square is an average member of the betting public. Most people are squares. We're all a little square sometimes.

If you're sensing judgmental undertones in the word, you're not wrong. To be square is more than just being unprofitable in the long run; it's about running with the herd. Being square also means that you not only are ignorant of but you also misinterpret and misunderstand key concepts in sports betting — to the detriment of your bank account.

(By the way, if you're looking for geometrical logic in these terms, you're not going to find it. Squares have 90-degree angles. I hit my head on the corner of a square table when I was a kid and it felt pretty sharp to me.)

In Figure 1-1, I attempted a Venn diagram of the betting population, but instead of circles and ellipses I used squares and triangles as an attempt to match the terminology. It's like a Cezanne masterpiece, except better, right?

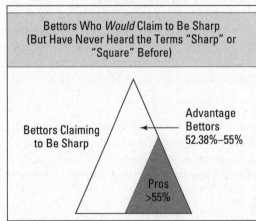

FIGURE 1-1:
Sharps versus
squares.

Do you track what's happening here? Bettors who know the word will always claim to be sharp. If you're sensing some b.s. in the sharp-versus-square distinction, you're probably onto something. Nobody *claims* to be a square, and many more claim to be sharp than actually could *possibly* show a long-term winning record. It's only natural: As humans, it is our solemn genetic duty to overrate our abilities and overstate our own success.

REMEMBER

The lesson to take out here: Don't put too much weight on these labels. Forget sharp and square. I want you to get better at betting and to have fun.

Advantage bettors

Somewhere along the continuum of betting skill and knowledge, a person moves *from* complete ignorance *to* a level of dangerous knowledge where you think you know more than you do and probably risk more than you should. Then on the far side of the spectrum are the dedicated professionals, who have as good an eye as anyone for sports wagers, who don't merely consume the market price, but they set the market price. The pros know more than is teachable in a book.

In between squares and full-on professionals is the territory you should target. You'll be a bettor who understands the marketplace, who has instilled discipline in your betting habits, who has a sound sense of your own abilities to evaluate both sides of a bet relative to the financial risks. When you're sharper than square, but maybe not ready to quit your day job, you're an *advantage bettor.* Being an advantage bettor is a reasonable goal for a reader of this book. Even if you can't get there, this book will offer a survey of methods, opinion, resources, and information that will help you evolve as a sports bettor, from less sophisticated to more sophisticated, from less profitable to more profitable, and hopefully from less fun to more fun.

Why 50 Percent Doesn't Cut It

Let's understand what we're up against first with a simple illustration. Imagine a game where you and a friend are betting on the outcome of a coin flip. You win $1 for heads and you lose $1 on tails. You could theoretically play forever, right? Sometimes you'd have nice winning streaks, and sometimes you'd go on losing streaks, but the longer you play, the more likely it is your expected return on this game would be absolutely 0. No gain, and no pain.

I talk more about calculating odds later, but on any bet, your expected return is the sum of the outcomes multiplied by their probabilities. In the coin flip game, it should be intuitive that your expected rate of return is 0, but just to show the work:

(50% chance of a win) × $1

(50% chance of a loss) × – $1

$.5 \times 1 + .5 \times -1 = 0.$

When you place a bet with a bookmaker, that bookmaker charges a commission that varies depending on the bet (and the bookmaker) that reduces the amount of your winning payout.

A bookmaker, or bookie, is an organization or individual (legally sanctioned or not) that accepts bets on sporting events. They're often associated with a casino. Bettors make a bet by staking cash or credit on a certain outcome, and are given a virtual or paper ticket receipt that describes the wager and the payout. In the event their bet wins, they exchange the ticket for the bet payoff.

REMEMBER

On average, a bookmaker keeps 1 cent for every 22 cents wagered: a 4.5 percent commission. If you were to make your coin flip bet at a bookmaker, the terms would be altered slightly to your distinct disadvantage. You still lose $1 on tails, but when heads comes up, you'd only profit 96-ish cents. Even if the coin is fair, the game is now tilted against you. It's a mathematical certainty that if you played forever, you'd give all your money to the bookmaker.

The good news with sports betting is that you're not dealing with a coin from your pocket. To drive the metaphor into the ground, you're the coin. You select which bets to make and which to pass on. The bookie, as a rule, has a stake on every game. But the bettor gets to pick and choose. Your ability to select which outcomes to bet on, and on which odds, means there's a possibility of flipping a coin that's weighted in your favor.

52.38 is the new 50

With a 4.5 percent commission, you'd need more than a fair coin if you hoped to play forever. In fact, you'd need a coin weighted to heads at least 52.38 percent of the time just to break even. I like to think of the number .5238 as the *Gambler's pi*, a number you'd be wise to commit to memory. I'll talk more about how the probability of a good outcome affects your success in later chapters, but for now, understand that the bookmaker's fee has a big impact on your ability to maintain this hobby over the long term.

Remember those newspaper writers from *The Dallas Morning News* earlier in this chapter? Six of the eight writers picked north of 50 percent but less than 52.38 percent. You'd be surprised at how often this subtle raising of the bar can hamper the dreams of sports bettors in the long run.

You'll read that "most people don't win in the long run" at sports betting. If you take as evidence the simple profit/loss numbers of the Nevada sports books, and you consider that companies are falling all over themselves trying to get in on the sports betting concession in newly legalized states, then it's clear that booking bets is a winning proposition, and the profits are paid for by losing bettors.

But that analogy should end at edge of the casino floor. Unlike in roulette or black-jack, there's no mathematical law dictating your eventual bankruptcy in sports betting. It's more akin to a poker room or a horse track, where there is an endless parade of dabblers and dilettantes providing losing bets for the benefits of the betting houses . . . and the winners.

So what's the profile of a winning bettor?

WARNING

Break-even bettors have to win 52.38 percent of their bets. Professional sports bettors would be thrilled if they could win a mere 56 or 57 percent of their bets in the long run. Yes, this is a warning, because 58 percent is devilishly hard to achieve, and if your expectations aren't in line, you're in for a disappointment.

How sports bettors win

Pros win by doing two things well:

>> Forecasting the outcome of games

>> Looking for tiny edges in the odds and seizing them in a timely fashion

Pros aren't quitting their day jobs to live on a yacht in the Caribbean; they're quitting their day jobs because being a pro is an up-at-dawn, number-grinding, pride-swallowing siege that entails immersive study and iron-willed discipline. Later in the book, I'll talk about handicapping games (picking the winning side), and I'll show you why shopping for the best odds is so critical to being profitable.

Comparative betting success

So let's review the narrow margins of sports betting:

» Throwing darts at a board: 50 percent winners

» Required to break even: 52.38 percent winners

» Fully immersed professional: 56 percent winners

If you're wondering what it looks like in terms of winning bets and losing bets, consider Table 1-2, where 3 levels of bettors make 6 bets per week:

TABLE 1-2

Comparing Bettors

Bettor Type	Wins	Losses	Win %	Units Won
Sharp Professional	181	131	58%	36.9
Break-Even (ish)	164	148	52%	1.2
Dart-Throwing Square	156	156	50%	–15.6

For now, just assume a "unit" is a dollar, or maybe $1,000. The point is, look at how thin the margin is between a victory and defeat: A break-even bettor and a dart-throwing square bettor are perilously close in terms of wins and losses. Over the course of a year, the square is slowly going broke, averaging 3 wins and 3 losses per week. To be a break-even bettor, the square need only convert one betting week out of every 6 from 3 wins and 3 losses to 4 wins and 2 losses. That means winning just one additional bet for every 36 placed! Giving you the tools to raise your winning percentage a few points seems like a reasonable goal for this book.

Of course, another thing you probably infer from having such thin margins between success and oblivion is that these results play out over a very long time scale. How will you really know if you've been promoted from square to sharp? It's not like you get a certificate in the mail. When I talk about bankroll management in Chapter 5, I discuss ways to judge your long-term success.

What Kind of Sports Bettor Are You?

Maybe you've placed a few bets before, or maybe you're an old hand. I'd suggest coming to terms with what you hope to get out of your sports betting career before going any further.

Financially interested fan

You're a big sports fan with an interest in betting on games, but you're not expecting to become a pro anytime soon. You'd be satisfied if you think and speak authoritatively on sports betting markets. You'd like to be able to walk into a bookmaker, understand the menu of games on the big board, and approach the betting window with the confidence of a seasoned bettor.

You follow some college and pro teams, and you want wagers on those teams and on games that you like to watch or stream. For the biggest games, you'll look at player props for extra action.

If you win money, great. But you're going to win some and lose some. For the financially interested fan, it's mostly about the fun of taking your fandom to the next level.

Ace Rothstein-esque

Sure, you're a fan, but you've got an eye for teams, coaches, and schemes. Maybe you played the sport you're betting on, but it doesn't matter because you have a feel for how athletes work. You look for hot streaks to ride and know when it's time to hop off. You know why the center is the most important position on the football field, and that on-base percentage is superior to batting average in terms of offensive baseball stats.

In the classical sense, you're a handicapper. You're an equal opportunity bettor, ready to lay a wager on a winning proposition regardless of the sports. You know the numbers pretty well, but you don't get caught up in whether a team's YPP is superior because handicappers evaluate teams and players on a qualitative basis first. You go by feel and look, and you're in tune with how situations and match-ups lead to betting advantages.

Success is possible as a pure fundamental handicapper, but just understand that you'll have to be better than Joe Sixpack and the rest of the general public when you go to the betting window, and that can be harder than you think, especially for the most popular betting sports like NFL football.

WARNING

Knock yourself out, Ace. It's always possible that your feel for the game is superior to the market's. It will be even more important for you to keep a good record of your betting history so you can prove that it's really true.

Data guru

In World War II, the generals called people like you *boffins*, which are people engaging in arcane scientific pursuits. But instead of inventing radar or the atomic bomb, you're going to find statistical angles on sports that nobody has thought of.

You're stats oriented; I daresay a stat-head. Did you watch the game? Some of it; at least the highlights. But the box score is far more important to you. You know the WHIP, FIP, and ERA+ for most pitchers in the league, and you're not afraid to deploy standard deviation and ANOVA.

As a bettor, your plan is to deploy numbers to your advantage. I'm guessing you already know Excel inside and out. The topics that will interest you in this book are the discussion of power ratings and technical analysis.

There's lots of good news for data-oriented bettors. Profitable angles are out there, and the proliferation and availability of data online makes your life easier. What's more, there's a growing literature out there for using mountains of data to find advantages, including Andrew Mack's excellent *Statistical Sports Models in Excel.*

WARNING

Now here's the bad news: Oddsmakers are now data-driven too. They employ their own boffins, who toil away in bookmakers' back rooms to identify the most important and predictive statistics. I'll talk in later chapters in detail about how odds are made, but it starts with a data-driven power rating for each team.

Spread shredder

Sure, you're willing to put time in on handicapping teams qualitatively and quantitatively, and that will get you some good days and some bad days. But if you're willing to put time into seeking out and betting on tiny edges, and repeating it over and over, you'll be flying in the rarified air of professional sports bettors. They lie in wait for situations where the expected return from their wager is slightly positive, and not only are they willing to pounce, they have the discipline to manage their bankroll to their advantages, and they maintain multiple options for placing bets: either accounts offshore, private bookmakers, or, if necessary, casinos. And they do it all without drawing attention to themselves by bookmakers who would limit their action.

If you're familiar with the world of professional poker, you know that winning players are able to evaluate risk and reward on the spot. They make only smart bets, knowing that sometimes the smart bets lose and the not-so-smart bets win. In the long run, they're comfortable that if they make enough wagers with a positive expected outcome, they'll come out ahead.

Professional sports bettors have similar characteristics: They're coupon clippers; they are grinders. If you have the time and discipline to invest yourself in the craft, your recognition skills will improve, and you'll eek out more and more long-term profit. To do this means moving beyond sports betting for fun and entertainment; it has to be a job that you commit to. Very few gamblers have what it takes to reach this level and have a long stay. If you're able to do it, I salute you.

A little of everything

When you start betting on sports, your eyes will be opened to a variety of prediction and betting techniques that all seem like they can put you on the road to profit. My recommendation is to take bits and pieces from each of the approaches I just covered. Each has its own costs, risks, and rewards.

But deciding early on how you want to approach sports betting can help set your expectations and focus your time and efforts. Chances are, you have natural inclinations one way or the other, so go with it. Put your time in and see where it takes you.

The Legal Landscape of Sports Betting

The laws surrounding sports gambling are a knotted web. In this section, I'll make an attempt to untangle it for you. Gambling on sports is as ubiquitous as the law is gray, and many states have laws overlapping and sometimes contradicting federal laws.

I'm not a lawyer but . . .

If you're taking legal advice from a paperback book that's referring to you (affectionately) as a "Dummy," you *might* consider getting a second opinion, so allow me to say this very clearly:

WARNING

Don't break the law. If you read anything in this book that you're construing as an encouragement to break local, state, federal, or international civil or criminal statues, you've misinterpreted it.

Federal laws

The good news for casual bettors is that state and federal laws have a host of anti-gambling statues, but they're aimed at people and entities booking bets rather than those placing bets. If history is any guide, the chances of you, as a bettor, getting into legal hot water for placing a bet is virtually zero.

The federal government has effectively restricted sports betting through a series of statutes with a variety of purposes and side effects:

» **The Organized Crime Control Act of 1955** was based on fears of mafia-led bookmaking businesses. The Ike-era law said any entity that took in $2,000 in gambling revenue or more and involved five or more people was illegal. You'd be hard pressed to find a bookmaker that can survive on four clients or less.

» Bobby Kennedy's war on organized crime put more restrictions on sports betting with **The Wire Act of 1961,** a broadly worded law whose aim was to starve the Sicilian beast from its sports and horse-racing revenue, which were heavily reliant on (federally regulated) interstate and international telecommunications lines. Contrary to popular belief, the original intent wasn't to make it illegal for the average Joe Kennedy to place a sports bet. In fact, its purpose was to give state and local authorities an easy excuse *for them* to pursue and disrupt betting outfits. Because making the act of placing a bet would run up against free speech issues, The Wire Act and other Kennedy-era laws criminalized activities that were related to running a bookmaking business, not on placing bets. (It's as if Congress wanted to make fishing illegal by outlawing standing next to water for more than a few minutes at a time.)

» The *coup de grace* for sports gambling was **The Bradley Act,** also known as **The Professional and Amateur Sports Protection Act (PASPA) of 1992,** which was passed in the wake of some unseemly sports scandals that saw college athletes shaving points and altering outcomes of games for a few six packs of beer. The PASPA explicitly prohibited any form of sports gambling operation, but in particular set out to take on states who wanted to turn sports betting into a source of tax revenue via lottery-like contests and sweepstakes. (If you're wondering, Nevada got an exemption. Their legislators ensured the casinos could continue to book bets to their shareholders' delight.)

» If you remember the online poker craze of the early 21st century, you might remember how it died at the hands of **The 2006 Unlawful Internet Gambling Enforcement Act,** or **UIGEA.** (I dare you to try and pronounce it.) Anti-gaming zealots in Congress stealthily attached a clumsily worded rider to an unrelated anti-terrorism bill that passed virtually unnoticed by most legislators. This law made it illegal for U.S. banks to transact with known offshore casinos and bookmakers. Millions of Americans had been quietly enjoying a peaceful activity in the privacy of their own homes, so the federal government did what came naturally: It passed a law that made it much harder to do. As was the case with earlier laws, the 2002 law did not make it illegal to play poker or place a wager online; it just made it much more difficult. Suddenly you couldn't simply put a deposit in your PartyPoker account with your Discover card. This restriction was enforced in a blanket way, affecting the various offshore bookmakers that had popped up in the early days of the internet. Many offshore casinos stopped doing business with American citizens as a preventative measure, and the poker boom was over.

REMEMBER

While federal laws have made running a sports betting business illegal and impossible in every state except Nevada, none of the above laws made it, or make it, a federal crime for an individual American citizen to place a wager on the outcome of a sporting event.

The Supreme Court to the rescue

In May 2018, the Supreme Court of the United States voted 6 to 3 to overturn the PASPA. (I urge you to offer a quiet word of thanks in honor of your favorite Supreme Court Justice who voted in favor of this decision every time you place a bet.)

The effect of the decision was to let states decide for themselves whether, and in what form, to allow sports betting. And dozens of states have jumped at the chance. In anticipation of this outcome, there were over 40 bills making their way through various state legislatures as of the day the ruling came down from the high court!

State laws

That brings us to 2020.

The state you're in (as in "Iowa" or "New Jersey," not as in "shock" or "non-plussed") defines the availability of sports bets to its residents and guests. We'd need a lot more pages to describe the ins and outs of every state's attitude toward gambling. Some don't bother with any laws at all. Others, like Washington (the state, not the district) actually has a law that forbids people from placing bets online.

The laws are manifold and variegated, but they can be summed up in the Table 1-3.

TABLE 1-3   **State Laws on Sports Betting**

STATE	STATUS	ONLINE BETTING ALLOWED?	NOTES
Alabama	No significant legislative action in progress		
Arizona			DFS = Illegal
Arkansas	Operational	Unclear	
Colorado	Awaiting governor action		
Connecticut	Almost there!		
Delaware	Operational	Approved	
District of Columbia	Lottery parlays only	Not approved	
Florida	No significant action		
Georgia	No significant action		
Hawaii			DFS = Illegal
Idaho			DFS = Illegal
Illinois	Approved	Approved	Trial period only; no betting on Illinois collegiate teams
Indiana	Approved	Approved	
Iowa	Approved	Approved	
Louisiana	No significant action		
Maine	Governor's veto was recently overridden; sports betting is on the way!		
Mississippi	Operational	Not approved	
Montana	Approved	Approved	Run by state lottery; DFS = Illegal
Nevada	Operational	Operational	
New Hampshire	Approved	Approved	
New Jersey	Operational	Operational	
New Mexico	Tribal casinos	Not approved	

STATE	STATUS	ONLINE BETTING ALLOWED?	NOTES
New York	Operational	Under consideration	
North Carolina	Tribal casinos	Not approved	
Oregon	Operational	Available via state-lottery-sponsored app	No betting on college sports
Pennsylvania	Operational	Operational	
Rhode Island	Operational	Approved	
Tennessee	Not approved	Approved	No college prop bets
Vermont	Legislative commission created		
Washington			DFS = Illegal
West Virginia	Operational	Approved	
Wyoming	No significant action		Charitable pari-mutuel wagering allowed

NO PURCHASE REQUIRED

Have you ever wondered why contests and promotional giveaways often get advertised with the statement "No Purchase Required"? That seems strange, doesn't it? The whole point of the giveaway is to get me to buy a magazine subscription or tickets to the opera, right?

The reason "No Purchase Required" appears is because of a legal concept called *consideration,* which is part of the legal definition of gambling. The law says for an activity to be considered gambling, both sides must have consideration; that is, they both put something of value on the line. If a purchase were required to win a drawing or sweepstakes, many states would classify that as a gambling activity. If you're not required to spend money for a chance, we can all pretend we're not gambling by the letter of the law. Prize-filled sweepstakes? Not gambling. Freemium apps on your phone? Not gambling. Customer loyalty contests that you can translate to real merchandise? Not gambling. Life insurance? Not gambling. (Okay, maybe that last one doesn't count.)

Sports betting and organized crime

When I was a kid, I thought racketeering was a tennis strategy.

Most people remember the basic contours of the Black Sox scandal, and a few know the names Art Schlichter or Tim Donaghy, both of whom used their position in their sport (Schlichter as an NFL quarterback; Donaghy as an NBA referee) to change the outcome of games on behalf of gamblers. You might also remember the Tulane point-shaving scandal from the late 20th century.

There is a natural fear that sports betting invites the nefarious influence of organized crime into the pristine territory of professional and amateur sports. After all, people like to gamble, and it is inarguable that organized crime finds its way into society where human wants and needs fall on the wrong side of the law and/or what society deems acceptable.

But if the Prohibition era offers any lessons, it's that passing laws against things that people want doesn't make people want that thing any less. Americans' demand for alcohol did not change by passage of the Volstead Act. Nor did Americans' taste for gambling disappear with various state and federal statutes.

The reality is that illegal bookmakers, whether small and independent or large and connected with friends of Tony Soprano, operate to make money. And while a quick buck can be made by influencing the outcome of games, in the long run, bookmakers prefer the consistent, reliable income provided by the *vig*.

REMEMBER

I already mentioned the 4 to 5 percent commission charged by the bookmakers. It has a cooler name than "commission": It's called the *vig*, or vigorish. Sometimes it's known as *juice*, and it's effectively a service charge collected by bookmakers.

When gray-market betting standards began to stabilize between the World Wars, bookmakers quickly came to understand that game-fixing and scandal would keep bettors at home. It's that simple: If betting customers suspect that games are fixed, they won't bet.

In this way, perhaps counterintuitively, sports betting, even if associated with criminal organizations, drives demand for games that are at least perceived to be fair by the betting public. There are other factors at work as well:

>> Athletes are paid well and are thus harder to influence.

>> Athletes and games are under greater scrutiny for odd behavior and outcomes.

>> Technology makes it easier to spot iffy betting patterns.

>> Betting houses limit wagering amounts on sports at risk for corruption.

I'm not telling you every contest is on the up-and-up, but if you think the fix is always in, you're mistaken.

What Can't I Bet On?

The sports betting universe is vast and varicolored. To start with, it's legal in scores of countries, in one form or another, with each country mixing in its own tastes and traditions. Rules and processes can differ across borders, and even from venues next door to each other. The internet, now in its full adulthood, is driving changes and advances in the market every day.

That means with offshore bookmakers, you'll be able to find one with nearly every level of professional sports. NBA bettors can bet on Summer League basketball. Tennis bettors can even bet on Challenger events (the equivalent of the minor leagues). And there are international sports galore. In Appendix B, I list the biggest online sports books and the range of bets they offer and specialize in.

Bookmakers are in business to take bets. If there's an event on the field of play with an unknown outcome, it's in their interest to find a way to take bets on it. State by state, the rules will vary, and some states are sensitive about taking bets on amateur sports like college football. When Nevada was the only legally sanctioned betting locale, there were strict betting limits on local teams (like the UNLV Runnin' Rebels). Today, the Nevada Gaming Commission keeps a very tight control on what bets are on offer, and they work to ensure fair markets and protection against corruption influences are in place before they tell bookmakers they can accept bets. But with all the competitive pressure, Nevada's menu is expanding ever faster. (For example, in 2019, you were able to vote on the Heisman Trophy winner for the first time.)

Setting Some Goals (and Limits)

In upcoming chapters, I talk about betting strategies and how to size your bets. To start with, you'll need to establish your *bankroll.*

REMEMBER

A bankroll is your pool of wagering money. It's a loose term that some people apply to the amount they allow themselves to bet when on a gambling trip with buddies. A bankroll is really two discrete pieces of information:

>> How much *money* you're comfortable losing

>> How much *time* you're comfortable losing it in before you add to your bankroll from other sources

If you don't set an amount, you're sunk. If you set an amount but adjust it once per week after you've emptied your piggy bank, you're sunk. This is realism, not pessimism, and when you place bets on sports with real money, only one thing is certain: Bookmakers always win; gamblers don't.

So think worst-case scenario where you can lose every bet over a time period of a week or a month (or maybe a pay period) and still meet your obligations in life. (Do I really have to tell you this? It feels patronizing, but it's the truth.) After a certain amount of time has passed in your betting career, you can reassess your bankroll and decide if it's still the right amount for you.

WARNING

Figure out your bankroll and stick to it. Tell a friend or write it on your hand in permanent ink — whatever it takes. Gambling as a hobby is fun and entertaining. As you learn more, you hope it will become profitable as well. But as you no doubt know, gambling has its dark side, and we need to talk about it.

This Is Your Brain on Gambling

What you'll read in these pages is about betting on individual games, sometimes even on individual plays or parts of games. And what I hope to convince you of is that the path to success relies on developing theories, finding small advantages, and *repeating those advantages over and over.*

That could be a problem, because for some people, repetitive actions like betting contribute to what the American Psychiatric Association defines as an *impulse control disorder,* a broad category of conditions related to things like biting your nails and pyromania.

(By the way, do you know how a crooked soccer team is like a pyromaniac? They both like to throw matches.) Yes, you're right: That was uncalled for. This is a serious subject, and I apologize to all pyromaniacs (and crooked soccer teams). Okay, time to be serious again.

There are millions of people in this country and throughout the world who are able to gamble as a pastime and not let it take control of their lives. Besides, can you really get "addicted" to gambling? Unfortunately, the answer seems to be yes. According to the American Psychiatric Association, 1 percent of the population suffers from a serious gambling *disorder.* Addiction, disorder, potato, po-tah-to.

Ferris Jabr wrote in a 2013 *Scientific American* article that psychiatric professionals are broadening their definition of addiction beyond the more common concepts of physical dependence on chemicals that we all know so well. Addiction, they say, can now include *any* activity that disrupts the normal risk and reward response workings of the brain. And here's the fascinating part about gambling: It's *not* the winning or losing per se that gets you into trouble; it's the time between placing a bet and the bet resolving that causes your brain scan to light up like a Christmas tree. It's the seconds when the slot machine reels spin, or the moment when your cards are dealt but you haven't looked at them yet. Or it might be the first pitch of a ballgame you have a big bet on. In this span of time, your brain sends little "thumbs up" circuits to itself. Over time your, brain rewires itself to require bigger and more enthusiastic thumbs ups for the same response.

Let's get one thing straight: This effect is an elemental force in our brains. Addiction-related compulsion is not an indicator of a character flaw; it doesn't mean you're "weak"; and it's certainly not something you can overcome through sheer willpower. That's because an addict's brain literally overwrites the normal checks-and-balances pathways in your brain that exist to keep you on the straight and narrow with new circuitry focused exclusively with a desire to do *that thing* — whatever it is. Instead of your brain commanding you to do common-sense things like "protect your children" and "don't poke yourself in the eye with a toothpick," it starts acting irrationally and whispering things in your ear like "You know, it's technically not *embezzlement* if my boss doesn't find out." Before you know it, you've maxed out your credit cards for that long-shot bet that the Washington Generals will finally beat the Harlem Globetrotters.

And worst of all, *it might be bad for you and you might not even know it.*

And before you ask, yes, it's different from playing fantasy football in many ways. For starters, you're chances of landing in the money are low (especially the way *you* draft). It's also normally a zero-sum affair where there's no commission being charged. Finally, the outcome happens in slow motion. Unfortunately, the path to sports betting success relies to some degree on the thing that makes it dangerous: repetition. You want to find small edges and bet them over and over, and you get paid in adrenaline in a way fantasy football never could.

The basic definition of a gambling disorder is that you continue to do it in spite of harmful consequences in other parts of your life. If you have millions in the bank but you're squandering small amounts of it through bets, it's entirely possible that gambling hasn't caused you any immediate harm, but that doesn't mean there's not a problem.

Here's a handy list of questions to ponder before you go any further, and you should revisit them periodically throughout your sports betting career:

>> Is gambling your only recreational activity?

>> Have there been multi-week periods where you're trying to think of ways to acquire money to gamble with?

>> Do you often exceed your gambling budget for a given time period (for example, a month or a pay period)?

>> Have you ever lied to someone important to you (a spouse, a parent, a sibling) about how much you gamble?

>> Has gambling ever cause serious, long-lasting problems with your family members or friends?

>> Has gambling ever interrupted or caused problems in your professional or academic life?

>> Have you ever felt the need to bet increasing amounts of money to maintain a set "level of excitement"?

>> Have you ever taken a long-term loan on money with the express purpose of using it to gamble?

>> Have you ever written a bad check or stolen money in order to gamble?

>> Has gambling ever caused you to be late on payments of your primary bills (mortgage, car, health insurance)?

>> When you aren't gambling, do you feel restless or irritable?

>> Have you ever tried and failed to stop, cut down, or control your gambling hobby?

>> Do you ever gamble to relieve feelings of guilt, anxiety, helplessness, or depression?

>> Have you spent the last year talking to people about gambling and/or writing a book with a black and yellow cover that tries to convince other people that they should do more sports betting?

Uh oh, I think my wife threw in that last question. Skip that one.

So considering all the other questions, if you answer yes to more than a handful of them, I would urge you to consult a professional to see if gambling is in fact a hobby you should avoid.

TIP

Fortunately, there are resources available to people who might be on that slippery slope. Start by calling 1-800-522-4700 for a confidential evaluation. Or check out the resources at ncpgambling.org.

If you think you might be a problem gambler, please burn this book and forget everything you've read so far. Maybe you have a pyromaniac friend who could help you out.

IN THIS CHAPTER

» Taking sides in a sporting event

» Making money on the moneyline

» Studying PHD-level point spread calculus

» Developing an overwhelming understanding of over/under

» Tackling teasers, parlays, and other exotic bets

Chapter **2**

The Basic Bets

t all started a few dozen centuries ago at the Colosseum in Rome. Two strangers sitting next to each other waiting for the contest to begin. These were good seats, Section E, Row 14, or rather, Row XIV, with a clear view of the action, but not close enough to be the victim of an errant thrown spear.

Being season-ticket holders, our two citizens both considered themselves expert judges of gladiators, but on this fateful day, they had opposite opinions of the competitors in the main event. Neither man could be convinced he was wrong, so somewhere between the pregame toga slingshot and the pregame ritual sacrifice, they hit upon a simple solution: The man who picked the wrong gladiator would owe the other a gold sestertius.

And so, with a final handshake (one of those weird Roman double-forearm grasps), sports betting was invented.

Whether it's the biggest college football game of the century, a regular season basketball game, a cornhole match between friends, or a gladiator fight to the death featuring a guy who could be Russell Crowe's identical twin, sports betting magic is in the air when you have these elements:

>> A regular calendar of sporting contests with well understood rules

>> A shared belief that the outcome is uncertain but "fair"

>> A critical mass of knowledgeable fans who possess a medium of exchange (like gold sestertii or some other form of currency)

Notice I didn't mention the necessity of a legal framework for making bets. Sports betting is like weeds (or maybe love): With the right starting conditions, it sprouts and grows. We know enough about human nature to say that where there's sports, there's bets.

Anyone can blurt out a prediction or opinion on an upcoming game. The essence of betting is having something to lose. If you like to predict the outcome of a game without risking anything, you're making what's known as a *gentleman's bet*. If that's your speed, this book is not for you.

The Betting Contract

When two people agree to a sports bet, they are creating an informal pact. Because money changes hands, a strong tradition has been built up around what bettors are expected to know, what words they use to describe their bets, and how they're expected to behave. These long-standing norms help pave the way for would-be gamblers to find and make the bets they want, and to avoid any misunderstandings when the game is over.

The premises of the promise

It might seem obvious, but both parties involved in a bet must agree ahead of time on what defines the winning side of a bet. The fancy way of talking about the possible betting outcomes are that they are mutually exclusive and collectively exhaustive. That means every bet has a winning side and a losing side, and any bet you make will unambiguously either win or lose.

For basic sports bets, one bettor backs Team A and the other backs Team B. At the end of the game, the bettor who backed the losing team pays the bettor who backed the winning team. What could be simpler?

As you might guess, gamblers are rarely satisfied with simple, and sports betting gets far more complicated. Have you ever been to a home poker game and witnessed a late-night argument over whether a royal flush beats five-of-a-kind? Tempers flare, chips fly, friendships are dissolved . . . all over the $1.81 worth of chips in the pot.

Lest you think sports betting is without its own royal flush versus five-of-a-kind arguments, consider these questions:

>> If I bet on a football team to win and the game ends in a tie, what happens?

>> What happens if I bet on a baseball game that gets called off after 7 innings due to weather?

>> Do overtime points count if I bet that a football or basketball team will score a certain amount of points in the 2nd half?

>> If a baseball player hits a game-winning home run but gets mobbed by teammates as he's rounding the bases (and never sets foot on home plate), does the run count or not?

>> If I bet on a football player to rush for 100 or more yards, and then one newspaper has him at 99 yards while another has him at 100 yards, which one counts?

>> If I bet on a QB to score a certain number of TDs, and in a fluke play he catches one of his own passes on a deflection and scores, does it count as both a throwing TD and a receiving TD?

I could go on. The good news is that most professional bookmakers have an answer to every one of the above questions, and I'll get to them later in the book when I cover the major sports in Part 3. Until then, you'll have to live in suspense. The important point to remember though is that every bet should be based on an outcome that is undeniable and obvious to all parties involved in a bet. Tempers can still flair, chips may become projectiles, and friendships can still dissolve over a sports bet, but hopefully, it won't be due to a lack of definition of the terms of the bet.

Once a bet is made and committed to, the terms of that bet are locked in. Neither party can renegotiate the amount risked, the payout amount, or any other conditions of the bet (like the point spread). As you'll see, this is a feature of sports betting, not a bug. Locking in advantageous betting terms is, well, advantageous!

Monetary policy

Bettors must also agree on the *stakes*, otherwise known as the amount each person puts at risk. If you lose the bet, you lose your stake — no more, no less. Two sports bettors making a wager with each other is no different than poker players sliding chips into a pot. That money is in limbo until the game is over. It's not yours to spend anymore, and yet at the same time, it represents your claim to a payment should your side of the bet win.

When two friends make a bet on a game, it's likely no more than a mutual commitment for the loser to hand over a $10 bill to the winner. Bookmakers don't operate on the honor system. Don't take it personally. As a requirement of making a bet at a professional establishment, you must hand over the amount you want to wager in cash, or in some cases, establish credit that you can bet against. The bookie is always kind enough to hold on to your bet until the game has been decided.

REMEMBER

Bookmakers don't make bets; they *book* bets. That is, they accept bets from the public as a business, and they don't do it for free. Whether you're betting with an online bookmaker or a real-world brick-and-mortar bookmaker, they're charging you a percentage of every bet you make. Unlike a bet between friends, the bookmaker pays you a little less than you risk. I'll dive deep on how bookmakers operate in the next chapter.

All's fair

While sports bettors agree to honor the terms of the bet, there is no commitment of any kind to an equal and open exchange of information. Bettor beware! It is the bettor's responsibility to collect any relevant information about an upcoming game before wagering on it. You'll get no sympathy (or refunds) from a bookmaker if you bet on a football team without knowing the quarterback drove his motorcycle into a tree ten minutes ago.

This is a contest of information gathering, interpretation, and prediction, with a healthy dose of randomness thrown in. All the injuries, crazy bounces, bad calls, freak weather events, and temporary coaching insanity that you see in major sporting events are considered part of the game and therefore part of any bet you make. When the whistle blows at the end of the game, the loser pays up, no matter how crazy the circumstances or unlikely the outcome.

WARNING

Believe it or not, there is a water's edge when it comes to a common definition of fairness in sports betting. For the entire enterprise to work, the outcome of the contest must not be in doubt. If the players and coaches have any motivation other than winning, or if the officials have an interest in anything other than calling a fair game, it's not a fair bet. It doesn't happen often, but if a bookmaker has any doubt about the integrity of the game, they reserve the right to cancel bets. And if you have any doubt about the integrity of a game, stay away.

Overloading the odds

It's worth mentioning the multiple ways the word *odds* can be used in sports betting. In any form of gambling, odds is always a term that describes the agreed-upon payout amount of a bet. More precisely, it's the ratio between what a bet pays relative to the amount wagered. ("I placed a long-shot bet at 50-to-1 odds.") The formal term for this *x*-to-*y* ratio is *fractional odds,* but you won't see that term very often, and as you'll soon find out, there are several other ways to express this same ratio.

Just know that in sports betting, the word odds is a casual catch-all for any and all betting terms: the payout ratio plus any other conditions that define the bet's winner and loser (like a point spread or a total, which I explain later in this chapter).

And finally, odds can also be a broad expression of probability ("odds are against that team winning ten games in a row"), where longer odds imply an event that's less likely and shorter odds are connected to a more likely event.

Illuminating examples

Armed with an understanding of the basics, let's go through some sample bets. These scenarios will demonstrate some of the important concepts discussed in the preceding sections. For now, it's a casual bet between officemates, and we'll expand from there.

Example 1: A decent proposal

Kim and Naveen are NFL fans and are looking forward to watching the Cardinals play the Ravens on Sunday. Kim is bullish on Cardinals QB Kyler Murray. Naveen thinks Murray is overrated. Like all patriotic Americans, they've agreed to make a wager on Murray's total touchdowns. Here's the terms they've agreed to:

>> **Outcome 1:** Kyler Murray scores 0, 1, 2, or 3 TDs: Kim pays Naveen $20.

>> **Outcome 2:** Kyler Murray scores 4 TDs or more: Naveen pays Kim $20.

This is as straightforward a bet as you can make. At the end of the game, either Kim or Naveen will have doubled their stake.

REMEMBER

Outcomes within a single bet will always be mutually exclusive: Only one outcome or the other is possible. When one side wins, the other side loses. Of course, there are caveats:

>> **Some sports bets have more than two possible betting options.** For example: Who will win the NBA MVP Award in 2027? (Answer: LeBron James, Jr. Duh!) A bookmaker might list a dozen players you can bet on. But when the bet is resolved, one bet wins and all the others lose.

>> **Bookmakers may offer separate bets where outcomes overlap.** (Example: Bet 1: Will the Padres score between 0 and 3 runs? Bet 2: Will the Padres score between 2 and 4 runs?) Again, for each individual bet, one side is the winner, and one side is the loser.

>> **Betting terms can change *over time,* causing outcomes to overlap.** (Best to save that discussion for a later, like Chapter 4. It's critically important, but honestly, you're just not ready yet. You need more marinating in the basics.)

For now, let's keep things simple.

REMEMBER

A quick note: Unfortunately, I am unable to predict future free agent movement in the NFL, so I can only offer examples from today's NFL, which is yesterday's NFL to you. So if you're reading this book in your autonomous-flying-car, personal-jet-pack-powered future, and Kyler Murray happens to no longer play for the Cardinals, please just play along. You're going to see dated examples over and over in this book. Thank you for your courage.

Example 2: Riskier business

Joan overheard Kim and Naveen and wants to get on the action. She thinks Kyler Murray is going to have a huge day and is willing to bet that Murray will score at least 6 TDs! Wow! Naveen, whom you'll recall doesn't think much of Murray, is glad to risk more money on Kyler having a bad day, so he suggests similar stakes as his bet with Kim. Naveen will pay Joan $20 if Murray scores 6 touchdowns and Joan will pay Naveen $20 if Murray scores 5 or fewer.

Joan wisely realizes she's betting on a scenario that's less likely to happen than the one Kim bet on. She decides a $20 payout for isn't worth the risk, so she declines Naveen's offer.

REMEMBER

Sports betting is like any financial endeavor in that as the risk of losing your investment grows, you'll demand a bigger reward. Consider one of the safest financial bets available: U.S. Treasury bonds. It's not a coincidence that both the probability of losing everything and the rate of return on these bonds are both very small. On the other hand, if you're looking for an investor in your fly-by-night tech startup with a 1 percent chance of success, you'll have to promise a fantastic rate of return. Rational people always connect risk and return, and gamblers are no different.

Joan correctly perceived she was at higher risk for losing her stake than Kim was, so she didn't take the bet. Naveen is so convinced that Murray will have a bad day that he's willing to sweeten the payout for Joan. He proposes the following schedule of payments:

>> **Outcome 1:** If Kyler Murray scores 5 TDs or fewer, Joan will pay Naveen $20.

>> **Outcome 2:** If Kyler Murray scores 6 TDs or more, Naveen will pay Joan $30.

By promising a higher payout for a relatively less likely event, Naveen has given Joan better odds on her bet. Specifically, because he thinks a 6-TD day is unlikely for Murray, Naveen is willing to pay a larger amount for that outcome. By making this bet, Joan is risking $20 for the possibility of winning $30.

REMEMBER

Naveen's original bet with Kim hasn't changed. Once they've agreed to their bet, the amount and terms are settled *regardless of what Naveen agrees to with Joan.* This is an important feature of sports betting that differs from pari-mutuel betting (for example, horse or dog racing or progressive jackpots). In sports betting, once a bet is placed, all the terms of that bet like the amount paid out to the winner and any numbers that determine a winning bet (like the number of touchdowns, or a point spread) are locked in and can't be changed by either party, even if new information comes out.

Extending the investment metaphor further, you should think of the entire sports betting arena as a *marketplace.* It has buyers (bettors) and sellers (bookmakers or other bettors). A bet is a thing of value to be traded because it is a promise of a future payment, or at least a potential promise of a payment. It's up to buyers and sellers to decide for themselves what a given bet is worth. Joan weighed the probability of Kyler Murray having a big day along with her appetite for risk and the potential joy of winning $30. Because Naveen and Joan had differing opinions on Kyler Murray and the Cardinals, they each found value on opposite sides of the same bet.

Example 3: Poor Tom

Let's do one more example in our hypothetical office (where it doesn't seem like much actual work is getting done). Tom from the next cube over hears about Naveen's bets with Joan and Kim. He's also a big believer in Kyler Murray and wants to make the same bet that Joan did. But Tom doesn't have a $20 bill, he's only got a fiver. So, Naveen agrees to make this bet with Tom:

>> **Outcome 1:** If Kyler Murray scores 5 TDs or below, Tom will pay Naveen $5.

>> **Outcome 2:** If Kyler Murray scores 6 TDs or more, Naveen will pay Tom $7.50.

Why $7.50? In sports betting, the odds are a ratio that describes the payout relative to the amount risked. No absolute dollar amount is implied. Naveen put $30 at risk against Joan's $20, so we could say Naveen gave Joan *3-to-2 odds* on Kyler Murray's big day. That is, he agreed to pay off $3 for every $2 Joan risked, regardless of the actual amount. Since he's getting the same odds on a smaller bet, Tom will pay Naveen $5 if the bet loses, and Naveen will pay Tom $7.50 should the bet win.

When you're betting against a real bookmaker, the bookmaker sets the odds, but the bettor chooses the amount to risk, subject to some limitations.

On Sunday, if Murray scores 7 touchdowns, Naveen will owe all his coworkers money. He'll owe $30 to Joan and $7.50 to Tom. Naveen would also have to pay Kim $20, who would no doubt have some regret that she didn't take the higher risk/higher reward bet. On the other hand, if Murray only scored 5 TDs on Sunday, Joan and Tom would lose their bets and Kim, with the more conservative play, would win $20 from Naveen.

An introduction to betting with odds

One thing you hopefully noticed in the examples of the preceding sections is that you need two people to make a bet. If you're a sports bettor, you need a counterparty willing to accept a common set of terms that define how to determine the winner of the bet, what each bettor must risk, and how much the payouts are for the winning bettors.

To continue the investment marketplace metaphor, if you think of bets as items being bought and sold, the odds — again, the proportion of dollars risked to dollars won — plays the role of price.

Buyers assess purchases by determining if the value they place on an item outweighs the price they must pay to own it. Rational bettors do the same thing: They assess the betting proposition (like a team to win a game, or a score to go over or under) and the associated odds on offer from a bookmaker. If the value matches the price, the bettor will place the wager. If the price is too expensive, or the perceived value isn't high enough, the bettor will pass on the bet.

What is value?

I've been freely throwing around the word *value,* and defining it requires me to briefly detour into some academic pointy-headedness. Value is a shortcut for quantifying the worth and usefulness of an item to an individual. It's another way of describing utility, whether it's financial, psychological, social, or really *any* way an item can impact a person, positive or negative. As you might suspect, there's no such thing as absolute universal value. It's always subject to a person's preferences, needs, and predictions of the future.

Bets are valuable to people for the possibility of winning money, in real financial terms as well as the emotional impact. When you buy a Powerball ticket, there's a possibility you'll win the jackpot, but most psychologists agree that the actual benefit you're getting is the license to daydream about spending millions of dollars. Value can be negative too! Being separated from your money not only decreases your bank account, but it also comes with the emotional pain of betting the wrong way.

In a basic way, when I place a value on an item that exceeds its price, I will buy it. That is, when the combined satisfaction and benefit I'll get from owning something outweighs the negative impact of handing over money, I'll make the purchase, even if all I get is the chance of winning money in an upcoming game.

Example 4: Connecting betting odds to win probabilities

Naveen's coworker Randy is a big Joe Burrow fan. He makes a bet with Naveen that Burrow's touchdown total will be higher than Murray's. He proposes the following schedule of payments for the bet:

>> **Outcome 1:** Naveen is backing Kyler Murray. If Murray throws more touchdown passes than Joe Burrow, Randy owes Naveen $20.

>> **Outcome 2:** Randy is backing Joe Burrow. If Burrow throws as many or more touchdowns, he'll collect $30 from Naveen.

We can infer that the two bettors must think Murray's chances are better than Burrow's or they wouldn't have both agreed to differing payoff amounts. Randy's risking $20 to profit $30. And Naveen's risking $30 to only win $20. That's another way of saying Naveen is offering Randy 3-to-2 odds on the bet.

You can translate betting odds into a set of *implied probabilities,* or the likelihood of each possible outcome of a bet as perceived by bettors. Probability is always expressed as a number from 0 to 1 and describes the chances of a certain outcome relative to all possible outcomes. If you divide the losing payout of the bet by the total amount of money in play, you get the implied odds of the winning side. In this case, the implied odds of Burrow throwing more touchdowns is $20 (the amount that Randy owes for a Murray win) divided by $20 + $30 (the total dollars in play by both bettors), or $20 ÷ $50, or .4 (also known as 40 percent).

It's more straightforward to calculate implied probabilities starting from bets with multiple outcomes. You can calculate each implied probability this way: In a bet with two possible outcomes, just subtract the first number from 1 to get the implied probability of the other outcome, or $1 - .4 = .6$ (or 60 percent).

Is this the same thing as saying a fair coin has a .5 probability of landing on heads? Heavens no! It's possible to precisely define the underlying probability of a repeating event (like a coin flip, a dice throw, or the decay of an isotope), but sporting events defy that level of precision. The probability of Kyler Murray outplaying Joe Burrow on any given Sunday is a matter of speculation.

Nevertheless, implied probability is a good starting point for analyzing the value of a bet. You can take your own estimation of the probability of an outcome and compare it with the odds offered by a bookmaker or a friend to see if the risk and reward are in balance.

Using our example above, if Randy thought Joe Burrow only had a 25 percent chance of outplaying Kyler Murray, the $30 payoff on a Burrow win is hardly enough. Randy should demand bigger odds from Naveen. How much bigger? Starting with the $20 payout for a Murray win, we can calculate: $20 ÷ ($20 + fair payout for Burrow win) = .25. After a brief algebra refresher, Randy realizes that a .25 probability of a Burrow win requires 3-to-1 odds from Naveen, which is a $60 payout against a $20 payout.

Consider this a shot across your mathematics bow. In Chapter 4, I'll wade deeper into the math behind sports betting.

TIP

For bets between friends, the total of the implied probabilities is always equal to exactly one. That equation changes slightly when a bookmaker is involved because they charge a small fee to book your bet. For professionally booked bets, the sum of implied probabilities is slightly more than one, depending on how much the bookmaker is charging.

Betting against a Bookmaker

Armed with these basic lessons, let's leave this little office full of football fans and shift the discussion to the way the vast majority of bets get made and paid: with a bookmaker. Unlike the officemates who have to dream up, discuss, propose, and accept wagers on their own, a bookmaker offers a handful of standard bets on every game (with a few exceptions) in every major sport.

I'll talk more about the business of booking bets later in the, uh, book, but there are a few concepts that you'll want to understand before we get into bet types.

>> Unlike a marketplace like eBay that attempts to match buyers and sellers, bookmakers accept all bets regardless of whether there's a counterpart on the opposite side. In other words, when you place a bet on Team A (to beat Team B), the bookmaker *hopes* another customer will come along and make the same-size wager on Team B. But if Team A wins, you get paid regardless.

>> A simple model of the bookmaking business requires that they set odds such that half the betting dollars are on one side of a bet, and half are on the other. Bookmakers are constantly adjusting odds to influence that betting split.

>> Once a bookmaker accepts a bet from a gambler, the terms of the bet at the time the bet is placed remain in effect even if the odds change later on.

The moneyline

Up to now, I've described odds as a ratio of the payouts for each side of a bet, like 3-to-1 or 100-to-1. It's time for you to get familiar with the way American bookmakers list odds. It's called a *moneyline*, and it's going to give you a severe case of the WTFs. But don't worry. You'll get the hang of it.

A moneyline is just a way to describe payout odds relative to the number 100. No, that doesn't mean you have to bet $100, it's just the notation. Here's what you need to know:

>> Moneyline odds are always shown as three (or more) digit numbers.

>> Each side of a bet has its own moneyline, whether it's two teams playing in a game, or a ten possible winners of the NBA three-point contest.

>> When a bet is listed with a negative moneyline, that means you have to risk more money than you'll profit.

>> When a bet is listed with a positive moneyline, that means you're going to profit an equal or greater amount of money than you risk.

It's easier to talk about the math behind the moneyline by separating out favorite bets from underdog bets.

The moneyline of any bet describes odds of a given bet. Every bet you ever make has odds that can be expressed as a moneyline. Don't get confused when you hear about someone making a moneyline bet. That just refers to betting on a team to win *straight up*, which just means betting on a team or a competitor to win the contest outright. To be even more specific, the bet is not helped or hindered by a point spread (which I'm getting closer to explaining).

Betting on a moneyline favorite

When you see a minus sign in front of a moneyline, you'll be staking more money than your profit. In fact, the number you're looking at shows you the amount you have to wager in order to profit exactly $100. Read that sentence again, take a nap, and let it sink in.

So if you see a moneyline listed as −300, it means for every $300 you risk, you profit $100 if your bet wins. Or if you choose to bet $3, you profit $1 if your bet wins. See how that works?

REMEMBER

If you win a bet, your initial stake is returned to you plus any profit. If you wager $50 on a bet with a −200 moneyline, the bookmaker will hand you $75 if you win. That's your $50 stake plus your $25 profit. To calculate your profits, divide −100 into the moneyline and multiply it by your stake. In this example, −100 ÷ −200 = .5, and .5 times your initial stake, which amounts to $25. Table 2-1 lists some moneylines and associated profits on a $100 bet for your reference.

TABLE 2-1

Moneylines and Profits for Favorites

Moneyline	Amount of Profit on a $100 Bet
−110	$90.91
−200	$50
−250	$40
−300	$33.33
−1,000	$10

Betting a moneyline underdog

When you see moneyline odds listed with a plus sign (or no sign at all), you can conclude that the bet is a moneyline *underdog*. An underdog bet just means the amount you profit on a bet is more than (or equal to) the amount you risk. Unlike the favorite moneyline, the underdog moneyline expresses the number of dollars you'd profit for every $100 bet.

For example, if you bet $10 on a team that's a +200 underdog and win, the bookmaker gives you $30 total. You get your $10 back, plus your profits, which are 200 ÷ 100, or 2, multiplied by the initial wager, which comes to $20.

As you just saw, calculating the ratio of risk and reward is much easier for an underdog. It's like a straight percentage: To figure out what your profit will be, take the moneyline over 100 and multiply it by your wager. A +300 moneyline means your profit on a win is three times what you risked. A +150 moneyline nets you 1.5 times what you risked.

REMEMBER

And again, there's no requirement to bet $100 or in increments of $1 or $10 or $100. You are free to bet anything you want, subject to the bookie's minimum and maximums. Collect all the spare change in your couch and bet $15.26 (it's a big couch) on a team listed at +200 moneyline odds. If the team loses, you get nothing back. If the team wins, the bookmaker owes you $45.78. That's the $15.26 you forked over for the initial bet, plus the profits of $30.52.

Just in case you're not following, Table 2-2 lists sample underdog payouts.

TABLE 2-2

Moneylines and Profits for Underdogs

Moneyline	Amount of Profit on a $100 Bet
+100	$100
+250	$250
+400	$400
+1,000	$1,000

TIP

The convention with moneyline bets is that a bet at exactly even odds, where your profit will be equal to your risk, it's listed as a +100 bet, not a −100 bet. Mathematically, they're identical, but for reasons I can't explain to you, the former is always used and never the latter. If you think about moneylines as a sequence of numbers, it goes from −102 to −101 to +100 to +101 and up.

The favorite versus a moneyline favorite

In any bet where the choices are listed with moneyline odds, the lowest number is considered *the favorite*. That is, the betting public considers that team or that betting option to be the most likely winner compared to the other possibilities. That doesn't mean other bets can't also be moneyline favorites.

Here's an example of a bet listing you might see on the menu:

2025 National Champs	Odds
Alabama	–250
Oregon	–105
Texas	+200
Houston	+450

Alabama is favored to win the championship. But the minus sign next to Oregon means you have to use the moneyline favorite equation to calculate your potential winnings from a Ducks triumph. Texas and Houston are both listed with underdog odds, but if you're looking to bet on the biggest underdog, take Houston at +450 and laugh all the way to the bank when the Cougars win it all and you get $4.50 for every dollar you risk.

REMEMBER

When you place a moneyline bet, it means you're betting on a team or a player to win with no handicap (like a point spread, which, not to sound like a broken record, I'm going to explain soon). If you place a moneyline bet on a team, when they win, you win.

Let's look at another example of moneyline notation and break down the math. Imagine the scenario where the NBA semifinals have just begun, and you can bet on one of the final four teams to win their last two series and take the trophy home:

NBA Champions	Moneyline Odds
Dallas Mavericks	–400
Denver Nuggets	+100
New York Knicks	+200
Miami Heat	+1,600

To win this bet, the team you bet on must win it all. What you get paid is dependent on the moneyline odds listed next to each team. The runaway favorites are the Dallas Mavericks. Bet them to win and you'll risk $4 for every $1 in profit. The longest of long shots are the Miami Heat. Every dollar you risk will be returned to you 16-fold if they win.

Let's say you put $60 on the Mavericks. The Mavericks' moneyline has a minus sign, so we're using the equation for favorites. Throw out the minus sign and plug numbers into this equation:

Profit = Amount of Wager × 100 ÷ Listed Odds

That is:

Profit = $60 × 100 ÷ 400

Or:

Profit = $60 × .25

Which comes out to a $15 profit in the event of a Mavericks win. With only 25 cents worth of profit for every dollar you risk, you'd better have a lot of confidence in Luka and his teammates.

TIP

Amateur bettors and dabblers love underdog plays. Let's face it: It's more fun to win more than you risk. Don't fall into that trap; there's just as likely to be good value in a favorite as there is an underdog. If someone asked you to risk $1 to profit 1 cent if the sun comes up tomorrow, that's a pretty good bet, even though you're betting on the equivalent of a –10,000 moneyline bet.

Back to our example. Say you bet $60 on the Heat, and sure enough, they go on a dream run to win it all. For an underdog, just multiply your bet times the moneyline over 100 to calculate your profit:

Profit = $60 × 1,600 ÷ 100

Which means:

Profit = 60 × 16

Profit = $960

That's a nice payday for a $60 bet.

TIP

If you recall from math class, it doesn't matter whether you do the multiplication first or the division. Choose your own adventure, dear reader.

There is absolutely no significance to the *order* of betting options. Traditionally, the favorite is listed at the top of the list, but because the odds can change, there's no guarantee that the bets will always be listed in favorite-to-underdog order. The only thing that matters to your wallet is the moneyline. Take a look at this listing:

Mavericks	–400
Heat	+340

It has exactly the same meaning as this listing:

Heat	+340
Mavericks	−400

A bet with no favorite?

For outcomes where you're picking a single winner out of a big field, the lowest moneyline is the betting favorite. But sometimes you'll see bets without any negative moneylines, like this:

World Series Champions 2025	Moneyline Odds
New York Yankees	+260
Portland Angels	+310
Texas Rangers	+500
Atlanta Braves	+850
Miami Marlins	+1,400

In this bet, the bookmakers consider the New York Yankees winning the World Series that year to be the most likely outcome. So the Yankees are favored. Don't get confused though. A bet with a plus sign means you're using the underdog equation to determine potential profits from your bet.

An evenly matched bet

What about a bet where you have two evenly matched teams competing on a neutral field? Bookmakers often list bets with equally likely outcomes as −110 bets, like the one below:

Winner — NFL Exhibition	Moneyline Odds
Lions	−110
Bengals	−110

The odds indicate that regardless of which side you bet on, the bookmaker requires you to risk $110 to win $100. Because the moneylines of the two possible outcomes are identical, we can infer the betting public considers these teams equal.

EUROPEAN ODDS

There are lots of ways to describe odds, which are, at the end of the day, just a ratio between two numbers. American sportsbooks publish odds as moneylines, where the positive numbers represent the profit on a hypothetical $100 bet, and negative moneylines represent the amount that must be risked to profit $100.

Gambling houses and sports books around the world have their own standards and formats for expressing the same concept. European sportsbooks use a format called *decimal odds,* which most people would argue is and easier format to grasp than American odds.

Decimal odds are expressed a single number that represents a multiple of the initial bet that a bookmaker would payout for a winning bet. The key differences are that it's written as a multiple of a dollar (or a Euro or a Pound or whatever), and even better, the number you're looking at is the combination of both the profit from the bet and the initial stake.

For example, an even-money bet where the amount of profit is exactly equal to the amount of risk would be a bet listed with odds of 2.0. When you multiply your wager times the decimal odds, you get the amount the bookmaker owes you for your winning bet. So a $10 bet pays you back $20, which is your initial $10 stake plus your $10 winnings.

For American odds bets listed with positive moneylines, the equivalent decimal odds are greater than 2.0. For favorites, or bets listed with negative American moneylines, the equivalent decimal odds would be somewhere between 1.0 and 2.0. If you're still feeling shaky on this, here are some examples that might help you get the hang of it:

American Odds	Decimal Odds	Fractional Payoff Odds
−400	1.25	1-to-4
−200	1.5	1-to-2
+100	2.0 (Even-Money Bet)	1-to-1
+260	3.6	2.6-to-1
+1,400	15	14-to-1

There are other ways to express odds as well. Asian sports books have a completely different standard that we'll skip for now.

If you walk into a bookmaker or casino in North America, you'll be dealing with moneyline style odds. If you bet online, your online bookmaker will be happy to show you odds on bets in whatever format you'd like.

If you play this out in your head, you might notice that if you placed a $10 bet on the Lions, and the next guy in line places a $10 bet on the Bengals, at the end of the game a little bit of money is missing, because the −110 odds mean the winner is only netting $9.09. That missing 91 cents is kept by the bookie as a fee.

A quick look at vigorish (the vig)

If Person A bets $110 on the Lions and Person B bets $110 on the Bengals, one of them will get paid $210 ($100 in profit plus their initial $110 stake). The bookmaker keeps the remaining $10 as a fee known as *vigorish*. Bookmakers stay in business because they take a small fee on every bet by paying out a few pennies less than what's wagered.

It's as if you were betting the coin-flip game with a friend where you paid her $1 for heads and she only paid you 96 cents for tails and kept the change! In the long run, assuming you had a fair coin, you'd lose all your money to your "friend."

REMEMBER

Vigorish, sometimes called the *vig*, or the *juice*, gets baked into every bet by the bookmakers. They never state it explicitly as a percentage or a fee. The bottom line is that since the bookmaker takes a small bite from every bet, you'll have to win slightly more than 50 percent of your bets to break even.

Point Spreads: Thumb on the Scale

The term *handicap* might be meaningful to you if you are a golfer or an aficionado of horse racing. Promoters long ago learned that competitions between mismatched opponents are boring. Bookmakers also learned that it's hard to coax bettors to place bets when the odds are long.

Sports fans and bettors like evenly matched competition. That's why there are weight classes in boxing and wrestling. It's why you never saw an aging Muhammad Ali fight an up-and-coming Sugar Ray Leonard. There's just no point in watching a race between a basset hound and a greyhound.

Early promoters of horse racing realized they could garner more interest in the race between Quadruple Crown contender *Paul Revere* versus a field of horses destined for the glue factory if they could somehow make the race more competitive. And so some genius in the distant past had a novel idea: They added weights to the faster horses to slow them down. This system of handicapping horses was a boon to the industry: More closely contested races meant more interest from fans and bettors — and more money for the race tracks.

Amateur golfers of vastly different skill levels compete through a system of handicaps where the better golfer's score is adjusted in a standard way. Even chess competitions have occasional informal handicapping systems where a higher-rated player will be forced to start without one of his or her pawns or bishops.

And that brings us to bookmakers, who use *point spreads* to artificially create an even bet between two mismatched teams. A point spread is nothing more than an adjustment applied to the final margin of victory to determine the winning bet.

A point spread is a number specific to a single game, and it might appear as either a positive or negative number, like this:

NFL Football	Spread
Dallas Cowboys	–7
Houston Texans	

Or like this:

NFL Football	Spread
Dallas Cowboys	
Houston Texans	+7

Or even this:

NFL Football	Spread
Dallas Cowboys	–7
Houston Texans	+7

These bet listings all mean the same thing: The betting public think the Cowboys are more likely to win this game than the Texans. The bookmaker wants to present a bet to the public that makes the bet closer to a 50-50 proposition, so they've added a handicap in the form of a 7-point spread.

When you're talking about this game, you could say the Cowboys "are minus 7" or "Texans plus 7." Both mean exactly the same thing. Regardless of which side you bet on, the bet is evaluated and paid out by taking the final margin of victory and adjusting it in the Texans' favor by 7 points. If the game results in a 10-point Cowboys victory on the field, they will have "beaten the spread" by 3 (10 points minus the 7 point spread). In that case, bets on the Cowboys' point spread win; bets on the Texans' point spread are losers. On the other hand, a 6-point Cowboys victory gets evaluated as a 1-point Texans victory for bettors. (Bets on the Texans win; bets on the Cowboys lose.)

REMEMBER

Point spreads are for bets between two teams, like an NFL football game. You won't see point spreads on multi-way bets like the 2023 Big 12 Basketball Champion.

Losing team, winning bet

Unlike with a moneyline bet, point spreads make it possible for one team to lose the game but be on the winning side of the bet, as in this example:

NFL Football	Spread	Final Score	Spread-Adjusted Final Score
Dallas Cowboys	–7	28	21
Houston Texans		24	24

The Cowboys in this case won the game on the field, but Cowboys bettors are losers because the margin of victory (4 points) was smaller than the point spread.

When you evaluate a point spread bet, there are a few things to get the hang of:

>> The favorite is always listed with a negative number, *or,* if one team is listed with a positive number, the opposing team is the favorite by implication.

>> The underdog is listed with a positive number. If only one team is listed with a negative number, the opposite team is the underdog by implication.

>> In American sports, away teams are listed on top, and the home team is listed on the bottom. (In this example, think of it as "Cowboys at Texans.") The order of the listing has no bearing at all on the point spread or how a bet is evaluated.

REMEMBER

When the margin of victory on the field is the same as the point spread, the bet is considered a *push,* which is a fancy word for "tie." In this instance, if you placed a bet with a bookmaker, you get your original stake returned to you.

Half is enough

If you're new to betting, you might be a little confused by a bet listed like this:

NBA Finals — Game 3	Spread
Knicks	
Mavericks	–5½

Point spreads are denominated in half points, colloquially known as *the hook*. No, unless you're talking about wrestling, your team can't score a half point. Half points are useful because they make a push (tie) impossible, and as you'll find out later, can have a profound impact on the value of a bet. Otherwise it's evaluated the same as any other point spread. Here's an example:

Super Bowl LXII	Point Spread	Final Score	Adjusted Final Score
Indianapolis Colts	–3½	27	23.5
Carolina Panthers		24	24

Here, Panthers fans can't be happy that they got so close to beating the hated Colts, but Panther *bettors* will be delighted. The 3½-point spread margin is enough to make them winners.

POINT SPREAD COLLOQUIALISMS

Like any hobby, sports betting has developed its own set of insider words and phrases. There are lots of ways to express what's going on with a point spread (or "spread"). Here are a few notables:

- **The line:** Another term for point spread. Example: "What's the line on the Lakers game?"

- **Laying:** When a team is the favorite, you can say they are laying points. Example: "The Lakers are laying 9 and a half tonight."

- **Getting:** When a team is the underdog, you can say they're getting points. Example: "The Warriors are getting 4."

- **Covering:** When a point spread bet wins, either a favorite wins by a margin greater than the point spread, or the underdog loses by a margin that's less than the point spread. Example: "The Mavericks lost last night, but at least they covered."

TIP

Standard point spread bets either win, lose, or occasionally push. The margin of your spread victory or loss doesn't affect your payout at all. It doesn't matter if the side you bet on beats the spread by a half point or by 50 points; your bet wins.

Point spread = 0

Sometimes teams really are evenly matched, and the bookmaker doesn't have to attach a point spread to either side. Rather than taking the easy way out, gamblers have invented a phrase for this situation: *pick'em* or *pick*, which means a game's spread is zero. It's expressed like this:

NCAA Semifinal	Spread
Butler	
Duke	PK

Betting on a point spread

Bookmakers charge vigorish on every bet, including point spread bets. If there's no moneyline odds listed, assume the odds are −110 for both sides of a point spread bet, also known as an 10-to-11 or 10/11 bet. That means you're risking $110 for every $100 you win when you bet on a point spread.

In this example, the Falcons are favored by 4:

NFL Regular Season	Spread
Atlanta Falcons	−4
N.Y. Jets	+4

Even though it's not stated, a bet on either side requires you to risk $110 for every $100 you win. That's the same as this:

NFL Regular Season	Spread
Atlanta Falcons	−4 −110
N.Y. Jets	+4 −110

Like every other bet, once you place a bet on a game with a certain point spread, the terms of your bet are locked in, including the point spread. The bookie might change the point spread after you place your bet, but it won't affect how your bet is evaluated.

For example, if you place a bet on the Bengals +14 against the Patriots, and then later that afternoon the bookie lists the spread at Bengals +13, it doesn't change your bet. You still get the benefit of an additional 14 points on the game margin. If the Patriots win 27–14, your bet is a winner, but people who were unlucky enough to place their point spread bet after the change to +13 spread will only get a push (tie).

This can just as easily work against you as for you. If you had bet the opposite side, in this case the Patriots −14 versus the Bengals, and the final score is 27–14, your bet loses, while later Pats bettors end up with a push.

Spreads and moneylines combined

When you see a point spread bet with no other notation, you can assume it's a −110 bet, where you're laying $11 to win $10. The betting market often causes the bookmaker to adjust the point spread up or down to alter the balance of betting action. The bookmaker can also use the odds themselves as a lever to attract bettors to one side of a bet or another. If a bookmaker gets too much action on the Cowboys −7 point spread bet, they might alter the odds on that bet from −110 to −115 to make it slightly more expensive to bet on the Cowboys. In fact, most bookmakers will tweak the moneylines *before* they change the point spread.

Look at this example:

NFL Football	Spread
Jacksonville Jaguars	−6 −115
Tennessee Titans	+6 −105

Instead of the normal −110 bet on each side, the bookmaker is offering adjusted moneyline odds. We can infer they've received a little more action on the Jaguars and would like to push a few more bettors to the Titans, so they've made the Jaguars odds a little more expensive than a normal bet, and they've made the Titans a little less expensive than a normal bet. That adjustment might not seem like much, but at the margins, it makes the Jaguars a little less attractive to bettors and the Titans that much more attractive.

An altered moneyline doesn't change the way you evaluate a point spread bet for a win or a loss. In the above example, the Jaguars must still win the game by more than 6 points for that side of the bet to win. The only difference is that Jaguars bettors have risked a little more for their potential profit.

Specialty point spreads

In Major League Baseball and the National Hockey League, there are standard point spread bets called the run line and the puck line, respectively. Like a point spread, these indicate adjustments on the final score to determine the winning side of the bet. Unlike basketball and football, however, where the point spread floats depending on market forces, the run line and puck lines never change; the bookmaker only adjusts the associated moneyline for each side of the bet. Here's an example of a run line in baseball:

MLB – Playoffs	Run Line
Baltimore Orioles	–1½ +140
Chicago White Sox	+1½ –155

These bets work just as you've come to expect. If you bet on the Orioles' run line, the final game margin is adjusted towards the White Sox by 1.5 runs. If the Orioles win with that adjusted score, you're the beneficiary of a +140 moneyline. On the other hand, if you bet on the White Sox, you'll get the benefit of a 1.5-run adjustment in your favor, but you will have put more at risk than your profit.

TIP

For basketball and football, if you like one team to win, you can bet either the moneyline bet (with no point spread) or a point spread bet (at –110 or something close to those odds). Even though these are two distinct bets, the bookie's adjustment of a point spread usually means the moneyline moves too:

>> When the point spread on a game gets further from zero, the two moneyline bets get further apart. For example, they might move from –150 (on the favorite) and +135 (on the underdog) to –160 and +145.

>> When the point spread gets closer to zero, the moneylines get closer together.

>> If the bookmaker decides two teams are exactly evenly matched, and the point spread gets adjusted to zero, the moneylines settle at –110 for each side. At this point, there is no difference between a point spread bet and a moneyline bet since the handicap on the game is zero points.

Over/Under Betting

I've discussed betting on teams, but if you'd prefer to just root for lots of offense or a defensive struggle, you can place bets on the other ubiquitous game bet known as an *over/under* bet (also known as the *total* bet). When you place a bet on the over/under, you're betting that the total combined points or runs scored in the game will either be over a certain total or under a certain total. Unlike a moneyline or point spread bet, when you place an over/under bet, the winner of the game and the margin of victory have no bearing on the outcome of the bet.

When you see an over/under bet listed, you'll notice the bookmaker has defined the total. As always, the bookmaker's goal is to set the total at a number that will split the action between over bettors and under bettors. By default, over/under bets are considered 10-to-11 or −110 bets, just like a standard point spread bet.

Bookmakers list game totals mixed in with point spreads like this:

NFL – Regular Season	Odds
Las Vegas Raiders	−3½
Seattle Seahawks	44

In this example, the bookmaker has combined the point spread bet with the over/under to save space. Since an over/under point total is always a positive number, in a menu of games and bets, they're simply listed opposite the favorite's point spread. In the example above, the Raiders are 3½-point favorites, and the over/under is 44 points.

This listing shows four possible ways you could bet on this game:

>> A point spread bet on the Raiders -3.5 points

>> A point spread bet on the Seahawks +3.5 points

>> A bet that the final game score will be over 44 combined points

>> A bet that the final game score will be under 44 combined points

The fact that no moneyline is listed next to either the spread of the total means these options are all standard −110 bets.

The mechanics of over/under bets are quite similar to point spread bets. Totals float on the whims of the betting market, moving up when there's too much action on the over and down when there's too much action on the under. In addition to moving the total itself, bookmakers sometimes alter the odds to slightly above or below −110 to alter the betting balance. Finally, totals can be denominated in half points just like point spreads. For example, you might see a game listed like this:

College Football	Odds
Florida	−9½
Miami FL	44½ U−120

There's lots of information available here in the Florida at Miami betting market. For starters, Florida is a road favorite of 9½ points. If you see two numbers in the game listing, the negative number is always the point spread. That means the total is 44½ points. The U–120 next to the total is an indicator that the bookmaker has made a bet on the under 44½ total slightly more expensive than the normal –110 odds. In this case, you'd have to bet $120 for every $100 you win.

Over/under betting creates a fascinating and different dynamic from betting a *side* (that is, betting a team with a moneyline or a point spread). If you have a bet on a total, you become a cheerleader for either both teams' offenses or both teams' defenses. And (especially in football) sometimes you'll have the odd case where, as an over bettor, you become a rabid fan of a team's *defense* because the game is tied near the end of regulation and the only chance of your over bet winning is for the defense to get a stop and send the game to overtime, where both teams could potentially score more.

Speaking of which, unless you've placed a bet that explicitly excludes extra time, overtime is always part of deal for your bet. Whether you've bet on a moneyline, a point spread, or on an over/under bet, overtime or extra innings is part of that bet. The final score, including overtime(s), is the only thing that matters.

So if you've bet on the Broncos +3 against the Vikings and the 4th quarter ends with the game tied, you can pat yourself on the back for having correctly predicted the Broncos would stay within 3 points for 4 quarters, but your bet hasn't won yet. It can be infuriating, as when you make an under bet on a basketball game that that is way under the total at the end of regulation but also tied. On the other hand, overtime can be a second chance if you've bet on a big favorite that's only able to pull away in overtime. I'll talk about nuances of over/under betting in Part 3, where we delve into each major sport.

Multi-Bet Wagers

Bookmakers have learned how to attract bettors, and an important innovation in the sports betting world was the creation of bets that connect the outcome of two different games.

Parlays: Let it ride

Imagine a scenario where you have a little money to bet and you find two NFL games you absolutely love. To maximize your returns, your plan is to place the first −110 bet and then put all the proceeds if you win onto a second −110 bet. That means your $10 stake will grow to $19.09 if the first game wins. Then you'll place that entire amount on the second game in hopes of turning it into $36.45. There's only one problem: The games start at the same time, so there's no way to let your winnings ride, right?

Fortunately, the bookmaker has an option for you to let your bet ride virtually in the form of a *parlay* bet. When you place a parlay bet, you're selecting two (or sometimes more!) bets and tying their results together. The parlay bet wins when all of the constituent bets win, and the payoff is roughly equivalent to your "let it ride" strategy described above.

Here's a quick example:

NFL Regular Season 10:30 a.m.	Spread
Atlanta Falcons	−4
N.Y. Jets	47
Las Vegas Raiders	43
Seattle Seahawks	−7

For these two NFL games, you decide to parlay both favorites listed above. Colloquially, you've "parlayed the Falcons −4 and the Seahawks −7 for $10. Your bet wins if both teams win their individual bets, covering their respective spreads. This parlay loses should *either* team fail to cover the spread. The payoff for parlaying two −110 bets like this is 2.6-to-1, or +260. So your $10 becomes $36 if you prevail.

Here are a few key facts about parlays:

>> **Most bookmakers will let you parlay up to a dozen or more bets.** Just remember that *every* bet must win for the parlay to cash.

>> **You can mix and match bets inside your parlay.** Not only can you parlay point spread bets, total bets, and even moneyline bets, but you're free to add bets across different sports inside your parlay.

>> **You are free to parlay games across times and dates.** In November, you can parlay a Wednesday night NBA game with a Sunday afternoon NFL game.

>> **In the event a leg of your parlay is cancelled or (more likely) pushes, your parlay is not dead.** The bookmaker just treats your parlay as if it was one size smaller in terms of payout odds. If there's a push in your 4-bet parlay, you'll have to win the remaining 3 bets and will get paid out according to the 3-team parlay odds.

Parlay odds

The odds for a parlay bet depend completely on the odds of its constituent bets. The good news is that when you parlay −110 bets, the payoff amounts are mostly standardized across bookmakers. It's good to commit the fair payout odds to memory, so check out Table 2-3.

TABLE 2-3

Parlay Payouts at −110 Odds

Number of Bets in Your Parlay	Approximate Fair Payout Odds (or Moneyline)
2	13 to 5 or +264
3	6 to 1 or +600
4	12 to 1 or +1,228
5	24 to 1 or +2,435
6	47 to 1 or +4,741
7	91 to 1 or +9,142
8	175 to 1 or +17,544

WARNING

Why am I qualifying these odds with the word "fair," you ask? Because sports books often charge a little more vig on parlay bets, especially when you get above four or five teams. I'll talk later in the book about how to spot when you're being overcharged by your bookmaker.

You don't have to restrict your parlay bets to −110 bets. You're free to parlay two −250 moneyline favorites together or two +250 underdogs if you want. Just know that the bookmaker isn't going to compensate you very well for parlaying two heavy favorites, and they'll give you a much fatter payout than the standard 13-to-5 for parlaying two underdogs.

How much is the payout on a parlay? The easy answer is: Ask your bookmaker. If you want to do the math yourself, there's no straightforward way to do it with moneylines. However, if you convert each moneyline to European-style decimal odds mentioned in a sidebar earlier in the chapter, you can multiply each leg of your parlay together. (Remember, decimal odds just show you the amount the bookie returns to you for every $1 bet.) For example a −200 moneyline is equal to 1.5 decimal odds. If you parlay 3 different −200 bets together, you'd turn every $1 bet into 1.5 times 1.5 times 1.5 = 3.375 or $3.37. That's your $1 stake plus $2.27 in profits.

Teasers: A little help

A teaser bet is similar to a parlay in that you connect two or more bets that must all win for your bet to pay off. The twist is that the games come with a built-in advantage over the market value of the point spread or the total. The bookmaker then compensates for changing the handicap on the games by reducing the payout odds of the bet.

An example will quickly bring clarity. Here are the two football games again from the parlay example.

NFL Regular Season 10:30am	Spread
Atlanta Falcons	−4
N.Y. Jets	47
Las Vegas Raiders	43
Seattle Seahawks	−7

To bet a teaser, you pick two or more bets, and then you select from a menu of spread or total handicaps, which then get applied to every game. For example, if you place a two-team 6-point football teaser on the Raiders and the Falcons, the spread on each game is adjusted by 6 points *in your teams' favor.* The market handicap on the Raiders is +7, but that leg of your teaser will get evaluated at Raiders +13. The Falcons are −4, so adding 6 points in your favor means that bet changes to Falcons +2.

In other words, when you tease a bet, those extra points mean you're raising the chances of winning each leg. The downside is that the payout is greatly reduced relative to a parlay.

The following table shows specific payouts for a pro football teaser plus specific payouts for a pro basketball teaser. As with a parlay, the more bets you include, the better your payout.

Number of Bets in Your Teaser	6-Point NFL Payout Odds	4-Point NBA Payout Odds
2	5 to 7	10 to 11
3	8 to 5	9 to 5
4	12 to 5	13 to 5
5	4 to 1	4 to 1
6	6 to 1	13 to 2
7	8 to 1	9 to 1
8	10 to 1	12 to 1

Here are some more teaser basics:

>> Like parlays you can include spread bets and over/under bets in your teaser.

>> The point adjustment on your teaser gets applied to each bet. If you place a 6-point teaser on the Falcons/Jets under 47 along with the Seahawks –7, the bets will be evaluated with an adjusted total of 53 in the former case, and Seahawks –1 in the latter case.

>> Teasers are most common in basketball (where you can select 4-, 5-, or 6-point teasers) and football (where you can select 6-, 6.5-, and 7-point teasers). Some bookmakers have other handicap options.

>> Because an individual point has a specific value depending on whether you're talking about football or basketball, pro or college, most experts would tell you not to mix sports when you make a teaser bet.

Variations on a Theme

Armed with full understanding of these major betting concepts opens the door to an endless variety of bets on sporting events. Here are some examples of bets you can make using the moneyline, point spread, and total concepts:

>> **Quarter/half/inning/period betting:** Bookmakers will list point spreads, moneylines, and totals that apply only to part of a game. For example, if you think UCLA has a tendency to start strong but fade late, maybe you should place a moneyline bet on them to win the 1st half.

>> **Alternate point spreads:** You can get a different moneyline if you're willing to place a bet using a different point spread. For example, instead of a –110 bet on Hawaii –6, you can get a +200 moneyline if you're willing to bet Hawaii –13. (How confident are you in the Rainbow Warriors?)

>> **Over/under team points:** Similar to an over/under bet on the combined total points, this bet pays off when you bet above or below the bookmaker's number for a single team.

Exotic bets

Exotic might be overstating it just a bit, but when you get into wagers outside the family of common sports bets (moneyline bets, point spread bets, and over/under bets), you're definitely not in Kansas anymore. These bets involve events on the field (and sometimes off) limited only by the bookie's imagination. While there's no hard-and-fast definition, most people classify exotic bets into a few broad categories:

>> **Prop bet:** A wager on a specific proposition within a single game. Examples are things like an individual basketball player shooting a certain number of 3-pointers, or a team scoring a specified range of points.

>> **Futures bet:** A wager on a specific sports outcome that requires multiple games to resolve, possible the entire season. Common futures bets include betting on an NFL team to win the Super Bowl or to make the playoffs.

Every sport comes with its own particular array of both prop bets and futures bets. Odds are usually given as in any other moneyline wager.

Prop bets

Before the internet, sports bettors had limited options at game time. You could bet what you saw on the big board: sides, totals, maybe halftime bets. In the bigger betting houses, a bettor could always request one-off bets on obscure propositions. ("Hey, Ace, what kinda odds you give me fer Mantle hittin' two dingers t'day?") Bookmakers could either come up with odds on the spot and book the bet, or they could simply refuse the action.

But remember, bookmakers seek to balance their action, and before the internet, there was no easy way to make a balanced market for a bet that few people were thinking about. So betting on props was limited, and the maximum bet amounts had to stay low to keep risk in check. In today's computerized, digitally connected betting market, bookmakers can offer prop bets to the public and set the odds to ensure balance. In the example above, a bookie might list this bet:

MLB 1966 All-Star Game	Odds
Mantle hits two or more home runs	+425
Mantle hits one or zero home runs	−300

That means bookmakers with an online presence can offer a huge variety of prop bets, secure in the knowledge that they can find a way to balance the action.

Later in the book, I'll talk about bets that go beyond moneylines, point spreads, and totals. There are combination bets that require winning outcomes across different games, and there are bets that take entire seasons to play out, and more. For now, let the basics soak in.

IN THIS CHAPTER

» **Understanding how bookmakers make money**

» **Placing a bet in person**

» **Betting online**

» **Using a local bookie (not recommended)**

» **Playing state lotteries**

Chapter **3**

The House

This chapter deals with any entity (or person) who books bets, that is, they act as the counterparty for sports bettors. This shouldn't surprise you, but *booking* a bet is another name for taking a wager from a bettor. Offering a menu of bets is one thing, but it's not official until its booked.

In the previous chapter, I talked about how the standard odds for a bet is known as an 11/10 bet, or in moneyline terms, a −110 bet. When odds aren't explicitly stated, you're usually looking at an 11/10 bet, which means you're betting $11 to win $10.

REMEMBER

A moneyline with a minus sign in front if it means you're looking at the number of dollars you'd have to risk to profit $100. If it has no sign or a plus sign, that's the amount you profit for risking $100.

If you and a friend wanted to make a friendly wager about who's going to win the Stanley Cup at the end of the hockey season, you'd likely have a brief informal negotiation to arrive at acceptable odds for each of you. For the sake of argument, let's say you like the Pittsburgh Penguins, a powerhouse this year, and your friend likes the Calgary Flames, who are middle-of-the-road at best. Your friend wants to take your bet, but expects you to acknowledge the higher likelihood of the Penguins winning, so he asks for you to risk $5 to his $1. You think that's a little much (the Pens aren't that good) and offer $4 to his $1. He accepts, so you've just made a bet at 4-to-1 odds. If Pittsburgh wins, he gives you a buck. If the Flames win, you owe him $4. (If neither wins, you agree that no money will change hands.)

Betting with odds provides a convenient way to balance reward with risk. If bettors see an outcome as more unlikely, it should command a higher return for a set amount of risk.

With this personal bet example in mind, you'll be interested to know that bookmakers operate differently from a private bet between friends in several important ways:

>> **The bookmaker offers a menu of bets they'd be willing to book.** Although if you go to an in-person bookmaker and you don't see a bet you want on the board, they'll sometimes be willing to provide odds for you on the spot.

>> **Bookmakers list odds for every bet, and as you'll find out in this chapter, it's practically the most important part of their business.** If you like the bet and its odds, you can make the bet. If you like the bet but not the odds, don't bet it. You're not going to change the bookmaker's mind on the odds.

>> **Bookmakers take bets that either win or lose.** You won't be able to find an "either the Penguins or the Flames" bet unless they were meeting in the Stanley Cup Final. (There are exceptions: When a bet you make results in a tie or if an unusual event happens surrounding the event, bookmakers will cancel the bet and give you back your original stake.)

>> **Handshake agreements are nonexistent with legal bookmakers.** To place a bet, you have to lay down cold hard cash (or a few equivalents) up front. Having said that, people who bet with "unlicensed" (read: illegal) bookmakers know you can bet on credit, which has its own risks and benefits.

The advantage you have over the bookmaker is that you can opt to pass on a bet. Bookmakers can refuse bets and limit action, but they are in business to accept wagers on a wide variety of bets. It's a business like any other, with competitive pressure to offer good service and a wide variety of wagering options.

The Sports Betting Business

Bookmakers have been around to take advantage of bettors' gambling proclivities for centuries. In the United States, the business started with horse races and then grew along with the popularity of various sports. Stories abound that there were as many bookmakers as there were fans at the parks and fields of professional baseball, which began its run as the nation's pastime after the Civil War. With money to be made on virtually any sporting event with an uncertain outcome, bookmaking spread to boxing, college football, pro football, and basketball in the 20th century.

Inventing the modern sports book

As Nevada become the last refuge for sports betting in the 1960s, and with the increasing ability of larger establishments to centralize information and accept risk, it was a natural fit for casinos to offer race and sports books, doing the business of private bookies on a larger, more comfortable scale.

If you're interested in learning to bet on horse races, let me recommend the excellent *Betting on Horse Racing For Dummies.*

While Nevada harbored sports betting through the dark ages following the Wire Act of 1961 (which effectively shut down sports betting across the rest of the country), the business flourished in the rest of the world.

Online options began to emerge in the late 1990s for Americans who wanted to bet on sports. Companies began setting up operations, sometimes shady and sometimes not, in the Caribbean and Central America to serve the U.S. market.

Today's business

After the fall of the federal proscriptions against sports betting in the 49 states other than Nevada (which I discussed in Chapter 1), companies are swooping in to scoop up concessions for states without incumbent establishments to take bets.

If you're in the United States, you have several options for betting on sports depending on which state you're in. if you want to stay on the right side of the law, you'll need to live in, or travel to, a state that allows sports betting. Some states have brick-and-mortar bookmakers where you walk up to a counter and make a bet; some have legally sanction mobile betting options; and some have both. Offshore bookmakers will take your business regardless of what your state lawmakers think about sports betting, as will local non-sanctioned bookmakers. The next few sections cover the ins and outs of both options.

In-Person Betting

The way most Americans legally bet on sports prior to the internet age is inside a casino (or betting parlor). Sports books come in all shapes and sizes. In smaller venues, the sports book is as simple as a single counter and bet taker with some form of display for current odds. In the bigger resorts, you just follow the signs for

"Race and Sports Book," and you'll find a big room that looks a little like NASA mission control, except instead of rocket scientists monitoring spacecraft, you'll see bettors monitoring the "big board" that lists games and odds and watching live broadcasts of ongoing sporting events and horse races.

When you're in a casino, the loudest place is often the craps tables, where gamblers hoot and holler after a dramatic roll of the dice. But race and sports books come in a close second. In the biggest venues, there are comfy chairs and gigantic TVs showing games going on at that moment. Watching a game from a big sports book is a little like going to the game. It's perfectly acceptable to cheer on your team; just know that there will be fans and bettors wanting the exact opposite outcome. Be a good sport. It's easy for peoples' blood to be up when there's money on the line.

Placing a bet in person is as simple as walking to a betting window, telling the bet writer what you want to bet on, forking over cash for your stake, and walking away with your betting tickets. If your bet loses, you can toss your tickets in the trash. If it wins, bring your tickets back to the same counter to receive proceeds from your winning bets. For most bets, a tie or cancellation means you turn your ticket in for your original bet amount.

TIP

Unlike the rest of the casino, race and sports books rarely stay open 24 hours. If you've got a winning ticket and the sports book is closed, you have a couple of options:

>> The casino cashier counter (also know as "the cage") can cash tickets in casinos of any size. They usually have the appropriate scanner to check your ticket and pay off your winning bets.

>> On the back of your ticket is instructions for receiving payment by mail. If the game hasn't finished as you're running to catch your flight, you can send your ticket in and the casino will issue you a check by mail. It sounds sketchy, but I've done it many times without issue.

The big board: Reading the betting menu

If you're in a domestic casino or sports book, the first thing you'll notice is the big board, which is a listing of all of the most popular sports, games, and proposition bets available for you to bet on. The board is divided up by sport, and the events are put in order of start time, with a few exceptions. Most electronic boards are kept up to date with scores for games underway. You're also likely to see final scores for recently completed games, along with that game's closing odds.

TICKET PARKING

It goes without saying that you need to keep your betting tickets in a safe place until your bet is resolved. Sports betting tickets are what lawyers might call *bearer instruments.* That is, if you're in possession of it, you're presumed to be the owner, just like a casino chip or a dollar bill.

But there are some easy ways to protect your sports bets beyond having a bad-ass wallet. First, if there's a loyalty or affinity program available at the sports book or the associated casino, join up! Make sure you present your membership card at the time you place your bets. Not only will you get the benefits associated with the program (maybe drink tickets or cash back), but your bets will be logged in the bookmaker's database, which can come in handy. Second, take a picture of your betting tickets and make sure you have a clear image of the unique serial number associated with each bet. With these precautions in place, it's much harder for a random person to cash your ticket if they find it on the floor in the men's room (yuck). And if you accidentally tear your ticket to shreds, the sports book can look up your bet and pay out your win (provided the ticket hadn't already been cashed).

One note of caution: Keep the images of your betting tickets off of the internet. Or if you insist on showing your bets off to your Instagram followers, make sure to blur out the serial number.

Reading the betting menu

With limited space available on the display, sports books have to cram a lot of information into a small area. You may have to do some searching to find what you're looking for, but as a rule, the most popular sports and bets get the prime real estate. If in doubt, walk up to the counter and ask where you can find odds for your preferred game.

At a minimum you will find the following data about upcoming games:

>> Header information:

- Date of competition

- League / Sport

- Game title or details (for example, Rose Bowl, NBA Playoffs 1st Round, or NFL Preseason)

- Wager type (for example, 1st Half or Regular Season Wins)

Then for each listed game you'll see the following:

>> Rotation number or Bet ID (see below)

>> Scheduled start time and TV information

>> Team names or abbreviations

>> Side and total odds (which can look different depending on the sport)

>> Starting pitcher (baseball only)

>> Indication if betting is limited

The rotation number

Since the 1970s, every major sports betting house has taken advantage of a standard system for identifying games, now known as the *rotation*. Every sports bet has a rotation number, which is a 3-digit (or sometimes more) code that is unique to that bet for that day. The most prominent games get two consecutive 3-digit codes, one associated with each team or individual athlete involved in a bet. The rotation number follows those teams regardless of schedule changes, and no other available bet will have that same number — regardless of sport.

Once a game has started, the sports book will often replace the rotation number with an updated score. Once the game is final, the display will show the final score and derivative scores (like halftime score).

Interpreting the big board

The following listing shows a small sample of the college betting menu on an early season Saturday.

College Football, Sept 7th

	Rot	Team	Spread/Total	ML	1st Half Wagering		
11a	101	TEXAS	–6½	–340	2101	–3–120	–180
CBS	102	OHIO ST	44	+260	2102	+3+100 / 22	+155
1115a	155	WAKE FST	49	+200	2155	25	+130
	156	RUTGERS	–5	–240	2156	–2½	–145
1120a	105	SYRACUSE	–11	–950	2105	–6	–310
ESPN	106	PITT	46	+600	2106	24	+290
1145a	107	FAU	39	+120	2107	20	+105
	108	MIAMI FL	–1½	–135	2108	Pk	–120

First of all, we're looking at odds for four separate college football games on September 7, and they're listed in order of start time, which you can see in the left-most column along with the broadcasting TV network. Then you'll see four columns describing full-game bets, and three columns on the right describing betting odds for the first half only.

The board lists games according to start time. The rotation numbers are assigned according to how games are scheduled prior to the season starting, but sometimes there are scheduling changes, so the games won't always appear in rotation number order. In this example, the Wake Forest versus Rutgers game was originally scheduled as a night kickoff, but it got rescheduled after rotation numbers had been assigned.

The two game participants will always have consecutive rotation numbers. And once they're assigned to a particular bet on a particular day, the rotation numbers never change. Every representation of these games, no matter which sports book you're in, domestic or international, brick-and-mortar or online, you'll see the same numbers.

The other thing you probably noticed is the columns on the right show 1st half betting odds. These bets — and any bets derived from the main game bets — will use that same base rotation number as the full game bet, but with a prefix of one or more numbers to set it apart from the whole game bets.

REMEMBER

Rotation numbers make it easy for people to clarify which bets they're talking about, but if you don't have to actually talk to a real person to place a bet, you may not need them at all. Online bookmakers, especially those not catering to North American bettors, sometimes don't bother displaying rotation numbers.

Multiway and futures bets

The main display at a sports book will often include bets you can make where there are more than two competitors or teams. For this week's NASCAR race or the next golf tournament, you'll get a list of competitors with updated odds. Make sure you read the description of the bet at the top of the display. Instead of betting on the winner, you might be looking at secondary bet, like odds to finish the car race, or odds that the player will make the cut.

2025 Masters — Champion

ROT#	PLAYER	ODDS
72701	McIlroy	+200
72702	Koepka	+320

ROT#	PLAYER	ODDS
72703	Morikawa	+600
72704	Willett	+900
72705	Chandra	+1,100
72706	Hovland	+1,900

Futures bet are listed and handled the same way as a multiway bet. The only difference is their time horizon. They're called "futures" because your placing on a bet that may not resolve for several months up to a year.

2022 Heisman Trophy Winner

ROT#	Player	Odds
79061	Ditto	+200
79062	Garrett	−120
79063	Staton	+400
79064	Vencill	+600
79065	Chandra	+1,100
79066	Cole	+1,300

For multiway and futures bets, you'll see the different betting options listed in rotation order, not in order of shortest odds to longest odds. And because odds can change over time due to intervening events and action from bettors, you'll sometimes find that the favorite for the event sits somewhere in the middle of the list.

2024 NFC East Champions

ROT#	Team	Odds
43202	Cowboys	2/1
43203	Eagles	6/1
43204	Redskins	9/1
43305	Giants	18/1

Multiway and futures bets are frequently shown with *fractional odds* instead of a moneyline. Regardless of what form they take, the odds are designed to show you how much a winning bet pays relative to the amount risked.

Proposition bets on the big board

When a big game is approaching, you'll often see a collection of associated prop bets listed together on the board. Read the description at the top of the bet, and before you place a wager, make sure you clarify any questions with a ticket writer.

Super Bowl LXI — First Team to 10 Points

ROT#	Team	Odds
130401	Miami Dolphins	–125
130402	Dallas Cowboys	–105
130403	Neither	+8,500

Super Bowl LXI — Highest Scoring Quarter

ROT#	Team	Odds
130435	First Quarter	+500
130436	Second Quarter	+175
130437	Third Quarter	+450
130438	Fourth Quarter	+205
130439	Two or More Quarters Have Equal Highest Score	+800

Again, the rotation numbers for the betting option in each prop are consecutive, and to keep it even simpler for bettors, all prop bets connected to a single event start with the same numerical prefix.

TIP

At most brick-and-mortar sports books, you'll find a display case with stacks of betting sheets or *odds sheets* for each major sport that's in season or for a big upcoming event. Odds sheets are meant to take the content on the big board and put it on a piece of paper for gamblers to take with them. All the pertinent betting information on upcoming games is there, and there are even sheets for prop and futures bets.

Sports books typically print a new sheet every day with that day's schedule for the major sports. Grab one for each of sport you're interested in and use it to make notes. Keep in mind though that the odds you see on paper might have changed since the sheet was printed. For the latest odds, you'll need to review the big board or ask a bet writer at the betting window.

Step by step: How to place an in-person bet

Your neck is starting to hurt from looking up at the big board, so it's time to make some decisions and place a few bets. If you're feeling a little intimidated, here's the step-by-step process to make things easy for you.

1. Make a list of the rotation numbers and bet type for every bet you want to place. The betting sheets are perfect for this.

   Write the type of bet next to each bet number: spread, moneyline, over, or under.

2. Check (then double-check) that you have enough cash or voucher credit to cover all your wagers. Credit cards will not be accepted! If you're in a big casino, they will sometimes accept chips at the betting window.

3. Make sure you don't cut in line. During busier times, the line will be obvious, but sometimes it's hard to tell the difference between a person waiting for an open betting window versus a person lingering in front of the counter watching a game. Ask!

4. When it's your turn at the counter, hand the ticket writer any winning tickets from completed games. If your plan is to place new wagers using proceeds from winning bets, tell the ticket writer before he starts counting out cash.

5. Give the teller the essential information about your bet, slowly and clearly. If you're going to place multiple bets, it doesn't hurt to start by saying "I've got four different football bets." While you don't want to waste their time with extraneous information, you also want to set the teller up for successfully translating your words into betting tickets.

   For each bet, the essential information is the rotation number, the type of bet (point spread, moneyline, or over/under) and the amount of your wager. For example, you might say "Bet Number 2101, moneyline, $50." (In the bet menu example earlier in this chapter, that's a bet on the Texas Longhorns to win the first half outright against Ohio State.)

   For a total bet on the Texas-Ohio State game, you might say: "Bet 102, over, $10" which means you're risking $10 on the Texas-Ohio State game to go over 44 total points.

REMEMBER

   When you make an over/under bet, you can use the rotation number of either team when you state your wager. "Bet 102, over $10" is the same as saying "Bet 101, over $10."

6. For multi-team bets like parlays and teasers, tell the bet writer up front what kind of bet you're placing. One bet might be "I want to do a two-team parlay on bet 102 and bet 106 under for $25," which tells the bet writer you're risking $25 on a parlay bet that includes the Ohio State point spread and the Pittsburgh-Syracuse under.

7. As you give the details of each bet, the ticket writer will punch the information into the sports book point-of-sale device, and the most helpful ones will state the name of the team that corresponds to the bet number you give as a way to confirm what you want. The printer will spit out your betting tickets out one at a time.

8. The ticket writer will tell you what you owe, so pay up!

9. Double-check your tickets before you leave the counter. The odds can move up and down, but make sure the big-three data points are correct: bet number/team, bet type, and bet amount. Once you walk away, the bet is final.

TIP

Finally, there are a few unspoken etiquette items to remember at the sports book that will make you a good betting citizen:

>> You know those signs at the pharmacy that ask you to wait a few steps back "for patient privacy"? Assume the same rule applies at the sports book counter. Your commentary on the next guy's wager choices or amount is best kept to yourself. Mind your own business while you're in line and at the counter; save your friendly observations and questions for when you're away from the betting window.

>> There is often a rush between early games and afternoon games on NFL Sunday, or on other big sporting days where games are scheduled close together. Bettors have to wait till early games finish before they can cash their tickets, and they often need the funds from their cashed tickets to bet the next round of games. If your transaction isn't time sensitive (like if you're cashing a final winning ticket without making additional bets), wait until the line goes down.

>> The other thing that will drive fellow bettors crazy is approaching the counter without a plan. You don't want to be standing there at the counter scanning the big board for rotation numbers, calling audibles on bets, and generally taking up everyone's time. If there's no line, chitchat is perfectly acceptable at the window. But if there are people waiting, make your bets and get out.

And in the end, the odds you get are equal to the odds you give

REMEMBER

The odds you see on the odds sheet or on the big board are subject to change until your bet has been accepted by the bookmaker and you have a ticket in hand. Your ticket will explicitly show the final terms of the bet, including any relevant numbers (like a point spread or a total that will determine whether your bet wins or loses) along with the payout schedule should your wager be a winner.

For example, a betting ticket might say "Redskins +3½ −110, $50 to pay $95.45." That tells you everything you need to know about the bet. Your stake is $50 on the Redskins +3½. At −110 odds, the profit from the bet would be $45.45. So if the Redskins cover the spread, the bookmaker will pay you $95.45 for your ticket, which is the initial $50 bet plus $45.45 in winnings.

And unlike pari-mutuel betting (think horse racing) where the odds are finalized once the race is over, the terms of a sports bet are locked in place at the moment it's accepted by the bookmaker and the ticket is printed. That can mean good news or bad news for bettors. The spread is said to move "with you" if you're able to place a bet before the odds get worse, and "against you" if you would have been better off waiting before placing the wager. If you have Redskins +3½ and the odds move down to Redskins +3 before kickoff, you're in possession of a bet that's at a slight advantage relative to the market. On the other hand, you're at a slight disadvantage if the spread moves to Redskins +4. I'll talk more about how the odds are created and evolve in the next chapter.

The morning after

Once the games are in progress, the sports book will often show results on the big board, such as halftime scores in college basketball. After a game raps, you'll see the final score and the closing spread and total. Game results will stay up as long as there's room, which usually means about 12 hours. So when you come back in the morning, you can check yesterday's scores.

Online Betting

If you're looking for betting in the convenience of your own home, workplace, car, or anywhere, you're in luck: The internet's tubes reach all the way to sports books that will book your bets remotely.

Betting online requires you to open an account, deposit money, and maintain a balance with an internet bookmaker. Your online betting account acts as a special-purpose bank account where you place bets against your balance. If you win, your balance goes up. If you lose and your balance drops to zero, you'll have to reload your account by making another deposit if you want to keep betting.

If you're winning more than you're losing and your balance grows to the point where you're ready to see the spoils of your hard work betting on sports, you can request a withdrawal and the bookmaker will (hopefully) send you the amount you request.

Betting online has its advantages:

>> **No-wait convenience:** Instead of waiting in line at a sports book, just fire up your laptop or your mobile device and off you go. For bettors looking to pounce on weak odds, this is a huge advantage over having to be physically present to make a bet.

>> **In-game betting:** Some sports bettors like the action of betting on the next play in football, the next inning in baseball, or even on the outcome of the next period or quarter. Sports book apps are so advanced that they can offer bets without requiring a human to analyze probabilities and decide on odds. That means a world of betting possibilities are just a click away.

>> **Deeper odds menus:** Online casinos make hundreds of proposition bets available that are too numerous to fit onto the board at even the biggest sports book. For example, it's not unusual for a typical internet bookmaker to offer several dozen bets on a single regular season baseball game.

>> **Better odds (maybe):** The sharpest sports bettors like to seize the moment and bet heavily on odds that have advantageous prices before the market can catch up. In the old days, shopping for the best odds meant physically going from casino to casino. Today, bettors with multiple online accounts can quickly compare point spreads and moneylines to find the best possible price. Having said that, individual sports books almost always cater to certain types of players. In the same way that a grocery store might offer cheap beer and wine but more expensive dairy and bakery products, if you've only got a single online sports betting account, you might be paying a premium for the kinds of bets you like to place.

And of course there are disadvantages to online betting:

>> **Too easy:** Winning at sports betting requires picking the right side at the right price, and being awash in betting options can make it tempting to make bets that have neither.

>> **No personal touch:** If there's a dispute about a bet, or a question about an event, or a request for the bookmaker to create odds on a custom event, the bettor operating through an in-person bookmaker has a far better chance of getting a response to their satisfaction. Online bookmakers are impersonal and automated.

>> **Delayed gratification:** There is a felicitous joy in standing at the counter at a sports book and having them count out hundred-dollar bills to pay off the bet you made on the game that just finished. Betting online means your balance can jump, but the tactile immediacy of cashing in a ticket is lost.

>> **Offshore hassles:** If you're betting through an offshore bookmaker, there is variability in how easy it is to deposit money, create an account, and make a withdrawal.

Online bookmakers often come with handy casinos too, just a click or two away. For some sports bettors, it's a feature: You can play blackjack while you're waiting for the game to start! But for some of us (including me), it's a distraction. And for a subset of the distracted types, it's a money sink that cuts into sports betting profits. And for yet another subset, it's hazardous. For people susceptible to gambling's dark forces, betting online makes things worse. When placing a bet is just a click away, it's easy for problem gamblers to weave destructive behaviors into every part of their life.

Domestic online sports books

Internet gaming grew in fits and starts as gamblers, gaming companies, lawmakers, courts, payment processors, and other stakeholders attempted to navigate the collection of laws and regulations concerning the act of placing bets on the internet.

Some of the states that have legalized sports betting have passed laws either specifically allowing or prohibiting online sports bets. Check out Table 1-3 in Chapter 1 to see the status of your state as of publication time.

Tight geolocation controls in apps mean they can limit your action to betting while you're in the state. Once you cross the border, the app won't accept any more bets.

Offshore sports books

If you're in a state that hasn't yet passed a law allowing in-person betting, your only option that doesn't involve travel is betting online through offshore sports books, which have been around as long as the internet has.

Many of them set up shop in the Caribbean and Central America to cater to American customers under a loose interpretation of the Wire Act that would let them operate just outside the reach of U.S. law enforcement. But the 2006 anti-gambling statues cut more American sports bettors off from offshore bookmakers when it became illegal for U.S. banks to process gambling payments.

But where there's a will, there's a way. The gigantic underserved American market prompted international casinos and bookmakers to innovate and find ways to process deposits and withdrawals without relying on American institutions. Although several major betting houses abandoned the U.S. market in 2006, there are now several dozen legitimate offshore bookmakers for Americans to turn to. In Appendix B, I provide information on some of the major players in the market.

Betting kiosks/casino apps

It's worth mentioning that many of the biggest casinos have an interest in letting you place sports bets as easily as possible, so some sports books make kiosks available that offer a blended experience for bettors. You insert cash or vouchers, make a bet through a touchscreen interface, and you're issued a betting ticket, just like you bet at the counter in the sports book. When you win, you insert your winning tickets and are issued a voucher that can be turned into cash at the cashier or the betting window.

TIP

Many big casinos have issued their own betting apps that work in concert with the in-person sports book. Go to the counter in the sports book and they'll help you open an account and establish a balance through cash or casino credit, and then you can bet on your mobile device with an app that's skinned (that is, branded with that place's logos and colors) to look like any other casino offering. While it may look unique to the casino, the guts of the skinned application are based on an application that casinos buy and dress up to look like their own.

I Got a Guy: Private Bookmakers

The traditional, unsanctioned way to bet on sports is with a private bookmakers, also known as your friendly neighborhood *bookie.* In the old days, bookies were the only game in town. But the world's second oldest profession has persisted, and, believe it or not, the private bookie still has a place in the sports betting universe, even with so many offshore betting houses and waves of states legalizing sports betting.

It turns out that there are niches the big companies and betting houses can't quite fill. Private bookmaker might do it full-time or part-time, but either way, they can't quite operate in the full glare of the law, so they get new clients on a referral basis. They maintain a list of anywhere from a few dozen to a few hundred long-term clients, depending on their tolerance for risk and their ability to handle the logistics of so many bettors.

As a new client, you'd be extended a small line of credit and tight betting maximums. Over time, as you prove that you're discreet and you pay on time, the limitations on your account get loosened.

Why go through a bookie when an internet casino is a few clicks away?

>> **The personal touch:** Private bookmakers establish relationships with their clients and provide credit and favors in proportion to your behavior, and that is your ability to pay on time and the level of self-control you can demonstrate.

>> **Flexible betting:** Some major betting houses are corporate-owned and have little tolerance for success among their bettors. For the select few sharps in the world, private bookmakers offer a way to bet more on big games. Even if you're not a big bettor, a private bookie often has looser rules on bets, accepting correlated parlays (which I will talk about later) or offering a special-order betting line on an obscure event.

>> **Accountability:** It's not an accident there are so many pawn shops in Las Vegas. Where a big impersonal company in charge of a sports book might not care if you start betting your rent on Bundesliga games, a private bookmaker can recognize when you're betting out of your depth and has the tools to cut you off. It's not really about altruism as much as it's about needing customers who can pay on a regular basis when they lose. But the personal relationship that develops means your bookie just might be the one telling you to slow down, while the big corporate sports book would be urging you to cash in your 401k.

Private bookies used to have a certain rhythm during football season: Everybody settles up their debts on Tuesday; then payouts come on Wednesday. It's not quite as rigid these days, but the expectation is that every player maintains their account within a certain range. For example, a beginning bettor gets $500 in credit, and his account range is negative $500 up positive $250.

Maybe every other week, the bookie looks at your account and determines where you stand. If you take some losses and you go down $700 after a football weekend, because it's below the $500 credit limit, you'd be cut off from betting until you can pay at least $200 off to back to your limit. You'd owe every penny of the full $700, but as long as you're keeping your account no worse than −$500 every week, you can continue to bet — within reason. On the other hand, if you win, you could either bet against your credit, or you could request a cash payout for any balance greater than $250.

Before the age of the internet, bookies might operate like bootleggers and spies of old, taking bets by phone through a set of secret client names and betting codes. Today, it's less Mario Puzo and more Jeff Bezos: Bookies give their clientele a white-label betting application (hosted overseas) and sit back and watch the bets roll in rather than manning a phone bank.

Okay, I know you want to ask: What about the baseball bat to the knee when I can't pay? Being in debt to anyone for an illegal activity is a bad thing. When your gray market creditor doesn't have the normal remedies available to collect on a debt (ruining your credit score, going to the courts), there's always a concern that things could turn ugly. But a skillful local bookie won't let you get to that point. It's not in his interest or yours. And at the end of the day, like any creditor, they'd much rather figure out a way to help you pay your debt so that you can keep playing (eventually). I would never claim violence has been eradicated, but it's probably greatly overblown. In the immortal words of Sollozzo in *The Godfather*, "Blood is a big expense."

WARNING

Gambling and betting on credit with a bookie is a bad mix for some people. It can be tempting to chase losses when you're not forking out cold hard cash as you would in an in-person sports book. A good bookie will stop you and have you pay down your debt. A bad bookie will recognize you're on a cold streak and let you make a big bet to even the score.

TIP

So this is great information, but where can you actually find a local bookie? Please. It's *illegal.* You shouldn't participate in law-breaking behavior, and you should absolutely never ask a bartender at a local sports bar if they know anyone who takes bets. If you encounter guys at a municipal golf course deli cheering on a big game, it would be quite rude to interrupt and mention how you wish you would've taken the points instead of laying the points.

State Lotteries

When sports betting outside of Nevada was made officially verboten by the PASPA, there were a handful of other states grandfathered into the law. Oregon, Delaware, New Jersey, and Montana (of all places) were given a window to explicitly legalize sports betting (in the case of New Jersey) or had the right to hold state-run contests that includes sporting events.

Now all states are free to transform their existing lottery infrastructure towards the sports betting market. The state of Oregon has offered lotto-like sports betting where players can pick the outcome of multiple sporting events just like buying a scratch-off ticket. Montana is in the process of introducing limited sports betting on its state-run lottery kiosks. There's no doubt many other states will follow suit.

WARNING

Betting through lottery-style games is better than nothing, but it's not quite the same as a full-service sports book. Here are some things to be aware of:

>> If you're hoping to win in the long run, you're going to need more than just a good side picking strategy, because the odds for state-sponsored lottery-style contests are often much worse than you'd get a mainstream sports book. At a normal bookmaker, the bookmaker takes a 4 to 5 percent of every dollar wagered. Professional bettors can live with that; they're looking for edges that can net them a few pennies per dollar wagered. But government run lotteries are not in the business of competing in the bookmaking market, as they have

effective monopolies on sports betting, and they keep as much as 30 cents of every dollar wagered.

>> The betting menu is limited, and the odds are fixed.

>> Check the rules before you play. In a normal parlay bet, a tie means your parlay reverts to the next lower-level bet. (For example, a 3-way parlay where one leg ends in a tie means it now behaves as if it's a 2-way parlay.)

>> The sports betting menus are listed as discrete pools, where each game gets locked on a certain date and time, in some cases several days before the game starts. For NFL bettors, you'll notice you can't bet on Sunday's games after Thursday.

PLAYING THE CANADIAN LOTTERY

Are you a Canadian tired of the America-first approach of this book? I think this paragraph will make you hosers happy, eh? While traditional sports betting is illegal in Canada, there are several government-sponsored contests you can take part in that rely on the outcome of the most popular Canadian and American sports.

While it goes by different names depending on what province you're in, the games are similar and will sound very familiar. Here are some details:

- Play in lottery retail outlets (or with the online app in some provinces).

- Select three to six outcomes from among point spread sides, over/under bets, and prop bets on any combination of games across sports. For your ticket to cash, all selections must win.

- Point spread bets are fixed: You can bet on either side to win big, either side to win small, or for the game to be a close shave or tie. In football contests for example, the win-big spread is always 8 points; the win-small spread is 4 points; and the close shave means the game ends up within 3 or fewer points either way. The ProLine oddsmakers in Ontario adjust the payout odds for each of the point spread options accordingly.

- Wager between C$2 and as much as C$100.

- Odds for each individual bet are listed (in decimal odds) and accumulate toward the payoff amount of your ticket, which varies based on the number of selections you make and how long the odds are. A C$2 ticket full of long shots is potentially worth thousands if they all hit.

Ontario's version, called ProLine, is the most popular, but the game is available by other names in other provinces. (*Mise-O-Jeu* in Quebec. Très joli, no?)

2

Betting Smart

Unravel the mysteries of sports betting odds, from moneyline to point spreads to totals. Learn how they're set and why they move.

Develop your understanding of highly effective habits of successful sports bettors, including winning approaches to bet sizing and bankroll management.

Feed your head with invaluable statistics and probability in a way that won't make your eyes cross.

Learn key concepts with fun gambling examples.

Compare information-based and numbers-based methodologies for picking winners, and develop your own power ratings.

Chapter **4**

Beating the Odds

n the first few chapters, I talked about the two key skills of successful sports bettors. Sure, you'll have to build up some muscle in some peripheral areas like bankroll management, record-keeping, and self-evaluation.

But above all, successful sports bettors must know first how to *handicap* games. That is, they take in information in the lead-up to a game, separating predictive information from noise, and they develop an accurate narrative of how things will play out once the contest begins. Second and less understood is the ability of a sports bettor to analyze and optimize odds. The best bettors are not only able to compare and evaluate the odds on offer from bookmakers, but they can also recognize and place a portfolio of bets that maximize the chance of profiting from a successful handicap.

In this chapter, I'll talk about where odds come from, who plays a role in their evolution, and how they change over time. There's more going on here than you might suspect!

A Tale of Two Numbers

The difference between winning and losing in this arena is winning one or two more bets out of every 20 you place. Sports bettors don't need a PhD in math to succeed, but you're going to need to develop a level of comfort with several mathematical concepts that will help you interpret odds and analyze your bets. I'll start by revisiting expectation, expected value, and break-even percentage.

Great expectation

In the last chapter, I talked about calculating the expectation, or expected value, of a given bet using this formula:

Expectation = (Chance of Winning × Amount Won) + (Chance of Losing × Amount Risked)

Expectation is like a bet's average outcome. You calculate it by adding up each possible outcome multiplied by that outcome's probability. Another example can't hurt, so here's one that's a little more complicated than the ones in the last chapter. You're playing a dice game with a friend, and she offers these rules:

If you roll a 6, she'll pay you $9.

If you roll a 1, 2, 3, 4, or 5, you pay her $2.

Is this a profitable game for you to play? Your intuition probably tells you it is for her, just not so much for you. And sure enough, calculating the expectation, you get this:

Expectation = (.167 × $9) + (.8333 × –$2)

We plugged in numbers from a fair die, where the chance of rolling any single number is 1 out of 6, or 16.7 percent. So the chance of success (rolling a 6) must be 16.7%, and the chance of rolling anything but a 6 must be the opposite: 1 – 16.7%, or 83.3%. So you get an expectation of $1.50 – $1.67 = –$0.17.

We've just calculated the *expected value* or *EV* of playing this dice game. Knowing that it's less than zero, we can conclude that this game is a bad idea if you're looking to make money at it. In fact, for a –EV bet ("minus EV"), if you were to play it over and over, you'll go broke.

Sports bets aren't like dice games or card games. Every game, every play, every swing of the bat is a unique event with singular circumstances. So assigning probabilities is not easy to do. Nevertheless, successful betting means thinking about every bet in a probabilistic way and betting accordingly.

The search for +EV bets (pronounced "plus EV"), or bets where the expectation is positive, is every bettor's mission in life, and it should be yours as well. The concept of expected value has specific implications of profitability in sports betting, but EV has growing cachet in any area where there's something to be maximized, profit margin, yards per play, point per game, and so on.

After successfully injecting itself into baseball over a decade ago, advanced analytics is in the process of infecting both basketball and football. Both sports are being thought about in and coached and played in ways that throw out traditional gut-feel conventional wisdom in favor of data-driven, empirical, evidenced-based thinking. Coaching and scouting staffs are worshipping at the altar of positive EV more than ever before. Run on 1st down to set up the pass? Analytics experts say that's a −EV approach, as evidenced by a growing number of teams passing on 1st and 10. Send receivers on routes past the line-to-gain on 3rd down? That used to make sense, but analytics says throwing *short* of the line and having receivers run for the first down has a better overall probability of success. Sporting decisions in the 2020s and beyond will revolve more and more around EV.

Sports bettors need to understand this concept because it helps them do two things. First, thinking about EV means you can identify coaching staffs doing things on the cutting edge of the game. Second, it's a mindset that encourages data-driven, mathematically rigorous betting.

Breakin' even 2: Electric boogaloo

I also touched on the concept of a break-even percentage in the early chapters of this book. For any bet with a set payout schedule, bettors must achieve a certain minimum winning percentage over time, or they can expect to eventually lose all their money.

The simplest example is a bet that pays even money ($1 profit for every dollar risked), where the break-even percentage is 50 percent. If you win half your bets, you'll survive. But the smallest player disadvantage (for example, a dip in the expected winning percentage to .495 associated with a crooked coin perhaps) will lead to eventual financial ruin for the bettor.

We calculate break-even percentage by taking the amount of the wager and dividing it by the total payout (profit plus the initial wager).

Here are some sample odds and their break-even winning percentages:

>> Coin flip example from above = $1 ÷ $2 = 50%

>> Standard –110 sports bet = $110 ÷ $210 = 52.41%

>> Betting on a 14-to-1 long shot at the horse track = $1 ÷ $15 = 6.67%

For each of the preceding examples, if you aren't winning at the rate listed for each set of odds, you'll be losing money in the long run. If you're winning more often than the listed rate, you can expect to grow your bankroll over time.

As long as you know the payment schedule for a single betting round, which is how much you win relative to how much you risk, then you can always calculate the break-even percentage. Bets that give you a big payday for a win have a much lower break-even percentage. That makes sense. If you can pick 14-to-1 long shots every now and then, you make a big profit, so you don't have to win all that often to be profitable. On the other hand, being on a heavily favored winning side is great, but the payout will be much more modest. You'll need to win these bets more often than your long shots. Either way, if you can't hit your break-even winning percentage for any bet, regardless of the odds, it's a –EV play.

REMEMBER

Start with the published odds and determine the break-even winning percentage. Now figure a realistic chance of winning the bet. As long as your probability is higher than the break-even, it's a +EV bet. Should you make that bet? Usually. Even if your only sports-betting talent is being a +EV picker of 14-to-1 bets, you'll still be subject to unlucky streaks, and that could mean a long time between wins. That can be bad for your psyche, and it makes bankroll management a challenge.

Positive EV, No Instructions Included

I've talked about two related calculations that come at the same question from different directions that answer a simple question: Is a bet worth making or not?

>> If you know the payout schedule determined by the published odds, you can calculate the break-even percentage. That indicates the minimum required win probability to make a bet worth making.

>> If you know the specific winning percentages for a bet (like a coin flip or a card game), or if you're willing to project a winning percentage of a bet, you can take the associated payout schedule and calculate the statistical expectation of a game. If that expected value is negative, don't make the bet unless it's just for fun!

Either approach is valid in assessing a bet.

The missing piece: Win probability

When you assume fair dice and no chicanery from the shooter, you know to a tee what the likelihood is of throwing any number combination, just as you can calculate the likelihood of catching the right card on an inside straight draw. So what about calculating the exact chance of winning a sports bet? Yeah, about that. Have a seat. We need to talk.

I don't need to tell you that athletic endeavors are unique to their moment in time and made up of a nearly infinite number of hard-to-predict and seemingly random events. Games get played using human brains and bodies, sometimes in the elements, sometimes with an oddly shaped ball or other equipment. So many factors that govern the outcome of sporting events are so opaque and unknowable to an outside observer that they have the appearance of being completely random. That makes calculating the win probability of any game inherently difficult.

There is of course no sharp-pencil, chalkboard way to determine the exact probability of a certain outcome in a sporting event. But that doesn't mean we give up on calculating bet expectation and expected values. The best sports bettors use historical data and projections to approximate future probabilities, and then use those probabilities in concert with the odds offered at sports books to determine optimal bets.

Pennies on the dollar

Sometimes the expectation is small. In David Hill's excellent article "Requiem for a Sports Bettor," he describes getting to know a professional bettor whose expectation was no more than a penny or two per dollar wagered. It doesn't sound like much, but if you find a tiny edge and apply it to enough bets, you'll make money in the long run.

Let's do some analysis on a real sports example to determine if we have a +EV opportunity or a −EV opportunity. Imagine you've found an angle on baseball underdogs where the average moneyline odds of the teams you're betting on are +200 (meaning, you risk \$1 to profit \$2). Additionally, you've done some historical work and found that these particular underdogs win 35 percent of the time.

Is this a good bet? You probably have an instinct one way or another, but let's do the math just to make our 5th grade teacher happy. You can either calculate expectation or break-even percentage.

>> Expectation on this bet is the sum of all possible outcomes, weighted by profitability. So .35 times \$2 profit for a win, plus .65 times – \$1 for a loss.

That makes 70 cents – 65 cents, or 5 cents. Since the expectation or EV is a positive number, we know it's a bet worth making.

>> The break-even percentage on a +200 bet is simply the amount risked divided by the amount returned including the initial stake. That makes $1 ÷ $3, or 33 percent. Since our expected winning percentage (35 percent) is higher than the break-even percentage (33 percent), it's a good bet.

TIP

If it's not obvious, the two metrics described above are directly related. If you have a +EV bet, it means your win probability is necessarily north of the break-even percentage. The goal of this section is to give you some different tools for getting to the profitability of an underlying bet.

Note also that it doesn't matter how many opportunities you get during the baseball season, and it doesn't matter what the size of your bet is. What makes a bet +EV isn't affected by the size of your bet and how often you get opportunities to make similar bets.

Staying positive

Finding +EV bets is how money is made in gambling. Notice I didn't say how *you* make money gambling, it's how *anybody* makes money gambling. Consider the variety of casino table games. Every single one of them is a +EV play for the house, making it –EV for gamblers.

Casinos know that every time a bettor puts $1 down on a hand of blackjack, even if that gambler plays "perfect strategy" blackjack, the house will keep a half a penny of every dollar bet. So the casino's goal is to make it easy for everyone to keep playing. The more hands you play, the more money the casino piles up.

In the case of blackjack, innovative players found a way to boost themselves into +EV territory by counting cards and varying the amount they bet to take advantage of player-friendly decks. Casinos retaliated by reducing the payout for a natural blackjack from 3-to-2 to 6-to-5 (oh, and by making card counting illegal).

The blackjack story illustrates a critical concept of identifying +EV bets: If you can change the win percentage while keeping the payout schedule the same, that bet gets more advantageous to you. Alternatively, if the winning percentage stays steady but you figure out a way to improve the payout schedule, that's another way to move your bet towards +EV territory.

Think back to fractions in school. You can make a fraction bigger by making the numerator bigger or the denominator smaller. Casinos and sports books know the math makes the average bettor's eyes start to cross in confusion, but astute bettors know that you can't find edges without paying close attention to both variables.

Here's a relevant sports betting example: You are considering making a straight −110 bet on the Colts −3 against the Titans. You think there's a 54 percent chance that the Colts win by 4 or more, and because that's more than the 52.38 percent break-even percentage on a −110 bet, you know it's a positive EV play.

But before you can get to the counter to place your bet, the odds change to Colts −3 −120. So the point spread is the same as before (you still win if the Colts win by 4 or more), but instead of a standard −110 bet, you now are expected to risk $1.20 to win $1. What should you do?

Because the point spread is still −3, your 54 percent chance of winning shouldn't be any different than it was before. But because the odds have moved from −110 to −120 on that bet, you're now risking a little bit more relative to your win. Before you bet, you should check to make sure this is still a +EV bet.

To get the break-even win percentage, take the risked amount (1.20) divided by total payout (1.00 in winnings plus the 1.20 risked), or 1.20 ÷ 2.20 = 54.54 percent. So you're expected win probability (54 percent) is now lower than the break-even (54.54 percent). That makes this a −EV play. All things being equal, stay away!

WARNING

Passing on the Colts in the preceding example — that is, refusing to bet because the payout schedule has changed slightly — is one of the hardest things for sports bettors to do. After all, we don't bet with the expectations of losing. Think back to the casino example where the house scratches and fights for every penny of advantage. A move from −110 to −120 odds gets ignored by the squarest amateurs, while the advantage bettors recalculate and reconsider as necessary.

TIP

Laying is a term associated with betting on a favorite. To lay $200 to win $100 just means you are risking $200 for a $100 profit. In a standard bet, you lay $1.10 to win $1. Another use of the word has to do with a point spread, as in "the Giants are laying a touchdown," which means the Giants are the favorite, and the point spread on the game is Giants −7.

Bookmakers and Odds

Now we can start thinking more about what, and who, we're up against as sports bettors. In the most basic sense, bookmakers do what any other gambling house does to separate gamblers from their money: They offer odds (that is, the ratio of profit to risk) that are slightly different from the event's underlying probability.

The bookie knows that if he pays a little less than a bet is "worth" and repeats that process over and over, he'll pile up money a penny or two at a time. In this section, I'll talk through the specific processes used by bookmakers to manage betting markets.

Holding onto the handle

Booking bets is a great business . . . if you consider it "great" to make mountains of money. The magnitude of the total market discussed in Chapter 1 is a testament to the fact that there is massive demand, across America and the world, for gambling on sports.

In that chapter, I discussed betting numbers in terms of the raw dollars bettors wagered on games. In this chapter, I'll talk about how those dollars translate into to bookmaking profits. And I'll start with identifying two key metrics that every bookie understands: *handle* and *hold*.

» **Handle** refers to a few stats related to all bets placed with a bookmaker, regardless of the wins and losses. Traditionally, handle only referred to the number of discrete wagers placed, but it's more commonly used to denote the total dollar amount bet in a given time period. Handle is a measure of both the popularity of the underlying event, plus the bookmaker's share of the marketplace, which in turn is an indicator of how well they market, cater to customers, and offer competitive services, attractive lines, high betting limits, and so on.

» **Hold** refers to the money retained by the bookie after the winning bets have been paid off. It's most often expressed as a percentage of the overall amount bet. So if a betting house takes in $5,000 in bets for the day, and as a result of the games, pays out (or owes) $4,200 to the winning bettors, the hold would be expressed as either $800 or 16 percent ($800 ÷ $5,000 = 16%).

A bookmaker's hold percentage is a useful data point for bettors because it creates a comparison point between different houses. Regardless of handle, a house keeping more money is an indicator they're offering less competitive odds. Of course, hold is also determined by the bookmaker's ability to balance action, react to events leading up to a game, and recognize or resolve situations when there's financial exposure from their position on a game. Secondarily, hold might tell you how well a bookmaker can attract bettors to high-margin events like contests, futures, prop bets, or parlay cards.

For a standard −110 bet, if you imagine a scenario where a bookmaker accepts the same volume of betting dollars on each side of a bet, the hold will be 4.54 percent. That number should look familiar to you because it also happens to be the vigorish percentage.

So what's the difference between the vig and the hold? The vig is the implied fee involved in every individual bet, but the bookmaker doesn't actually net that percentage unless the action is balanced perfectly on all sides of every bet. That's why they sometimes call the vig the *theoretical hold* percentage.

If the world's simplest bookie offers a single −110 bet, and Bettor A lays $110, and Bettor B lays $110, the winner will walk away with $210, and the bookie will keep $10, or 4.54 percent. In the real world, with scores of bets available per day at the mercy of the betting public, betting sides are rarely perfectly balanced. So the actual hold is what the bookmaker realizes when all the bets are added up. If you've ever managed a budget, you can think of vig as the "forecast" and the hold as the "actual."

Book balancing

As always, a good example can be worth a thousand . . . something.

Consider a very *un*balanced bet. A bookmaker takes $1,000 of bets on a hypothetical Silver Team −7 points, but only $150 worth of bets are made on their opponent, the Gold Team +7 points.

With unbalanced betting volumes, the bookmaker is exposed to swings in their financial results, which is not what they prefer. Sure, the Gold Team might cover the spread, in which case that $1,000 worth of Silver Team bets lose, and the bookmaker only has to pay out $150 worth of winning bets. Cool! The bookmaker's hold would be over 80 percent! But if the Silver Team wins and covers the spread, the bookmaker would have to swallow a big loss on the game, and they don't like that. To quote Gordon Gekko from the movie *Wall Street*, "I don't throw darts at a board, kid; I only bet on sure things."

Win some, lose some, make some

Unless you're betting on the Harlem Globetrotters, or against the 1919 White Sox, there is effectively no such thing as a "sure thing" sports bet. Bookmakers would not be successful if they set out to purposely bet on one team or another. They're not trying to outsmart the public into betting heavily in one direction or another.

That doesn't mean bookmakers don't passively end up with incidental interest in the outcome of some games. But they take measures to limit that exposure so that they can make money on the sure thing: the vig. And the best path to maximizing that fee is to *balance* the action, which means to attract an equal amount of money bet on each side of an event.

REMEMBER

Action is an overloaded term in the gambling world. It usually simply means "wagers" or "dollars wagered," as in "I heard the Golden Nugget sports book took a lot of action on the Packers because there were a bunch of Wisconsinites in town at the International Cheese Convention."

Stop me if you've heard this before, but there's a second, slightly more refined meaning that implies a bet has been accepted, is valid, and will be honored by the sports book. That distinction is necessary because there are some circumstances where a bet is considered *no action*, or void. The best example is when you bet on Major League Baseball, where bookmakers set the odds based on the projected starting pitchers actually taking the mound in the first inning. On tickets for baseball bets you might see a note to this effect: "Listed starting pitchers <at the time the bet was placed> must throw first pitch or this bet is NO ACTION."

Starting pitching is such an essential part of the odds offered to bettors that the bookmaker reserves the right to declare the bet to be "no action" if there's a late change. In that case, your bet is voided and your initial stake will be returned to you.

Achieving balance

Trying to balance bets to the penny would be like a manager at a grocery store and demanding that every cash register ends the day with the same number of quarters. Bookmakers take bets right up to game time, and bettors are fickle, inconsistent, and unpredictable.

Bookmakers can still be profitable with a certain amount of betting imbalance, but you might be asking yourself: Bettors are free to bet whatever amount they want on any side of a bet they choose (both with some limits), so how do bookmakers exert any control at all?

They actually have several tools at their disposal to influence how bettors behave at the betting counter:

>> **The odds:** Bookmakers can't force you to make a bet on one side or another, but by changing the ratio of risk and reward, they can make certain bets very attractive and others equally unattractive.

>> **The handicap:** Bookmakers alter the point spread, the total points on over/ under bets, and other terms that define the bet.

>> **Betting maximums:** During certain time periods, bettors may be restricted to lower maximum bets. And in some cases, bookmakers can limit specific bettors.

>> **Delayed approvals:** High dollar bettors who have been identified as sharp gamblers by a bookmaker may not be able to place their wagers immediately when they go to the betting window.

>> **Lay offs:** Just like an insurance company, bookmakers have the ability to reduce their lopsided bets by moving action to a second bookmaker.

TIP

Betting metadata — that is, information about how much the public is betting on each side of a game, the number of individual bets, odds movement over time, and other data — is available to the public on a number of free apps and websites. In later chapters, I'll talk about how to use this information to your advantage. I also include a list of free resources in Appendix A. If you just can't wait, take a look at www.pregame.com or load The Action Network's app on your smartphone. There's lots of free data for every bet on the menu.

Looking at betting skew

Let's open the books at a hypothetical betting parlor on a day where there are six games on the schedule. This example looks at a standard bet on each game (maybe it's a point spread or a total bet) and assume –110 odds. The sample listing below shows the total number of dollars bet on each side of the game just prior to kickoff:

Bets Available	Side A	Side B	Skew
Game 1	$4,000	$3,800	2.6%
Game 2	$1,200	$1,360	6.3%
Game 3	$1,550	$1,500	1.6%
Game 4	$2,940	$3,150	3.4%
Game 5	$5,275	$4,900	3.7%
Game 6	$1,100	$1,100	0.0%

Game 6 is the only one where the amount bet on each side is exactly even, so the financial outcome for the bookmaker on that single game is easy to predict: The bookmaker will collect $2,200 worth of bets and pay out $2,000 to the winning side regardless of who wins.

So is the bookmaker worried about Bets 1 through 5?

No. For all games except one, the skew amounts are lower than the vigorish percentage. Below is the worst case scenario for the bookmaker, where the winning side on every game happens to be the side they've received outsized action on. Spoiler alert: The bookmaker still shows a profit on the day.

Bets Available	Side A	Side B	Skew	Result	Collected	Paid Out	Net Profit
Game 1	$4,000	$3,800	2.6%	A	$7,800.00	$7,636.36	$163.64
Game 2	$1,200	$1,360	6.3%	B	$2,560.00	$2,596.36	–$36.36
Game 3	$1,550	$1,500	1.6%	A	$3,050.00	$2,959.09	$90.91
Game 4	$2,940	$3,150	3.4%	B	$6,090.00	$6,013.64	$76.36
Game 5	$5,275	$4,900	3.7%	A	$10,175.00	$10,070.45	$104.55
Game 6	$1,100	$1,100	0.0%	A	$2,200.00	$2,100.00	$100.00

Before the bookmaker undertakes any effort to balance the betting, here are some things he'd consider:

» As mentioned before, the 4.545 percent vigorish on the bets allows the bookmaker some leeway in taking unbalanced action on a game. As long as the skew of the bet totals doesn't exceed 4.545 percent, the bookmaker is guaranteed to make money.

» In certain situations, the bookmaker might fear that acting to balance bets could lead to reducing the total handle and would therefore be willing to accept the risk of a higher skew to increase the overall money wagered. The bookmaker certainly doesn't want to get swamped on a bad bet, but high handle means lots of customers coming to the betting window. If a single bet attracts bettors in the door with questionable odds, it might also prompt them to spend money on more profitable bets or services. (It's like a grocery store taking a loss on laundry detergent, knowing customers will buy other items that are marked way up.)

» Bookmakers assess their risks as they would any financial portfolio; that is, they consider all the bets in aggregate. I've presented a single day when there are only six games happening. But on an average college basketball Saturday, there might be a hundred games plus derivative bets available. More individual bets means diversity, and as stock market investors know, diversity reduces the possibility for big swings in either direction.

» In this example, there are only –110 point spread bets, but in the real world, moneyline odds float above and below –110. Additionally, each game would have derivative bets as well (like first half wagers), which would be closely related to the full game odds. Because the derivative bets' outcomes are tied to the outcome of the full game, they can sometimes act as a direct offset of an unbalanced full game bet.

>> All wagers are not created equal. Sure, a dollar is a dollar, but bookmakers also do their best to track which person is doing the wagering. They regularly assess some bettors as sharper than the rest and therefore more likely to bet on winners. More square means slightly more likely to lose, so the bookmaker would consider accepting a higher skew in the direction of Bet 2/Side B.

I'll talk about different sources of betting dollars next, then I'll talk about tools at the bookmaker's disposal to equalize the dollars bet.

Balancing the Books

I've talked about bookmakers taking measures to ensure they aren't overexposed on any given bet to ensure they reduce risk and maximize profit. The primary action they take is by adjusting odds and handicaps, and it's critical that every bettor understand these mechanisms. In this section, I'll dive deep on the forces at work that set and change the bookmakers' betting terms.

Odds as a price

The odds on a game — moneylines, point spreads, totals, props, derivatives, and futures — behave as prices do in any marketplace. Bookmakers are the sellers; bettors are the buyers with freedom to act or pass; and the odds on each bet represent a price that is either attractive enough for a bettor to stake money, or not.

A hypothetical rational bettor makes a prediction on a game like this:

The upcoming game will result in the following score: Bengals 27, 49ers 24.

Then that bettor walks into the bookmaker and sees the following odds on the board:

Team	Spread / Total
Bengals	–2
49ers	48

Being completely rational, the bettor would then naturally place a bet on the Bengals –2 (since he has predicted a 3-point win) and a bet on the over 48 (since he has predicted 51 total points in the game). What if the same bettor had walked in and seen these odds:

Team	Spread / Total
Bengals	–3
49ers	52

The bettor would have *not* bet on the side, because the point spread matches his prediction precisely, and he would have bet the under 52 instead of the over because he predicted 51 total points.

As I'll discuss later, betting like the above rational bettor is actually a good way to approach sports betting. In an open marketplace, the odds act as a price, and rational bettors should bet on one side or another based on that price.

We know most bettors don't actually behave in the way I just described on an individual level, but taken as a whole, the market actually does behave that way. If you lined up 100 people looking to bet on the Bengals/49ers and asked their predictions on the game, the distribution might look like this:

Bengals will win by 10 or more: 2 bettors

Bengals will win by 7–9: 3 bettors

Bengals will win by 5–6: 10 bettors

Bengals will win by 4: 20 bettors

Bengals will win by 3: 30 bettors

Bengals will win by 2: 20 bettors

Bengals will win by 1 or tie: 8 bettors

49ers will win by 1–3: 3 bettors

49ers will win by 4–7: 2 bettors

49ers will win by more than a 7: 1 bettor

So the betting public on average thinks the Bengals will win by 3, which prompts the 30 people who think the Bengals will win by *exactly* 3 to pass on the game. The 35 people who think they'll win by 4 or more to bet on the Bengals, and the 35 people who think they'll only win by 2 or less, or tie or lose, will bet on the 49ers.

Now imagine the point spread was instead initially set at Bengals –3.5. How would these same 100 bettors behave? The only change would be that those 30 folks who passed because they think the Bengals will win by 3 now see a price that makes it worth betting on the 49ers.

You can continue doing this on down the line: Set the spread at Bengals −4, and we'd see the 20 who predicted a Bengals win by 4 would decide to pass on the game instead.

Even though a half-point change in a point spread doesn't seem like much to you, if the betting market is big enough, there are people whose opinions sit right on the razor's edge, for whom that half point will represent a change significant enough to alter their betting behavior.

If you studied economics, you know that having a large enough group of either buyers or sellers in a marketplace means you can describe the market as a continuous curve. Since every actor in a marketplace acts with their own individual outlook, constraints, information, and risk tolerance, you have to assume that when conditions change ever so slightly, there are actors at the margins who react by altering their behavior. A small dip in the price of oil doesn't affect most drillers, but because there are so many companies in the market, you can assume there's one that needed those few pennies per barrel to keep operating. Have I lost you? Okay, back to sports betting.

What I'm presenting here is obviously a simplistic model of bettor behavior. But there are some critical takeaways here:

>> Odds (as in profit-to-risk-ratio plus handicaps like point spreads) are nothing more than prices for a service offered by the bookmaker.

>> Bettors' behavior in the aggregate is determined by the odds.

>> Different odds activate different bettors at the margins.

>> Odds aren't predictions of the game; they are predictions of the betting market's predictions of the game.

An odds life

Every sports book has its own inflection points for adjusting odds in hopes of altering bettor behavior. In some cases, it's as simple as tacking on a half point to a point spread and adjusting the moneyline accordingly. But there are some nuances that I'll discuss later in Part 3, because every sport's odds get adjusted in their own unique way.

Pre-game odds

Although in-game betting is becoming more popular, most of the time, you're placing a bet before the game kicks off. Odds can change any time between the game opening and the start time. You can watch the odds change in the run up to game on any of the free services that monitor odds across the big sports books. Changes can literally happen to spread, totals, and payout odds on a minute-by-minute basis.

Consider this simplified look at how odds might change over the course of a week for a single regular season football game that kicks off on Sunday afternoon. Let's pretend the odds only change once at the start of each day at this bookmaker:

Cardinals at Ravens, 3 p.m. Sunday

Day	Cardinals Handle	Cardinals Odds	Ravens Handle	Ravens Odds	Skew
Tues	$3,902	−2	$6,399	+2	−24.2%
Wed	$7,912	−2 +110	$12,043	+2 −120	−20.7%
Thurs	$10,560	−1.5	$14,500	+1.5	−15.7%
Fri	$17,050	−1.5	$15,050	+1.5	6.2%
Sat	$19,880	−1.5 −115	$22,800	+1.5 +105	−6.8%
Sun	$24,180	−2	$25,800	+2	−3.2%

The table shows the running total of bets on each side of the Cardinals/Ravens game, along with the point spread, for the week leading up to the game. When you see a negative skew, that (arbitrarily) means it's towards the Ravens, and positive means it's towards the Cardinals.

When the game opens on Tuesday morning, the oddsmakers have set the number at Cardinals −2, and they receive far more bets on the Ravens than they do the Cardinals. At the end of the day, the book realizes they have an imbalance that's big enough to justifying altering the odds of the game. In reaction to that 24 percent skew, they adjust the odds by making the Ravens slightly more expensive (+2 −120) and the Cardinals slightly cheaper (−2 +110) in the hope it will lure bettors toward the Cardinals.

The skew dips to 20.7 percent by end-of-day Wednesday, but that's not enough to make the sports book director satisfied. So the oddsmaker makes another change for Thursday bettors by moving the spread down to 1.5. Over the course of

Thursday and Friday, so many bets come in the other way that the skew actually reverses and starts favoring the Cardinals. The bookmaker, concerned about the action slipping too far in that direction, tweaks the –1.5 point spread to make the Cardinals slightly more expensive. By kickoff on Sunday, action on the game has pushed the line back to –2, where it closes at kickoff.

REMEMBER

If you bet on the Cardinals on Thursday or Friday, your spread is –1.5, even though the game opened and closed at Cardinals –2. Your bet is settled according to the odds at the time you placed the bet.

You can see how the math can start to get a little complicated when it comes to calculating the bookmaker's financial outcome for this game. Because the line fluctuated between 1.5 and 2, a Cardinals win by exactly 2 means a push for some bettors and win for other bettors. And because the odds moved from a standard –110 bet to –115, the hold calculation requires doing math for each separate day. In the real world, bookmakers' accountants have a big task to add up and summarize their position on each game, because the odds may have changed dozens of times between opening and kickoff.

In-game odds

Sports books now take advantage of the internet to maintain a spread and total that float with the action of the game. Making these bets is called *in-game betting*, and it's a whole new world for bettors looking for an advantage.

In fact, it's common in a football game to be able to place a bet on more granular results than the score. For example, you can bet on the current drive, the outcome of the current set of downs, and sometimes whether the next play is a pass or a run. All major sports books offer some kind of in-game betting for the major sports.

How do they set these odds? Things move too fast for a person to continually reset the odds over and over. So bookmakers rely on complex algorithms that assign probabilities to in-game outcomes based on all the factors you'd expect: score, time remaining, down, distance, and so forth, combined with a massive amount of historical data that points to the likelihood of certain outcomes. The systems take the probabilities and converts them to betting odds that are made available to gamblers to wager on.

Betting limits for on-the-fly bets are usually quite low, and the hold is relatively high. For example, it's not unusual for a standard point spread bet placed after kickoff to require you to bet at –120 odds regardless of which side you take. Nevertheless, bettors who know their teams and sports can often identify profitable betting niches.

WARNING

If you are trying to do live betting on your sportsbook app or website, make sure you understand whether the method you're using to monitor the game is on a broadcast delay or not. Regular TV and radio broadcasts operate with a delay of a few seconds, but some internet TV providers operate with a 20- to 30-second delay. Those few extra seconds can make all the difference when it comes to assessing a situation on the field. You might think you're betting on the outcome of an inning with bases loaded and no outs, but your broadcast hasn't caught up to the fact that there was a strikeout-pickoff double play a moment ago. Would your bookmaker take advantage of having a more up-to-date game feed than you? It depends on the bookmaker, but I'd make sure I knew the relative delays before committing to in-game betting.

Quarter points?

Sometimes you'll hear or read about a spread being −3.2 or −3.25. This is shorthand for a spread that's listed at −3, but with associated odds that are more expensive like −120 or −125 odds instead of being a standard −110 bet. To reiterate, a point spread bet or an over/under wager has implied −110 odds. That is, for every $1.10 you risk, you stand to profit $1. (Or if you risk $1, you profit 91 cents.)

So if a bet is −3.2, it means you're laying 3 points, but your payout schedule is slightly more expensive than a standard −110 bet.

Sharp objects

As you know by now, bookmakers continually adjust odds after they've been released for two main reasons:

>> The volume of bets coming in on one side is lopsided relative to the other side, requiring the bookmaker to alter the price in such a way that drives more equal action.

>> Bookmakers alter the line to reduce their exposure to an extraordinary loss by paying close attention to how the sharpest bettors are wagering and shading the line that direction, even if it means being out of balance overall.

The second reason is a concept that even experienced bettors struggle with. In a world where every bettor is equally skilled and knowledgeable, the bookmaker would alter the line in a way that evened out the action as closely as possible.

But the reality is that bookmakers know some bettors are more likely to be on the winning side of a bet. If you assume that the general public has a 50 percent chance of being right about a bet and sharp bettors have a 55 percent chance of being right, you'd minimize risk by taking action that was slightly weighted away from the sharp side.

In Figure 4-1, the bookmaker is taking bets on the Oregon Ducks versus the Utah Utes, and it looks like they've taken more betting dollars on the Ducks +3½. But this bookmaker considers this bet in balance because the sharp money is tilted toward Utah. Given that information, the oddsmaker will likely leave the spread where it is and accept the imbalance in action. If the sharp money indicates the Utes have a 55 percent chance of covering the listed spread, the bookmaker will happily accept a little more public money on the opposite side.

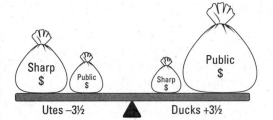

FIGURE 4-1: More sharp money is on the Utes, so the overall imbalance is acceptable to the bookie.

Heads you lose, tails they win

Knowing where the sharp bets are being placed is another dimension to how the bean counters at sports books assess their exposure on any given week. Remember the six game skew table from earlier in the chapter? The sports book's accountant knows that over the long term, a game that perfectly splits betting volume will make money for the sports book. And she also knows that if the oddsmaker sets the odds skillfully such that each side has a 50-50 chance of covering, the sports books will make money in the aggregate even with some amount of betting skew on each game.

Why? If probability is truly a coin flip, then half the time the sports book will be on the winning side of the skewed game, and half the time they'll be on the losing side. I adjusted the earlier table by skewing the betting amounts well above the 4.545 percent vigorish/ideal hold amount. The sports book's risk manager calculates the expected return the same way we did earlier, but calculating the possible returns and averaging them (when Side A wins and Side B wins).

Bet	Side A	Side B	Skew	If A Wins	If B Wins	50/50 Win Expectation
Game 1	$4,300	$3,800	6.2%	$(109.09)	$845.45	$368.18
Game 2	$1,200	$1,360	6.3%	$269.09	$(36.36)	$116.36
Game 3	$2,300	$1,500	21.1%	$(590.91)	$936.36	$172.73

Bet	Side A	Side B	Skew	If A Wins	If B Wins	50/50 Win Expectation
Game 4	$2,940	$3,370	6.8%	$697.27	$(123.64)	$286.82
Game 5	$5,275	$4,450	8.5%	$(345.45)	$1,229.55	$442.05
Game 6	$1,100	$1,100	0.0%	$100.00	$100.00	$100.00

REMEMBER

To calculate expectation, you add all possible outcomes, which consist of the chance of winning times the resulting profit/loss. For a bet where each side is equally likely, you'd calculate it like this:

.5 × the result of Side A winning + .5 × the result of Side B winning

To calculate the result of a winning side, you start with the total money collected and subtract the payout amount, which is initial bet plus winnings. For an −110 bet, winnings equal the initial bet times .909.

Note that even though negative outcomes are possible, the expectation remains positive for every game. In the short term, an "imperfect storm" might cause the book to be on the wrong side of every bet, causing a losing day. But in the long run, they'll win closer and closer to 50 percent of their bets, meaning they'll be profitable.

Here's another example where all the games look pretty close in terms of how even wager volume is, except for Game 3, where it's nearly 15 percent towards Side A.

Bet	Side A	Side B	Skew
Game 1	$3,902	$3,679	2.94%
Game 2	$4,010	$3,900	1.39%
Game 3	$7,310	$5,410	14.94%
Game 4	$5,940	$6,150	1.74%
Game 5	$7,270	$6,990	1.96%
Game 6	$4,450	$5,100	6.81%

But now we know that all bets are not created equal. If the sports book director assumes every game is a 50-50 coin flip, he's incentivized to balance the action to get as close as possible to the 4.545 percent hold percentage. But if sharp bets are flowing in on Game 3 Side B, he might tweak that 50-50 assumption to more like 45-55. (In other words, Game 3 Side B is slightly more likely to win based on sharp betting.) That might prompt him to adjust his target skew on that bet based on some simple expectation calculations.

Think about it: If the sharp money is an indicator that Game 3 Side B is more likely to win than Side A, the bookmaker would be wise to set the odds to balance the action accordingly, which means skew toward Side B.

I inserted 45/55 odds into the equation below and you can see that by letting the bets skew toward Side A, the bookmaker's expected return from Game 3 improves.

	Side A	Side B	Skew	50/50 Win Expectation	45/55 Win Expectation
Game 3	$7,310	$5,410	14.9%	$578.18	$759.55

You might think that sports books are always working in opposition to winning players, and sometimes that's true. After all, betting houses are in business to make money from gamblers, so players who bet big and demonstrate an ability to win over the long run are often profiled by the bookmaker and restricted to lower-limit bets.

Playing with steam

When known sharp bettors make a bet, sports books often assume the odds they posted are vulnerable in some way, and react by making that bet more expensive. If you're at a bookmaker standing in line behind a professional, you might see the odds change in the seconds after he leaves but before you step up to the counter.

THE SHARPS ARE ALRIGHT

As any bookie will tell you, for any given game, the sharp side isn't always the winning side. The saga of the 2020 college football National Championship game between LSU and Clemson is a perfect illustration of how bookies attempted to adjust the odds in response to public and sharp betting imbalances, but it doesn't always work out how they predict.

When the game opened with LSU as a 3-point favorite, the public piled on the Bayou Bengals, driving the spread as high as LSU –6. But even though the betting continued to pour in on LSU, the best-known sharp bettors were backing Clemson. That support for the underdog made oddsmakers hesitant to make Clemson any cheaper than they already were at +6. By kickoff, many big bookmakers had taken so much public money on LSU that they had a significant rooting interest in Clemson at kickoff. The result? LSU rolled to an easy cover, winning the title to the consternation of the sharpest minds in sports betting.

Betting alongside the sharps seems like a good idea, right? They pick 56 percent winners, so why not bet with them? In sports betting parlance, trying to identify when pros have made a play on a big game, and then mimicking that bet, is called a *steam play*, or *chasing steam*, or a similar steamy metaphor. If you read enough sports betting media, you'll hear this term. Insert your favorite cliché here about taking it with a grain of salt, buyers being aware, treading carefully, and so forth.

There are some problems with this strategy that make it hard to profit in the long term:

>> If you detect a steam move, it's usually because the odds have already changed. That means the +EV play the pros jumped on has theoretically now become a –EV play.

>> Chasing steam requires monitoring sports betting metadata closely and having the ability to bet at many different sports books with large bets. If you're an average bettor, the juice won't be worth the squeeze.

>> Gleaning the intentions of the best bettors is not straightforward. Sudden, drastic odds changes might be the result of professionals loading up on a bet because they think it's a good bet. Or not. Sometimes the pros' intent is to create a rumor of a steam move and tempt the public to bet up the other side. Then when the odds rebound in the other direction, the pros jump on the opposite side they started with.

Monitoring steam moves has value to the average bettor as another piece of information you can use before placing a bet. I'll talk about putting metadata to use in the next chapter. So steam might have a silver lining, but it is no silver bullet when it comes to long-term profits.

WARNING

You might think your long-term goal is be identified as a sharp bettor by the casinos. Think of the comps! Well, it's not all good news. Laws vary state by state and country by country, but in most places, casinos have the right to refuse bets from anyone, and that right is extended to sports books too. They don't do so lightly because it's not good publicity, but make no mistake, sports books know who the sharpest bettors are and will often limit them to small bets, or they may simply refuse to serve them altogether. It's a conundrum that should lead you to behave very carefully if you find yourself winning over 55 percent over stretches of hundreds of games: Some sports books won't tolerate a bettor who wins a lot.

Bookmaking Business Models

In this section, I'll talk about how bookmakers manage odds throughout their life cycle, from their introduction to the public through the end of the game.

Market makers: The odds stork

If you read through the chapter to this point, you know how the market gets moved. But how do the odds get established and moved in the first place? The easy answer is that sportsbooks have a room full of analysts, sports experts, and researchers who model both the sports factors and public opinion to produce numbers to get listed on their betting menu. Once the game *opens* (listed on the betting menu for the first time), several things happen in sequence to shape the spread and total:

1. Bookmakers that are willing to publish early lines are often known as *market-making books*. They'll release games and allow bettors to wager on these games at lower limits until they're comfortable that they've accurately gauged the pulse of the market.

2. Known sharp bettors are allowed to place reduced-amount bets against the early totals, which give strong hints to the bookmaker on whether and how much to alter the odds. (The bookmaker/sharp-bettor partnership seems like an odd couple, but it's a true symbiotic thing for many betting houses. Sharps get a piece of early weaker numbers, and bookmakers get to shape up their numbers.)

3. As time goes on and spreads and totals get released into the wild, the maximum bet amount allowed goes up until just before kickoff or tipoff.

Different bookmakers play different roles in the marketplace. Market-makers use their rooms full of propeller-headed analysts to get an early bite at the betting market. Market-following bookmakers won't release games early, and they pay the price by not getting those early market advantages.

Market followers

Market-following bookies keep a close eye on the market makers and let the market makers set the opening odds and watch the early market stabilize before they set and release their own numbers. In the Ed Miller/Matthew Davidow book, *The Logic of Sports Betting*, they label these bookmakers as retail sportsbooks, who specialize in servicing the average bettor rather than offering innovative or market-leading plays.

With the wave of legalization in the United States, some clear market makers are establishing themselves. Draft Kings, CG Technology, MGM, and William Hill are big corporate bookmakers that set lines and distribute them to retail bookmakers. Having said that, there are still plenty of independent houses out there like The Golden Nugget, where Las Vegas legend Tony Miller still runs a fully self-sufficient operation, as he has for many years. Pretty much every other book falls into the retail category.

The SuperMegaCup odds life cycle example

Here's some detailed factors that impact how odds originate and move. Imagine a dystopian alternate universe where there was a only a single sporting event that people are allowed to bet on. Let's not even worry about the sport. We'll just say it's the SuperMegaCup, and it happens on December 31 every year.

The process for creating odds looks a little something like this:

1. Starting the summer before the game, the biggest bookmakers have PhD analysts, researchers, and even former SuperMegaCup competitors on staff. They combine intrinsic data about the players and coaches with external factors such as weather, referees, and a healthy dose of research on public perception to come up with an initial moneyline, point spread, and total for the game.

2. Based on the key odds (moneyline, point spread, and total), the team also establishes derivative odds: quarter and half betting, team totals, and so on.

3. The odds are released to the public with low betting limits. If the team of analysts has misjudged public perception, it will be very apparent early because bets will flow in on one side or the other in disproportionate amounts. The bookmaker also tracks whether known sharp players are betting one side bigger than another.

4. The bookmaker carefully analyzes betting patterns and tweaks the odds on the primary bets and the derivative bets. As time passes, the bookmaker slowly starts raising betting limits as they feel more comfortable that they're line becomes more stable and the risk of releasing a line that's way off gets lower. As the SuperMegaCup kickoff gets closer, the bookmaker also starts releasing alternate lines and prop bets at both the player and team level.

5. When the SuperMegaCup kickoff is a few weeks away, the market maker raises its betting limits to maximum. At the same time, sports books around the country offer opening lines based on the market maker's established line. They follow the same pattern as before, just in a more compressed time period: low

limits to start with to ensure the bets they're taking have stabilized. (After all, every sports book's pool of bettors is slightly different, so there's no guarantee they'll receive the same pattern of bets as the market maker.)

6. Gradually, each betting house raises its own betting limits, but they carefully monitor their own bet skew for the SuperMegaCup. A bookmaker can't change the odds too drastically in either direction or it will expose itself to arbitrage and middle opportunities, where sharp bettors take advantage of discrepancies in lines between casinos to create no-risk bets for themselves.

7. In some cases, the betting houses will work together: If one is skewed heavily towards under bets and another is skewed heavily toward over bets, they can go through a process of laying off bets in a mutually beneficial way that ends with each bookmaker reducing its skew.

Early money/late money

From the time a bet becomes available to the public to the time a game starts, a narrative grows about the game that has some valuable information for the average bettor. By simply comparing the opening line to the current line, you can see how close the oddsmakers predictions lined up with public sentiment. When news comes out about an injury, suspension, or any other factor that might affect the game, you'll be able to see how the line reacts, from which you can make inferences about the perceived value of certain players.

World premier odds

Sports book directors are of two mindsets on when to release lines prior to a game. On one hand, it's good for business to be first to market. The earliest book to offer wagering on a game stands to attract more business. After all, bettors like to bet. When a Saturday slate of college football ends, gamblers have fresh memories of that day's games, new information on their performance, high levels of interest, and, for some, a pocket full of winnings.

But offering betting too soon can be risky for a sports book. It's an immutable law about predicting the future: The earlier you make the prediction, the less information you have. If you've ever dealt with any kind of planning or forecasting function, you're probably familiar with the concept of the *cone of uncertainty*. The concept is straightforward: The further you look into the future, the more variance there is, as illustrated in Figure 4-2. If you can picture a weatherman showing the predicted path of a hurricane, you'll remember the possibilities start out narrow and get wider with time.

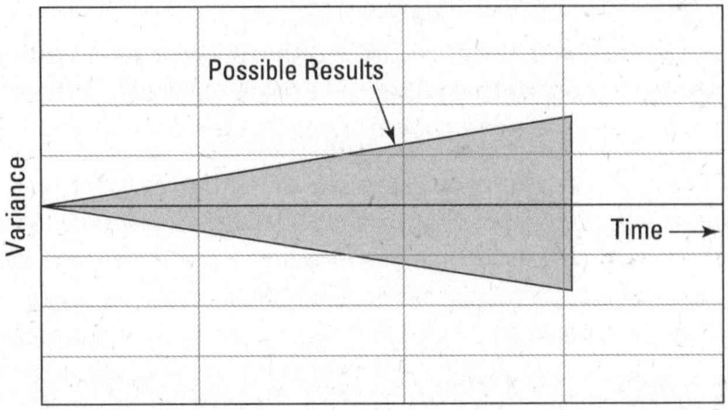

FIGURE 4-2:
The cone
of uncertainty.
As we project
time out into the
future, things
get harder and
harder to predict.

The cone applies to predicting sporting events as well. When the weekend's games are over you have available all the information you can possibly get about on-field performance, but what about midweek practices? Or coaches' comments to the press? What about injuries and suspensions? Or weather at game time? A lot can happen between the end of week 1 and the kickoff of week 2; a lot can impact the public's perception of the upcoming game; and none of it is knowable until it actually happens. In theory, if the goal was to set odds with a 100 percent complete set of information leading up to a game, the only way to do that would be to not set the line until a moment before kickoff.

So opening a game up for betting represents a compromise between these two forces. The bookmaker wants to serve its customers with a competitive product, but they also need to collect and process as much information as possible to feed oddsmakers' predictions about the market.

The early bird gets the risk (and the reward)

Early lines mean less information, and that translates to higher risk for sports books. Sports book directors and oddsmakers manage this risk through clever use of betting limits. If you walk up to the counter a minute after a sports book offers odds on next week's games, you might not be able to make as big a bet as you'd like. It's not uncommon to limit early betting to 5 to 10 percent of what's available later in the week. Where a casino sports book would let you bet up to $50,000 at a time on a football point spread just before kickoff, they might restrict the "early bird special" bettors to just $1,000 on the same bet. As the week goes on and the odds stabilize, betting limits start to climb.

There's also a game-within-a-game happening with sports books offering early betting because an important part of the universe of information is how bettors themselves will react to the odds once they're released. If bettors swarm on one particular side during the early betting phase, oddsmakers gain valuable information that they need to make that side more expensive if they expect to balance their action.

Odds at odds

Because of different business conditions, bookmakers make their own choice about when and how to change their odds for a game. The slight difference between bookmakers is a function of the nature of the bet volume they've received and their own risk tolerance and projections. To illustrate the utility of this exercise, I picked a random baseball game and copied the moneyline and total from the DonBest.com free website that shows information across several major sports books.

	Opener	Westgate	Mirage	Station	Pinnacle	SIA
Cardinals	9	8.5	9.5	8.5	8.5	9
Diamondbacks	–110	–113	–120	–120	–116	–121

(Just to set your expectations, baseball does not have a floating point spread like football or basketball. The most common baseball bets are the over/under bet and the moneyline bet, where you're just betting on the team to win straight up.)

It should be obvious to you that a bettor with multiple sports book accounts who takes the time to shop around to find the most advantageous odds will improve his winning percentage and profits over the course of a season. For this game, a bettor at the Mirage who bet over 9.5 would, based on overall baseball statistics, lose that bet 10 percent more often than a bettor who was able to bet over 8.5. That translates to a lot of lost opportunity and money.

Chapter **5**

The Best Bettor Habits

The goal of this book is simple: to help you develop tools and process for becoming an advantage sports bettor. Your personal goals might vary for what you want to get out of sports betting, but everyone wants to win.

Predicting wins gives you verbal bragging rights. But the real indicator of success is making your wallet fatter from betting. To do that, you'll need a good eye for bet selections, a disciplined approach for finding the best odds, and the skill of bankroll management, which means tracking your money carefully and responsibly.

To claim success, or acknowledge failure, means being able to answer a few critical questions:

» Where do I stand financially? That is, if I stopped betting this instant, can I claim to be winning or losing?

» At what rate am I winning or losing?

» Am I gambling within the limits I've set for myself?

REMEMBER

The upshots you need to take away from this chapter: At the very least, have an approach to bankroll management, bet sizing, and bet allocation, and then stick to it, whatever it may be.

What leads many sports bettors to ruin is not following their plan. Maybe they hit a losing streak and start chasing their losses with bigger bets or long-shot wagers.

Or maybe they win and overestimate their ability and start betting bigger and bigger. The systems in this chapter will help you maintain discipline, and discipline will help guarantee your success as a sports bettor.

Winning Habits: A Quick Review

In the first several chapters, I've given you a look at how advantage bettors approach sports betting. Any successful bettor does these activities well:

>> Evaluating teams, players, and situations

>> Using your evaluation to predict the most likely game narratives, situations for the upcoming event

>> Throwing out games where you predict a high variance of outcomes, or where you can't make predictions with confidence

>> For remaining games, identifying bets that will win if your prediction of likely game outcomes comes true.

>> Shopping among multiple bookmakers to find the best prices for your identified bets

>> Recognizing when there are no +EV bets available, and passing on any bets that you suspect are -EV

Most of the above is review. Those six items get you to the door of success; now it's time to look at the final two steps that help you walk right on through:

>> Sizing your bets according to your bankroll management and bet allocation plan

>> Finally, tracking your action; keeping good records of bet history and having an accurate view of your financial position at any time

Betting Approaches

In this section, I'll get into detail about the best way to select an amount of money to bet on game day, how to break that dollar amount up between games, then how to size individual bets. Of course, a lot of how you do this depends on your personal preferences, risk tolerances, and your goals as a sports bettor. But you'll find some key principles to put to use when it's time to put your money down.

An idealized bet selection process

I'll talk in Part 3 of the book about betting angles on each of the major sports. Every bettor has his or her own style, focal points, and interests. As you evolve in this hobby, you might build some mental (and computerized) tools to help you.

Zooming out for a moment, here's how it all comes together on game day for many gamblers.

1. **Initial handicap.** You look at the games on the slate for the upcoming season increment and put some initial thoughts down on teams in good spots, teams who caught your eye previously, or matchups you like. (This step is largely dependent on what kind of handicapper you are.)

2. **Create straw man scores.** Many handicappers skip the first step and rely on their power ratings, which you'll learn how to develop in Chapter 9. Power ratings are a simple quantitative tool to compare two teams and to develop a preliminary score for each game. You might note places where you're relatively more or less confident about your power rating.

3. **Filter down to candidate games.** Starting with their initial power rating scores, you might introduce available odds to your process. Where your scores represent a big mismatch with the odds. (For example, you put the game at Wisconsin 45 Illinois 28, but the published odds are Wisconsin –20 with a total of 70.) so your power ratings indicate that betting on Illinois and the over has value). The games with the biggest gaps between your estimate and the odds are your candidate games.

4. **Perform a deep handicap.** For each of your candidate games, you want to add quantitative analysis, like the spot, crowd, motivation, travel concerns, team injuries, matchup, scheme, coaching questions, and rivalries. Anything that goes on between the players' ears, rather than in their muscle, counts as quantitative.

5. **Do an odds deep dive.** If you have multiple sports books available, you want to look for the most advantageous odds for the plays you like. This is the point where you consider the entire attack surface of a game.

6. **Apply betting and bankroll strategy.** With your candidate games and your bets selected across the entire attack surface, now it's time to select and place bets. How do you split your dayroll up for the games that day? This step is as important as any other in the betting process, and I'll talk about it next.

TIP

I'd never want to take the fun out of it for you, and there's not always adequate time to execute each of these steps perfectly. But in general, you're looking to throw out games you're not interested in or can't predict with confidence. For the remaining games, you want to look for questionable lines and then build some analysis steps that support or refute your impressions.

The goal of bet allocation

Bet allocation involves the action of optimally allocating your bankroll across the bets available to you. I say "optimally" because it's quite possible to do this badly and to lose, not because you picked the wrong teams but because you failed to shop for the best lines and then bet too much on the wrong bets and not enough on the right bets.

A betting motivation anecdote

My good friend Shope and I go to Vegas together frequently. Our bankrolls are similar, but our betting approach is very different because we derive utility from different gambling outcomes. Of course, we both want to win, but I'm delighted to stand up after our blackjack session with a $100 profit in my pocket, and I'm infuriated if I've lost $300. Shope, on the other hand, derives no value from either of these outcomes. In fact, he doesn't consider his blackjack session a success unless he's up at least $1,000. He's not in Las Vegas to win enough to fund a nice dinner; he's there to go for broke. He wants to tip the cocktail waitresses a $100 chip for bringing him a Miller Light. He wants to surprise his wife with an emerald pendant. After many trips to Vegas together, I can say we end up in about the same place. I'm usually a little up or a little down. Shope often comes home down $2,500, but every few trips, he cashes out a tube of black and purple chips before he leaves for the airport. Which one of us has the better strategy? Neither.

Why are *you* betting? Of course you want to make money, right? Beyond that, everyone has different goals, both long term and short term, and they are often in direct conflict with each other. Imagine you place a $10 bet at 100-to-1 on Louisiana Tech beating Alabama, and at the end of the 3rd quarter, the Bulldogs are up 24–21. Pop quiz: If the sports book offers you $300 for your ticket, would you take it?

The answer, of course, is: It depends. It depends on whether you're Shope or me. It depends on how the rest of your day has gone, if not the rest of your month. You might have lost $300 worth of bets earlier in the day, and taking an early cash out on your bet would mean a lot to you. Or you might be committed to that needle-in-a-haystack win.

Answering why

Here are some possible betting goals. Which ones match you the best?

>> Betting on games/teams you're interested in

>> Betting on games in which you have high prediction confidence

- » Maximizing lifetime profits
- » Maximizing profits in a finite period, or over a set number of plays
- » Maximizing wins and losses over ROI
- » Betting to avoid going bust
- » Betting to lock in profits (also known as hedging)

I'll talk about some general principles of bet allocation first, and then I'll discuss some common approaches to bet allocation before wrapping up the chapter.

Financial diversity

Money market managers and financial planners tout diversity as a way to increase odds of investment success and reduce the odds of ruin. In the cliché world, it's known as not putting your eggs in one basket. What's wrong with having your life savings wrapped up in shares of the company you work for? If the company flourishes, the stock will go up and you'll get raises, promotions, and bonuses. Great! But the flip side of that is that if the company struggles, there's a higher chance that your savings will be wiped out at the precise moment you lose your job in a layoff.

The value — and limits — of diversity

Diversity in financial markets says that you want to have an array of investments that react in different directions, or at least at different intensity, to a certain kind of external event or economic environment. That's why you might hold stocks that respond well to high oil prices but also own stocks that thrive when prices are lower, or you might hold both stocks and bonds because they behave differently during recessions.

Stocks, bonds, and other financial instruments often have predictable correlations with each other because broad market forces, which makes diversifying holdings a complex, scientific pursuit. In sports betting, games are completely independent events. Although there are a few exceptions (like when one team's playoff hopes are pinned to the result of the outcome of a different game), in nearly every other case, games will play out completely independent of one another. That doesn't mean you should ignore the diversity concept.

Diversity: The slightly imperfect casino analogy

If you walk into a casino and look out across table games, every gambler you see has money on a −EV bet. It's a tiny disadvantage, but it is all but certain that with so many gamblers on various tables playing repeated hands/rolls/spins with a 49.5 percent chance of winning, the results will be good for a casino.

To paraphrase Joshua from *War Games,* if you're looking at a −EV bet, the only winning move is not to play. (Do we call him Joshua? Mr. WOPR?) However, if you insist on playing, the best chance you have of avoiding ruin is to put all your money on a single bet rather than spreading it across many smaller bets.

Picture a scenario where 100 people show up at a casino with $1,000 each, and each person sets out to play 100 consecutive $10 hands of a table game with a 1- or 2 percent house advantage. The casino bosses know that after those 10,000 hands have been played, there will a tiny number of people who got lucky and added $400 to $500 to their bankroll. There's a big pile of people who are somewhere in the middle, up a little, down a little. Finally, there are the people who got smoked and lost $400 to $500. Casinos know if you add it all up, though, the casino will be keeping a good chunk of that $100,000. The house wins by celebrating the "big winners" and letting the far more numerous losers quietly skulk back to their room with their free drink tickets. Then they rinse and repeat, draining money from bettors on an average of a few nickels and dimes per $10 bet. As long as there's an endless train of people walking through the door, the math will always work in the casino's favor.

But you could make a casino *momentarily* nervous if you could corral everyone in the casino and suggest that instead of betting $10 per hand, they pool their money to make a single $100,000 play. It feels all wrong, but it's true: If your goal is to double your money, you're far more likely to get there by placing a single bet with a 49 percent chance of winning than by making 100 $10 bets.

(Clearly, the casino would be fine with the above scenario as long as they have a parade of $100,000 bettors, because they know that over the long run, 51 people would lose their big bet for every 49 that win.)

If those thousand players played $10 hands continuously until they had either doubled their money or gone bust, there would be precious few who double their money before going bust. Betting −EV bets, even if they're only slightly negative, means playing longer makes you more likely to lose. If your play is −EV, maximizing financial outcome requires you to put it all on a single throw of the dice, or a single hand of cards.

Betting small advantages: Rinse and repeat

Conversely, if you have a small betting advantage, you should do the opposite of the single one-time bet. In fact, you should do what the casino does with *their* 51 percent advantage: Spread your bets out. A 51 percent advantage is a goldmine if you have enough time to make a small bet over and over. Now you stand a far greater chance of doubling your money than you do going bust.

I'm not saying with absolute certainty that *you* have an advantage in sports betting. Remember, if you bet straight -110 bets, you must win bets at a 52.38 percent rate just to cover the vig. But my suggestion is to bet like you have a small advantage — that is, make lots of small bets rather than a few big bets. The results won't seem dramatic, and going 5–4 on a weekend isn't nearly as fun as going 2–0, but if you accept that you're in this for the long haul, and you're going to pile up winning weekends with small profits, you stand a better chance of not breaking your bank.

Betting more comes with a cost: It means you'll need to find more bets worth making. If you're used to picking out your favorite game or two from the NFL weekend that you feel strongly about while ignoring the others, then you'll need to adjust your approach. Instead of only putting money on bets you've fallen in love with, move down the chain to bets you merely have a crush on, or even those bets you'd like to be no more than platonic friends with.

The wisdom of placing many small bets lies in the benefits of diversity and the profitability of repeating a small advantage over and over. Whether you bet for fun, or bet to not lose, or bet to win, placing lots of small bets is the way to go.

Of course, there's formal math to figure all this out, but I'm always tempted to simulate it. I built a simple Excel script that simulated a casino where cohorts of gamblers started with $1,000 and bet $10 per round on a game with a set winning percentage per round. They played continuously until they either doubled their money or went bust:

Win% per Hand	Doubled	Busted
45%	0%	100%
49%	2.3%	97.7%
49.5%	14%	76%
50.5%	94%	6%
51%	98.6%	1.4%
55%	100%	0%

When you play a long time, those tiny edges matter a ton. If you're playing a 45 percent game, you've got no hope of doubling your money before you go bust. Even for a game where the disadvantage is only a half percent, only 14 percent of the simulated players were able to double their money before running dry.

I also simulated what how things would go if you had a limited number of rounds. Here are the results for the same winning percentages, but limited to 1,000 rounds of play:

Win% per Hand	Winners	Losers	Doubled	Busted
45%	.1%	99.9%	0%	55.5%
49%	26.3%	73.7%	.02%	1%
49.5%	36.9%	63.1%	.08%	.4%
50.5%	63.12%	36.8%	.56%	.08%
51%	73.9%	26.1%	1%	.4%
55%	99.9%	.06%	56.5%	0%

Because these simulations were limited to 1,000 rounds of play, we need new columns to describe the winners and losers. Look at the amazing difference between 49.5 percent and 50.5 percent: The number of gamblers who are ahead after 1,000 rounds jumps from 36.9 percent to over 63 percent.

REMEMBER

Professional sports bettors can quit their day jobs if they can win anywhere close to 60 percent of their bets. Advantage bettors and money-making hobbyists are satisfied as long as they're between 53 percent and 55 percent. It's not uncommon for pros to place bets they have no more than a few points of advantage on. That works in the long run because they identify lots of bets, and they stick with their approach.

The value of outs

I've alluded to this concept before, but it's worth saying it explicitly: Good bettors maintain many *outs*. For a sports bettor, an out is any venue where they can place a bet.

For most people, having lots of outs means maintaining active accounts and positive balances at multiple online sports books. If you're betting in person, it means having multiple sports books you can walk into and place a bet.

Avoiding profiling

Maintaining outs is a constant challenge for pros because people who bet big and win frequently are often targets of *profiling*. That means the sports book has identified them as bettors who bet a lot and win a lot. Or these bettors may engage in behavior that the bookie decides is suspicious. When you get profiled, the bookmaker either closes your account altogether or severely reduces the amount you can bet on a game.

How much is a lot? I had a friend who was betting between $500 and $1,000 per game and went on a hot streak right after he got his online account established. After he had won eight or nine NFL games in a row, he got a terse note from the sports book saying they would be sending him the proceeds from his account but his business would no longer be welcome. And profiling can sometimes happen at lower average bet sizes too.

Pros use multiple outs to bet multi-thousand-dollar bets in a way that allows them to obscure the fact that they're winning. If they've won too much at sports book A, they can shift their attention to another out and play some throw-away −EV bets at sports book A while they put their high-quality wagers elsewhere.

Odds shopping

For the average bettor, having multiple outs is important for a different reason: odds shopping. A half point might not seem like much to an beginning bettor but once you've identified a +EV you want to make, taking the time to shop around for the best odds is well worth your time. In Part 3, I'll talk about how tightly the point spreads and totals match the actual outcomes, but just to give you an idea of what I'm talking about: If you win 10 bets out of 20 at −110 odds, you'll lose long term. If you can turn one of those 20 into a push or a win through odds shopping, you've transformed yourself from a losing bettor to a winning bettor. And it might surprise you how many games finish within a half point of the spread.

Of course, there is a real cost to maintaining multiple outs. Odds shopping takes time and patience. It's also harder to keep good records if you have several off-shore accounts. At any one time the amount you're up or down requires you to look in multiple places. Finally, if you're an online bettor, offshore books often require transaction fees when depositing or withdrawing money. So while I firmly recommend maintaining multiple outs, you'll have to balance the value against other considerations.

TIP

If you're dipping your toe into sports betting, a single account is fine. After you've decided you enjoy it and want to make a real effort to start winning money, I recommend setting up accounts so that you have at least five outs.

Bet sizing

Whether you're betting lots of wagers, or only putting money on your favorite few, you should also do some thinking about how big those bets should be.

>> How much money should you bet on each game?

>> How much should your bets vary in size relative to each other?

There is some controversy over bet size. Most bettors like to think about bets in *units,* which has no formal definition but usually means about 1/20th of the total amount you have available to bet. When those bettors are feeling more confident, they bet more units. When they feel less confident, or for long-shot future bets, they bet a single unit. Other bettors prefer a flat amount, regardless of how much money they have available, and still others adhere to a more directly proportional betting scheme where they bet a certain percentage of their money depending on their confidence in the bet.

Flat betting

I am a proponent of picking a bet size that works for you and sticking closely to the same amount for every bet. If that size is $10 per bet, you stick to it. If you only find a single bet in a day where you were prepared to wager $50 total on different bets, it's still at $10 bet.

How do you set the amount of your flat bet? It depends a little bit on how many sports you track and your preferences, but a good rule of thumb is five to ten flat bets per betting session (like an NFL weekend or a basketball weekday). Focusing on sessions is helpful because it gives you a limit to the number of games you're evaluating, and when the bets resolve, the winnings will be available for funding wagers in the next session.

I am a mostly flat bettor because it simplifies the math when I want to figure out how I stand financially. I also like flat betting because unit betting and proportional betting require differentiating confidence levels between different bets, something I don't like to spend time doing. On top of that, I've found that my winning percentage doesn't vary all that much between bets I love and bets I like.

As a mostly flat bettor, I calculate the amount I can bet in a month (which is a cycle in which I pay my bills). I take that amount and divide it into 50 even-size bets, and I put 15 to 20 percent of those bets to work for me in each betting session (less if there's only a game or two). In very rare cases, I will place multiple bets on a game, or place a double-sized bet on a game.

TIP

A minor exception to flat betting comes with high return/long odds prop bets. You might not want to place a full bet on some 1,000-to-1 long shot that your cousin who plays for Southwest Nowhere State is going to win the Heisman Trophy.

Multiple unit betting

An extension of flat betting is unit betting, where, as I covered earlier, you start with the amount you want to bet in a month, divide it into a number of flat bet amounts called *units.* Some units are bigger than others. (Insert your own joke here.) Instead of betting a single unit per pick, you'll be betting one unit for most picks and then two units for your favorite picks. For example, if a unit in your world is $10, most of your bets would be $10. On the rare occasion when you encounter a pick you fall in love with, you'd bet two units on it ($20).

TIP

Unit betting is a good approach, and it's quite common in the betting world. Everyone will understand what you mean if you say you're betting 1 unit on the Cowboys, Redskins, and Raiders, and 2 units on the Bengals. But don't get carried away with the variations: Have no more than 3 or 4 different levels of unit bets. Maybe it's 1u, 2u, and 5u, for example. Maybe you like the Fibonacci sequence and you want to do 1, 2, 3, 5, and 8 units. However you do it, consider these caveats:

>> Have your higher unit bets occur at decreasing frequency relative to the lower unit bets.

>> Don't go any higher than 10 units. If you're 10x confident in one pick versus a second pick, you should probably pass on the second pick altogether. When you monitor sports betting social media, you'll see people talk about 100-unit picks and 1,000-unit picks. Don't buy into it. It's marketing hype and pure balderdash.

Percentage session betting

There are more sophisticated bet allocation systems available if you're willing to go to the trouble. Some bettors like to take the money they've profited from one session and recalculate their unit size in the next session as a way to take advantage of win streaks without spending too much of what they've budgeted.

This system will look familiar: Divide the total dollars you want to bet per month into betting sessions that make sense for the sports you're interested in. At the beginning of each session, make your selections and divide your session bankroll by the number of bets you want to place.

If you lose it all, you're back to the original budgeted amount for the second session. If you win, you can make your selections for the next session and let the proceeds from the first session "ride" by adding them to the numerator to determine your second session bets. In this way, you're doing a recalculation of your bet size with every session. An NFL bettor who wins on Thursday night would roll that money into the early games on Sunday so that the bet sizes would increase slightly.

It's a simple way of saying "I'm going to bet 10 percent of my monthly betting dollars per weekend and 2 percent per session. If I win, I'll put those profits to work. If I lose, I'll be starting from scratch." With this strategy, you limit your losses, and you give yourself a chance to ride a win streak.

Mathematicians would tell you the problem with this method of bet allocation is that your bet stake should be changing according to the risk of the underlying bet rather than how much money you happen to have at that moment. That's not wrong. There's been research on optimal betting strategy, and it's led to some straightforward conclusions about how to bet, which I'll get to in the next section.

Kelly Criterion betting

The idea behind the Kelly Criterion system is to maximize the profit of each bet. As we know, that's not always your goal, but it's a common enough north star that it provides a basis for sound wager sizing.

The mathematicians who proved this system started with the idea that you should assess the probability that a bet would win, and then you assign a portion of your bankroll that's in proportion to that probability. At the risk of getting too deep in the weeds, the best approach in fact for long-term growth of your bankroll is to maximize the natural logarithm of the expected payoff of each bet. This is related to the fact that as bet size grows in proportion to bankroll growth, payoffs increase exponentially. The thinking behind the Kelly Criterion math is not important, but here's the formula for bet sizing:

Betting fraction of bankroll = (prob of win × Euro odds) – 1 ÷ Euro odds – 1

The Kelly system doesn't say anything about how much you should bet in any one session, but it is implied in the number that you spread bets out. Only a handful of bets will have probabilities of winning north of 50 percent, and very few will be much more than 60 percent likely to win. So if you take that handful and apply the formula, you (often) naturally come out with several bets per session, each representing a fraction of your bankroll.

Take a straight bet with a .55 winning percentage. Applying the formula you get:

1. Probability of a win multiplied by European odds = .55 × 1.91 = 1.0505

2. Taking that number and subtract 1 = .050505

3. Dividing it by European odds – 1 would be .050505 ÷ .91 = .05555, or in this case, 5.5 percent of bankroll.

WHY KELLY IS SO POPULAR

In theory, gambling with Kelly gives you the optimal fraction of your bankroll to wager on any bet. In theory, betting the optimal fraction would mean your bankroll will climb to infinity. If you set up a test in Excel, you'll see the mathematical advantage of Kelly, and it really does out-earn other similar bet allocation systems. It gives higher returns and minimizes the time taken to reach a specific bankroll objective (for example, if you want to double your money). The Kelly Criterion is widely used and well understood in many different situations, including poker and financial markets.

PROBLEMS WITH KELLY

So what's not to like?

For one thing, the math behind Kelly is based on continuous betting that goes to infinity, where bankrolls start arbitrarily large. That's not what's happening with sports bettors in the real world. Consider that . . .

>> Losing streaks are real. Even very good handicappers and bettors experience gut-wrenchingly inexplicable losing streaks. A 55 percent bettor can easily lose seven or eight 55 percent bets in a row. Kelly would have that bettor placing larger and larger bets on the way down into oblivion.

>> Hopefully this occurred to you already: All probabilities of a bet winning are merely estimates. Sports betting isn't dice or cards, so you don't actually know the win probability. A miscalculation can have you over-betting or under-betting, which fouls up the Kelly equation.

TIP

There's a place for Kelly Criterion in sports betting, but many bettors accept its application blindly. Losing streaks can lead you straight to bankruptcy with the raw Kelly Criterion, so lots of sports bettors execute what's known as a *half-Kelly*, which sounds like a dive at the Olympics. Doing the half-Kelly is to calculate the optimal bet percentage of bankroll and then cut it in half. This causes your growth rate to be less than optimal during win streaks, but it protects you during losing streaks.

The Importance of Record-Keeping

Maintaining good records of your sports betting activity has two primary goals. The first is financial: You want to ensure you're staying within the limits you've set for yourself and you want to be in a position to evaluate where you stand in terms of money won and lost at any moment. Second, you want to evaluate your betting performance. If you have more money than you started with, you can call yourself a winner. But good record-keeping lets you go one click deeper. What's your record in each sport? Do you have more success with a certain kind of bet?

When you lose bets, are they close or are you getting blown out? Are certain betting systems working better than others for you? When you have success, you want to be able to repeat it, and when you've lost bets, it's good to know why so, if you can identify a mistake, you can avoid it in the future. Without a disciplined approach to record-keeping, you're just spraying money onto bets and hoping for the best.

WARNING

In any form of gambling, the bottom line is the bottom line. If you end the day with more money than you started, you're a winner for that day. But there are also many opportunities for self-deception.

It's never too late to start keeping good records. In your document, you'll want to track this data I cover in the following sections so that you can answer the associated questions.

Measures of success

How successful has your betting and money management been?

>> **Win-loss record/percentage:** How well do you pick winners and optimize odds being offered at the sports books? The coin of the realm in sports betting is being able to claim a winning percentage and/or a basic profit/loss as a result of your bets.

>> **Profit/loss:** What is the magnitude of the change to your bankroll? When you add up your amounts won along with amounts lost plus other expenses, where do you stand for a certain time period?

>> **Bankroll:** How much money do you have available to bet with today, this week, and beyond? Have you been betting more than you wanted to?

>> **Liquidity:** Where is your money right now? What is the amount of money at each sports book that you could cash out today?

>> **ROI:** How efficient are your bets? What was the "return" on each dollar bet?

Bet records

What bets have you placed? Did they win or lose? Do you have bets that are still open?

>> **Bet type:** Are you betting sides and totals or derivatives, props, parlays, and so on?

>> **Sport:** What sports are you the most profitable betting?

>> **Bet details:** What odds did you get? How early did you place the bet? Did you get any *CLV?* (Closing Line Value, which I'll discuss later, in essence means the sports book payout odds changed after you put your bet in.)

>> **Open bets:** What bets are still to settle? What's their expected value? Should you consider placing hedge bets to maximize your position?

Bankrolling

In the most basic sense of the word, your *bankroll* is the pool of money you draw from to fund wagers. Your bankroll shrinks temporarily when you place bets; hopefully it grows larger than before when your bets settle as wins, and sometimes it shrinks below the starting point if you lose more than you win.

The bankroll concept can be deceptive and confusing. When you deposit money in your online account to bet against, is that online balance your bankroll? If you budget $1,000 to bet with over the course of a year, is *that* your bankroll? If you have bets pending, do the wagered amounts count as part of your bankroll or not?

The time dimension

REMEMBER

Before I dig into those questions, you should understand that a bankroll is more than just an amount of money. In fact, bankroll is best thought of as a defined amount of money over a defined amount of time.

When you go to Vegas for a weekend of gambling, you might bring $1,000 with you. "This is the most I can possibly lose at the tables. If I lose it all in one night, I'm staying in the room." Good thinking! Limiting yourself is important. In this case, that $1,000 is your bankroll for the trip. On that same trip, you might sit down at a blackjack table with $100 in chips, a $50 bill in your shirt pocket, and a promise to yourself that you won't lose more than $150 at this particular table.

In each instance, there's an implied time period along with a dollar value. Every time you go to the racetrack, sit at a blackjack table, or make a trip to Las Vegas, there's a dollar amount that you have in mind along with a level of self-enforcement that you apply to that bankroll.

Time as a flat circle

But modern sports betting isn't time-bound like a Vegas trip or a poker game. It's more like a never-ending ballgame, where you might fall behind, but there's always time to make up the points deficit.

Adopting sports betting as a hobby means there's no easy start and end point. After all, if you have an account with an online sports book, or if you have legalized in-person gambling in your state or province, sports betting is a year-round activity. There's no clear start and end point where you cease playing, run the numbers, and declare victory (or defeat).

So you'll need a way to manage your bankroll without clearly defined breakpoints. That means you need a way to measure as you go, or to create artificial break-points, or both.

Where do you stand?

Your sports betting hobby is a "going concern," which means bookkeeping can be a challenge. Picture this scenario:

1. You establish an account with an online sports book, and you deposit $100. There was a $5.90 fee tacked on because it was an international transaction.

2. You get a 50 percent sign-up bonus from this sports book that comes with a 5× rollover requirement. (That means you get $50 more to bet with. However, it's not your money to withdraw until you've put it at risk at least five times over.)

3. You bet some, you win some, you lose some, and at the end of the month, here's your status:

   - Your balance is $105.

   - You have $75 in pending futures bets that will resolve at various dates in the future ranging from 1 to 6 months from now.

   - Your $50 bonus has been put in play 3.5 times, so you'll need to put $75 worth of additional bets down before it's all available for you to withdraw.

   - The amount available to withdraw from the account is $55.

Pop quiz: Are you a winning or losing?

I have no idea either. I'll show you a more precise way to get at that number later in this chapter, but in the meantime, I wanted to give you an idea of the number of factors in play when it comes to sports betting accounting. And with all that, I've left out another big complicating factor, the maintenance of multiple outs.

Establishing a fiscal period

The first step in making sense of it is establishing some time periods and terminology when it comes to keeping the books on your new hobby. First, think about the money you're going to spend.

TIP

I hope you're a big winner at sports betting, but I'm going to say something you might not want to hear: When you try to determine your initial bankroll, you should assume you're going to lose it all. When you ask yourself how much money you want to gamble with, the *real* question is how much you're willing to part with.

Just like any risky investment, you should start with the most conservative financial scenario in which you lose every bet you make. Does that mean you will actually lose everything? Probably not. But it's always possible, and if the worst-possible-luck scenario would lead to problems paying bills, rent, or cause a material increase of your consumer debt balance, then you need to make it a smaller number.

And here's the good news: In-person sports books accept bets as small as $5 or $10, and online sports books take bets of $1 and sometimes less. So if the goal is to just to have a little bit of fun gambling on games, it doesn't require a huge commitment of wealth.

For now, I'll use bankroll as a blanket term that refers to the pool of money you're going to bet with, but before you start gambling, I urge you to set up some kind of record-keeping system in a spreadsheet or a notebook. Make note of a few key numbers (some of whose names I made up) you're going to want to keep at the top of your mind, which I cover in the following subsections.

Dayroll: A betting session

The amount you're willing to risk (and lose) in any one betting session. What's a betting session? A single day's games usually makes sense, like the nightly slate of basketball games, or the Sunday NFL games. Consider the initial game and prop bets as well as halftime or follow-up wagering.

WARNING

Start with your dayroll; don't end with it. Your daily limit and minimum bet amount will determine the number of distinct bets you can make in a day (again, assuming no wins). If you come from the other mathematical direction and start with bet size and then multiply it by the number of bets you want to make to come up with your bankroll, you risk defeating the purpose of setting an overall limit.

A week in the life

If a day limit is too finely tuned, and your favorite sports have an obvious one week cadence, calculating a *weekroll* — a maximum betting limit for a single week — might make sense. You can also stretch your weekroll to mean a certain period of time between a day and a month to suit the periodicity of the sports you bet on. If you like tennis, your weekroll might cover two-week periods for tournaments. The PGA week usually ends on a Sunday, and the NFL week often ends on a Monday. I like to call this time period a *season increment*. It's an easy way to divide up your favorite sport's season. It's usually a week, sometimes more, sometimes less. The season increment might be divided up into increment *sessions*, like rounds of a golf or tennis tournament. In EPL soccer, around half the games usually fall on Saturday with the other half on Sunday with a few outliers. For the NFL, there are five distinct sessions: Thursday night, Sunday early games, Sunday late games, Sunday night, and Monday night.

TIP

You might calibrate your weekroll to your job's pay periods so that your "just for fun" money gets refreshed at the end of it. However you define it, the point is to settle on a single amount you're willing to risk and lose and connect it with concrete dates on the calendar.

Monthroll: Connecting it to your bills

For lots of people, mortgage and bills come on a monthly cadence. If your sports betting hobby is going to involve more than a few dollars, have a monthly checkpoint for yourself, and a set dollar amount that you will not go beyond. (That dollar amount could be derived from smaller increments if you like.)

Wealthroll

This one's a little different because it's probably not a fixed amount. Presumably every non-problem gambler has in mind a percentage of their income, wealth, or cash flow that they are willing to risk (and lose) before they consider themselves a problem gambler.

These numbers are different for everyone. It depends on the amount of joy and overall utility you receive from betting on sports. It depends on your sports and betting preferences, the limits and constraints of your betting options, and of course how much disposable income you can afford to spend.

TIP

However you define it, if you're a regular gambler, you should set a hard limit in terms of the fraction of your income you can afford to part with for the love of the game.

How to think about a wealthroll

Establish your wealthroll first. Consider the disposable money you have available to spend on entertaining yourself, and decide what share of that you want to spend on sports betting. For most people, this should be a share of income or wealth, or a percentage of your liquid worth.

If you're the type who goes through a strict process of budgeting every paycheck, that will make sense to you. If you're less of a planner, it might sound grandiose or strange to put sports betting expenditures in terms of income and worth. But I would argue that we do exactly that for every hobby, whether it's through a conscious budgeting process, or whether you arrive at your preferred spending level by unconsciously balancing the various forces pushing you toward and pulling you away from that activity.

For example, I like playing golf. Every year, if I added up the money I spend on greens fees, club dues, lessons, subscriptions to golf media, buckets of balls at the practice range, clubs and equipment, funny pants and hat, tips for the beer server, and so on, it would probably average about 30 percent of the disposable part of my income, which is the part of my paycheck I spend on feeding, clothing, and entertaining myself and my family. While I don't start with 30 percent in mind via some sharp-pencil precise calculation, I know that in the recesses of my mind I am striking a balance between the joy and satisfaction I get from the game against my finite resources of time and money, in addition to factors like opportunity cost of not doing other fun stuff like mountain biking, or pressure I might feel from my family, my time constraints, and, of course, the fact that I have a finite amount of money to spend on entertainment for myself and my family.

If next year my income dropped, or if my wife started voicing more frustration at my weekend absences, or perhaps if I just stopped enjoying the game as much, the change in forces would probably lead to a new equilibrium point: I'd play less, and I'd only spend, say, 25 percent of my disposable income on golf rather than 30 percent. (Can you tell I was an economics major in college?)

WARNING

Sports betting isn't golf. Don't try to find your "natural level of utility" when it comes to gambling. Even if you don't think you're susceptible to gambling's siren song, when you wing it, a lot can go wrong. It's often a private activity and can be easily hidden. Because betting can potentially take nearly zero time to do, there are basically no governors to slow down your spending, and there are no refunds if you're, uh, dissatisfied with your purchase. (Think about golf by contrast: You can return the $600 shoes you bought on impulse; you can only play so much golf in a weekend; and it's a difficult activity to hide.)

ESTABLISHING A WEALTHROLL

Here are the steps you can take to start with big-picture rules for what and how you're going to spend money on sports betting:

1. If this is a one-time experiment to see if you like sports betting, set an initial amount you're going to have some fun with. But don't stop there. Be conservative: Assume you'll lose and you'll love it, so set some rules for when and how you'll reload your account or reset your bankroll.

   How much is your "experimental" bankroll?

   How long do you expect that to last?

2. Define the limit of your recurring financial outlay:

   Set an assessment time period where you're going to take stock, reload your account if necessary, take a withdrawal from your account if you're winning, and so forth. Pay periods work, but months are better because most peoples' bills come due on a monthly cadence.

   Define an amount money you're willing to dedicate to the hobby based on the time period you describe.

   Think about circumstances that would cause you to reassess the amount downward. Write them down. "If I lose my job or if I have a medical emergency, the gambling budget goes to zero."

   Think about what happens if you win. If you decide to gamble $100 per month and you find that you win enough so that a $50 deposit in an online account lasts for three months before your account is empty, do you allow yourself to "catch up" and reload your account with the $250 you thought you would have spent by now? (Obviously that would be a problem if you already spent that money on . . . golf.)

Hopefully you've put these terms into an Excel worksheet or a Google spreadsheet (or whatever document you're going to use for record-keeping) so that it's easily accessible and the data is sortable. Being able to look at your betting records from different angles can be a very valuable practice.

Rolling your own

As important as setting up your bankroll parameters, it does you no good unless you track it. Everyone has different appetites for record-keeping and different systems for limiting their expenditures. If you can keep it all in your head and feel your way through, that's bully for you. But if there's any doubt in your mind about your ability to keep sports betting in its proper place in your life, I highly recommend a more permanent record-keeping system. Whether you're using an online document or use an old-fashioned legal pad and pencil, you'll want put this information at the very top:

>> Bankroll amounts or percent.

>> Associated time period.

>> For weekroll and monthroll, define the end dates for each time period. While you're at it, make calendar reminders in your smartphone.

>> Reevaluation dates.

What's a reevaluation date? These are preset dates, maybe a day or two, where you take stock. You should keep handicapping and betting to a minimum and instead focus on past results: your betting, your bankroll management, your record-keeping, and of course, the financial outcome. Your early reevaluation dates should be more frequent, maybe every few weeks. As you get the hang of things, you can spread them into once-a-month-or-two events.

Reevaluation dates should be spaced far enough apart to allow time to place and settle a good sample size of bets. I suggest no fewer than 20. They should be spaced close enough together that you can do a full assessment of what you did and why you did it. And if you found you've made bookkeeping errors or betting mistakes, or that you need to change your approach, you're not far enough down the road with a bad plan that it's impossible to dig out of the hole.

On every reevaluation date you should ask these questions:

>> How well did you stick to your bankroll constraints?

>> What was your financial position and betting performance per time period?

>> What is your current overall financial position?

>> And finally, does your bankroll setup need to be adjusted?

The last question is the one you should consider the most carefully. If you lost money, are you comfortable with your losses in terms of your overall personal financial health? Are there reasons to adjust your bankroll numbers downward? Look ahead in the sports calendar to make sure you're budgeting such that you have money available to bet on your favorite events.

WARNING

Make a promise to yourself: Winning or losing, you will only adjust your bankroll upward during reevaluation periods, and never in between, even if you're winning mid-cycle.

Metric Superiority: Winning Percentage versus ROI versus Profit

Earlier in the chapter, I touched on some questions you can only answer through record-keeping. This section will provide a more detailed breakdown of some of those concepts.

ROI

ROI, or return on investment, is a common financial metric that describes the amount won or lost in terms of a percentage. ROI is useful because you'll get a feel for how well you're doing regardless of bet size, regardless of bet type, and regardless of the number of bets you've placed. It's a good measurement if you've placed 100 $1 bets or 2 $50 bets, or if they're parlays or straight bets. ROI is an indicator of how well you're putting your betting dollar to work, whether you're betting too much or too little, and whether your selecting the right kinds of bets.

ROI has its weaknesses too. It's a measurement that doesn't mean much if you've only made a few bets. It doesn't mean the number you get is wrong, but it's just not a fair measure of your return on investment with such a small sample size. Because it's a percentage of your investment, it's also not going to tell you the real dollar amount you're ahead or behind. It's also tricky comparing ROI across multiple time periods if you're not making close to the same number of wagers in each increment. ROI should be calculated using the amount you've put at risk, not the amount you've deposited in an online account. That means ROI doesn't show you how "liquid" your position is. Having said all that, ROI is a helpful number to keep an eye on in the medium and long term.

REMEMBER

To calculate ROI, divide your profit by the total amount you've invested, with profits being the amount you've won from betting.

ROI example

If you've placed $1,000 worth of bets in the last month, Table 5-1 shows what your ROI worksheet might look like.

TABLE 5-1

Sample ROI Worksheet

	Stake	Result	Profit
Bet 1	110	210	100
Bet 2	110	200	90
Bet 3	50	–50	–100
Bet 4	50	230	180
Bet 5	200	381	181
Bet 6	110	–110	–220
Bet 7	50	–50	–100
Bet 8	110	210	100
Bet 9	110	–110	–220
Bet 10	50	–50	–100
Bet 11	50	230	180
Total:	$1,000	$1,091	$91

Profit = $91 — Risked = $1,000 — ROI = 9.1%

WARNING

I've put a lot of emphasis on setting and sticking with time periods to measure your betting and financial success. ROI is like win/loss record in that it helps you assess your financial success over a set period of time. Once you decide the time periods you're going to use to measure ROI, don't change it. It might be tempting to tweak the start and end dates of your measurement to make your ROI look better. Like your bankroll, I recommend you track ROI as follows:

>> **Season increment or week:** If you place 10 or more bets in a single week (or a season increment, like a single golf or tennis tournament), you might be interested in tracking your ROI for that discrete event. If you only bet a few bets a week, save the ROI calculation for the end of the month.

>> **Monthly ROI:** The first of the month is a good, straightforward, easy-to-remember spot to look back on your ROI. The benefit of tracking ROI over a month is you can make a determination if changes in one or more elements of your betting approach are changing your return on investment.

>> **Lifetime ROI:** If you can maintain a positive ROI over the entirety of your sports betting career, you're doing well.

How should you account for long-horizon "investments" like futures bets? Like most metrics, calculating ROI should be done against wagers made and settled.

That causes a couple of bookkeeping problems for ROI and other financial calculations because . . .

>> You'll have a disproportionate number and dollar amount of futures bets settle at a single point of the season (for example, often at the end).

>> Because many months can elapse between when you make a futures bet and when it settles, it's possible your sports betting strategy will have evolved (and hopefully improved). So having a slew of past futures bets settle may not be a good indication of how you're betting today.

>> But if you count your futures bets in the time period they were made, you'll have to "leave the books" open until the end of the season, so your ROI calculations will only be preliminary measurements until all of those long-term bets finally settle.

TIP

I prefer to let my futures bet fall in the month they are settled, if for no other reason than I like to close the books on earlier months. I'm sure there are CPAs out there who would argue differently, but the key is this: Make a system that works for you and stick with it.

Profit (and loss)

Calculating profit and loss tells you where you stand overall. And it's actually quite simple to do. The problem with ROI is that it's a percentage, so it doesn't clue you in on the overall volume of betting you've been doing. You can be extremely efficient with your betting dollar, as indicated by an ROI of 50 percent, but if you've only identified one game per month to bet on, your excellent ROI won't amount to much in the way of profits. Calculating profit is as straightforward as tracking the net gain or loss from each bet. Specifically, in any form, this number should include vigorish.

Basic profit

To calculate basic profit, sum up the net result of each bet you make, setting aside the wager amount. If you risked $1 on a game at −110 odds, your win nets you 91 cents. (You gave $1 to the bookmaker, and he returned $1.91 in exchange for your winning ticket.)

Your tracking spreadsheet would show this as a 91-cent profit. If the same bet lost, you'd record that as a −$1 profit in your tracking sheet. When you add up the net results of all of your bets, you get a look at how much you've grown or shrunk your bankroll. Check out Table 5-2.

TABLE 5-2

Sample Profit Worksheet

Date	Bet	Wager Amt	Odds	Result
1-Nov	Nets-10	23	–115	–23
1-Nov	Jazz 1H-2.5	11	–110	10
2-Nov	Rockets/Lakers Under 220	10	–110	9.19
4-Nov	Wizards ML	5	+170	8.50
4-Nov	Jazz 3pt Attempts 18 Over	26	–130	–26
4-Nov	Hawks Team Total 113 Over	10	–110	9.19
5-Nov	Mavericks/Jazz Under 230	11.50	–115	10
6-Nov	Heat+6.5	5.50	–110	–5.50
7-Nov	Clippers 1Q -4.5	12	–120	10
7-Nov	Warriors ML	20	–200	10
			Profit	9.38

This sample table is an excerpt from your tracking spreadsheet with a week's worth of early-season NBA betting. As you can see, there are many different kinds of bets listed, with a variety of odds. Regardless of the odds or the wager, the results of each bet are recorded in the far-right column.

For the week, your profit was $9.38; that's your bottom line. If the number was negative, you'd say that was a loss. As long as your profit is positive, you're adding to your bankroll. When you go through your regular review periods, you should look at your overall profit/loss to see where you should adjust the amounts you bet on each sport and also to determine if you're being a discerning-enough customer in terms of how profitable each sport is. It's possible you're not betting enough on sports you're good at, and maybe you're betting too much on sports where you can't pick winners.

Profit/loss complexities

Like ROI, if you have additional expenses, you should include them in your overall profit or loss calculation. A good tracking sheet will have categories for subscriptions, services, or other expenses. When you want to consider the overall cost or financial benefit of your sports betting hobby, include all these expenses.

Long-range wagers, or futures, are hard to account for, because you might place the wager in July and not see the bet settled until the following February. I prefer to list future bets as losses in my tracking sheets, and unless future betting occupies more than a few percentage points of your overall gambling dollar, you should do the same. After all, I'm not running a long-lived mutual fund. If the bet loses, it's already been recorded and "paid for." If the bet wins, I record it as a windfall gain at the time of the settlement. (Besides, futures bets are often done at long odds, so most of them are bound to lose anyway.)

Unit profits

Bettors often do away with absolute dollar amounts and express their confidence in picks by assigning them unit values. Regardless of whether you're a $1-per-game bettor or a $1,000-per-game bettor, describing your bets as flat *units* gives you a level of accountability when you describe your win/loss record. For the most common bets, you'd describe it as a one-unit bet. For those bets you feel more confident in, you call them a two-unit bet and go up from there.

In *Sharper*, the excellent book that takes you inside the world of professional sports betting by an author under the pseudonym of Poker Joe, among professional bettors and sharps, a unit is defined to be 1 percent of bankroll, and for everyone else, it just means a standard-sized bet. Sounds important and well-defined, right? Hey, the pros must have it all figured out! Except, nowhere in that book is there a precise definition of unit. I got a definition from a professional bettor I know who told me a unit is 2 percent (or 50 bets' worth) of the amount you'd have to be down before you'd have to take a long break from betting on sports.

Having the precision of 1 to 2 percent of your bankroll is very helpful. But if 1 unit equaling 1 percent doesn't fit for you, it's fine to define 1 unit as being the lowest flat amount you're willing to bet on any game. Describing a play as a one-unit bet that wins implies that you're wagering the odds amount for a favorite and a flat unit for an underdog. So a 1-unit win on a −110 bet means you're +1 unit. A 1-unit loss means you're −1.1 units. If the bet was −150, you'd be −1.5 units.

Unit betting is helpful for standardizing your bet size and also standardizing your level of confidence in a bet. It also allows you to speak in abstract terms with other bettors whose bankrolls are different than yours. Most bettors settle into the value of a "unit" for them that depends on their bankroll and risk tolerance. It's often a flat percentage of their monthroll. For example, a player who is willing to bet $1,000 per month might divide that up into 20 wagers of $50 each. That bettor's unit is $50. A bettor with $50 per month to play with who likes to bet smaller on more games might have a $1 unit. The key is that one unit is their standard bet amount.

Betting in units also lets you obfuscate the actual amount of money you're wagering if you want to communicate with other bettors but prefer to keep the financial details private. Calling something a "1u bet" or a "2u bet" is a good starting point for indicating your commitment to that selection.

Win/loss records

A win loss record is a great way to understand if — on a basic level — you are picking winners successfully. A win% or Win/Loss record says nothing about the efficiency of your gambling. Gamblers like to tout win/loss records, but there's an inherent weakness in them in that you should only add up wins and losses meaningfully if you bet the exact same amount at the exact same odds every time. That rarely happens.

If you make moneyline bets, a single win might be 10 percent of what you risked, or it might be 400 percent of what you risked if you bet on an underdog. That means if you bet on a +200 underdog and win, you shouldn't count it the same as a win on a −200 favorite. It's far easier to eschew any version of a win/loss record and instead focus on ROI and profits.

Chapter **6**

Full Frontal Nudity (and Some Statistics and Probability)

y editor said nobody would read the chapter unless we spiced up the title. This chapter is both one of the most important in the book, and it's one that an average reader is likely to skip, so I had to get your attention somehow.

Have you ever looked at a map on a placemat at the local diner or pancake restaurant and seen the warning "Not to be used for navigation"? That's my approach to the statistical and probability concepts contained in this chapter. I want you to take the first steps in adding some mathematical rigor to your approach to gambling and sports analysis, but beware: I am not prepping you to defend a Master's thesis on Bayesian inference or stochastics. This chapter is a map on a placemat. It will be simplified and conceptual, and you might learn something new, but it is not to be used for navigation purposes.

Dry or not, I'm including this chapter because the reason is as simple as this: Sound use of mathematics is so critical to sports betting that you simply can't function successfully without a solid foundation. And I'm not just talking about addition and subtraction. If you don't possess a mastery of a few key statistics and probability concepts, you will draw dubious conclusions, make spurious attributions, and almost certainly lose at sports betting over the long term.

I understand this topic causes some heartburn. Heck, I always thought I had a knack for math, but I get lost easily in the deep waters of "standard deviation" versus "standard error" and "binomial distribution" versus "normal approximation of the binomial." Fortunately, going deep isn't necessary. I'll present these concepts in layman's terms, I will not throw a bunch of formulas at you, and I will avoid using Greek letters at all costs. Your job is to grasp the concepts and then let Excel do the spadework for you.

WARNING

This is the most likely chapter to skip in the whole book, but don't do it. Even if you think you know this stuff inside and out, I urge you to adopt the Zen practice called "beginner's mind" or "original mind," which means you set your ego aside along with any assumptions and prejudgments you might bring to these subjects. Open yourself to the universe, and be ready to learn how to do what every acolyte in a Himalayan monastery seeks to master: kicking the bookmaker's ass.

And now, onward to Enlightenment. . . .

Thanks for Nothing, Ancestors

The modern human brain came into being a hundred thousand years ago, give or take 10 minutes. It is literally the most complex thing we know about it in the entire universe, other than the Chapter 3 Fortnite map.

Part of the software that's been installed in that lump of gray matter on top of your neck is an innate sense of numbers, statistics, and probabilities. Hey, that's super helpful, right? You can imagine a Cro-Magnon doing some caveman mental multiplication when trying to figure out how many elk skins they'd need to dress every member of the clan for the upcoming fertility dance. That Egyptian architect trying to convince the King not to build his new palace so close to the river? He couldn't describe a normal distribution to you, but he would know without a doubt that annual Nile floods cluster around a certain reading on the Nilometer, with more extreme floods and droughts being the most rare.

Unfortunately, those intuitive math skills that saved our species from lurking sabre-tooth tigers and allowed Egyptians to build the Pyramids (with a little help from the Sky People) have limits, and they come with certain deceptive flaws. While we have the ability to grasp essential calculations with small numbers, when the numbers get big and are fueled by a desire to predict and to recognize grand patterns, the results have not been good.

Narratives instead of numbers

It's proven difficult for humans to move beyond thinking anecdotally, and as a result, human history has been driven by what writer Michael Shermer called "folk numeracy," where people just like you and me convince themselves the world works a certain way based on bunk math. Comets bring plague! Groundhogs bring cold weather! Eating a stolen egg on a Sunday gives you heartburn! Our lack of intuition about probability led us, and continues to lead us, to attach meaning to the meaningless, to find nonexistent signals amid a sea of noise, and, in general, to fail to connect the dots between evidence and consequence.

Think of the people who won't think twice about the safety of getting in their car but are morbidly afraid to fly in spite of the far greater relative danger of the road. If you're a fan who thinks the pitcher won't succeed if you utter the words "no hitter" before the game is over, or if you're a gambler who has discovered teams with names that start with N through Z beat teams whose names start with A through M 60 percent of the time, you're not so different from the person who won't fly.

We are not simple computers, discerning the most rational choice in any decision tree (as evidenced by the tattoo on my shoulder). The process we use to evaluate and make decisions rely on a complicated layer-cake of neuron groupings that includes physical, emotional, and computational components layered on top of memory, experience, and the stress of the moment. No wonder it's hard to think straight!

That's why formal definitions and advanced concepts in statistics and probability took so long to come up with, but now that we have them, they're clearly worth the wait. Think about it: So much of life exists outside the realm of the certain. So when faced with uncertainty and we are tasked with finding the optimal path forward, the most profitable choice, the safest option, or the most likely diagnosis, statistics and probability toolkits are what we turn to.

And guess who we have to thank for advancing the statprob cause? Gamblers.

Probabilities and Single-Outcome Events

Celebrity forecaster Nate Silver put Donald Trump's chances of winning the electoral college at something like 38 percent the night before the 2016 election, and when Trump won, many observers howled with delight at the failure of pollsters and prediction markets to anticipate the surprise result, and in the process, exhibited a fundamental misunderstanding of the value of probability. I saw the same reaction when Silver tweeted the chances of a 49ers' win in Super Bowl LIV was 92 percent with the Chiefs down 10 with 9 minutes to play. The joke is on the mockers, and I'll get to that momentarily.

When you're predicting the probability of a certain hand appearing from a deck of cards, you can calculate it precisely because you know the entire universe of possible outcomes. When you predict the probability of radioactive decay of an atom, you might not know it as well as you do a deck of cards, but your prediction is based on a long pattern of observations and a deep understanding of the physics of the atomic nucleus.

WARNING

For events like these, describing the probabilities is not quite the same as making a hard prediction of the future. If the outcome aligns with the highest probability event, it's not a vindication of the latter, and if the outcome *doesn't* align with the probabilities, it's not a repudiation either. Probabilities give us information about possible outcomes. They are not meant to be a crystal ball.

Nate Silver's published probabilities were akin to saying "the 2016 election is like reaching into a bag with four red marbles and six blue marbles; a Trump win is relatively less likely than a Clinton win."

That is not the same as predicting "Clinton will win; Trump will lose."

For sports watchers of Super Bowl LIV, Silver's statement of the 49ers' chances of winning was based on historical data that pointed to exactly that situation. It's still true! Any NFL team with a 10-point lead in the 4th quarter has over a 90 percent chance of winning if we use history as a guide. The fact that Pat Mahomes and the Chiefs pulled it off doesn't make that history less true and doesn't change the probability in the next NFL game that sees an identical situation. I'd like to see a show of hands of folks who'd like to bet even money against Mr. Silver on future NFL games with the same setup. I'm guessing there would be no takers among those who mocked Nate, because that winning percentage is likely to hold going forward.

When is it appropriate to generalize about a sporting event? And when is a play or a game a singular event? Statistics and probabilities inform our actions and provide a *window* on an upcoming event, and they provide guidelines for thinking about it, but they shouldn't be treated as hard determinants of every bet. The best sports bettors have to consider many lines of analysis because sports outcomes, like elections, are singular events. These players and coaches, at this moment in time, with their accumulated experience and memories, in these conditions, have never occurred before, and will never be repeated again.

Alternate universes would be nice

As singular events, we can't determine probabilities with absolute certainty. For elections and next week's stock market results and sporting events, we can only run the experiment once.

REMEMBER

Sports bettors, like the rest of us, live in a world of singular events. And yet, we must assign a probability of winning that almost always looks strange when compared with the eventual score of the game. If the 49ers and Chiefs were able to replay that 4th quarter a hundred times starting from the 9-minute mark, who knows what we'd see? You might make the case that nine times out of ten, the 49ers don't let Tyreek Hill run free for that fateful 3rd and 15 play. Nine times out of ten, on the what ended up being the 49ers' final offensive play, the ref blows the whistle when the play clock expires before the snap, and the 49ers get a second chance to run a play that doesn't result in a game-ending sack.

When we talk about the probability of Clemson versus Oklahoma in the 2023 College Football Playoff semifinal, it can often be helpful to think about it as if these players, coaches, and conditions were transported to 1,000 parallel universes at kickoff to play out the game. As far as we know, it's not actually happening, but the hypothetical parallel universe game simulator is a good way to think about probabilities and predictions.

Once the games start in each parallel universe, normal randomness takes over: The crazy bounces, bad calls, crowd noise, coin-flip catches, and wind gusts play out like a normal game. As each game goes on in its own universe, the players, coaches, and crowd react to their own unfolding narrative so that by the end, each of the 1,000 games wind up differently. When you think of games in this way, a 65.2 percent probability of a Clemson win takes on a new meaning. You're simply saying that there are 652 parallel universes where Clemson wins, and 348 where OU wins.

The challenge is that we don't know which of those outcomes is on order for our own universe. But the lesson that Nate Silver teaches us is that just because the ball didn't bounce your way doesn't mean your probabilities were wrong. It just means that sometimes the less likely event actually happens.

The ball will not bounce your way every time, but in the long run, a sports bettor who can assign good probabilities to events will win.

Statistical analysis as a process to find truth(iness)

Even if you are a purely instinctive handicapper who evaluates teams on fundamentals, you simply can't win without math. What's worse, even if you think you're winning, if you can't calculate something as straightforward as a winning percentage or a return on investment, nobody will believe you.

Statistics and probability are a pathway toward the truth. They won't get you the whole way there, but they're a great start.

The basic process for assessing and betting on a game looks like this:

1. Sports bettors assess a sporting event using one or more of the methods I discuss in this book.

2. The bettor creates a narrative for the event of varying depth and quality, such as "Team A's pace has been improving in the last several games; several key offensive players are finally fully healthy; Team B's travel and schedule is unusually arduous; there are multiple historical angles that favor Team A beating the spread."

3. Assuming a simple moneyline bet, the bettor assigns a straw man probability to Team A beating Team B, such as "Team A has a 65 percent chance of winning."

4. The bettor compares the probability to odds being offered by sports books.

5. If the probability and odds combine to make a +EV bet, the bettor decides to make a bet.

6. For some advanced bettors, the level of EV positivity informs the size of the wager: the greater the value, the greater the amount of the wager.

In this way, the sports bettor is going beyond where Nate Silver goes with assignment of probabilities to the outcome of an election. With apologies to the cliché gods, sports bettors put their money where their mouth is by converting those probabilities into a prediction.

Overdue: The Gambler's Fallacy

If you've ever been on a casino floor, you've probably seen displays at the roulette tables that show you the results of the most recent dozen spins, the number itself, and the color: black, red, or the dreaded green zero and double zero.

I can remember before the fancy displays, the casino would hand out little pre-printed sheets and golf pencils to help customers who wanted to write in results from each spin. Why go to all this trouble for customers? It's simple. It is not only difficult for gamblers to shake the idea that previous spins have an impact on future spins, but casinos know that if they encourage it, customers will feel they have more control over the game and will sit and play longer. And playing longer means losing longer.

WARNING

Independent random events have a probability of occurring but no memory about what happened in the past. As a gambler, you'd be wise to sear this lesson into your brain and learn to recognize when an occurrence is independent, and understand how to think about independence.

A roll of the dice or a draw from a deck of the cards is clearly an independent event. A spin of the roulette wheel is an independent event. Even if a red number has appeared 10 times in a row, it doesn't matter.

"But wait," you say, "if there's a 48 percent chance of getting a red spin, getting an 11th red after 10 reds in a row has a vanishingly small probability. To be precise, it's .48 to the 11th power, or .48 times .48 times .48 and so on, which comes out to .0003, or 3/100ths of a percent. So there's no way it's coming up red again!"

There's a tale of a casino in Monte Carlo where the roulette wheel hit an astounding 24 black numbers in a row one night, a one in a few hundred million outcomes. Was that wheel crooked? Not necessarily.

Let's be clear about what that probability represents. It does not mean the 11th roll has 3/100ths of a percent chance to come up red. That percentage hasn't changed; it's an independent event, and it's still .48. What does have a 3/100ths of a percent chance is that any random group of 11 consecutive spins of a roulette wheel would come up all reds. You've already climbed most of the way up Mount Improbable once 10 reds in a row appeared. Now that it's happened, future spin patterns are as likely as they were when you walked up to the table. There's a 48 percent chance of getting another red, a 23 percent chance of getting two reds in a row, and yes, 3/100ths of a percent chance that the wheel will hit 11 more reds in a row.

How Randomness Masquerades as Non-Randomness

When I was just starting my career in technology, I got an opportunity to do some freelance data analysis work for a guy who owned a small business North of Houston (or so I was told). I imagined an entrepreneur with a growing business in oil patch consulting, or maybe a reseller of pipe valves and fittings. I imagined doing some important work, setting up a database to record results of his well logs or client contacts. As I followed the directions off the freeway and deep into the woods, the question-mark bubble over my head began to grow. When I finally pulled up in front of the small temporary structure in the forest, my optimism had turned into doubt, and when I heard about the project he wanted me to undertake, I began immediately coming up with excuses for why I couldn't do it.

The project I was asked to do was, drumroll, to predict numbers in the Texas Lotto. Every Wednesday and Saturday, the Texas Lottery commission picked six random numbered balls from a drum, and the person who matched the grand prize won a minimum of $3 million. My prospective client had been tracking the winning numbers for months and was convinced there was a pattern to it. The basis for his conviction was a graph he had created that looked something like Figure 6-1.

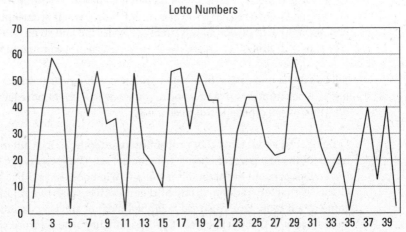

FIGURE 6-1: Lottery number patterns.

I looked at the chart he had diligently drawn and could feel his eyes on me. What we were looking at was as obvious to him as it was unclear to me. Finally he said, "Look, the numbers just keep going up and down, over and over. I want you to write a computer program that describes that movement and predicts what the numbers will be next week."

After a few minutes of digging into his "theories," it was quite clear that he was doing what many gamblers do. He was doing the same thing as those ancient people who overlaid the shapes of their gods and myths in the constellations. He was doing the same thing that a soothsayer did with chicken entrails and the color of a comet tail. He had convinced himself that there was a pattern in a completely random set of numbers, and he was quite convinced that with a little help from a computer, he'd be on his way to lotto riches.

(In case you're wondering what I did, dear reader, I can report with great pride that I wrote him a fancy random number generator that used about 20 lines of code, waited for a few weeks to make it seem like I had put a good deal of work into it, and then cashed his check and changed my phone number.)

The fundamental assumption of randomness

As a sports bettor, there should be a constant question at the back of your mind at any point when you're looking at statistics: What if I'm looking at a set of completely random numbers that just happened to come up this way?

In fact, it shouldn't be a question; it should be an assumption. Sporting events, with all their wacky bounces and results that change because a player's toe was a millimeter in the wrong direction, are mostly random events. So it's not a stretch to assume betting outcomes like moneylines, point spreads, and over/under bets are basically random too.

Sports bettors are confronted with assertions of non-randomness all the time. You might be looking at a win-loss record of a fellow bettor, or analyzing the spread results from an angle you found in the historical data for a team. Heck, it doesn't have to be betting-related; it might just be someone arguing with you about certain players being more "clutch" than others.

TIP

More often than not, assertions of non-randomness are perfectly normal streaks that appear in totally random numbers.

Inserting randomness into sports assertions

Let's dive deeper into the fundamental assertion of randomness. Embedded there is a well justified suspicion that the numbers sports fans and bettors bathe in every day are, in fact, meaningless. Let's take a few common examples and explain why they it is perfectly sensible and non-cynical to chalk up each argument to randomness:

1. College basketball teams that lost their conference championship game are more likely to get beaten in the first game of the NCAA Tournament. In the last five years, those teams have lost 11 games and only won 7 in the first round of the tournament.

2. The Cowboys come into tonight's game with a turnover margin of –4 on the year, and the Saints are at –1. Clearly, being able to protect the ball better is an advantage for the Saints in their upcoming game.

3. Bellinger bats .405 with runners in scoring position, so he will be a real threat in the game tonight if the top of the Dodgers lineup can get on base.

4. Elliott's yards per carry average is down this year from 4.8 yards to 4.3 yards, so clearly there is an issue either with him or the Cowboys' offensive line.

In each case, the speaker is attaching statistics to a storyline and presenting the numbers to you as if they definitively back up his or her assertion. But I desperately want you to be a skeptic in these cases about how statistics are deployed to support a story that could very easily not be true. Here are possible rebuttals for each assertion:

1. 7 wins and 11 losses doesn't represent anything close to a statistically meaningful data set. You could flip a coin 18 times and quite easily come up with 7 heads and 11 tails.

2. Sure, the Cowboys raw turnover number is lower than the Saints, but there are many possible explanations that make this argument nonsense. First, it is possible that turnovers are completely random events, in which case, teams will be randomly distributed along the bell curve, but their relative position to each other is not predictive. Second, the Saints have had their bye week while the Cowboys have not. Third, the Cowboys have played against much tougher defensive competition.

3. Cody Bellinger hit .406 with runners in scoring position this season, but did you know he hit .431 on games after a rest day? Did you know he hits .289 against pitchers with odd numbered jerseys? Did you know he only hit .260 with a runner only on 3rd base, but he hit .418 with a runner on 2nd base or runners on 2nd and 3rd? There's no pattern to be found here. Slice the data enough ways, and you'll inevitably find one slice with a higher batting average.

4. Maybe the Cowboys have played better defenses this year. Or there was that one game last year where the defender who was about to tackle Elliot for a loss tripped over his shoelaces. Most of all, Elliott and his offensive line could be performing just as objectively effectively as the year before, and the

difference between 4.8 and 4.3 could simply be due to random variation. If you roll a pair of dice 50 times, you know each roll will be between 2 and 12, but a 50 second trial of 50 rolls could easily result in an average being .5 higher or lower than the first trial.

TIP

If you're facing an argument by statistic, your sports rebuttal should have two parts:

>> **First, there may be circumstances that weaken the underlying statistical argument.** This is most common in comparison arguments, where someone is showing you two measurements that, to be meaningful, require the circumstances to be identical.

>> **Second, look at the numbers themselves.** Do the numbers really support the narrative being propounded? Or could they be the result of looking at a fortuitous window on a totally random process?

Descriptive versus predictive

A third part of rebutting sports arguments, which deserves its own subsection, is the idea of data being interesting but by no means an indicator about the future.

REMEMBER

The job of statistics is to describe the past. There is an abundance of tools that help you tell a story about existing data. Yay math! But a lovely and complete description of the past does not automatically equal a prediction of the future.

If you're an NFL bettor, this essential truth is thrown in your face over and over again in the early part of the season when 2–0 teams lay an egg and 0–2 bust out with a 45-point performance. We have to constantly remind ourselves that next season will be very different from the last season, and the next game is likely to not resemble the last one.

"Pat Mahomes has passed for more yardage than the previous week for three consecutive games" is the kind of statement that masquerades as being predictive, but it is really nothing more than an interesting descriptive statement about the past.

Take a pair of dice and roll it a few times. In one of your trials, you'll get a couple of low numbers to start with. Imagine a sports pundit telling you that because you rolled a 2, 5, and 6 to start with, it's clear that those dice are "above average" and "are performing better than normal dice because they're averaging north of 3.5." Is it possible your dice are extra awesome? Sure. But it's much more likely you're just looking at a narrow slice of a larger non-pattern of randomness.

TIP

Again, these questions are among the most important you can make a habit of asking: Is it possible I've assigned meaning to a random process? Have I looked at enough data to justify the conclusion I'm drawing? Are there circumstances that invalidate a numerical comparison? And finally, even if a pattern is evident, do I have reason to believe it is predictive or merely descriptive?

The statistical numeracy that you build in this chapter and hopefully from other sources, is designed to answer that question. I call it the fundamental question because it is so very important. At the heart of any sports bettor's work is an attempt to separate signal from noise. If you want to win, you want to be able to tease out predictive and meaningful information from an ocean of meaningless numbers.

Predictably random: The bell curve

If you're a visual person and you want to understand how randomness works, the bell curve is a valuable aid. If you're not familiar with the bell curve, it's the shape that's created when you graph the results of a finite number of trials of normally random numbers.

A trial is a fixed length set of repeated experiments, such as 10 flips of a coin, 20 rolls of a pair of dice, or 30 baseball games. Each event has one or more associated measurement (respectively, the number of heads, the total value of all dice rolls, and the number of runs, hits, errors, or a zillion other possible metrics).

When a random number is normally distributed, that just means it's a variable, like test scores or batting averages, that center around a certain most likely outcome. When you have repeated trials of events, normally distributed variables produce a bell-shaped pattern based on the probabilities of the outcomes of your experiment.

Let's use a coin to demonstrate this. Take a worn out fair coin and flip it 100 times. You know intuitively that the average result of 100 flips will be 50 heads. But you also know that in any single trial of 100 flips, you're unlikely to get exactly 50 heads. But you will certainly get results that seem to orbit around 50 heads: sometimes 46, sometimes 58, sometimes 49. And most important, the farther you get from 50 — higher or lower — the more rare that number comes up. Occasionally you'll be in the 40s and 60s, and once in a blue moon, your heads will be in the 30s or 70s.

If you graphed the result of each trial of 100 coin flips, where the horizontal axis is the number of heads and the vertical axis is the number of times that head count has come up, your graph would start to look like the curve shown in Figure 6-2.

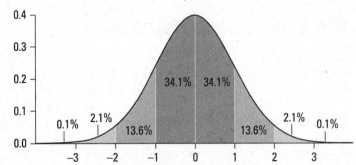

FIGURE 6-2:
A bell curve of coin flip results.

With the first few trials, the curve won't resemble anything. But inevitably, the more trials you measure, the more clearly the bell curve will be outlined. Every bell curve has a few descriptive statistics that you'll want to get to know:

>> **The *mean* is the apex of the curve, also known as the average value, around which all other results cluster.** Track 100 flip trials of a coin and the bell curve will cluster around 50 heads because 50 is that's the halfway mark between getting 0 heads and getting 100 heads.

WARNING

Just because the mean is at the top of the bell curve doesn't mean it's a likely result. In fact, it would be quite rare for you to flip a coin 100 times and get exactly 50 heads and 50 tails. But the mean represents the most likely outcome relative to all other outcomes.

>> **Another aspect of the bell curve is its *variance*, which is the amount to which values cluster tightly around the mean.** We often express the amount of variance with the more useful mathematical term called standard deviation. Your curve can be skinny and tall, or it can be shorter and wider, but it's still a bell curve, and that makes it useful for statistical analysis.

The Matter of Sample Size

Proving correlations and demonstrating that observed probabilities represent a real-world effect is always better when you have a larger sample of events.

If you notice the road team covered the spread earlier in the day in the NFC Championship game and conclude that result represents sound evidence for betting the road team in the afternoon's AFC Championship game, you've succumbed to anecdotal reasoning. That doesn't mean you're wrong, but you're a long way from proving that road teams have a spread advantage if you only have a single example of it happening in the past.

The Law of Large Numbers

When statisticians try to make sense out of information, they view it through the filter of sample size. There's an idea known colloquially as the Law of Large Numbers, which says the more data you collect, or the more experiments you run, the more likely that data maps to what's going on in the real world. For example, if you measure the height of the 4th graders at the nearest elementary school, you get a fair idea for the average height and variance of all American 4th graders. If you visit a second school, then a third, your results will be an increasingly more accurate picture of what the bell curve for those 4th graders' height is.

Sports bettors spot angles and trends all the time that they try to match with betting results. In the story above, we have a single example of the road team covering the spread in the Conference Championship games. Trying to infer that the way your single example (or "experiment" in statistician speak) is actually a universal rule about Conference Championship games is a serious stretch. You would be able to learn more with a bigger sample of data. If you found that road teams were 10–2 in the last six years and 65–38 in the Super Bowl era, you might be on to something.

Sports betting results with only a handful of instances are virtually meaningless. If somebody tells you they've picked 4 out of the last 6 World Series winners, the message they want you to receive is that they're good sports prognosticators. That may be true, or it may not be true, but the numbers neither prove nor disprove that narrative. Demand more data.

How much is enough?

Before you can draw any conclusions about your data, you have to consider whether you've collected enough data. Clearly one example isn't enough. What if you find an angle that's 4–0? Or 12–7? If you find an angle that's won 4 and lost 0 against the spread, it's certainly profitable . . . in the past. But with only a few instances of it occurring, you really can't make any claims that you're not simply looking at a random set of about its predictive power.

How much data is enough? It actually depends on what you think the data is saying.

In general, as your sample size increases, the more confidence you can have that the results of your data represent what's happening in general. If you're interested in doing a deep dive on this topic, you can look into the statistical tool called *confidence intervals,* which indicate how likely your sample measurement matches the underlying measurement, and it's arrived at through a calculation involving the number of samples, the resulting measurement, and confidence level chosen by statisticians. You've no doubt witnessed this in the form of an opinion poll's margin of error. For example, an opinion poll reports that 58 percent of the population prefers strawberry ice cream to chocolate, with a 3.5 percent margin of error. That means the researchers are 95 percent certain the true strawberry lover proportion is between 54.5 percent and 61.5 percent (that is, 3.5 points above and below the sample measurement). The researchers could have chosen different confidence levels.

Proof of above average-ness

Sports bettors are very often trying to find trends and angles that beat the spread. Remember, with the vigorish, you have to beat the spread 52.4 percent of the time, so if you find an angle that wins 53 percent of the time, you can call it profitable and call it a day, right?

Not exactly. But this is the part when all the mental exercises with coin flips pay off. If we assume that wins and losses on straight bets (that is, 11/10 point spread and over/under bets, where the probability is theoretically 50-50 either way) are like coin flips, then finding an angle that shows something other than 50 percent lets us use mathematical tools that might otherwise be used to prove a coin is weighted based on the result of heads and tails. And I'll formalize those tools in the sections that follow, but in the meantime, the essential concept will probably make sense to you intuitively.

REMEMBER

If you want to prove a coin is weighted, the amount of data you need to prove it is inversely proportional how far away your experimental results are from the expected result. And the same process you use to think about weighted coins applies to proving statistical significance in sports betting trends and angles.

If that sounds complicated, it's not. If I told you I thought a coin was weighted unfairly towards heads because I flipped it 100 times and got 53 heads and 47 tails, you'd tell me "nope, that's probably just random variation." But if I ran an experiment and got 53,000 heads and 47,000 tails, it's much more convincing because of the Law of Large Numbers (among other things). Each experiment resulted in 53 percent heads, right? But the second experiment had 100,000 trials rather than 100. With such a massive number of data points, it is extremely unlikely that a fair coin would result in such a discrepancy between heads and tails.

Here's the, uh, flip side of that same concept: If the result of my experiment was 30 heads and 9 tails, or 17 tails and 1 head, it would be powerful evidence that the coin was indeed crooked, even though the number of data points is quite small.

When the results of your experiment land far away from the expected result, you don't need as much data to make your case. The closer you get to the expected result, the more data you need.

TIP

For sports bettors, this essential statistical truth means you should beware of a handicapper or analyst trying to tell you a betting system is worth betting on if . . .

>> You have a ton of data points but fall under 52.4 percent. For example, "home favorites in college football are 1041–959 over/under in the last three years." Poppycock. Even if it were true, betting this trend blindly doesn't win enough to cover the vigorish.

>> The spread results of that betting system are hovering close to 50 percent without a lot of data points. For example, "road college football teams following a 30-point loss at home are 45–35 against the spread." Balderdash. Yes, a 56 percent trend would be profitable. But you should have very little confidence that this angle reflects some deep truth about college football teams overperforming, because 56 percent with only 80 data points is totally inconclusive. Again, think of the coin flip. If you flipped a coin 80 times and got 45 heads, would you think anything of it?

So again, you might be asking, how much data is enough? We're building to it; bear with me.

Standard deviation: You can do this

If the words *standard deviation* send a shiver down your spine, I'm here to tell you there is nothing to be afraid of. In fact, standard deviation is a straightforward concept that even the most statprob-illiterate folk can digest and put to good use.

WARNING

I want your focus to be on the concepts, not on the specific math, so wherever possible, I'm going to skip the detailed formulas and caveats.

First, I am going to assume you understand what an average, or arithmetic mean is. (If you don't, let me recommend a thing called Google.) You no doubt know exactly how to calculate an average, but it's worth remembering that the concept behind "average" is to give meaning to a set of data. The average of a group of numbers helps you understand the point those numbers cluster around. It's a shortcut to describing a set of data.

TIP

Like average, variance is just another characteristic of a set of data. The variance of a data set describes how widely dispersed the elements are. And like average, standard deviation is just a number that's a descriptive shortcut to help you give meaning and context to a set of underlying data.

Let's look at a quick example. Below are two data sets, each having an average of 5:

(4, 5, 5, 6, 5)

(8, 5, 1, 9, 2)

But you can see right away that despite their common average, the second data set has values that stray much further away from 5 than those of the first data set. Calculating the standard deviation of each set gives you an exact number to describe how much variability is in the data.

In this example, a few seconds of Excel work reveals that a standard deviation on the first set is equal to about .6, and for the second set it is equal to about 2.9.

Standard deviation's special purpose

So what can you do with standard deviation?

>> **It gives you a basis for talking about data across different data sets.** If you see a measurement that's .6 units different from 5 in the first data set, it represents the same level of variance as a measurement that's 2.9 units above or below 5 in the second data set.

>> **It makes a specific statement about just how unusual a certain measurement is.** For a normal random variable, about two thirds of all measurements fall within one standard deviation of the average (that is, one standard deviation to the left of the average and one standard deviation to the right of the average). About 95 percent of the measurements fall within 2 standard deviations. 99.7 percent of the measurements fall within three standard deviations.

So if you measured the heights of the kids in the nearest elementary school's 4th graders and calculated the average to be 49 inches and the standard deviation of 2.5 inches, you might draw the conclusion that a random 4th grader from a different school has a 68 percent chance of being between 46.5 inches and 51.5 inches tall (each height being one standard deviation away from the mean).

Standard deviation for binary results

There will be many occasions when you need to analyze the results of a betting strategy or validate a certain angle or trend. So instead of taking measurements, you're counting something like wins versus losses or overs versus unders.

It turns out you can deploy standard deviation in these scenarios as well, even though you are working with categories of data rather than specific measurements. If you're curious, you simply take the number of data points and multiply it be the probabilities of each outcome, and then take the square root of the whole thing. So if you're looking for a standard deviation on 100 coin flips (or on wins and losses against the spread), it's

Standard Deviation = Square Root of $(100 \times .5 \times .5) = 5$

Remember that .5 is the probability of both heads and tails. And like other square roots, you express this in terms of the underlying measurement. We could say, "When you flip a coin 100 times, the mean number of heads is 50, and the standard deviation is 5 heads."

As you can see in Figure 6-3, since 1 standard deviation = 5, getting 45 to 55 is within 1 standard deviation of the mean, 40 to 60 is within 2 standard deviations of the mean, and so on. Beyond 3 standard deviations and you might have a weighted coin!

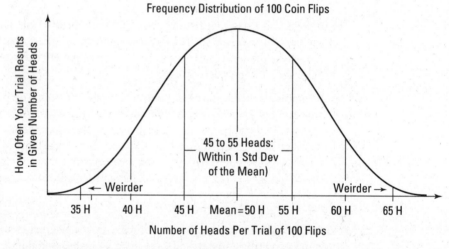

FIGURE 6-3:
The bell curve resulting from many trials of 100 coin flips each.

Example: Standard deviation in sports

Say you're analyzing the offensive output of a certain soccer team, so you build a table of the number of goals they've scored in the first 18 games:

Game	Goals For
Game 1	4
Game 2	1
Game 3	3

Game	Goals For
Game 4	3
Game 5	2
Game 6	0
Game 7	5
Game 8	2
Game 9	1
Game 10	2
Game 11	4
Game 12	2
Game 13	4
Game 14	2
Game 15	0
Game 16	2
Game 17	4
Game 18	3

The average here is 2.44 goals per game, and the standard deviation is equal to 1.38 goals.

In today's compute-enhanced, Excel-driven world, the math behind a standard deviation is not as important as understanding the concept. What makes it a "standard" deviation and not a deviation unique to this particular set of data is the idea that you can use standard deviation as a measurement of variation across any data set that results in bell curve–ish data. So if this team were to score 4 goals in their 19th soccer game of the season, we know it would be above average. But standard deviation lets us describe just how unusual it is. Since 4 goals is 1.56 goals higher than the mean of 2.44, and since we know a standard deviation for this team's goals is 1.38, we could describe that result as being 1.13 standard deviations away from the mean.

So what? Well, for one thing, it gives you an intrinsic feel for how unusual the result is. We expect 68 percent of all results to be within 1 standard deviation of the mean, 95 percent of the values to be within 2 standard deviations of the mean, and 99 percent of the results to be within 3 standard deviations of the mean.

TIP

As a bettor, this concept is valuable because it helps you interpret results and characterize them as being out of the ordinary or not. You'll start noticing analysts and so-called experts often peddle data points as being far more remarkable than they really are.

The Wonderful, Life-Changing Beauty of the Amazing Gambler's Z-Score

If you take away one thing from this chapter, it's an understanding of randomness and a level of comfort with what statisticians call a *Z-score*. Oops, that's two things. If you take two things away, it's randomness, Z-scores, and an understanding of what a standard deviation is. Oh heck, that's three things. Let's move on.

If you've come this far, I hope you're willing to go a little further into statprob literacy and gain mastery of the incomparable *Gambler's Z-score,* one of the most useful weapons in your sports betting arsenal that you'll use over and over. In some ways you've already deployed it earlier in the chapter, but we're going to get focused on it in a sports betting concept.

Zee origin story

The Gambler's Z is an offshoot of the Z-test. No, the Z-test is not a pop quiz in math class that only Taylor Zalinsky and Andy Zimmerman had to take. It's a test in the statistical sense, in which researchers evaluate data to see if the numbers validate or disprove a previously stated hypothesis, and to what degree.

The subject is way more complex than I can get into here, but suffice it to say the Z-test is when statisticians have two sets of data and they want to figure out whether there is a significant amount of difference between them. Say we wanted to test that antibiotic: We'd take a bunch of petri dishes full of bacteria, apply the antibiotic to some of them, and then apply chocolate milk or something to the others (I would make a terrible biologist), and count of the bacterial cells. The result would be two sets of data, and for each, we'd calculate the average and standard deviation. The Z-test is a way to look at those numbers and determine whether the difference we see in the average bacteria count is statistically significant or not. After centuries of people eyeballing data, putting their thumb in the air, or asking the gods if there was any difference in the two sets of data, the Z-test actually tells you once and for all that yes, chocolate milk is the perfect agent to fight bacteria.

The Z-score and sports betting

Why would comparing two sets of data be useful? It all goes back to that essential question about whether the results we're looking at are the result of random luck or not. Imagine you are presented with an NFL trend that says "In the last 20 years, teams that score fewer than 17 points three weeks in a row and then score 28 or more have gone under the total 23 times, and they have gone over the total 7 times. It only happens once or twice per season, but you'll win 78 percent of the time."

Before you start setting aside money to make this bet, you'll want to ask yourself three questions:

1. Does this trend make sense logically, and is there a reason why bettors or teams would behave in a way that makes this trend predictive? I'll talk about how to answer that question in later chapters.

2. Does the data I'm looking at represent a material difference from a completely random set of data?

3. Related to question 2, if it's not random data, how unusual is this result relative to a random result?

The Gambler's Z helps you answer questions 2 and 3, because the question we're really asking is what the statistical Z-test asks: Would a coin flip trial that resulted in 23 heads and 7 tails be inconsistent with a fair coin that had a 50-50 chance of landing on heads and tails?

We know that if we did repeated trials of 30 coin flips, we'd get a bell curve centered on 15 heads. The Z-score will determine where on that bell curve that 23 heads trial is.

Doing the Gambler's Z calculation

To get the Z-score, take these simple steps:

1. Get the standard deviation of a 30 trial coin flip for a 50-50 coin, which is the square root of 30 times the probability of heads times the probability of tails, or $30 \times .5 \times .5 = 7.5$. The square root of 7.5 is 2.74.

2. Take the difference of the result with the expected result. In this case, the expected result is 15 heads, and we got 23 heads. So $23 - 15 = 8$.

    Note, what you care about is the distance between your result and the mean. The sign is not important.

3. Divide the result in step 2 by the result in step 1 to get the Z-score, which is the number of standard deviations away from the expected result.

In this case, 8 ÷ 2.74 = 2.9, or nearly three standard deviations.

A Z-score of 2.9 would indicate that your result is in the 95th to 99th percentile in terms of rarity. If you did 100 trials of 30 coins, you would only get a result that far away from 15 heads in only two or three of the trials.

TIP

If you calculate a Z-score of less than 2, you should treat it as a random result. Between 2 and 3 standard deviations is open to interpretation, so I'd look for more evidence that it's a meaningful trend. And at 3 standard deviations and more, I consider it at least a statistically viable trend. That doesn't mean it's predictive of future results, but I feel comfortable that it's not simply a random result.

Example: Random or not?

Look at the table below that shows the results of your friend flipping a coin 50 times. By the end, he's come up with 25 heads and 25 tails. No big surprise there.

H	H	T	H	T	T	T	T	T	H	H	H	T	H	H	H	T	H	T	H	T	H	H	H	T
H	H	T	H	T	T	H	T	T	H	T	T	T	T	H	H	T	H	T	H	H	T	T	T	H

Now imagine that you only walked in the room starting at flip 10 and witnessed the next 18 flips. You witness the coin going 13–5 in terms of heads and tails and conclude the coin must be loaded. The Z-score helps you quantify how unusual that result is.

Again, let's go through the steps to find the Z-score:

1. Take the difference of the result you got and the expected result (or the mean). In this case, we got 13 heads when we would have expected 9 (that is, in 18 attempts with a 50-50 coin), so that gives us 4.

2. Now we divide that by the standard deviation of this data set. It just so happens the standard deviation for a coin flip is the square root of the number of trials (18) multiplied by the probabilities of each outcome (.5 for heads and .5 for tails). That gives us a standard deviation of 2.1 heads. In layman's terms, it would be perfectly normal to get between 6.9 and 11.1 heads on 18 flips (one standard deviation away from the mean), and hardly unexpected to get as few as 4.8 or as many as 13.2 heads (two standard deviations from the mean).

3. Calculating 4 ÷ 2.1 gives us a Z-score of 1.88.

If you find a trend with a Z of less than 1.96, the results are not unusual enough to say definitively that you're not just looking at statistical noise. I structured this example on purpose because I wanted you to see the vulnerability of the Z-score to misinterpretation. As good as 13–5 seems in the moment, we can see in the context of all the flips that it's meaningless; you've stumbled into a lucky streak and nothing more. It's also entirely possible that you're on to something, that you've identified a non-random phenomenon, but you'll have to keep measuring to prove it statistically.

Last word on the Z

I've just given you a very simple use case for the Gambler's Z, and I am completely comfortable that even though this version of it may seem like a cartoon to a formally trained statistician, it does the job it was meant to. Be aware that there are subtleties and caveats and twists that you'll encounter if you dig deeper into the Z. My advice is to keep it simple. You're not using it for your PhD or to find the source of a global pandemic. Don't make it overly complicated.

Chapter 7

Handicapping the Fundamentals

I've talked about the mathematical importance of finding the best odds, and I've also walked you through the systems for allocating your bankroll toward wagers. Now it's time to spend a few chapters talking about different methodologies for that all-important activity we call picking winners. It is part art, part science, part instinct, part witchcraft, and it is known as *handicapping.*

Handicapping is an overloaded term in the world of betting, but in essence, it's about finding winning bets. More specifically, handicapping is the process of looking at the menu of available games to bet on, and analyzing games in order to identify situations where the betting market has misjudged or mispriced a bet.

While there are common approaches, there is no set recipe for handicapping. To handicap a game is to analyze all factors you think are important enough to impact the outcome of the game, with the result being a prediction of the likely final score. The difference between your predicted outcome and a game's published odds inform your final betting choices. For example, if you handicap the Clemson/ Notre Dame game and determine Notre Dame is 7 points better, you'd consider betting on the Irish if they are favored by fewer than 7 points, and you'd consider betting the opposite way if the Irish are favored by more than 7 points.

WARNING

Successful bettors focus on *numbers*, not teams. They use their handicapping skills to predict the outcome of a game, and they then make bets that provide the highest expectation of return. The road to ruin is paved with sports bettors who start a handicap by picking a team first and then going through the handicapping process to justify their pick.

REMEMBER

Bookmaker odds and payout schedules represent market expectations, so you're looking for ways the market has misjudged odds. For point spread bets, you're trying to identify favorites that will win by more than the point spread and underdogs that will lose by less. For total bets, it means over bettors think the game will be higher scoring, and under betters think the opposite.

Successful fundamental handicapping is about gathering and distilling information. It's about finding an underappreciated angle on a game (something connected to a team, maybe an offense, defense, or a single player, or perhaps something to do with the weather, a referee or other factor) and then finding the bets on the menu that don't properly reflect that factor in the odds.

The Challenges of Fundamental Analysis

Fundamental analysis is a vast universe of research opportunities. Here are the big challenges for you, which I cover throughout the chapter:

>> **Finding fundamental factors that have an *actual* impact on game play.** Handicappers pursue all manner of theories, looking for situations and settings that cause a team to play above or below their market expectations on a given day. There's a near infinite amount of information out there, but very little of it affects the game. While you don't want to follow the herd and focus only on the most common fundamental factors (weather, rest, injuries, coaching, motivation), it's also important that you quickly throw out unimportant theories and information.

>> **Even when you find factors that influence the outcome of games, you need to make sure that you can actually bet based on that factor.** Though sports books offer a huge number of bets, you can't just bet on anything. If you spend hours developing a rock-solid theory that Jimmy Garoppolo is more accurate during minutes 5 through 10 of each quarter, that's great, but is there a way to bet profitably using that knowledge? Maybe, maybe not, but the lesson is that your handicapper should always be informed by what bets are available to make.

>> **Make sure the fundamental factor you want to bet on hasn't already been priced into the marketplace.** There is very little true insider information when it comes to the major sports. If you hear a change in a key player's injury status via primetime media, your first assumption should be that the public betting market has heard the same thing and bet accordingly. That means the odds now reflect this new piece of information and there is no way to profit from it. Profiting from good fundamental handicapping is the art of finding novel angles that the public isn't paying adequate attention to, or by finding information that the betting markets are aware of but have fundamentally misjudged.

REMEMBER

A lot of data is available online. Some is crap; some is good. You may have to combine it in creative ways to get what you want. Therein lies the joy in fundamental analysis: You get to be creative and explore any of the endless number of angles that exist.

Outside the Lines, between the Ears

Fundamental handicapping is a family of handicapping largely distinct from technical handicapping, although there are areas of overlap. Fundamental analysis is a fancy way of saying qualitative analysis, which itself is a fancy way of saying the activity of looking for an information edge when assessing specific players, teams, and situations. Fundamental analysis requires judgment calls about where advantages exist and where there is value in the betting markets.

As you'll learn in the next chapter, technical analysis is far less reliant on the handicapper making judgments about teams, schemes, players, and external factors. Technical analysis relies on numbers and broad patterns of behavior that lead to +EV bets.

Fundamental analysis comes from a deeper level of understanding about the sport. If you're an expert or just a dedicated fan, the more you watch the games, the more you'll develop qualitative conclusions about which teams are good and bad, how certain situations and setups can cause a team to underperform or overperform relative to the betting markets' expectations.

That's not to say it's all thumb-in-the-air touchy-feely guesswork. Fundamental factors can often be proven mathematically to be true. It's not uncommon for a handicapper to start with a fundamental factor, develop a theory about its impact on the betting markets, and then back-test that theory against historical game and betting data.

The home-field advantage example

The original sports fundamental factor that is the best demonstration of the concept is something we all know to be true today: Most professional teams play incrementally better in front of their home crowd. Why is this important to a bettor? The impact is big enough that if the oddsmaker set the point spread and moneyline for a game on both teams' bodies of work without regard for where the game is being played, the odds would be much less accurate and therefore vulnerable to astute bettors like you who realized that blind-betting on the home team would be extremely profitable.

I talk in more depth about home-field advantage for each specific sport in Part 3, but to give you a taste of how it affects football outcomes, NFL home teams average 3 to 4 points more than away teams, and college football teams average about a touchdown more. We take it for granted now that this factor is big enough for oddsmakers to consider when they set point spreads. And there's an easily understood chain of logic why this would be the case.

First, there are the mental and emotional factors:

>> Athletes often say they are energized from the noise and enthusiasm of a home crowd and distracted by a hostile crowd.

>> The comfort that comes from the familiarity of the home court or field.

>> Playing at home spares players from the fatigue and hassle of travel.

Then there are some measurable, real-world advantages that teams get from playing at home for a handful of sports:

>> Baseball fielders have more familiarity with the contours of the outfield wall and the shape of the obstacles in their home stadium's foul areas, so their defense is likely to be statistically better when they play at home.

>> Baseball general managers also have the ability to shape their team to fit the park over the long term in terms of both batting and fielding.

>> Football requires players to communicate with calls at the line on both sides of the ball; a noisy crowd makes it more likely for a miscommunication.

The benefits of fundamental analysis

The wonks can play money ball, running endless regression analysis on mountains of data. But it takes somebody who understands the game as it is played, who rely on their eyeballs to tell them which teams are overrated and which teams are underrated. If you are into the strategy and sweat, fundamental analysis just might be for you.

REMEMBER

Fundamental analysis works best in the hands of those who have this kind of visceral understanding of the game. And fundamental handicappers recognize that technical analysis, or looking at games through a stats-only lens, comes with some built-in weaknesses:

» Game stats and player metrics describe the past, not the future. Past results do not always presage future results.

» Technical analysis usually misses situational factors like injuries and weather.

» Stats don't just hide the underlying truth; sometimes they lie outright. If you judge a football team on the final score and yards per play, you'll miss the fact that in the last game, they were the beneficiaries of three lucky takeaways and a 99-yard run that occurred because the two safeties ran into each other.

The numbers tell a story, but they are only a model of the truth, or the truth told in a certain way.

And remember, if you rely on metrics and stats, you're a slave to those aspects of the game that can be recorded, encoded, and quantified. If you watch a game, you'll agree that there's plenty that can't be boiled down into a number or a flag. Because of that, experienced fundamental handicappers have access to parts of a game that are inaccessible to number crunchers and modelers.

In 2018, an enterprising fundamental handicapper noticed that Vikings QB Kirk Cousins's performance was sensitive to the time of day. Where Cousins can be masterful on Sunday afternoon, he seems to turn into a pumpkin with regularity during primetime games. And the thing is, his stats aren't that much different if you were simply looking at box scores. It's not an obvious angle; it's only one you would pick up on if you watch games, make careful notes, and tease out conclusions from what you see.

The downside of fundamental analysis

One of the biggest issues with a fundamental analysis is its ubiquity. Every bettor and oddsmaker does fundamental analysis to some extent. In fact, more than any kind of mathematical method, a fundamental approach to sports betting is the default. This is the level of analysis you'll get from most analysts: "Rice looked awful out there this week. They got pushed around by Louisiana Tech, so I'm not optimistic that they'll be able to cover the spread against Baylor next Saturday."

While there's not much value to be had in statements like that, it is a species of fundamental analysis in that it's a person putting a team to the eyeball test rather than relying on box scores and stats.

Beating the crowd

That basic, unsophisticated level of fundamental analysis is what most of the betting public has to offer. Most bettors learned everything they know about a team from a handful of 20-second clips on *SportsCenter,* and you can rest assured those impressions are factored into the odds being offered from sports books.

WARNING

Conventional wisdom is *not* useful in sports betting. By definition, it implies most people have drawn the same conclusion about a team or a player. When information and impressions are widely traded in public, there will be zero betting value available to you. Has Steph Curry been dominant in the playoffs? Great. Everybody knows that. You can rest assured the Warriors point spread already reflects the roll that he's on. Did you notice that Clayton Kershaw has some kind of mental block that prevents him from performing well in the playoffs? Congratulations, you and the rest of the baseball-watching planet know this "secret," which means it's already been factored into the game odds.

Fundamental handicapping requires you to be more perceptive than the average bettor. If you rely on the bog standard assessment of teams and players to give you an edge over the market, you're not likely to win in the long run.

Assessing the correctness of your wacky theories

Did that game go under the total because of you correctly assessed that Sam Darnold's robotic shoulder doesn't function well when the barometric pressure is low? Maybe so! Did the Steelers cover because you correctly theorized that September games are hardest on teams with older rosters because they have to deal with the stress of their kids going back to school? Maybe so!

Or maybe not. It can be particularly difficult to trace a path from your predictions about a game to the betting outcome. If you believe the Nuggets play a style of defense that will be particularly confounding to the Trailblazers, and Denver goes on to win and cover the spread, it's possible you were right on, or it's possible your theory was totally wrong and they won for completely unrelated reasons. Even when data is available, untangling causality is a tough proposition.

TIP

Fundamental analysis is not just about doing qualitative assessments on teams and players in order to determine where there's betting value. The best handicappers do a second-order assessment to see if their prediction came to pass in the game. That means when the game is over, you can't just rest on your laurels and count your winnings; you'll want to do a post-mortem to see if the Nuggets defense really did cause the Blazers' offense to struggle.

Data availability

The nature of fundamental handicapping means you're evaluating teams in a way that goes beyond the numbers. That means it's tough to find historical data to validate or back-test your theories.

For example, maybe you theorize that younger defensive rosters will struggle more with unusual offenses like Georgia Tech's option attach. Great theory! If you want to make an attempt to quantify your qualitative assessment, it would be great to look back in time and find teams who have been in this exact situation. So how do you propose doing that? You'll not only need to find data on defensive roster age, but you'll need to identify oddball offensive schemes that played in the past. It's not that data like this impossible to find, but it's just going to be time-consuming and difficult to get it sourced and put into one place.

TIP

Fundamental analysis is often impossible to quantify and prove. That doesn't mean you're wrong, and it doesn't mean you'll lose, but I urge you to find ways to back-test your theories whenever you can. If you're short on time (or if you're just lazy), fundamental analysis can hover very close to the neighborhood of betting on a gut feeling. Speaking of which . . .

Universal Fundamentals Concepts

There are certain factors that come into play in all team sports that you can use when you do your fundamental handicapping.

Matchup

Matchup is about differences in style and quality of play. Sometimes a certain player or team has strengths that perfectly exploit their opponent's weaknesses. It's as if they were built to beat them. When you focus too much on macro stats and team records, you lose track of the fact that teams and players have different strengths and weaknesses.

A simple example of matchup analysis in football might involve looking at how well a team's offensive identity mixes with their opponent's defensive scheme. A defense that leans heavily on man-to-man coverage will be vulnerable to an opponent running highly evolved mesh plays on underneath routes. This is an insight that would be difficult to tease out of a table full of statistics, but basic mismatches like this often determine the course of games.

Player quality

Advantages in the trenches are the easiest to identify and quantify. And most sports fans can think of a situation where a single matchup dictated the outcome of a game that wouldn't have been otherwise predicted based on stats or teams' overall record.

If you were a football fan in either Dallas or Atlanta, you'll probably have memories of the 2017 regular season matchup that saw the 5–3 Cowboys facing the 4–4 Falcons. Close observers would have realized the import of Cowboys All-Everything left tackle Tyron Smith being out with an injury, because his replacement was second-year guard Chaz Green. Not only did Green lack much NFL experience, he was playing out of position in Atlanta that day. That changed the entire complexion of the Cowboys offensive line, and the result was that Green looked like a matador to the Falcons defensive end. Adrian Clayborn didn't even start the game but wound up with 6 sacks on the day — twice as many as he got in the rest of the regular season combined! The Falcons won the game handily and beat the spread by 17 points. The Cowboys would struggle to replace Smith for the rest of the year and would go on to lose their next two games straight up by a combined 42 points, handing easy spread winners to those handicappers who recognized the fatal flaw in the Cowboys offensive line.

If you want to pursue player-level fundamental handicapping, I always recommend building a simple spreadsheet that tracks teams' first and second string players, with a basic rating for each player. It doesn't have to be complicated, just enough to know the difference between Chaz Green and Tyron Smith.

TIP

If tracking all first- and second-string players for 30 NFL teams sounds like a lot of work, don't worry. There are shortcuts. And the great thing is, you don't even have to be the person who rates the players. There are plenty of pundits, groups, and websites that will provide player ratings for you. While it's true that you'll find the most betting advantage in creating ratings that see beyond what the general public sees, the simple act of taking time to track player movement and injury status will put you ahead of a lot of the betting public. In Appendix A of this book, I provide you with some free online resources where experts rate players in all the major sports.

I recommend a simple model that rates players 1 to 5, where the ratings are as follows:

> 1 is an inexperienced backup, a player playing out of position, or maybe an average player who's injured.
>
> 2 is an average, serviceable, experienced player.
>
> 3 is an above-average player.

4 is a Pro-Bowl caliber player.

5 is an All-Pro caliber player.

In a theoretical matchup tracker from November 2017, your view of the Cowboys offensive line might have looked like this:

Player	Position	Rating	Notes
T Smith	LT	5	Out; backup is untested 2nd year G C. Green
J Cooper	LG	2	
T Frederick	C	5	
Z Martin	RG	5	Limited snaps post-injury
L Collins	RT	2	

Before each game, run down each team's injury report and make updates to your worksheet for each team. In the case of the Cowboys, you would have quickly realized that Dak Prescott's blind side was in big trouble with Green playing next to a player who only ranked as an average guard.

Let's take another example. In the case of the 2019 Texas Longhorns football team, if you had tracked their lineup, you would see that they had lost so many RBs to injury early in the season that they were down to a handful of walk-ons and water boys by the beginning of October.

You can make your player matchup tracker as sophisticated as it needs to be. I've seen analysts who include other fields, such as percent of play, level of experience, length of tenure with the other players on the team, and so on.

You can even use player-by-player ratings to quantify the advantage one team has over another. What's the impact of a team losing their top shutdown cornerback to injury? You could quantify that by matching the defensive back ratings up against the wide receiver ratings for the opponent. In fact, you could use player ratings to derive a projected point spread for the game. After all, the projected winner of a game is some combination of the quality of players and coaching, combined with spot factors like home-field advantage, travel factors, weather, and more.

TIP

If it feels too daunting to track the rosters of every NFL, NBA, Major League Baseball team, there are a few shortcuts you can take:

>> Narrow your tracking down to a handful of teams that you follow at all times, and then construct their upcoming opponents' player ratings trackers as needed before they play.

>> Learn some Excel automation so that you can run a script that will automatically populate your spreadsheet for you. Easier said than done, I know, but if you have any programming background at all, you'll find Excel VBA to be extremely straightforward. Learning to automate the work of handicapping games is one of the most valuable investments of time I could recommend to anyone interested in winning long term.

>> Build and maintain unit ratings strategically instead of individual player ratings. For football, you think in terms of the offensive and defensive lines, the receivers and defensive backs, and so forth. In baseball, you might rate the middle relievers as a group but assign a score to each starter.

Scheme

There's no escaping the fact that some teams struggle against certain strategies and thrive in others.

>> **In basketball, there are a few obvious dimensions of scheme.** Some teams have high-pace, fire-and-forget, fast-break offenses whose only goal is to wear you down by running you up and down the court. In the college game, think of the 2018 North Carolina team that averaged 74 possessions per game. In the NBA, it's teams like the 2019 Houston Rockets, who couldn't spell the word "defense" if you spotted them the D and the E. While the 40-minute full-court press has fallen out of fashion in college basketball, there are still teams like the 2020 Syracuse Orange, who try to discombobulate their opponents with non-stop pressure. Fundamental handicappers' first stop for Syracuse games it to check how skilled and experienced their opponents' point guard is.

>> **Football teams can be classified simply as run-heavy and pass-heavy, but any football fan knows very well the limitlessness of offensive and defensive strategies.** Thankfully, network and cable sports finally realized the huge market that exists to unpack the Xs and Os of football for fans (and bettors). Another scheme dimension of football is the fact that NFL and college teams often construct their rosters specifically to beat their division and conference opponents. Are you in the AFC West with Pat Mahomes and Philip Rivers? You better prioritize cornerbacks and safeties in the draft. Are you in the Big Ten? Then you'll be playing Wisconsin and Iowa every year, so you might consider finding the biggest gap-filling run-defending high school seniors in the country and beg them to attend your school. Good fundamental handicappers will take note of how rosters are constructed and will get their wallets out when these teams are facing off against teams they aren't built perfectly for.

>> **Lest you think otherwise, there is scheme to consider in baseball.** For example, there's lots of emphasis on having the right set of batters for the home park. Consider the 2018 Texas Rangers, who assembled some powerful left-handed bats for the short right porch in Arlington. Unfortunately, after some key righties went down with injury that season, it seemed like the entire line up was left-handed. As you might expect, as the season wore on, they were susceptible to left-handed starters and relievers, and they ended a year of misery at 67–95.

Rest and fatigue

In baseball and basketball, teams play multiple times per week, leaving very little time in between for anything except travel and minimal rest. (The phrase of the moment in the NBA these days is "load management," which refers to how many minutes that superstars can be expected to play and remain effective.)

Conventional wisdom says that rest should be central to any fundamental handicapping process. If you read or listen to any analysis of upcoming games, you'll inevitably be told to *fade* (that's gamble-speak for bet against) any team playing the second night of a dreaded back-to-back, or to avoid a team who's been on the road for a long stretch of time.

TIP

When you hear anything that sounds like conventional wisdom from would-be betting experts, be skeptical unless there are numbers to back it up. A casual look at the last few seasons' worth of back-to-back games in the NBA reveals a forgettable 210 wins and 219 losses against the spread. That means either NBA teams are unaffected by playing without rest, or the impact of playing without rest has been priced into the odds.

I am not saying rest doesn't matter! I believe rest is an important factor to consider in any handicap. The lesson is that when it comes to sports betting, conventional wisdom and rules-of-thumb are often just meaningless bromides that get passed around without thought. To profit from the rest variable, you'll need a more sophisticated approach.

Rest is a critical fundamental factor in football too, maybe even more than basketball given the brutal violence of the sport. Normally, teams have six days off between games. Team processes are optimized to those six days, so good handicappers look for situations that disrupt the standard schedule. When a team on a bye week spends two whole weeks not playing in the middle of the season, are they recovering and refocusing? Or are they getting rusty and out-of-rhythm?

Travel

Professional sports as we know them are impossible without travel. One team is always at home and one is away (except in the rare case of neutral ground games in which, usually, both teams must travel). It turns out travel has a huge impact on how teams play for a few key reasons:

» **Being away from home is tough for everybody, professional athletes included.** You sleep in a strange bed; you don't see your family; the places around you are unfamiliar. In other words, comfort is hard to find on the road.

» **Time zone changes affect sleep patterns and biorhythms.** While biologists still aren't sure of sleep's purpose, we all stubbornly continue to do it anyway. Sleep is known to be a critical performance factor in all walks of life, whether you're a student, a pilot, or a judge deciding a big case. And sleep is universally understood to be a contributor to all things that affect athletic performance, like muscle control, coordination, concentration, and decision-making. When players cannot sleep well, they cannot perform to their standard.

» **Flying is bad for you.** Anyone who has ever spent hours in an airport only to spend more hours on a plane knows that it is anything but relaxing. Prolonged time on an airliner means dehydration, reduced immune function, extended periods of mild hypoxia, reduced mobility, and sensory-related sleep deprivation. Even if you're a pro athlete on a luxurious team charter, you can't get away from the negative impacts of travel.

If you look at a map of professional teams, you'll notice that some are obligated to travel further on average than others. The Seattle Seahawks, for example, are the most geographically isolated of all the NFL teams. That means that, on average, they will have to travel farther than other teams in the course of the season. Where the Seahawks might travel 50,000 miles over the course of a season, an East coast team like the Eagles flies less than half that amount. In fact, the distribution of big cities in the United States is such that west coast teams in general must travel outside of their time zone more than teams in other time zones. (Teams based in the Pacific time zone have won just a single Super Bowl in the last 20 years. Coincidence?)

The NBA in particular has sought ways to ease the travel impact on players. With 42 road games per season, NBA teams spend far more time in the clouds than any other league, which has proven to cause many different problems. Not only does travel reduce athletic performance, but it's also been proven that NBA players are significantly more likely to suffer an injury on the road than they are at home.

TIP

Travel and rest provide many avenues for further research, and these factors just might give you an angle you can bet on reliably. Some ideas for further exploration might involve the length of road trips and what impact they have on a team. Do teams with older rosters get impacted more or less than teams with younger rosters? Are certain cities more distracting for young, wealthy pro athletes? Do football teams' travel habits vary and does it matter? (For example, for cross-coast games, does every NFL team travel the day before the game, or do some arrive in the host city earlier?) The possibilities are endless.

Recent performance

Recency bias is the mental shortcut we all take where we apply more importance and significance to more recent events than to events that happened further in the past. A team's last game is important for a couple of reasons. One, it provides the most recent snapshot of how well a team is functioning. If a team played a great all-around game two weeks ago but suffered through a clumsy loss last week, which version of the team is more likely to take the field this week? Second, recent performance shades behavior of the players themselves. Does a win or loss last week change the approach of a team for their upcoming game? Do teams stockpile confidence after wins that they can draw on going forward? Does a heartbreaking loss cast a shadow over a team's next game?

Recent performance is a critical fundamental handicapping factor because teams and individual players follow certain mental and emotional patterns that can be tracked and predicted. I believe game narratives induce reactions among players, and those reactions lead to subtle changes in preparation, focus, and effort leading up to the next game. And because the difference between teams in the professional leagues is so small, anything that affects preparation has the potential to have a major impact on the game.

Team-specific factors

Although I'm not a fan of team-specific angles, it's possible that recent performance is a factor that differs team by team. Teams develop mini-cultures all their own as a function of their coaches, captains, and the personalities on the roster. I read once that San Francisco 49ers players under Bill Walsh used to have a minor sense of dread of winning because they knew Walsh would hammer them in practice the next week to ensure they didn't lose focus. For some teams, a humiliating loss might lead to pessimism, loss of cohesion, and infighting. With others, getting beaten badly inspires a doubling-down of effort and a greater sense of resolve.

BET on great rebounders

Certain coaches instill a culture of accountability and improvement in their teams that manifests itself as resiliency in the face of adversity. History has proven that certain skippers can transform an ugly loss into a market-beating win.

> In an NBA game where a team's head coach is either Rick Carlisle, Eric Spoelstra, or Nate MacMillan OR
>
> In a college basketball game where a team's head coach is either Murray Garvin, Scott Nagy, Brian Dutcher, or Robert Jones AND
>
> That basketball team lost their last game by double digits
>
> **BET** on the team's point spread.

Betting on these coaches after a bad loss has netted a 64 percent spread record in the last five years.

That betting setup leads to the other major reason recent performance plays such an important role in fundamental handicapping: The betting public is intensely focused on what a team did in their most recent game. Square bettors are infected with a severe case of recency bias, and sharp bettors take full advantage of it.

Strength of competition

Does a team vary its play based on the level of competition? There is a common phrase about teams that play to the level of their competition rather than playing "their game."

When underdogs prevail, it's tempting to build a narrative about it. Sometimes the two teams were closer than we thought in terms of talent. Sometimes it's just random variance. We know the outcome of games is largely random, so every now and then, the most likely outcome doesn't happen. But there also might be an *underdog effect:* Facing tough competition forces otherwise bad or mediocre teams to rise to the occasion. In this view, being the underdog can act as an advantage. The reward for beating a heavy favorite is huge, while the reward for beating a big underdog is a big yawn.

Motivation

Lopsided motivation can be a significant factor for fundamental handicappers.

Rivalry games

"Throw out the record book" is another old saw in sports that we love to repeat when it comes to big rivals. I'm not so sure.

When the stakes are not just a usual victory but a hero's welcome (or not just a normal loss but an embarrassment), you might expect the players to put more into the game than into a normal game. Of course, this holds true for both sides of a rivalry, so be careful when thinking that the motivation that comes with a rivalry will change the outcome much from what it would have been otherwise.

More interesting to me are one-sided rivalries, where a traditional powerhouse school is the highlight of their opponent's schedule, regardless of how good they are that year. Every Pac-12 team wants to whip USC, whether they are in the hunt for the national championship or not. The same holds true when Texas Tech or TCU play Texas, or when Northwestern or Illinois play Michigan. Every school loves to beat the team with the most tradition, the most history, and the most hardware in the trophy case, even if they aren't as good as they once were.

In-season revenge

Betting on revenge as a motivational factor is an attractive narrative, but it's more of a fairy tale when it comes to betting. The underlying idea is that revenge causes players to somehow play beyond their intrinsic talent and, in turn, outperform spread expectations.

Most college basketball teams play their conference opponents twice per year (home and home), as do NFL division rivals. Every now and then, the NFL playoffs will line up so that division rivals have to play each other a third time in one season. Major League Baseball and NBA teams will usually catch the opposition multiple times.

Does the previous result have an impact on play? I could find no profitable system where teams facing each other multiple times in a season had an advantage or disadvantage worth betting on.

For NFL division rivals, teams are what they are. If one team won the first game, it usually wins the second game as well. Holding other variables equal, it doesn't appear that the NFL betting market makes any major adjustments for revenge either. I read a theory that the under bet should be profitable in NFL rematches because defensive coaches and players are more able to take advantage of offensive tendencies the second time around, but the results could easily be chalked up to random variance.

Win or go home

Though every league handles its playoff structure differently, there will always be games that a team must win if it wants to advance to the next round of the playoffs. This could be the NBA playoffs game 7 or literally any of the games in the NFL playoffs. Not only are these games more fun to watch (the drama is real and the stakes are at their highest), but they also give each team the ultimate motivation.

These games can also be one-sided. A team down two games to three in the NBA playoffs faces two win-or-go-home games; a loss in either means the beginning of their off-season. Players with a strong mental game, those that can keep their head together and not succumb to the pressure, are those that are best suited to persevere.

Playoff implications

Games with playoff implications are like miniature versions of win-or-go-home games. Maybe there are still a few games left in the season, but if the team doesn't win this one, then the regular season is all they'll get. Just like in win-or-go-home games, these can be one-sided. Unlike the standard win-or-go-home games, these can also have implications outside of their participants. Winning a late-season game in the NFL can change the wildcard picture for other teams in the conference. Bettors who are working long bets need to pay attention to what intra-conference games mean to the playoff picture as a whole.

REMEMBER

Every study I've read shows that in general, the market correctly accounts for whatever motivation effects there are with the playoffs or a bowl game on the line. Teams play their best, and oddsmakers know this and factor it into the spread.

Team Sports Factors

A lot of the betting you'll do will be on the most popular sports — the major league team sports. It's not enough to just know the individual players but also the way that whole teams operate and the way they match up against each others. These are the technical parts of the game that a deep knowledge of the strategy involved will help you spot angles and opportunities for handicapping.

Overall talent and speed

Most professional leagues are capped. They have rules in place in to make sure that teams have roughly equal amounts of talent so that every matchup is exciting. This usually means that a salary cap keeps teams from spending more than other teams to acquire the best players possible.

But in non-capped leagues, the overall quality can vary wildly from team to team. You see this in college sports where schools are not allowed to pay their athletes a salary and so must attract talent other ways. They do this by building the reputation of their programs and spending money in other non-regulated ways to make sure that they always have the best of the best. That's why you'll see the same schools consistently field better teams than others year after year.

Game plan

Some games, like football and basketball, depend a great deal on the strategies employed on game day: the whiteboard Xs and Os and the proper execution of those specific plays. You can know that teams generally play a certain way, with a certain style. You can know the strengths and weaknesses of a team and how those factor into the matchup. Knowing the game plan for the day of game is the sort of nuts-and-bolts knowledge that could give you an edge.

Perhaps you know going into the game that a football team is going to rely on rushing plays as opposed to the pass in order to stymie their opponent's well known zone defense? Maybe it's obvious that a certain star player will pull a double-team all night long. What consequences will that have on how the rest of the team plays offense with one fewer defender to account for? These sorts of questions have a major impact in how you evaluate the game.

Coaching

Any given team is made up of more than just the players. A good coach means as much to a group of players as a good manager means to a group of workers. And like managers (there are also managers in sports though they tend to focus on the business side of teams as opposed to the on-the-field and in-the-locker-room leadership), coaches play a central role in the successes and failures of their teams.

Also like managers, coaches have diverse styles both during games and outside of them. The latter matters when talking about the so-called culture of a team, but when making bets on games, you need to care more about the coach's decision making.

Much has been written about the best coaches like Bill Belichick of the New England Patriots. The Belichick Patriots have notably failed to score in the first quarter of their Super Bowl appearances. Knowing that the coach intends to slow-roll the first part of the game tells you that maybe the under is a good bet.

Likewise, another great, Nick Saban of the University of Alabama, is known for running up the score in his games. If he's helming the team, maybe you should take the over.

Looking at coaching trees can help you evaluate coaches with whom you are less familiar. A coaching tree shows you the relationship between coaches, much like a family tree. It turns out that in professional sports, many of the coaches have been assistants for past greats (or current greats), and knowing their career pedigree can tell you who they might share similar styles and strategies with.

Schedule/spot analysis

Experienced handicappers pay attention to a team's *spot*. The spot refers to how an upcoming game fits into the rest of the schedule, in terms of travel, rest, and strength of opposition. When you hear analysts talk about a look-ahead game, or a sandwich game, or a bad travel sequence, they're talking about the spot. It has nothing to do with the team's talent level; it's all about how friendly or unfriendly the schedule is for that week. Because most games are planned well in advance, you can look at spot factors as soon as the schedule comes out to decide if there's an advantage or not.

The following are a few fundamental handicapping items related to spot:

>> **Look-ahead games:** The idea of *look-ahead games* comes up often in the world of sports betting. The idea is that a team will perform poorly in one game because they are saving their energy, or spending more of their time preparing, for a future game against a better or more prominent opponent. When teams get caught looking ahead, they let their guard down against a lesser team in anticipation of facing a tougher team the following week. College teams are possibly more susceptible to this pitfall than professional teams, but it's just human nature. When you have a meeting to ask your boss for a raise in an hour, you're more likely to not be 100 percent in your current meeting.

>> **Sandwich games:** The *sandwich game* theory is essentially just a rephrasing of the look-ahead game. When a team goes from a high-leverage game to a low-leverage game to high-leverage game, the theory that is the middle game, or sandwich game, will not get their maximum effort.

External Factors

Fundamental analysis doesn't stop with the teams and coaches. Anything that can have an impact on the outcome of a game has to be taken into account.

Weather

Wind, temperature, barometric pressure, humidity, and numerous other factors can affect the game in both obvious and subtle ways. Many studies have been done talking about how the weather affects the flight of a baseball. And though you can't see it on television, the wind in an NFL stadium can play a huge role in the distance of field goal kicks.

TIP

You might find that betting under in adverse weather conditions is a good idea. When players literally have a harder time playing the game, you should expect them to score less.

And this is borne out by the data. In fact, game weather data is available for every major sport. Such a wealth of numerical information can be of great use to anybody trying to build a fundamental handicapping model. You can check out Appendix A of this book for a list of useful resources. I'll discuss weather-related handicapping in the appropriate sports-specific chapters of Part 3.

Rules changes

If you follow the NFL, you know that in recent years, in response the controversy around the long-term effects of concussions, they've changed a lot of rules around how defensive players are allowed to make contact with offensive players. This has led to real measurable changes in points scored. If you had a system where you were betting on totals at a certain level, but didn't take this rule change into account, your system has probably lost its efficacy.

Consider how rules changes might affect some teams more than others. In the 2019–2020 college basketball season, the 3-point line was moved back. Teams like Georgia Tech and Rutgers won't see much impact because their offenses are built around getting points in the paint. But teams like Auburn and Villanova have offenses heavily weighted toward 3-pointers and will have to contend with getting fewer points per attempt.

Astute handicappers monitor rules changes as well as officiating approaches to find edges they can exploit.

Officiating

If there's one thing sports fans love as much than watching their team win its complaining about the refs (or umps or whatever they are in tennis). But past just being blind or stupid, it turns out that certain officials have their own tendencies. Some are more likely to call certain fouls, some less.

The data for specific judges is readily available and can be a great boon to any sports bettor. If, for instance, you know that the ump in an upcoming MLB game tends to call more strikes than others, you might expect the game to be lower scoring.

Leagues can also change the way that officiating is done instead of changing the rules themselves. In the 2018 college basketball postseason, the NCAA released a statement saying that the refs were instructed to be looser in their interpretations of contact, which meant they were going to call fewer fouls. Astute gamblers intuited that more physical teams like Texas Tech and Kentucky would benefit from this change.

Venue and crowd

Where games are played can affect betting outcomes beyond the simple idea of a home point advantage. Different buildings and fields have their own unique wind and weather patterns, acoustic characteristics, and degrees of crowd participation in the game — especially in basketball, where the fans are only a few feet away from the action.

Some buildings are known for their rowdy crowds and intense. Allen Fieldhouse in Kansas is one of the loudest arenas in college basketball, if not in all of sports. Modern NFL stadiums are designed with acoustics in mind so that crowd noise is reflected back in to make the game louder, more exciting, and, for the visiting player, potentially more distracting.

Measuring Performance Variance

If you want to prove that any of the aforementioned factors matter, you're going to need more than just a hunch. As discussed earlier in this chapter, going from a gut feeling to an actual fundamental handicapping system requires research and deeper analysis on the part of the bettor. You should think hard about how you perform your analysis. These steps can help:

1. **Gather a ton of historical data.** The internet makes this easier than it used to be in the sense that tons of historical data are readily available. But more data means even more tables that you'll need to comb through to find the factors that you're looking for.

2. **Establish how you measure performance.** Ideally, you're measuring results against the spread, as that is the way most bets on games get placed, but maybe you think that total points, or rushing yards, or WHIP are a more reliable factor to judge your theory against.

3. **Make measurements with and without the factor.** Whatever fundamental factor you've identified as a way to handicap games, you must ensure that you are using a *control,* just like all good scientific inquiries do. In order to see if a factor matters, say back-to-back road games, you must also examine those cases where the factor is not present, say back-to-back home games, and compare the difference. Establishing a control in experiments that rely on historical data can be tricky as you don't get to design the experiment yourself.

Chapter **8**

Technical Analysis and Modeling

I would argue that men and women who get heavily into analyzing stocks, bonds, and other investments for a living are essentially feeding the same drive for making order out of chaos as those who take up sports betting.

In the investment community, there are two basic ways to evaluate whether a stock is worth buying or not. You perform fundamental analysis when you're trying to determine a company's intrinsic value by examining its marketplace, leadership, competition, and product array.

On the other hand, technical analysis doesn't really care about any of the things you can touch and feel. Technical analysis is about watching charts and finding patterns in the way stock prices move up and down in the market. A technical analyst operates under the assumption that in big liquid markets (like the NASDAQ), certain repeatable patterns emerge from the what may look like a chaotic set of individuals buying, selling, and reacting to news.

This is a good analogy for bettors who spend far less time studying teams and schemes in favor of finding broad patterns in the numbers. Technical handicappers look at past data for patterns that result in winning bets, and being familiar with this approach will, at a minimum, protect you from statistical nonsense that gets presented in every sport as a crystal ball. And if you're like me, you'll make technical handicapping the main weapon in a winning arsenal of selecting games to bet on.

When my high school football team beat our hated rival by 40 points, that outcome had a direct impact on the next week's game: We were so busy celebrating our win that we could never quite focus during practice. And in the next game, we lost to an inferior opponent. For a team with scant history of winning, getting a surprising upset win against a rival (a blowout no less) was a recipe for disaster.

As a technical handicapper, you'll look for recipes just like that one.

Winning bets with technical analysis is about identifying behavioral and statistical patterns that are connected to on-the-field outcomes that provide betting opportunities to the astute handicapper.

Like Math, but Fancier

More handicappers than ever are relying on advanced statistical methods, sometimes known as *analytics.* And there are now many important voices in the sports betting world who subscribe to *modeling* as a superior path to picking bet winners.

These topics are often tightly intertwined and deserve entire independent books of their own. In the meantime, here's a summary so you have some working knowledge.

Analytics

Analytics is a field that has hopped from baseball to other sports, and it is now a permanent part of the competitive fantasy football arena (and other sports) as well as daily fantasy sports (DFS) through such companies as DraftKings. It is, in essence, using statistics as a way to draw more complete and predictive conclusions about a team's quality of play.

In fact, you could just say analytics is nothing more than smarter statistics. The major betting sports — baseball, football, and basketball — all bring with them some basic legacy statistics that are still heavily used today. For basketball and football, the same stats have been around for many decades, and for baseball, we're talking more than a century. In the last several years, sports statistics have undergone a minor revolution due to a few key factors:

>> The general public's fascination with (and understanding of) statistics has grown steadily. Subsequently, stats have pervaded every aspect of how teams evaluate their own talent and performance. An athlete from the 1960s would be shocked at how much statistics have become intertwined with professional contracts in the form of incentives.

>> The media explosion started in the 1990s and accelerated by the spread of high-bandwidth digital technologies has allowed for much more detailed and intricate statistics to be tracked for every player, every game, and every team. In the so-called old days before widely available high-definition game video, how could you possibly measure a quarterback's catchable throw ratio? Or the spin rate on a pitcher's fastball?

The world of minutely detailed statistics and success metrics has grown. If you want a few standard bearers, look no further than Pro Football Focus, who provide advanced metrics for fans, analysts, and teams alike who want to break down and quantify every single move made on the field of play.

WARNING

I realize I'm going to sound like the old-school scouts in *Moneyball,* but the endless talk of analytics gives me some pause. While I like the emphasis on identifying value and quantifying choices made by coaches and players in the midst of a game and a season, there is one truth I have learned over the years: Being able to describe the past 100 different ways does not mean you are better equipped to predict the future. So while I think certain activities like normalizing metrics against the level of competition makes those metrics more telling, I also believe that every metric and stat deserves scrutiny for what it's actually providing the purveyor. Does it give us insight we didn't otherwise have? And for the bettor, does it make it easier to predict the outcome of the next game? Or are we simply describing the past in increasingly flowery ways?

Modeling

There is value in recreating a team, a play, a game, a season, or any complicated future activity in digital form and then replaying that virtual reality over and over until a clear pattern shines through. The activity of using computing power to simulate what happens in the real world is also known as *modeling.* And you might be surprised at how easy it is to do on your own.

The Daily Double puzzle

I once had dreams of being on the gameshow *Jeopardy!* And as I pondered what I might do on that stage with Alex Trebek and the rest of the world watching, I came up with a question I couldn't answer mathematically: What's the optimal Daily Double betting strategy?

To rewind for a moment, in *Jeopardy!* contestants earn points as they answer specifically valued questions correctly. And if they happen to select a certain category and value of question, there's a chance it might be a Daily Double. When a contestant gets a Daily Double, the contestant can wager up to the amount of his or her current point balance.

With the majority of money available in the second round of the game, I suspected it would be optimal to always bet everything you had on the first Daily Double. But I couldn't prove it with math. Since I can't persuade the next 1,000 contestants on the show to try my strategy out, the next best thing is a model, or a simulation of the game show. Using my old friend Excel, I started writing code that would assign random point balances, playing styles, right and wrong answers, and other variables to the three contestants. I'd force the first Daily Double contestant to bet his entire balance, and then I'd simulate the rest of the show to see if I could quantify the cost or benefit of that strategy.

The beauty of modeling complex situations with computer code is that you don't need to venture into the dangerous territory of mathematical theory. You can easily set up a simulation to run over and over again, tweaking the initial conditions until you get your answer. In the case of my *Jeopardy!* simulator, James Holzhauer ended up proving in person what my simulation had shown me years before, which was that people were way too conservative with their first Daily Double bet, given the low stakes involved.

To bring it back to sports, the same simulation techniques can be applied to just about any sporting situation if you can write some simple code loops in Python or VBA or just about any other programming language.

Are you curious about whether it's better to shoot a 2-pointer or 3-pointer with a 5-point deficit and 40 seconds left on the clock? Have you ever wondered about (and questioned) the mythical go-for-two strategy card that many in football rely on? Simulating these tricky situations lets you not only figure out the best choices to make, but with the right level of detail in your simulation, you can also start predicting any level of detail you desire, including individual player performance and (gulp) spread and total outcomes.

A quick modeling example

If you wanted to simulate an NFL football game and you had some basic programming skills, you could start off with code that used the average NFL home score and the average NFL away score, produced random numbers and fed them into a function that put the random numbers onto a normal curve (in Excel, something like NORMINV) and you'd have a simulated football game. Unfortunately, that would lead to scores like 23–18, which fit in with the overall scoring averages but aren't very realistic scores given the denominations of 3s, 6s, and 7s in the real world of football.

Fine, let's improve the previous simulation (which was really just a random number generator) and assign each team a number of drives in the game via a random number. Then the model can loop through each drive for each team and use more random numbers to determine whether the drive ends in a touchdown, field goal, or no-score. Now we'd have a real-sounding football score at least.

To make it one step better, you could score a team 6 for a touchdown and use another random number to determine if the team made or missed their extra point. You could also add a 2-point safety as another possible ending to a team's drive. Once you have the basic loop in place, you can make the simulation as intricate as you want!

Let's go one step more and add field position in. The new simulation would be the same as before, except you'd calculate (with random numbers of course) how far punts and kickoffs go. Then you could make the likelihood of a team scoring a touchdown inversely related to how far they had to drive.

Still another refinement would be to insert unique scoring probabilities for each NFL team, depending on their talent level and coaching quality. Maybe you could even use defensive talent to offset the other team's offensive talent in order to arrive at a combined probability for each scoring type.

And so it goes. I'll stop there, but you can follow the concept. The more detail you're willing to code into your model of reality, the more the simulation is likely to match reality. You could see how making the leap from drives to individual plays would allow you to start projecting player performance. And with all the computing power you have at your fingertips, you could run a game simulation thousands of times to draw a conclusion about who's likely to win, and by how much.

De-randomizing historical data

If you wrote the details of every NFL football game over the last 20 years onto individual marbles, put them into a bag, and then drew 100 random marbles, you could make a pretty good prediction about the entire population of marbles just from the 100 you selected. The home team would beat the spread around 50 percent of the time. The favorite would beat the spread about 50 percent of the time. The over and under bets would each win, you guessed it, 50 percent of the time.

REMEMBER

Oddsmakers mostly work to split the betting market between overs and unders, and also between bets for and against the favorite. And history has shown that they do a great job. In fact, any grab-bag of 100 marbles with historical NFL data will result in point spreads and totals that are right down the middle of the actual result. Home teams, road teams, favorites, underdogs, teams off of a win, early in the season or late in the season: For big categories of games, the oddsmakers' numbers are so efficient that no blind-betting strategy would have shown a profit over the last 20 years.

But as you slice further down into more specific groups of games, the betting results start to land farther from 50-50. That should be no great revelation of course. Imagine the side of a big red barn is randomly covered with 10,000 magic marker dots, 5,000 black and 5,000 red. If you compared the top half of the barn with the bottom half, the split would be 50-50, just like if you compared the left half from the right half. Split it into quarters, or tenths, and you'll continue to get something close to 50 percent red and 50 percent black. But as you zoom in closer, maybe dividing the barn into 50 equally sized squares, you'll start to encounter squares where red and black dots come in wildly varying proportions. That's just the nature of randomness.

The essential premise of technical handicapping is that the entire barn might be divided 50-50 between red and black dots, but there exist squares on the side of the barn that are in fact not random at all. The technical handicapper can describe a set of identifiable conditions that cause certain squares to be non-random, and in fact, he would be willing to bet that if more dots were to be added to the barn, he could predict with some certainty which squares would get more red dots than black dots, and vice versa.

Okay, I think I've taken the barn metaphor as far as it can go.

Systems and Angles

In the most common parlance, there are two flavors of technical handicapping: *systems* and a subset of systems known in the business as *angles*. Technical handicappers and system-based bettors follow these basic steps:

1. Get access to historical data for a sport or team.

2. Search through historical data for patterns of circumstances leading to a result that can be bet on profitably. Typically, you're looking for conditions leading to ATS (against the spread), wins/losses, or over/unders.

3. Monitor the sport on an ongoing basis, waiting for the patterns you identified in step 2 to occur.

4. When the setup conditions occur, place the appropriate bet as indicated by the historical data.

Betting systems

Systems are identifiable patterns of events leading up to a game that have a statistical association with a certain betting outcome (like point spread win for the home team). Systems may involve many variables and conditions, but they are not specific to a certain team or player.

Setup and payoff

A typical system has a set of predicate conditions, sometimes known as a *setup*. The conditions are linked with logical operators like AND and OR. Here's a typical example of a setup:

In NFL regular season games

The home team is an underdog AND

The home team won their last game AND

The home team was favored by 3–7 points in their last game AND EITHER

The home team's last game wasn't played on Sunday OR

The home team's last game was on a Sunday AND it went into overtime.

When this group of conditions has been met over the last 20 years of historical data, the game has gone over the total 13 times and under the total 1 once. (That's an actual system, by the way.)

When the technical handicapper sits down each Tuesday morning to start the process of identifying games and bets for the following week, he will check each game to see if the conditions listed in the setup are in effect. Each step is a filter. You start with every game and filter out next week's games where there's a home favorite, leaving you with only games where the home team is an underdog. With the remaining list of teams, you go one by one to check to see if they met the next set of conditions.

If you get to the end of the list of conditions and you have any teams left, you place the bet indicated by the system's historical record: in this case, a bet on the over.

TIP

The example system didn't have any other qualifiers. System betting means you're placing a bet on the over regardless of how you evaluate the teams. You're not worrying about whether the home team's yards-per-play stat is ranked last in the league, or whether there's snow in the forecast.

Sample size revisited

In fairness, a system with only 14 historical games doesn't have enough data to represent a strong trend. 13–1 looks good, but I wouldn't use it by itself to place that over bet. I'd want to find corroborating evidence that the over is the right play. If I had another system that pointed to the over, or some statistical or fundamental conditions (see Chapter 7), I'd feel much more comfortable using this system as supporting evidence.

In Chapter 6, I talked about the importance of sample size when trying to prove a point with statistics. One of the benefits of using systems with lots of historical data is that the more data you have, the more likely it is any countervailing circumstances (like the ones I mentioned earlier: low yards per play, snow in the forecast) are already baked into the system. In other words, if you're playing an over system with a historical record of 84 overs and 51 unders, you have enough data to assume there are some snowy games in there too, and it still wins 62 percent of the time.

An imperfect analogy might be appropriate here: Imagine you run a survey of random people on the streets of Chicago asking which state was more scenic: Colorado or Hawaii. The results come in and you find the answer is 60 percent in favor of Colorado. But then you worry that your survey results might not be valid. For example, Chicago is geographically closer to Colorado, and if you included more Coloradoans in the poll, they would bias the statistics to their own state.

It might be a concern if you only surveyed 10 people. But provided you asked 80 people or 100 people, the biasing impact of a few Denver tourists are most likely to not affect the poll all that much. Sure, you can assume you got a few tourists from Fort Collins in your poll, but the preponderance of data swamps whatever bias they introduced.

Betting angles

Angles are close cousins to systems, but they have a key difference in that they apply to a specific team, player, or possibly a coach, official, or even a venue. The point is, angles are not universally applicable in the sport. Implicit in angles is that the target person or team differs in some key way in their behavior from their peers.

Other than that, angles behave the same way as systems: Bettors identify a pattern in the historical data that has resulted in a profitable betting outcome. Bettors monitor conditions for the angle's setup, and when it happens, they place a bet as per the historical data.

Here's an example of a setup for a player-specific angle:

> NFL regular season game
>
> Kirk Cousins is the starting QB AND
>
> The game is on a Monday or Thursday

The result is:

> The Kirk Cousins-led team is 2–11–1 ATS.

Systems and angles are sports betting's version of data mining. The handicapper looks back through history to find profitable patterns in the past and then bets as if those patterns will continue in the future. And as you read in Chapter 1 of this book, past results are not guaranteed to continue into the future.

REMEMBER

Nevertheless, technical handicapping is a powerful approach. If you are willing to invest the time and brainpower and apply a level of discipline, it can be profitable over the long term.

The Benefits of Data-Driven Analysis

Old-school game pickers and handicappers might heap scorn on the new data-driven handicapping methodologies. Never fear. Let your winning do the talking. If in doubt, here are some things to keep in mind:

>> **Unlike fundamental handicapping, it doesn't make you a bad technical handicapper if you don't watch the games.** I am a testament to this. I won 55 percent of my 2018 college basketball bets, but I couldn't have named more than a two or three players and rarely watched more than a few minutes of highlights every week.

>> **Great tools and resources become available every day.** In 1995, I built my own database and search engine of NFL data using a programming language I learned in high school. Today, I rely on Excel. But if hacking your way through your own data doesn't sound fun, there are lots of online databases that you

can use, and many of them are free. (I list some of the best online resources in Appendix A of the book.)

» **Technical handicapping lends itself to Kelly Criterion betting strategies (covered in Chapter 5).** It provides you with a historical winning percentage, which you can translate into a win probability, which you can plug into the Kelly formula to produce bet size. Using the Gambler's Z-score, you can also use the historical results to assign a level of confidence to your selections.

» **Most sports bettors rely on their eyes and their gut when placing bets.** And most sports bettors lose more than they win. Technical analysis lets you test your theories against actual data to see if they're as strong as you think they are.

» **The barrier to entry of data-driven handicapping is higher than it is for game pickers who go on instinct.** That's a good thing, because it makes you more likely to be a contrarian bettor. Being a contrarian means better prices on the bets you want, and when that majority of gamblers out there goes down, it's not just the sports book that benefits. Contrarians like you benefit as well.

» **Technical analysis usually takes the betting market into account.** You can be an excellent fundamental handicapper who can identify better than anyone when teams have an advantage. Maybe you develop a feel for when travel and injuries are getting to a soccer side, or your playing experience helps you perceive that a particular golfer is struggling with his short game. And you could be correct about all your conclusions, but that doesn't always mean there's a betting advantage available to you. Technical analysis takes any combination of factors you can gather data on and connects them with historical spread results. That tells you directly if the pattern you've spotted has been profitable to bet on in the past.

» **There are huge swathes of undiscovered territory.** Systems and angles using the most commonly considered factors and statistics have been widely explored, but as of this writing, there's still tons of opportunity out there in terms the setup as well as the result. In particular, I see very little in the way of systems and angles for derivative bets (like first quarter spreads and totals in NBA basketball) and for live wagering.

» **Finally, technical analysis is easily combined with other approaches to handicapping.** There's no reason you cant start with fundamentals and power ratings and then see if there are systems or angles that reinforce (or contradict) your conclusions.

What Gets Lost in the Numbers

Working with data requires an investment of time. You can buy systems and angles from services, and you'll find some for free as well, but if you're determined to explore on your own, you'll need to either subscribe to or build your own data tools.

There is great temptation to find causality where it doesn't exist, or to invent a narrative that it fits perfectly into your system. Good systems come with good rationales. The worst systems are those where you've convinced yourself there's predictive value when there isn't.

Systems, like all handicapping, require patience

If you have discovered a legitimate 56 percent MLB total system that happens 50 times during a baseball season, the nature of randomness means you're likely to suffer through some frustrating losing streaks that might cause you to discard your system. The diabolical thing is that you won't really know if your system has become obsolete or if it's just a random losing streak.

Games change over time

Although more data is almost always better than less data, the further back in time you go, the more likely it is you'll be crossing eras of the sport. NFL scoring is up a point and a half compared to a decade ago, probably due to all the pro-offense rules changes. In Major League Baseball's 2015 season, there were 4 games with a total over 11 runs; in 2019, there were 109. If you have an over/under system where one of the conditions is betting on a certain total, you better make sure it's still relevant.

Teams change over time

As much I rely on systems when I bet, I am a skeptic on angles that require me to believe that teams have some kind of mysterious institutional memory that gives them certain tendencies. When I hear an angle like "The Texas Longhorns are 18–6 ATS in September night games," about half a dozen alarm bells start going off in my head. I don't doubt the historical numbers being accurate, but I doubt their predictive value.

There is no such thing as a single spread or total

In most historical data source, you'll see a single spread and a single total. As you learned in earlier chapters, the odds get released to bettors, but then they are changeable leading up to the start of the game depending on how the game is bet. Is the spread listed with last season's games the opening number? The closing number? Or something in between? This variance can have a huge impact on systems and angles because the opening numbers get pounced on by professionals, so they exist for only very short times.

REMEMBER

Every change of the odds matters! I built a database of Major League Baseball games that I used to find what I thought were valuable system plays. But because I was using opening odds rather than closing odds, my systems were much less profitable than I had calculated. When I added closing odds to my database, I had to throw half of my systems out because they simply no longer worked once the market had a chance to move the odds.

TIP

There is wisdom in the line moves! I recommend finding a database that includes odds metadata in it, which means opening and closing spreads, moneylines, and totals, as well as percentages of dollars wagered and tickets written for each game. This information can be used as conditions in your systems. After all, you're modeling the behavior both on the field and at the betting window.

The betting market assimilates winning systems into the odds

If a system is well known, such as the NBA Zig-Zag playoff system or the Wong teasers in NFL football, the oddsmakers will account for it. And if the oddsmakers don't account for it, there's a good chance that bettors will, driving the advantage out of the odds unless you're able to wager right when the bets become available.

As an example of how this works, consider the famous JR Miller over/under strategy in the NFL where blind betting any high total game to go under and any low total game to go under produced 59 percent winners over 20 years.

At first, the sharps took advantage of it, pouncing on an opening total of 49 and betting the under, forcing the bookmaker to lower the listed total to 48.5, then 48, and so on. By the end of the week, the advantage was gone.

Then the bookmakers figured out the weakness and began pricing this system into their opening odds so that not even the sharps and pros could take advantage of it. Where they might have listed a game at 49 in previous years, the oddsmakers started giving those high totals a haircut before they were released: 49s became 47s, 53s became 51.5s, and so on. And so the system that worked so well for two decades dried up completely in 1997.

The simpler the system, the larger the impact it has on games. That's great, right? Unfortunately that also means it's going to be part of the public discussion. The result is that oddsmakers will recognize the system and price it into their lines. Keep this advice in mind:

>> Systems and angles don't last forever; profits are ephemeral.

>> Good bettors are diligent about looking for new systems and angles.

>> The best bettors recognize when a system has dried up.

There's no such thing as a permanent recipe for winning. Picking games using systems and angles is an ongoing process. When you find a good one, build your bankroll before it gets assimilated into the betting hive mind.

Complexity and the Scourge of P-Hacking

The term *system* is an appropriate one because it has scientific overtones. Formally speaking, a system is a group of components that work together to some effect. Our setup conditions represent certain events in the real world, and when they happen together as prescribed, another piece of the overall system (the teams, the players, the oddsmakers, or the bettors) tends to behave in a non-random way. Scientists call this an *emergent behavior.*

An emergent behavior, sometimes called an emergent property (or just plain emergence), is a pattern of structure of some kind that is the result of the components in a complex system, where the individual components are acting and interacting according to their own set of rules and constraints. And it's often the case that the pattern that emerges would have been hard to predict by merely looking at the underlying conditions. Markets, traffic jams, consciousness, hurricanes are all examples of emergent behavior, as they are all larger structures or patterns with characteristics all their own that are the product of the individual components and forces.

Who cares about all this?

Simple technical handicapping systems and angles can be more logically connected to a real-world result. (For example, bet against a team that's had a big, surprising, on-field success because they're likely to be overvalued in the betting markets. Bet under games below a certain temperature because it's hard to catch and hold footballs with cold hands.) But they're also more likely to be already accounted for in the marketplace.

Does that mean complicated and obscure systems are better? Maybe. Off-the-beaten-path systems or angles are less likely to be part of the oddsmaker's formula, and they're less likely to be used as a basis for placing bets by the general public.

If your complicated system is connected to an emergent behavior in teams or bettors, it can be extremely profitable, and will remain unknown. The problem is that it's difficult to know if you've discovered a profitable emergent behavior or if you've simply sliced your historical data so many times that it's no longer predictive. This is a common misstep in statistics known as *overfitting.* I prefer the colloquial known as *p-hacking,* where p stands for probability.

P-hacking is a rampant problem with would-be technical handicappers or anyone with a limited grasp of statistics. It happens to anyone trying to find meaningful or predictive patterns in a set of historical data.

Here's a simple example. Imagine I'm in a room of 1,000 random people, and I ask everyone to raise their hand if they were born on January 1. I gather the 9 people that raise their hand together and begin asking them questions looking for facts and characteristics that all of them have in common. After quizzing them, I announce a system with this setup:

> If you have at least one "S" in your first or last name AND
>
> You have visited the Empire State Building at least once AND
>
> You went to a high school where the mascot was a mammal AND
>
> You are more than 15 years old and less than 62 years old.

Here's the result:

> If these four conditions are met, there is a 100 percent chance that your birthday is January 1.

Hopefully you see the problem. When you look at a set of data, it's tempting and not all that difficult to invent a pattern that correlates perfectly but has no causal connection and no predictive value.

REMEMBER

So when you sort through historical data, your goal is to find statistics and conditions that are highly correlated with a result you cold bet on before the game starts. But a parallel goal is to identify setups that have some kind of logical connection to the outcome, where causality is at least plausible.

Characteristics of a Good System or Angle

Technical analysis means finding situational patterns that lead to a profitable game bet. Your goal should be to find and bet on systems and angles that have characteristics described in the following sections.

Statistically significant

The biggest mistake bettors make is pretending there's a story in the data when there's only randomness. I talked in depth about how randomness often comes cleverly disguised as patterns in Chapter 6, and I also discussed some things you can do to protect yourself from these tall tales. Remember that a "trend" that gives you 12 wins and 6 losses is numerically a 67 percent system, but 18 data points isn't really enough in this case. Think about it: If only 2 of those games went the other way, you'd be looking at a 10–8 trend, which you wouldn't give a second thought about. And if you watch enough sports, you know that in any collection of 18 results, there will be a few coin-flip or lucky-bounce games that could have gone either way.

Predictive

If you can't find a causal connection, or at least a chain of logic that connects why the predicate conditions of your system or angle lead to a certain outcome on the field, you've either stumbled upon an emergence or a coincidence. Most of the time, it's just a coincidence.

Given a large enough universe of variables and games, you'll find all sorts of patterns that are statistically stunning, but they are unlikely to have any predictive value. If you find that games between NFC West teams where the opposing starting quarterbacks were born in the same time zone go under 72 percent of the time, don't bet on that. Just count it as an interesting coincidence and move along.

Bettable

Your system should be tied to the outcome of a specific bet. So your setup should correlate with point spread wins, overs or unders, or other common pregame bets.

This might go without saying, but in some cases, you might come across a system or angle that predicts an on-the-field outcome that doesn't tie closely to a profitable bet. Here's an example: You've found a setup that results in a certain quarterback throwing more passes to his left than his right. That's great information if you're the defensive coordinator for the opposing team, but how will you profit from that information at the betting window?

Timely

If your sought-after pattern doesn't appear in enough time for you to place a bet, it's not of much use. For example, if you discover that the first drive of a football game ending in a punt leads to 60 percent unders, that's great, but by the time that punt is fielded, the starting game total will be a distant memory, and the live-betting total you can actually bet on will have dropped several points.

A subcategory of timeliness is your systems' ease of visibility. If finding betting opportunities requires a 16-step mathematical adventure and manually tabulating some obscure data points, it might be too much work to be profitable.

Frequent (enough)

Your system should involve a pattern that appears often enough to make it worth tracking. If your can't-miss system only comes into effect when the Super Bowl is tied at halftime, keep working. Congratulations on placing that winning wager a few times per decade, but don't quit your day job.

A First Look at Trend-Spotting Tools

The technical handicapper makes money in betting markets by finding profitable systems and angles. If you hope to find these yourself, it will be nearly impossible to do so without building some kind of data collection and search tool.

There are several for-pay systems online. For now, what's consider the industry standard in sports databases is the SDQL. If you've ever worked with SQL (Standardized Query Languages) used by databases of all stripes, you'll find that working with SDQL has a familiar feel to it. SDQL is a language invented in 2015 by Joe Meyer, a developer and sports betting hobbyist. Joe's vision was to create a crowd-sourced dataset with historical box score information for all major sports, and that quickly evolved into creating a flexible web-based tool for querying the data.

The result is SportsDatabase.com, and it's a go-to for serious technical handicappers who are looking to explore historical data, test theories against spread and total results, and to interact with a community of similar-minded sports bettors and handicappers who collect and trade trends and angles.

How it works

The query page on SportsDatabase.com (and affiliate site Kiillersports.com) doesn't look like much: It's a no-frills web experience with a single text box and "Submit" button. This is where you enter your *query string* and see the results.

The query string is nothing more than a recipe to filter the vast store of sports data on the site. Technical handicappers translates their system or angle setup into a series of text phrases according to the standards of the SDQL language. For example:

season=2019 and A and points>40

For this simple college football query, I've specified the following setup:

During the 2019 season

For teams that were away (or simply "A" in SDQL)

Show game results where those teams scored more than 40 points.

Within a few seconds, the games that match this setup are returned and summarized on the screen. Although there are multiple ways to show the game data that gets returned, the default summary shows the straight-up results (that is, with no regard for the point spread), plus the point spread and over/under results followed by a handful of aggregated statistics:

SU: 127–17–0

ATS: 121–22–1

O/U: 122–19–3

	Team	Opponent
Rushes	41.3	35.8
Rush Yds	239.2	141.8
Passes	28.8	37.1

	Team	Opponent
Pass Yds	284.7	256.8
Comp	19.6	21.1
TOs	1.1	1.7
Q1	11.0	5.9
Q2	14.1	7.9
Q3	11.5	5.5
Q4	10.4	7.8
Final	47.6	27.8

Below the aggregated results is a table listing the 144 games that met the criteria of my setup, although there's a limit to the number of individual games that it can display.

Before you get too excited about the amazing spread results of this particular system, note that it does not meet the "timely" criteria from earlier in the chapter because I'm asking the SDQL system to return and summarize games where the team scores more than 40 points. Since there's no way to know ahead of time whether a game will meet these conditions, it's not possible to bet on it.

Querying previous games

But SDQL is amazingly flexible in that your setup can include a string of past games. For example, by adding the prefix "p:" you're asking the database to identify previous games. Here's an example that will look similar to the last one:

season=2019 and p:points>40 and p:A and A

By adding the p: prefix, our setup now reads like this:

In the 2019 season

Look at all games where the away team meets these characteristics:

They were away in their previous game (p:A) AND

In their previous game they scored more than 40 points (p:points>40)

The results show only games that match the data filter we specified in our setup:

SU: 15–28–0

ATS: 19–24–1

O/U: 23–20–1

Note that because we specified "A," we are getting the spread results from the perspective of the away team. If we replaced the "A" with "H," the results would come back reversed:

SU: 28–15–0

ATS: 24–19–1

O/U: 23–20–1

When the home team loses against the spread, the away team wins, and vice versa. And the over/under results stay the same regardless of which perspective you're looking at these games through.

This is just a tiny sliver of the data that's available. In addition to a variety of fundamental factors like rest, weather, time of day, game location, and other situational data, you can filter games on common team and individual statistics. The SDQL site has data available for the most popular team sports (from an American perspective, at least).

Today's games

There is one more benefit to the basic SDQL interface: The data is kept mostly up to date with current game data. So provided you include the current season in your query, if there are any games that match your system, they'll show up in the table of returned games. So not only can you use it to research systems and angles, you can use it to determine if any of today's games meet your criteria. If so, you know where to put your bets.

Chapter **9**

Power Ratings

I f you find your way into the back offices of a sports book, there's no top-secret room with a collection of omniscient alien beings producing odds for upcoming games. There's no pool full of clairvoyants spitting point spreads out inside billiard balls. And there's no all-powerful computer spitting out the Great Answer to the Universe alongside the totals for next Sunday's games. (You would know if there were, because the total would always be 42.)

In fact, point spreads and totals and moneylines are produced by teams of very smart people who watch teams and players, analyze market behavior, monitor external factors, and apply statistics and probability to come up with the best guess possible of what's going to happen in the upcoming games. Wait a second, this sounds familiar. This sounds like what *you're* doing.

REMEMBER

It's true: The odds are set by people. They just happen to be quite smart, and they get paid to analyze sports betting. They have biases, weaknesses, and blind spots, just like you. But that's the key: They're just people. And almost every point spread, total, moneyline, and derivative bet that you see listed as odds on offer from a sports book starts life as a humble power rating that was imagined, invented, and adjusted by a person, just like you.

A *power rating* is a numeric value, or values, assigned to a team that is designed to provide its owner with a measure of the team's quality, with quality being its ability to prevail over other teams. Power ratings are designed to be used in tandem: When you combine one team's power rating with their upcoming opponent's power rating, you should be able to derive a prediction for both the margin of victory and the total runs or points scored in the game.

REMEMBER

It's virtually impossible that you're a sports fan and have never been exposed to a power rating of some kind. It's a simple, straightforward definition, but it's important to make note of a few things we're *not* talking about here.

Ranking, Rating? What's the Difference?

Power ratings are different from power *rankings*. You can derive a ranking from a power rating, but you can't derive a rating from a simple ranking. The simplest example might be the AP Poll in college football. In the simple example that follows, the ranking is in the left-hand column and a power rating is in the right-hand column:

Ranking	Team	Power Rating
1	Ohio State	108
2	Alabama	99.5
3	Texas	94
4	Florida State	92

From this table, you know which team is ranked higher. But the power rating (derived from a snapshot of the Sagarin rating) can actually give you some intelligence about how a future game would go.

If Ohio State played Alabama, you'd expect them to be favored by 8.5 points (108−99.5=8.5). If Texas played Florida State, you'd expect them to be favored by 2 points (94−92=2). In this way, a well designed power rating provides not just a ranking of teams but also a sense for how much better one team is compared to another.

Totally rated

The previous example showed you a power rating that provided information about the relative difference between two teams. For many sports bettors, betting on point spreads and moneylines is the best way to make a profit long term. I urge readers of this book to consider the entire attack surface of a game, which should extend at the very least to betting on totals and derivatives. So a more useful set of power ratings might include enough information to predict the point differential as well as the total amount of points scored. Consider a power rating like the one below where the number is reflective of the actual points scored as well as the point differential:

Team	Power Rating
Rams	33
Cowboys	30.5
Patriots	28.5
Steelers	24.5
Ravens	24
Cardinals	23.5
Browns	22
Bengals	21

For this example, you can derive not only the point differential but a game score. If the Rams were to play the Cowboys, this power rating would predict not only that the Rams would be favored by 2.5 (33−30.5=2.5), but the total would be 63.5 points. Should the Ravens play the Bengals, you'd see the Ravens favored by 3 (24−21=3) with a total of 44 (24+21=44) for the game.

You're probably starting to see both the strengths and weaknesses of a power rating like this. As convenient as a single number is to describe the likelihood of a team to win its next game, it's a tall order to wrap up all the complexities of offense and defense and external factors into a single number.

Power ratings are based on quantitative, objective team data, but they can have pieces that are numerical versions of subjective information about a team's players, coaching staff, injury status, or the game situation (sometimes known as the *spot*).

REMEMBER

Power ratings use data from previous games, but they are designed to be predictive. Knowing which teams have put together the best resume so far on the season is interesting, but it's not quite the same thing as predicting the score of next week's game — and that's the only thing that matters to a bettor.

Power rating strengths

Most hardcore game-pickers and handicappers develop their own power ratings for every major sport. This provides the backbone of their initial quantitative handicap of an upcoming game. Here's why that's a good thing:

>> **Power ratings can be applied to any sport.** Team sports, individual sports, it doesn't matter. Although some sports lend themselves to power ratings more than others, you can always quantify the quality of a competitor in a sporting event.

>> **Power ratings are data-driven.** Once you settle on a formula for your power rating, and provided you don't adjust it to fit your biases and opinions, you have a non-subjective take on your team.

>> **Making changes to power ratings isn't the end of the world.** What makes it objective is the fact that you're going to apply those changes across the board. For example, if you decide you need to count yards after the catch more than you have been previously in your NFL power rating, go ahead. It's going to be applied to every team in the league, so the chances of introducing a single-team bias is lower.

>> **Power ratings are fast.** That's the great thing about math. You can find free sources of data and put your laptop work. No more agonizing over box scores: With power ratings, you update your inputs, and the calculations are what they are.

Power rating weaknesses

Did I say they were perfect? No I did not. Power ratings are a good way to ground yourself, but they aren't the be-all and end-all of a handicap. Here's why:

>> **Power ratings represent the past.** In most cases, no matter how advanced your model is, the inputs to your model are based on data from the weeks and months before. What's wrong with that? A couple of things:

- Just because a team behaved one way in the past doesn't mean it will behave that way in the future. In 2018, the Dallas Cowboys slipped to 3-5 and looked so pathetic that a local Dallas sports radio host made a bet that he'd get a mohawk if head coach Jason Garrett wasn't fired. A few months later, that very team would complete its season turnaround with an NFC East title and a playoff win. (The radio host kept his promise and got the mohawk, to the great consternation of family and neighbors.)

- Last week's team isn't next week's team. People get better. They heal. Backups become starters and vice versa. From the outside looking in, all the major players might look the same, but — especially for football with 22 starting roster spots, where backups play a major role — there may be a galaxy of difference from one week to the next that you can't see by watching highlights on TV.

>> **Power ratings don't account for fundamental factors.** As discussed in Chapter 7, when a power rating is just a single number or a pair of numbers representing offense and defense, how do you account for an injured player? Or an unusual weather pattern at game time? How do you account for teams with disadvantageous schedules? Or revenge on their mind? Or with a middle linebacker who's about to go to trial on an espionage charge? You could make the case that motivation and external factors matter more than past results in many sports, but it's difficult to capture that in a power rating.

>> **The data problem.** Power ratings are most often built on a team's performance to date. The data accumulated from those games provides the input for the predictions, but what if there aren't any previous games? What if there are only a few previous games? Power ratings are great once the season gets going, but you can't really count on them until several games are played and you gain some comfort that the stats are fair representatives of the team's performance.

REMEMBER

The better the power rating, the harder it is to maintain. The most sophisticated power ratings start as simple Excel formulas but quickly start taking into account more in depth factors like the quality of backups at certain positions. To have a good power rating means constant updating as new information emerges about teams and players.

Developing a Power Rating of Your Own

Now that you know what they're good for, let's go through a step-by-step process of building a power rating of your own. I'll start with an extremely simple example and give you ideas of how you can expand it from there.

TIP

You're going to need some kind of spreadsheet software. I highly recommend investing in Microsoft Excel because it has the most advanced set of formulas and tools available, and it lets you run VBA (Visual Basic for Applications) macros and programs to retrieve and manipulate data. If that's not in the cards for you, you can always use the Google Docs spreadsheet application for free. It should handle most of the basic formulas you need for building a power rating.

Plagiarism is the sincerest form of flattery

Before you take the step of building your own power rating, consider that in this, the internet age, with all its wonders, you'll find a number of different power ratings available to you out of the box — for free. They are of varied quality and predictive ability by themselves, but for the time-constrained would-be sports bettor, borrowing somebody else's power rating has great advantages.

When you come across a long-standing power rating like Jeff Sagarin's or Jeff Pomeroy's, you can rest assured that these guys have spent years thinking about and improving them. In some cases, these power ratings have been back-tested against historical data to make them more accurate. Are you willing to do that?

WARNING

Some sports bettors think they're gaining an advantage if they find multiple power ratings for a single sport and combine those ratings together in some way. On one hand, it can help you eliminate weaknesses that a single power rating might have. On the other hand, what are you really gaining by using multiple power ratings?

In terms of power ratings, the internet overfloweth. I list some great information sources in Appendix A. If you think you can do better, knock yourself out.

Your first power rating

I'll talk about specific factors to consider adding into a power rating in later chapters on specific sports (Part 3), but for now, let's pretend we're setting out to create a simple NFL power rating, and the goal of that power rating is to determine the winning margin for each team.

We want to be able to take the power rating(s) for Team A, compare them to those of Team B, do some simple math, and produce a prediction for the point difference in the upcoming game.

We're going to keep it extremely simple. Because the ultimate arbiter of football wins and losses is points scored and points allowed, let's start there. Here's a hypothetical list of average points scored and allowed for a miniature league:

Team	Avg Points For	Avg Points Allowed
Giants	28.5	18
Redskins	27.1	23.3
Falcons	25.5	19.9

Team	Avg Points For	Avg Points Allowed
Titans	24.9	24.1
Patrios	24.5	21.5
Browns	23.2	24.3
Raiders	23.1	16.5
Texans	21	21.9

As you can see, it's sorted for offensive points scored. In the simplest incarnation of a power rating, you can predict the outcome of a particular matchup by taking a cross average of two teams. In other words, the Giants versus Browns would mean the following:

Giants to score 28.5 points averaged with the Browns 24.3 points allowed = 26.4

Browns to score 23.2 points averaged to the Giants 18 points allowed = 20.6

After some minor rounding, your first power rating has produced the following prediction:

Giants	–6
Browns	47

Compare prediction to real odds

Now go compare that prediction to the odds available at various sports books and bet accordingly. If you find a sports book where the Giants are handicapped at fewer than 6 points, bet on the Giants! According to your prediction, they'll win by 6, so if you only have to lay 3 or 4 points (for example), you'll win your bet on the G-men should your prediction hold.

Alternatively, if the Browns are getting more than 6 points, you'd want to bet them. If you find a real-world point spread of Giants –8, your prediction says the Giants won't win by enough points to cover the spread, so the Browns are a better bet.

The same thing works for the total. Your predicted total is 47, so if you find the odds listed with a lower total (like 46), you'd place a bet on the over. If you see the odds with a total above your prediction, you'll want to bet the under.

Many into one

This was just a primer. No doubt you can see plenty of weaknesses in just looking at average points for and against. The idea of the power rating is that you blend many pieces of data into a single metric or a few metrics that (you hope) describe some aspect of a team or a player. In the sports-specific chapters, I cover some of the key metrics you should look at, and then in Appendix A, I list sites with prebuilt stats and power ratings you can use. For now, it's important that you just understand the concepts and a little of the math involved.

P.E. class

Any user of power ratings should understand that concept of *Pythagorean Expectations,* or P.E. for short. If you have visions of right triangles dancing in your head, you're on the wrong track. P.E. is a team metric that establishes a simple measure of quality for a team. It's a concept you'll want to be comfortable with because you might encounter it in the wild, and you might want to use it in your own power ratings.

By way of background, Bill James, the godfather of baseball analytics, concluded that while a team's wins and losses ultimately determine who, uh, wins, they didn't provide you much insight about the team. Sure, we determine who the best teams are in most sports by who wins the end of season tournament, which you qualify for by, you know, winning a lot. James' insight was that wins and losses per se are an imperfect measure of the inherent strength of a team; they only tell part of that story. Games are won and lost as a function of the strength of the opposition, external factors, luck, and more.

(Imagine measuring starting pitchers by nothing but their win/loss record. Baseball pitchers of course can pitch a lights-out game but get zero run support from their team and be stuck with the statistical loss. Baseball scouts and fans realized a long time ago that wins and losses were interesting but not adequate for describing a pitcher's quality.)

James decided that runs scored and runs allowed, rather than wins and losses, were much more accurate measurements of a team's quality, and the P.E. was born. Although the invention was in the context of baseball only, and while James didn't have sports betting in mind, the P.E. is a useful statistical concept and a great example of how it's possible to both derive more meaning and create more predictivity from standard statistics.

The P.E. equation

Deriving a basic P.E. is pretty straightforward. In the case of baseball, you take the runs scored and runs allowed, and insert them into this formula:

Win% = runs scored squared divided by runs scored squared + runs allowed squared

The result is a percentage that, when applied to the total games in a season, should reflect a projection of that team's number of wins. So a team that's scored 256 runs and allowed 211 runs will have a P.E. of .59, which translates to .59 times 162 total games in a season = 96.5 wins on the season. Not bad!

A few notes about the math:

» A team with equal runs scored and allowed will be expected to win 50 percent of their games.

» The result of the squaring magnifies the difference between the two numbers, which is a closer match with actual team performance.

P.E. across other sports

After its invention, statisticians and baseball enthusiasts have back-tested hundreds of team-seasons' worth of data and refined the formula in various ways, adjusting the exponent (that is, the "squared" part of the equation) and giving slight tweaks to make a baseball P.E. that matches quite closely with actual results. But P.E. has also been applied across multiple sports, including basketball and football.

Game-by-game data

Most people build power ratings by using season-to-date summary statistics, but if you want to take it a step further, you can pull game-by-game data to incorporate in your power ratings. On one hand, the data sources can be much more difficult to locate, and incorporating game data increases your spreadsheet work exponentially. But game data gives you the freedom to refine your power ratings with much more precision. Consider the possibilities covered in the next subsections.

Time weighting

Teams and players evolve over the course of a season. Some sophisticated power ratings give more weight to more recent games, the idea being they're more reflective of a team's "true" character and also more predictive of how they'll perform in the future. This is especially common in football power ratings where the season is so brief that a statistical outlier of a game can have a dramatic impact on the team's stats.

Here's an example where we have a power rating for college football teams where we use total yards per game as an input for the final rating. But because we have game-level stats, we can ascribe more meaning to the recent games and less meaning to games from early in the season. Here's the data for Michigan, including the raw total yards stat and the weighted total yards stat, along with the weights by game:

Michigan Offense

Date	Opponent	Total Yds	Weight	Weighted Yds
31-Aug	Oregon	443	0.3	132.9
7-Sep	Western Mich	509	0.3	152.7
12-Sep	Toledo	410	0.3	123.0
21-Sep	@Purdue	542	0.7	379.4
28-Sep	Penn State	295	0.7	206.5
5-Oct	@Notre Dame	195	0.7	136.5
12-Oct	@Indiana	267	1	267.0
19-Oct	Michigan St	233	1	233.0
9-Nov	Iowa	284	1	284.0
		Raw Avg		Weighted Avg
		353.1		319.0

The weight value for each row reflects that game's relative importance to the others in the final weighted average. The rows with a 1 have the most impact on the final average, and those with .3 have the least impact, and that's exactly what we're after here. Once we have the raw data and we've decided on the weights, computing a weighted average is simple.

The raw average means all items count equally, whether they're first in the list or last. And since we have data for nine games, every item contributes exactly 1/9th to the final average.

For the weighted average, we first multiply the raw value for each game by the weights to get weighted total yards for each game. Then we add those weighted total yards for each game up, and then we divide by the *weight denominator.*

What's the weight denominator? That's the sum of all the weights. In this case, if we add up the weights, it's 6, but we can make the weights equal anything you choose, as long as we use that sum as the denominator when we calculate the weighted average.

REMEMBER

If you think about it, every average is a weighted average. It just so happens that all items have a weight value of exactly 1.

So what was the result of all this math? By time weighting Michigan's season, we end up giving the Wolverines' total yards stat a 10 percent haircut before it gets incorporated into our overall power rating. That makes sense: Their offensive swoon in October and November doesn't bode well for their upcoming games. We want a power rating that is as predictive as possible, and that means being an accurate reflection of how the team is performing.

WARNING

If you're going to use any kind of weighting system, make sure you apply your weighting approach to every team in exactly the same way.

Other weighting applications

Once you grasp the concept of weighting, you probably realize there are many ways you could apply it to game data. Here are a few ideas:

>> Home/away performance

>> Strength of opposition

>> In conference/out of conference

>> Critical points versus non-critical points (which is almost the opposite of P.E., where teams don't get credit for running up the score late in the game)

What to do in early season

If you're thinking about how you might construct your own power ratings, you've probably spotted a weakness or two. The big one is that power ratings rely on data, and before you've played games, what data is available? Not only that, but if you're relying on average team statistics as inputs to your power rating, you'll need to wait till several games are played before you have enough data to make the power rating meaningful.

Last season stats

Depending on the sport, you can build power ratings based on last season. This approach is fraught with peril, even for teams that stay mostly intact from season to season. But at least it's a starting point, and you can embellish it using partial preseason data in the big professional sports.

Contribution share

An approach that has popularity among a certain segment of power ratings connoisseurs is to develop offensive and defensive power ratings based on players, particularly according to their contribution to the team. This is most common in basketball, where a team has 5 starters and probably no more than 7 or 8 players who contribute 90 percent of the points. If you build a power rating from player data, you can then add and subtract from season to season when players come and go.

Derive power ratings from odds

The entire purpose of a power rating is to predict game outcomes that provide you betting stances. Wouldn't it be great if we could take a peak at the power ratings used by the biggest bookmakers to give us a starting point?

It turns out you can do that in an indirect way. Before the season starts, bookmakers give clues about how they view teams in the form of season win total over/under odds, win-the-division and win-the-conference odds, and so-called *look-ahead* odds on regular season games.

For 95 percent of sports books, odds only get released after both teams' prior games have been played. For football, that means you won't see odds posted until 5 to 6 days before the game. There are, however, a few books that will issue odds on every game of the season (at least for football teams). You can even bet them, albeit at low limits.

With all that odds data out there, you can grab your magnifying glass and deer-stalker hat and cry "The game is afoot!" No, on second thought, don't do that. But all these odds represent clues into what bookmakers are thinking, and clever interpolation can lead you to a surprisingly precise list of power ratings.

As a very simple example is below with the first few weeks of look-ahead odds for the Jaguars:

Jaguars Look-Ahead (Regular Season)

Week 1	Jaguars	43
	Cowboys	−6
Week 2	Jaguars	41
	Patriots	−9
Week 3	Titans	39
	Jaguars	−1

What can you learn from three games of odds? At a minimum, you could draw these conclusions:

» Oddsmakers think the Patriots are 6 points better than the Jaguars, and the Cowboys are 3 points better than the Jaguars when considering home-field advantage

» The Patriots are favored by 9 and the Cowboys are favored by 6. So oddsmakers must think the Patriots are 3 points better than the Cowboys.

» The Jaguars at home are favored by 1 against the Titans, but again, removing home field advantage, we can infer oddsmakers must consider the Titans to be 2 points better than the Jaguars.

As a starting point, you might build a power rating that looks like this:

Team	Rating
Patriots	6
Cowboys	3
Titans	2
Jaguars	0

By removing a standard 3-point home field advantage, you are left with the raw difference between the teams.

WARNING

Leave home field advantage out of your power ratings. Create a "neutral field" metric that shows you the difference between teams' talent levels independent of home field advantage. The conceit is that if the two teams played on a completely neutral field where neither team has any external advantage, the oddsmakers would set the point spread at the difference in the power ratings.

If the NFL scheduler were to schedule a surprise game between any two teams, you could derive a basic spread and apply a home field advantage. For example, if the Patriots played the Titans in Tennessee, they'd be listed as 1-point favorites (4 points difference in the power rating minus 3 points because Tennessee is at home).

Putting it all together in Excel

In Chapter 16, I'll discuss some basic Excel tips and tricks to help you speed up some of the math and statistical manipulations that will help you maintain your records and power ratings. You could certainly use an online tool or a notebook of some kind to keep records, but if your plan is to maintain your own power ratings, and those ratings draw on external sources of statistics, I don't even want to contemplate the work involved in maintaining the data manually.

Without getting too deep into the weeds in the specific Excel formulas and VBA commands, let me give you a quick overview of how I track data and feed it into a power rating.

Of course, before you do anything, you want to think about what you're measuring. Are you trying to determine a team's offensive production? Are you trying to predict a pitcher's performance in his next outing? Do you want a power rating that creates a strawman total for upcoming NBA games? The power rating concept is versatile, and it can do all these things and more.

Step 1: Think about the inputs

Establish the power factors that you believe make a good team, and consider inputs that are predictive of future performance. For basketball teams, a lot of people think offensive rebounding percentage is what separates the men from the boys. For football, lots of sharps like yards per play.

Borrow and copy from others with vigor, but don't be afraid to look for stats and metrics that other people aren't considering. A great handicapper I know has an NFL power rating that weights game statistics according to the strength of the defense. I know of a baseball handicapper who builds pitcher power ratings that include game temperature in each pitching performance. Opportunities abound and are only limited by your imagination.

Step 2: Find sources

Find a reliable data source online for each one of your results drivers. It's entirely possible that you won't be able to go to a single place for each of your power rating components. (For example, with my NFL power rating, I rely on ProFootballReference.com and FootballOutsiders.com for my primary statistics.)

Keep in mind that the betting markets have not yet permeated all the mainstream media sports news websites. If you want to do any kind of back-testing or automatic validation of your predictions against the spread or totals, you'll need a good source for historical odds data.

These data sources need to have a couple of key characteristics:

» **They should be based on standard statistics for the associated league.** Don't pick a wildcard website that counts an NFL sack as a QB team rushing attempt (for example).

» **More granular is better.** Even though it might require a little extra work, it's never a bad thing to have flexibility with your data. And while you can always aggregate data up into larger grains, once it's there, you can't go backwards into smaller grains.

» **Your data source should be kept up to date consistently.** If it's a basketball or baseball site, the updates should match the league schedule — that is, every night. If it's football, you'll want to see up-to-date stats at least once per week.

» **No weird formatting.** Online data needs to be copy and pasteable at the very least. And when we talk about Excel and VBA commands, you'll start to get a taste for data that is structured in tables that are easily read by macros and scripts.

Step 3: Load and normalize the data

This is the step where I'm waiving my hands and casting magic spells. Much of this step has to do with your spreadsheet acumen. Even if you're still improving your Excel skills, take a look at how power ratings are constructed.

Start with a list of all teams down the leftmost column of your power rating worksheet. Assuming you've found well formatted web data, you'll be able to either Copy⇨Paste or perhaps find a way to Copy⇨Paste Special to make neat columns of data. As a last resort, you'll be able to use Excel's data import tool.

TIP

I like to simplify power ratings by translating actual statistics into rankings. Be warned that you lose a certain amount of precision by reducing raw statistics to rankings. As a simple example, consider the top 3 NFL teams' yards per carry are 5.8, 5.1, and 5.0, respectively. Translated to rankings, they're just 1, 2, and 3, so some information is indeed lost. The difference between #1 and #2 is .7 yards, and the difference between #2 and #3 is merely .1 yard, but by ranking them, those subtleties disappear.

In the example below, I've taken several underlying offensive statistics for NFL teams and applied a simple ranking system to each. At the end of this step, you'll have a worksheet that looks something like this:

	Pts/Drive	Yards/Play	3rd Down Conv%
Arizona Cardinals	5	3	13
Atlanta Falcons	19	17	16
Baltimore Ravens	1	1	3
Buffalo Bills	28	28	27
Carolina Panthers	2	4	1

In this example, you can see that the Ravens are the top team in terms of points per drive, yards per play, and near the top in the other category.

WARNING

Note that the best teams are ranked lower than the worst teams. Watch the order of your rankings and maintain consistency! If you're ranking your offense, higher sacks allowed means you're worse than a team with a lower number of sacks allowed. But if you're ranking a defense, a higher number of sacks means your defense is better! Make sure you're applying a consistent order to your stats.

Step 4: Calculate the final power rating

In the table below, I did some simple math to add up the rankings of the three offensive categories to come up with a composite score for each team.

	Pts/Drive	Yds/Play	3rd Down Conv %	Final Offensive Power Rating
Arizona Cardinals	5	3	13	21
Atlanta Falcons	24	23	32	79
Baltimore Ravens	1	1	3	5
Buffalo Bills	30	30	5	65
Carolina Panthers	2	4	1	7
Chicago Bears	32	32	20	84
Cincinnati Bengals	6	2	8	16
Cleveland Browns	4	5	6	15

When you add up each of the ratings, you get a composite score of these offensive categories. In this example, we see that the Ravens are clearly the best offensive team with the Panthers close behind.

You can certainly end at this step if you want, or there are more permutations you can peruse:

>> You can re-rank the final power rating, which again will obliterate, er, simplify the numerical distance between teams down to a simple 1 point.

>> You can weight one or more of the statistics. For example, if you think 3rd down conversion is the most important offensive statistic, you can alter the math of the formula to ensure that piece of the composite score dominates the others.

>> You can apply subjective factors to your objective power rating. For example, if you've built your power rating on past game data, but you know there's a key injury on the offense that might reduce their effectiveness, you can apply it to the final number.

Whatever you do, take note of your steps, and make sure you can back out of them if necessary.

3

Winning One Sport at a Time

Work up a basic understanding of the sports betting markets and nuances of NFL football, college football, NBA basketball, NCAA basketball, and Major League Baseball.

Acquire systems along the way that you can bet on immediately and learn how to make adjustments to them over time to keep them winning for you.

Ratchet up your understanding of the most popular betting sport of all: football. Get useful tips for the preseason, regular season, bowl season, and the playoffs.

Find opportunities beyond the bracket with a deep dive on NCAA basketball betting.

Learn how scoring upticks in the NBA and Major League Baseball have changed the way gamblers approach these sports, and how spotting broad trends in a sport gives you an advantage over the betting public.

Chapter **10**

Betting to Win on the NFL

There is no doubt that NFL football is the marquee product in the sports betting world. Sure, basketball betting has been growing over the years, but what those gamblers in New Jersey and Pennsylvania (and all the other states who jumped at the chance to legalize betting after 2018) are really focused on is football.

There are several elements to the modern NFL game that have led it to become the most watched sport in the country as well as the perfect target of opportunity for bettors.

The parity in the league, borne out of wise management of the sporting world's best player salary cap, means teams can rise from the depths quickly so that fans can always retain hope. It also results in competitive games on the field every week, with just enough surprise outcomes to keep the games interesting.

Most of all, the weekly cadence of football makes it perfect for betting. The six (or so) days that elapse between most games gives fans time to digest last week's league action; dig into box scores, injury reports, and roster moves; listen to mid-week analysis; and discuss the games with their friends. Bettors know that watching football odds evolve throughout the week often comes with its own micro-dramas. The break between games has always been just right to make football a talkin' sport as well as a bettin' sport.

Not that there was a shortage of football bettors in the past, but fantasy football has not only primed a massive crop of potential bettors, but it's also helped to usher in the analytics age, where companies and media outlets compete with each other to offer advanced statistics to fans and bettors.

College football likes to brag that every game matters, but that wasn't always a good thing. It used to be that an early season loss meant kissing championship dreams goodbye, and that created an incentive for contenders to play a pillow-soft nonconference schedule. The NFL has no such issue. The 16 games are each important and dramatic and memorable, but they are only very rarely life-threatening. On the other side of the spectrum lie basketball and baseball, where the seasons stretch out across so many games that there's a clear forest-trees effect, making it hard to attach significance to an average game.

Today's NFL Game

The NFL looks much different than it did a decade ago. Kids, let me tell you a story of a time back in the old days when creatures called fullbacks walked the earth and teams did something called a huddle. And yes, it's true, there used to be three linebackers on the field at once, and running backs were highly valued positions!

It may sound like a fairy tale, but it's all true. The college game successfully injected some life into the offenses in the mid- to late-2000s, and convinced teams that they could win with multi-faceted athletes playing quarterback. Helped by a wave of freakishly talented stars and a cascade of rules designed to protect quarterbacks and give succor to offenses, scoring rose from 37 points per game in the early 1990s, topping out at nearly 47 points in the mid 2010's. In Table 10-1 you'll see the last several years of NFL regular season scoring and the biggest rules changes enacted that year.

TABLE 10-1   ## NFL Major Rule Changes and Scoring Summary

Year	Home PPG	Away PPG	Rule Change
2007	23.7	20.3	
2008	23.3	20.7	
2009	22.7	20.3	No tackling QB's legs; no return wedge
2010	23	21.1	
2011	23.8	20.6	Kickoffs moved to 35 yard line

Year	Home PPG	Away PPG	Rule Change
2012	24.1	21.3	OT can't end on single-possession FG
2013	25	21.7	Defenseless snapper rule
2014	23.9	21.2	
2015	22.5	22	Expanded defenseless receiver; extra point try moved back to 15 yd line
2016	24.1	21.5	
2017	23.2	20.5	WRs treated as defenseless player
2018	24.6	22.2	No lowering head to make contact; expanded roughing calls
2019	22.8	22.9	Partial year

When road teams won all seven games in the 2019 World Series, wise bettors might have seen it as an omen for the home team advantage in the 2019 NFL season. For the first time in living memory, pro football teams scored more points on the road than they did at home.

In terms of quarter by quarter scoring (see Table 10-2), NFL's 2nd quarter continues to be where the offenses find themselves. Even with big point spread favorites, betting on the 1st quarter derivative usually involves a spread of a half point or a point.

Note how the change in overtime rules led to an increase in OT scoring, which is important if you're a totals bettor.

TABLE 10-2   ## Quarter-by-Quarter Scoring by Season

YEAR	Q1	Q2	Q3	Q4	OT
2007	8.75	13.35	9.28	11.82	0.6
2008	8.97	13.61	8.83	12.43	0.5
2009	8.5	13.91	8.53	11.78	1.8
2010	8.58	13.66	9.49	12.15	0.5
2011	8.84	13.23	9.67	12.42	0.5
2012	9.27	13.05	9.66	12.71	4.5
2013	9.17	14.14	10.12	12.95	2.0

(continued)

TABLE 10-2 *(continued)*

YEAR	Q1	Q2	Q3	Q4	OT
2014	9.08	13.47	10.07	12.17	3.6
2015	8.75	13.75	9.62	12.81	2.9
2016	9.15	13.99	8.99	12.99	3.0
2017	8.27	13.48	9.15	12.42	0.5
2018	9.36	14.28	9.77	12.81	5.8
2019	9.34	13.78	9.78	12.61	4.4

The Evolution of NFL Spreads and Totals

The NFL market is notoriously efficient, with any systematic discrepancies in the odds being quickly pounced on by the betting markets.

Table 10-3 shows you the average home point spreads and totals over the years, along with the home team's spread results and over/under result. The lesson to glean here is that the standard 3-point home-field advantage seems to be shrinking while the oddsmakers have (mostly correctly) bumped the total number up nearly 5 points in the last decade. You can track the narrative yourself. When there's a big disparity in one side of either bet, the oddsmaker adjusts the next year, so the big year for overs in 2010 led to totals being significantly higher in 2011.

TABLE 10-3 **Spreads and Over/Under Results**

YEAR	Avg Home Point Spread	Home ATS Wins	Home ATS Losses	Avg Total	Overs	Unders
2007	−2.5	126	119	41.3	135	116
2008	−2.7	115	136	42.5	122	124
2009	−2.7	118	133	42.6	120	132
2010	−2.5	123	126	42.5	140	108
2011	−2.6	124	122	43.6	124	126
2012	−2.3	118	131	44.8	122	126
2013	−2.6	133	115	45	131	119

YEAR	Avg Home Point Spread	Home ATS Wins	Home ATS Losses	Avg Total	Overs	Unders
2014	-2.5	121	131	46	115	133
2015	-2.2	115	131	45.2	115	128
2016	-2.1	120	125	46.1	128	120
2017	-2.1	125	114	44.2	111	132
2018	-2.4	119	124	46.1	118	129
2019	-1.86	103	140	45.27	122	122

The reason you're not seeing a result for every one of the 256 regular season games is due to the number of point spread pushes that happen every year. And remember, the 2019 season was in progress as I wrote this, so the numbers are incomplete.

Common NFL Bets

Bookmakers offer the widest variety of action on regular season and playoff NFL games, including moneyline odds on both favorite and underdog, plus a standard −110 point spread along with alternate lines for both favorite and underdog. NFL totals are almost as popular as betting the sides, and are also listed as a standard −110 bet along with alternate totals at odds.

Notation

Nothing should surprise you about the basic odds listing of an NFL game. Figure 10-1 gives you a summary.

TIP

In compact settings, bookmakers don't bother telling you that the favorite's point spread is −4 and the underdog's point spread is +4. They assume you know that's the way point spreads work, so they use the space to list the favorite spread and the total.

Derivative betting and props

NFL football has a full slate of derivative bets on each of the big three (moneyline, point spread, and total), where bettors can bet 1st quarter and 1st half pregame nearly everywhere, and preemptive bets on all quarters and the 2nd half at some of the larger books. Other popular derivative bets include team total points for the full game, halves, and quarters.

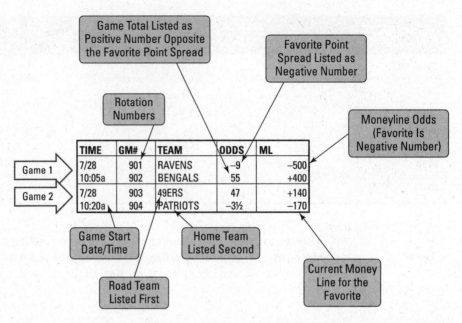

FIGURE 10-1:
How odds for
NFL games are
displayed.

NFL prop bets are some of the most extensive on offer due to the stat-heavy nature of the game now. Plus it helps that there's no squeamishness with betting on individual athletes on performance stats like yardage totals, total carries, total catches, scoring, and more.

TIP

Depending on the betting venue, NFL games are set up perfectly for in-game betting on propositions like whether the next drive will end in a touchdown, field goal, punt, or turnover. Some bookmakers even offer app-based betting on whether an upcoming play will be a run or a pass.

Futures betting

NFL bettors have a full menu of off-season betting options, the most common futures being the following:

>> Team regular season win total (over/under)

>> Team to make the playoffs (yes/no)

>> Division championship (multiway moneyline bet)

>> Conference championship (multiway moneyline bet)

>> Super Bowl champion (multiway moneyline bet)

>> Individual player season stat totals (over/under)

Most major bookmakers leave team futures open starting before the season and continuing through until the bets are resolved, adjusting odds along the way.

Betting sides

The public loves betting the favorites in NFL football. You need to aware of some key numbers.

I use the term *key number* to define a score or margin that is relatively more likely to appear. Because football is most often scored in 7s and 3s, games tend to end at a final margin derived from them. That's why 10-point wins or 13-point wins are more likely than a 12-point wins.

Bookmakers take this into account in football point spreads and totals, not just when they set odds, but when they move odds. You've learned in earlier chapters that if the action is too lopsided on one side of the betting, the oddsmaker responds by altering the odds to make the "overbet" side more expensive, thus making the other side of the bet cheaper.

In a game where all outcomes are equally likely, the bookmaker would have a set level of betting imbalance that would trigger a point spread change. But the wide variation in the likelihood of football outcomes means oddsmakers have corresponding variance in the amount of over-betting they have to see before they'll move the odds in a football game.

Look at Figure 10-2 and you'll see the frequency of NFL final margins. For example, because a football game margin of 12 points is just as likely as 13 points, oddsmakers (and sharp bettors) don't see much difference between those two spreads. But 14 is a key number, so bookmakers require a much bigger market signal before they'll move a point spread from 13½ to 14.

Key spread numbers

The lumpy nature of the NFL's margins leads to certain point spreads being stickier than others. Fully 40 percent of NFL games end with a margin of exactly 3, 6, 7, 10, or 14. A bookmaker who opens a team at −7 will require significantly more action to move the spread to −7½ because it's such a major stopping point for game margins.

And 3 points is another key number. Fully 8 percent of NFL home teams win by exactly 3 points, which means there's a huge difference in betting on a home favorite at −2½ versus −3½, even though they're only an extra point apart. If this were a game scored one point at a time (like volleyball perhaps), the oddsmaker would be indifferent about moving the point spread smoothly up or down as action becomes unbalanced. Not so with football.

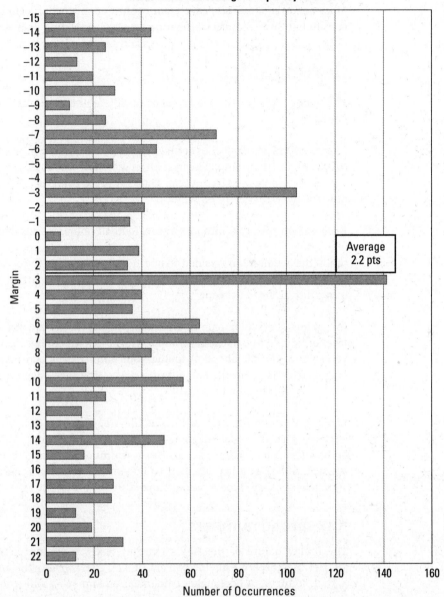

FIGURE 10-2:
NFL key numbers for point spread betting.

TIP

The lesson: Shop around. When you're thinking of betting a side that's lined in the neighborhood of +3 points, shop around and see if you can find +3½. And by the same token, as an underdog bettor, you can't consider +2½ and +3 to be in the same probability neighborhood as you might think of +4½ and +5.

Betting at +5 rather than +4½ will almost never matter. Five is an incredibly rare game margin. In the last 20 years, there have been 77 games lined at +4½, and in only one case (1.2 percent) did a team getting 4½ points lose the game by exactly 5 points. That means the difference between those two point spreads is almost nothing. In fact, if you were betting on a team at +5 and you had a chance to sell a half point, it just might be worth it.

Selling points

Selling points is an action you can take with some bookmakers when you're finalizing a point spread bet. By giving back a half point on your point spread (for example, from +5 to +4½), the bookmaker gives you a more advantageous payout schedule. (For example, instead of a –110 bet, or risking $110 to win $100, the bookmaker will ask you to risk $102 to win $100 as compensation for your half point.)

Let's look at the same half-point difference between +2½ and +3. There have been 152 games in the last 20 years where the home team was a +2.5 underdog. In 13 (7.5 percent) of those games, the home team lost by exactly 3 points. So you might say for underdog bettors, the half-point that moves you to 3 is worth 7 times as much as the half point that moves you to 5.

Is it worth it? Let me work it

If you treat NFL margins and total score patterns as actual probabilities for the future, they become good-use cases for putting our knowledge of break-even winning percentage to work for us to compare two bets.

In this case, we're contemplating selling a half point back to the bookmaker in exchange for a more advantageous set of payout odds. Again, the bookmaker has offered to move our odds from –110 to –102 if we'd be willing to move from +5 down to +4½. Should we do it?

At –110, the break-even winning percentage is 52.38 percent. At –102 the break-even winning percentage becomes 50.2 percent. It might seem like small potatoes, but professionals are constantly on the lookout for advantages like this, as they would welcome a 2.18 percent edge because they know — like casinos — that tiny edges make a big difference in the long run. So now we look at what we lose when we give away that half point. As I discussed earlier, a 5 point margin is extremely rare. It only impacted 1 out of 77 games lined at +4½, and a home team losing by 5 points at any spread has only happened about 1.5 percent of the time. But since the 2.18 percent advantage gained is more than the 1.5 percent advantage lost, you should make that bet. It's a positive EV play, so sell that half point!

What about moving from +3 –110 down to +2½ at –102 odds? We already know that at –110 we need to win 52.4 percent of the time to break even, and –102 gets us to 50.2 percent. But that 2.18 percent advantage we gain is outweighed by the fact that at +2½, we know that 7.5 percent of the time, a bet that would have previously won for us will now only push. Stick to the three points unless the bookmaker can give you a better price for moving from +3 to +2½.

There is a generic rule of thumb that the correct price for moving off of a key number in the NFL is 25 odds points, or in our case, moving from −110 to +115. In other words, if a bookmaker isn't willing to up your moneyline by at least 25 odds points (and most won't), don't sell that ½ point. There are some excellent free calculators online that can help you work through the math on buying and selling half points on NFL bets.

Moneyline betting

Oddsmakers offer the usual handicap-free moneyline bets to bettors who aren't interested in the point spread. The only thing you need to know about NFL moneylines is that they are tied into to the key numbers I talked about in the previous section.

Table 10-4 that shows a rough equivalent between an NFL moneyline and point spread (assuming −110 odds) on some key numbers.

TABLE 10-4   **NFL Moneylines and Point Spreads**

Favorite Point Spread	Moneyline	Historical Straight Up Win%	Underdog Point Spread	Moneyline	Historical Straight Up Win%
−2	−130	59%	+2	+110	41%
−2½	−140	58%	+2½	+125	42%
−3	−155	58%	+3	+140	42%
−3½	−175	63%	+3½	+155	37%
−4	−200	66%	+4	+170	34%
−6	−270	72%	+6	+210	28%
−6½	−300	84%	+6½	+220	16%
−7	−330	75%	+7	+250	25%
−7½	−360	82%	+7½	+280	18%
−9½	−400	76%	+9½	+300	24%
−10	−450	75%	+10	+325	25%

These numbers are from 2013 onward to incorporate the most recent rules that had a direct impact on scoring. That means for some of the oddities you see, it's entire possible there's not enough data yet to smooth out the curve. And in case you're wondering, no, it's not an accident that the winning percentages associated with each point spread are the inverse of each other.

WARNING

These are rough equivalents. While point spreads can make the odds look placid and calm on the surface, moneylines are more prone to churn beneath the waves. Moneylines don't automatically move in perfect sync with spread moves, and it's not uncommon for bookmakers to use the moneyline as a way to fine-tune action on either side of a game. A typical NFL Sunday might have two games where the favorites are both listed at −3 +100, but one moneyline is set at −155 and the other is set at −145. The lesson? If you're a moneyline bettor, shop around.

Total bets

Where other sports have smoother distributions of total scores, football does not, with it's 6-point touchdowns and 3-point field goals. Bettors should treat totals like they do point spreads: warily. Some point totals are much more common than others, as you can see in Figures 10-3 and 10-4.

NFL parlays

NFL moneylines, totals, and point spreads are available for betting in multi-way bets called *parlays*. A parlay is the equivalent of betting on one game and then automatically putting the winnings toward a second bet. The bookmaker kindly does this for you automatically. Best of all for NFL bettors, you don't have to worry about the timing of the games; you can parlay games that start at exactly the same time, and they're treated as if they get bet in sequence.

Standard parlay payouts are as follows:

2 bets	2.6 to 1
3 bets	6 to 1
4 bets	12 to 1

WARNING

Parlay bets come with restrictions. Most bookmakers forbid you from parlaying an NFL spread and total on the same game.

For a parlay bet to win, every leg must win. Should one of the legs push, the parlay bet reverts to the odds of a parlay with one bet fewer. For example, if you were to bet a three-way parlay, three wins pays 6-to-1. If one of the best were to push, your parlay would be treated as a 2.6-to-1 two-way parlay.

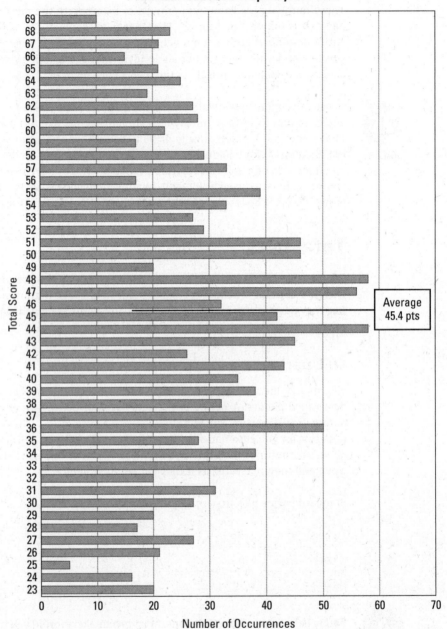

NFL Final Total Score Frequency 2013–2019

FIGURE 10-3:
NFL total scores average around 45.4 points.

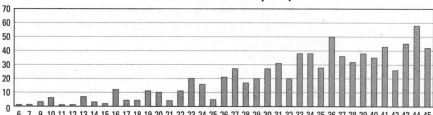

Total Game Score Frequency

FIGURE 10-4:
The frequency
of total game
scores.

NFL teasers

NFL teasers are a popular multi-way play. Bettors get the benefit of a set number of points for as many different point spreads or totals as they choose.

>> For a 6-point teaser to break even, bettors must win each single leg 72.3 percent of the time.

>> For a 6½-point teaser to break even, bettors must win each single leg 73.8 percent of the time.

>> For a 7-point teaser to break even, bettors must win each single leg 75.1 percent of the time.

Betting the NFL Preseason

Pop quiz: In what way are you and I exactly like All-Pro NFL players? Answer: We are all spectators when it comes to preseason football games.

In football, summer is springtime. No wait, springtime is summer. Well, anyway, after the six months of gloom that follow the final whistle of the Super Bowl, with occasional brief glimmers of the other side at draft time and during OTAs, preseason NFL football is, for a brief moment, a welcome sight.

But preseason football almost as quickly wears out its welcome. As of this writing, NFL teams play four preseason games during an excruciating mini-season in August and early September. Teams will typically play twice at home and twice on the road, but there are occasional promotional games in non-NFL cities.

WARNING

There is serious talk among the powers-that-be of finding ways to reduce the number of preseason games without losing the associated gate and media revenue with the two home games each owner gets per year. One proposal is to trade preseason games for a longer regular season. I'll believe that when I see it, as the NFL

Players Association appears to be solidly against adding two regular season games. It will all come down to the renegotiation of the Collective Bargaining Agreement between players and team owners.

What makes preseason NFL football so underwhelming as a fan is the uncanny valley: It resembles a real NFL game in every way, from the announcing voices to the stadiums to the uniforms, but something is just disturbingly out of whack. The new normal is to keep veteran players quarantined. Stars often play no more than a series in the first few games and not at all in the last preseason game.

Thankfully, we have gambling to keep us cool in the dog days of summer. Preseason football doesn't have to be a choice between the lesser of boring and who cares. In a meaningless game, populated mostly by spare players running a playbook straight out of last year's Pro Bowl (erp), at least you have the ability to make it interesting through a wager.

Preseason NFL football get a surprising amount of betting action. In fact, many sports books report there's more money wagered on the Hall of Fame Game (the first preseason game) than on the rest of that day's events combined, which includes a summer Sunday of baseball, tennis, golf, and summer league basketball.

Preseason lines and limits

The fact that sharps make bets on the preseason should tell you that it's worth pursuing. In fact, sharp action often outweighs the public on individual games, and that means you'll see bigger odds moves, and when it happens, you can derive more meaning from it because it's less likely to be fueled by the tourists and occasional squares.

If you are a high-dollar bettor, you'll notice that preseason betting limits are much lower than regular season limits. Some bookmakers limit bettors to 20 percent or even 10 percent of a maximum bet they might take in the regular season. Bookmakers are constantly trying to balance opportunities for increasing handle against the risk of getting beaten, and they have extra risk in high-variance games. Bookmakers want contests between two teams that put winning above nearly everything else. Because preseason games are meaningless, team and coaching motivation can be hard to pin down, which means outcomes are harder to model. Preseason carries an elevated risk of a single piece of information about the game might confer a big gambling advantage (like a coaching staff's plans for playing their 1st string quarterback), and there's nothing oddsmakers hate worse than losing the information battle with gamblers.

We know the NFL regular-season side and total markets are efficient: The oddsmakers models are accurate, there are lots of bettors who process and bet on new information, and oddsmakers quickly adjust lines. A good research idea might be to compare the efficiency of the preseason and regular season betting markets. With lower limits and more professional bettors, are there any systematic weaknesses in the preseason market that aren't in the regular season market?

You can get a sense for how efficient the market is by measuring the average distance between closing lines and winning game margins. This is sometimes called the spread margin. The lower the spread margin, the closer the game margin was to the spread. In recent seasons, the preseason NFL number has actually shown itself to be tighter (9.2) than the spread margin for regular season games (9.5).

So are preseason games as hard to beat as regular season games? The tighter spread margin difference between regular and preseason could be attributed to swings in points scored. (If an oddsmaker sets a game at a pick'em, you'd see a lower spread margin if the game ended 42–0 rather than 44–0, but it would be hard to say that the former score represents a materially better spread on the game). And the golden rule of bookmakers is that they lower their betting limits when they feel vulnerable. That makes me think the preseason is worth looking into if you're a bettor.

Preseason as predictor

Let's start with a basic question about NFL team performance: Do teams that win in the preseason go onto win in the regular season? The answer is appears to be no. Writer Chad Langager did a study a few years ago where he looked at ten seasons of data and found very little correlation between preseason winning percentage and the subsequent regular season winning percentage.

But of course, we're not trying to predict regular season winning percentages. We're looking for *betting opportunities* in the preseason.

Betting on head coaches

The surest spread play in the NFL preseason revolves around coaching tendencies. If you played a sport competitively, then you undoubtedly had a coach tell you that it was important to "practice like you play" and that winning had to become a way of life, not just an outcome. On the flip side are the coaches who treat preseason as the fans see it: basically meaningless, and wins are certainly not worth risking player health over. I can see both sides of the argument, but really, I'm just glad there are coaches out there who can be so easily profiled.

Coaches come and go, but there are some who stand out when it comes to the preseason.

Preseason win-obsessed:

>> John Harbaugh

>> Mike Zimmer

Preseason win-oriented:

>> Bill Belichick

>> Jon Gruden

>> Mike Tomlin

>> Pete Carroll

Preseason losers:

>> Jason Garrett

>> Dan Quinn

>> Matt Patricia

Jury's still out:

>> Doug Pederson

>> Sean Payton

>> Ron Rivera

I separate out Zimmer and Harbaugh because together they have won nearly two-thirds of their preseason games and have spread records to match. The approach is simple: Bet on the coaches who like winning; bet against the ones that have losing tendencies (if they're still in the league); and on the occasions when one type plays the other, bet a little bit bigger. And in case you're worried about tracking coaches and their straight-up winning percentage, understand that preseason spreads rarely stray beyond 4 or 5 points, so the straight-up winner is usually the point spread winner as well.

TIP

If you're reading this book in 2020 or beyond, there will inevitably be some new names in the coaching ranks, and some of the guys in the above list will have faded away. More important, some of the coaches I didn't list will have accumulated enough data to reveal themselves to be a Zimmer-type or a Garrett-type.

Before August comes around, do yourself a favor and look up the current coaching crop's preseason ATS record.

Considering the coaching angle is so widely discussed, it's surprising that it has not been priced out of the market yet. During the 2019 preseason, some analysts claimed the Zimmer-coached Vikings and Harbaugh-coached Ravens had more expensive point spreads than they normally would have. Maybe so, but they both continued to win.

Other potential factors related to coaching include coaches on the hot seat. It's been theorized that they're more likely to try and get wins in the preseason. After all, when you're fighting for your job, every non-losing result helps. In an admittedly unscientific look at this, I counted 7 "consensus" hot seat head coaches going into the 2019 season. I threw out two of them (Garrett and Zimmer) who had already been profiled. That left 5 hot seat coaches who, drum roll please, went a combined 7–14 in the preseason. Clearly this needs a deeper look.

BET on week 2 losers

Systems are hard to come by for preseason NFL, but this here's one that's intuitive, well known, and surprisingly has not been squeezed out of existence:

In the NFL preseason

Both teams are playing their second preseason game AND

One of the two teams lost their first preseason game outright AND

The other team won their first preseason game outright

BET the point spread of the team that lost last week.

Statistically, the correlation between the winning percentage of a team in the preseason and their winning percentage in the regular season is 0.0944. Values between −0.1 and +0.1 suggest no correlation between two variables.

Other preseason betting factors

Here's a list of basic factors to consider when assessing a preseason game:

>> **How long will starters play?** Most coaches have playing time recipes determined well before the game. Look for games where one team plans to leave starters in longer than the other; consider a 1st half or 1st quarter wager.

>> **The 2nd string quarterback is often the pivotal player when it comes to preseason results.** Beyond the quarterback, look at differences in overall depth of bench talent for the two teams. In the salary cap era, it's hard for teams to be both good *and* deep at the same time.

>> **In preseason games 3 and 4, watch for skill position players on the bubble.** If the team is only planning to keep two quarterbacks, find prop bets to take advantage of a third-string quarterback who's likely to be going for the big splash to save his skin. Interceptions, anyone?

>> **Skip it.** Spare yourself from watching it. Do some calisthenics. Play with your kids. Call your mother.

NFL Fundamentals

The NFL salary cap, draft structure, standardized schedule, and other forces aimed at maintaining parity reminds me of a stock car racing league. In car racing, there are tight standards for how powerful the cars can be to reward the superior drivers. What fun would it be if a pit crew could add a jet engine to the roof of the car? Actually that would be very fun, but I digress.

Because NFL teams are constructed according to strict rules, the talent level from top to bottom occupies a narrow band. That means successful teams have superior coaching, schemes, preparation, treatment, technology, process, contingency planning, and so on. The sections that follow discuss non-football factors that have an impact on the game. Some of the best handicappers and analysts will tell you that winning bets is gaining mastery over these elements of the sport.

Schedule spot (travel, bye week)

When we build a mental model of what an NFL team is, it's tempting to imagine it as a static list of players, slotted into positions, each with a statistical profile that, when combined with the other players on the team, reveal themselves to be a big deterministic machine. Generalizing is a habit: "This team is good" and "that team is bad," but it's a terrible habit for someone trying to predict performance.

Teams are a function of their players, but its important to remember that they function in context. The way they perform on the field is as connected to who they're playing against, how healthy the teams are, how rested they are, and so on. Yes, the teams you're watching this week has the same names and jersey numbers as last week, but they aren't really the same.

Travel

There have been scads of studies devoted to travel effects on pro football teams. A 2013 Stanford study expanded on previous theories about circadian advantages enjoyed by west coast teams playing night games on the east coast due to their body clocks being set to "afternoon" while the east coast team's body clocks were set to "bedtime." Other studies have tried to determine if the stress of travel has a detrimental effect on teams crossing time zones in either direction.

I twisted the data every way I could for teams going coast to coast in either direction and couldn't find an angle. That's probably an indication that the betting market has priced these travel factors into the point spread. Having said that, in the last four years betting *against* Eastern Time Zone teams playing at *any* time on the west coast has netted a 34–19 spread record. Not much to hang your hat on.

TIP

You can take advantage of the market when it underreacts *and* when it overreacts. In an ideal world, you find a factor that affects betting outcomes of games that nobody has considered. Bet it for profit until other people start mentioning it. Then when you finally hear other bettors mention it, consider betting the other side.

A Boston College research team led by Kyle Waters took the Stanford study one step further and tried to isolate specific travel distance as it impacts winning percentage. They concluded that NFL teams' winning percentage drops 3.5 percent for every 1,000 km traveled, with bigger impacts when the team changes time zones and when they play outside. That's a built-in disadvantage for teams in the west. If your team is in California, Arizona, or Nevada, your team spends easily twice the time in the air than a team in Ohio or Pennsylvania.

BET on early season wanderers

I didn't want to drag you through that discussion without giving you a system to look for. This system takes both time and space variables into account:

In the NFL regular season

It's the first half of the season (week 9 or less) AND

The home team is based in the Eastern time zone AND

The road team is based in the Pacific time zone

BET the road team's point spread.

This system comes up a few times a year and has gone 42–23 (64 percent, with a modest Z-score of 2.3). It is possible, after all, that both the Stanford and Boston College research studies are correct (that winning percentages drop with more travel) *and* for the betting markets to have totally overreacted to this phenomenon in the form of plum point spreads for the visiting team.

Rest

I am a believer that rest is a useful add-on characteristic when evaluating match-ups. While I think the oddsmakers build bye weeks into their models, I think it's helpful to set aside preconceived notions of what player rest actually does for betting outcomes. Rest is very likely a net positive in terms of improving player health, and for most coaches, more time is good for game-planning activities. But there's also value in routine and focus, which are sometimes at odds with rest.

By far most NFL games are played on the reverse-Genesis schedule: Work on Sunday, rest for six days, work again the next Sunday. But with Monday and Thursday night games interspersed with bye weeks, plus Thanksgiving day and a few Saturday games late in the season, there are a lot of rest possibilities, as you can see in Table 10-5.

TABLE 10-5   ## Rest Days in the NFL

Rest Days before Regular Season Games	Home Team	Away Team
3	6.3%	6.2%
4	<1%	<1%
5	8.9%	8.6%
6	60.6%	59.1%
7	6.1%	5.4%
8	<1%	<1%
9	4.6%	6.3%
10	<1%	1%
12	<1%	<1%
13	5.1%	5.5%
14	<1%	<1%

BET the curse of the well rested

Look what happens in the latter half of the season when a home team is playing after an unusually long rest period:

> During the NFL regular season
>
> It's week 9 or higher AND
>
> The home team is playing after more than 8 or days of rest AND
>
> The home team lost their last game
>
> **BET** on the road team's point spread.

This system actually works with or without a loss in the previous game, but this setup has gone 65–28 ATS since 2012 (69 percent with a Z-score over 3) and went 10–7 in 2019. I like this approach, and I think there's much more to be discovered when looking at rest.

Rest differential

The NFL takes pains to pit teams against each other that have a similar rest profile so neither team is at a major disadvantage. Obviously it doesn't always work that way. Table 10-6 shows the distribution of rest differential.

TABLE 10-6

Rest Differential

Rest Differential	Frequency
Road team more than 3 days extra rest	7.3%
Road team 1–3 days extra rest	14.6%
Home team's rest = road team's rest	62%
Home team 1–3 days extra rest	12.3%
Home team more than 3 days extra rest	5.2%

Injuries

Injury creates uncertainty around games. Uncertainty means higher variance of possible results. This you probably already knew. The biggest challenge for some-one examining the games is not when a player is hurt; it's deciphering injury information for players who might play.

A Football Outsiders study looked at NFL injury reports and calculated that when a player is listed as Probable, they play 95 percent of the time, and 32 percent of the time when Questionable. But teams, general managers, and coaches have different approaches to reporting injuries. Perhaps not a major factor, but if there's a player who's key to your handicap listed as probable, it's a good idea to understand the team's history in reporting injuries.

Teams also demonstrate their ability — or lack thereof — to make adjustments to scheme and style in the event a key injury. The 2017 Philadelphia Eagles won the Super Bowl in spite of a rash of injuries, which most people credited to coach Doug Pedersen's adjustments to play-calling, personnel groupings, and so on to fit the strengths of the remaining healthy players. As a Dallas fan, this is doubly painful because the Cowboys of the last decade have shown the opposite skill: They collapse like a house of cards when key players sit.

TIP

The final point on injuries that sharp analysts watch for is that players will play before they're at 100 percent speed. Going at 80 percent if you're a precision-route wideout like Amari Cooper can mean the difference between a 9-catch day and a 2-catch day. I like these three approaches with skill position prop bets:

>> Fade a yardage total for a skill position player returning from a minor injury that's kept him on the sidelines for at least two games.

>> Watch for big performance dips from skill players that occur without explanation during a win, and fade the yardage total prop the following week.

>> Is there such thing as "injury prone"? And are certain injuries subject to re-aggravation more than others? Yardage total prop bets for skill players are usually built on assumptions of full speed, but going under that total on a player with even a 10 percent or 15 percent chance of having to come out of a game can move the bet into positive EV territory.

Weather

Football is an all-weather sport, although the NFL has sensibly started pausing games if they're in the eye of massive electrical storms. When it comes to whether effects, we're interested in three basic factors: wind, precipitation, and temperature.

It should go without saying that everyone reacts differently to weather. I can think of some notable examples of skill players who had particular issues with certain conditions. Hall of Famer Troy Aikman, who played high school and college football in Oklahoma and Southern California, was vocal about not being able to comfortably grip a wet ball.

Data scientist Josh Mancuso studied three decades of NFL data and drew a handful of conclusions about quarterback play in bad weather:

>> Games played in high wind (20 mph or more) have the greatest negative impact on QB production.

>> QB efficiency doesn't change much in bad weather, but production metrics (touchdown passes, and yards passing) take a hit.

A different Stanford team led by Rory Houghton–Bery drew some fascinating conclusions in a 2017 paper about weather when they tested differential effects for the home and road team.

>> As a rule, rain and snow are an advantage to the home team and produces statistically significant increase in point differential toward the home team. The inference they made was that home teams are more used to the bad weather. Makes sense to me.

>> Teams playing in a dome see more home-field advantage than a team that plays their home games in the open.

>> Run-heavy teams (if there are indeed any left in the NFL) get less of an advantage in bad weather than a pass-heavy offense.

>> Wind is the great equalizer; it's bad news for both teams' offensive expectations. Bet under the total on a windy day.

Multiple teams have looked at the impact of temperature on a game. If you've ever tried to throw or catch a football in bone–chilling cold, you might be surprised to learn that cold weather — by itself — has not historically limited total points in a game. If anything several studies have found that extremely hot weather has more of a negative impact than cold weather.

A numberFire.com article written during the 2017 season is probably the most useful of all. In 256 regular season games, 20 percent of the games were played in moderately windy conditions (7–12 mph) where average total scores dipped by a point, and 15 percent were played in high wind (over 12 mph), where total scores were down over 6 points on average, with the under bet winning 19 times and losing 11.

WARNING

Wind looks like a promising angle for a fundamental handicapper, but it's hard to pass final judgment on an angle like this without more precise data. The biggest question is always this: Does that betting record represent wins and losses against the consensus closing total, the opening total, or some total in between? What wind data is being used? Was that wind as measured at the stadium? If you looked up the wind speed for Hot Springs, Arkansas (or a random city of your choice) on May 2, 2010 (or a random date of your choice), you'd probably see a single vector representing an average direction and velocity, but that doesn't necessarily represent what's happening at the stadium.

NFL Systems and Angles

As you'll read in these pages, I don't have much patience or appreciation for team-specific angles. When I hear someone tell me that the Raiders are 15–6 ATS in their last 21 visits to the east coast, I roll my eyes (in the nicest way possible). If there's no connecting logic behind a trend, I dismiss it.

If you read the preseason section however, you'll see I'm an advocate for some coaching systems. Long-tenured coaches develop and retain tendencies that get passed onto their teams.

BET Belichick's slow starts

It's a strange one, I know. But as successful as the man has been in all aspects of his NFL coaching career if you're reading this and Coach Belichick is still in the business, take a look at his team's performance in late-round playoff games. It's downright eerie how slow the Patriots start in these high-leverage games. In 10 games, the Pats have scored a touchdown in the 1st quarter once, a field goal once, and 0 points in the first quarter in all 8 other games. Sure, it's a little flimsy, but I had to mention it.

In an NFL playoff game

If Bill Belichick is the coach AND

It's the Conference Championship or the Super Bowl

BET under the 1st quarter.

BET a case of the Mondays

This germ of this idea came to me from Las Vegas sports betting media mogul R. J. Bell. I've tweaked it slightly from his version, but I'm not sure I understand the reasoning other than an MNF win is a shot in the arm. It comes up a few times a year and has gone 39–13 ATS in the last two decades (75%, Z–score of 3.47). Most importantly, this system was a perfect 4–0 in 2019.

In an NFL regular season game

The home team's last game was at home on Monday Night Football AND

The home team's most recent game resulted in a win AND

The home team played less than a week ago AND

The home team is favored by less than 7 or the home team is a dog

BET the point spread of the home team.

BET restless on the road

This is an example of the rest conundrum. It makes sense that more rest is better, but there are many situations where that's not the case; this is one of them. This system has gone 39–15 ATS (72 percent, Z–score of 3.1) in the last 7 years, but more interesting is the fact that it's an 85 percent winner as the leg of a 6–point teaser, which rises to over 90 percent when the home team's rest is a day more than the road team's rest.

In an NFL regular season game

When the road team is favored AND

The game total is greater than 42 points AND

The home team has at least one extra day of rest

BET the point spread of the road team.

INCLUDE the road team in a 6-point teaser.

BET growing totals

It's slightly more convoluted than I'd prefer, but the results are real: 54 overs and 25 unders (74 percent, Z–score of 3.15) in the last 15 years of results. I like this system because I believe it identifies a hole in the betting market. The market recognizes there's a good reason to think both teams will score more than they did before, but there are enough bettors who aren't convinced and who continue to bet the under. The result is the total isn't quite as high as it should be.

In the NFL regular season or playoffs

If the game total is 4 points or more than the home team's previous game total AND

If the game total is equal to or greater than the away team's previous game total AND

Both team's previous game over/under results were either under the total or no more than 1 over the total

BET over the total.

Chapter **11**

Betting to Win on College Football

In spite of its many problems, college football has proven incredibly popular among the sporting public and the betting public. The National Football Foundation claims that college football games regularly dominate the most-watched programming among cable TV channels. (For you kids out there, "cable TV" is this thing where you paid for hundreds of channels to be broadcast straight to your TV so that you could watch shows on maybe three of them.)

There's a lot of college football happening outside the games you can bet on, but this chapter will look specifically at the Football Bowl Subdivision (FBS), the top level of American college football — the artist formerly known as Division I.

Why bet on college football you ask? Ah, such are the joys of college football compared to the NFL. You have the raucous students and the bands, the way-cooler trophies and end-of-season awards, the silly century-old traditions and oddball mascots. (What do you mean it's a single Cardinal? Mascots are supposed to be plural!) There's the charm of the mid-size college town that gets 100,000 visitors six times per year. In essence, college football has spirit and personality in a way that the NFL has successfully filtered out of its league.

To be certain, college football has its share of problems, starting with the fact that it's the only major sport where the champion gets chosen (at least partly) off the field of play. Not only are teams shackled to their preseason perception and longtime name recognition (sorry, Baylor, TCU, Iowa, UCF, and others), but the act of ranking and polling teams is problematic, as it's done by people who don't actually watch the games, and it's done according to an unwritten set of rules-of-thumbs and decades-old norms that nobody dare explain. (How beautiful were your wins? How well-timed was your loss?) We have a term for a sport that picks its champion by committee: figure skating.

So yes, the line of aggrieved fans and players who missed out on "their chance" to play for it all forms up to the left. But the NCAA helped itself by finally introducing the four-team playoff in 2014. That effectively bumped teams' complaints down a notch. So instead of "We were robbed of a chance to play for the national championship," now you have schools saying "We were robbed of a chance to play for a chance to play for a national championship." Progress!

For bettors, college football is a smorgasbord of delights, with the familiar week-long rhythm of the season, offering just enough time to get caught up on last week's results and to plan for the betting Saturday ahead. Compared to the NFL, college football offers a very different set of betting challenges with its much wider and diverse set of teams manned by a revolving door of still-evolving players.

The College Football Schedule

College football doesn't have a tidy schedule like the NFL, with its 16 games and one bye week over a span of (let me do the math: let's see . . . carry the one . . .) 17 weeks starting the weekend after Labor Day.

The "week number" concept is not as prominent as the NFL's either, but when we handicap games, it's important to keep in mind where we are in the season. Week 1 starts with a handful of early kickoff games, usually the last Saturday in August. Near the end of the season are the conference championship games in early December (Week 15 or so), followed by bowl season (Week 18 and beyond).

College football has been adding games to its schedule steadily. National champs 30 years ago ended the season with 11 wins. 20 years ago, it 12 wins. But today's national champions play as many as 15 games: 3 or 4 nonconference games, 8 to 9 conference games, a conference championship game, and then the national semifinal followed by the championship game.

Scoring Overview

College football has more scoring than professional football, mostly due to some points-friendly rules:

>> The clock stops on first downs, which leaves more time to play (and score).

>> The college football overtime system, introduced in 1996, eliminated ties, and unlike NFL overtime, introduced the possibility of a lot more points added to regulation time.

>> College receivers only need one foot inbounds for a catch.

If you're used to betting on the NFL, you'll notice very quickly that college football has higher average scores and higher scoring volatility, as you can see in Table 11-1. While the pro game is steadily evolving toward more points, the college game is already there, orbiting close to its 10-year average of 56 points.

TABLE 11-1 ## College Football Scoring Averages

Year	Total Points	Avg Home Points	Avg Road Points	Avg Spread	Home ATS W	Home ATS L	Avg Total	Overs	Unders
2009	52.48	29.9	22.5	–8.1	345	383	52.5	330	366
2010	54.57	30.9	23.6	–7.9	353	377	53.3	352	339
2011	54.86	31.6	23.2	–8.1	367	365	54.6	369	355
2012	56.15	32.3	23.8	–8.6	368	377	55.7	315	331
2013	57.32	33	24.3	–8.9	373	374	56.8	379	370
2014	56.4	32	24.4	–8.5	363	397	56.6	354	397
2015	57.4	32.5	24.9	–8.1	361	412	56.5	369	372
2016	58.3	33.1	25.2	–8.5	362	398	57.8	358	397
2017	56	31.7	24.3	–7.9	347	407	56.5	351	414
2018	57.56	32.7	24.8	–8.4	379	413	56.9	396	394
2019	55.8	32	23.8	–7.7	390	400	55.9	382	412

In Chapter 10, I listed rules changes that affected NFL teams, but college football rules have stayed mostly steady where it concerns scoring patterns. One thing that Table 11-1 reveals is that the home-field advantage is more pronounced as well, given that by proportion it's much larger than the NFL home-field advantage. In terms of raw averages, home teams score 8 more points than road teams.

But hold on a second: 8 points is due to the big, powerful schools disproportionally inviting (and paying handsomely for) second-tier schools to visit and get drilled. If you take conference play by itself, home-field advantage drops to a more familiar-looking 3 points. Table 11-2 shows the ten year averages broken out by the Power 5 conferences, restricted for just intra-conference games.

TABLE 11-2

Ten-Year Averages of Power 5 Conferences

Conference	Home PPG	Away PPG	Home Field Adv
Pac-12	31.7	27.8	3.9
SEC	27.6	23.9	3.7
Big 12	31.9	28.8	3.1
Big Ten	27.5	24.9	2.6
ACC	27.9	25.8	2.1

A quick study of Table 11-2 reveals that you should . . .

BET under the SEC

The setup is simple enough:

> In a college football FBS game
>
> Where both teams are SEC schools AND
>
> The game total is less than 53 AND
>
> The home team is favored, a touchdown underdog or less, or the game is a pick'em
>
> **BET** under the total.

We all hear about how the SEC is the dominant conference, infused with talent from top to bottom. But dominance doesn't automatically mean offense. It appears there's a general market over-estimation of conference games to the point that unders have won over 62.4 percent of the time in the last 10 years (88 overs and 146 unders, Z-score of 3.73). This system has only produced more overs in two of the last 15 seasons, and 2019 was a banner year, with 24 bets that resulted in 6 overs and 17 unders.

College Football Bets

If you read the last chapter, you're familiar with all the essential football bets: the sides and totals, the futures, props, and derivatives. In this section, I'll also discuss multi-way football bets like parlays and teasers. The bottom line is that any bet you can make on an NFL game you can also make on a college football game.

WARNING

If you're a high-roller in the market for wagering your bookmaker's maximum bet-size on a single college football game, you'll find that number to be about half the size of the NFL max. Why? The college game is more volatile than the pro game, and some bookmakers protect themselves by accepting smaller bets.

College football sides

Moneylines in college football operate much the same way as moneylines in any other sport, and there's not much to recap here. Point spreads are the same way, but since there are no ties in college football games, you won't see games lined at a ½ point.

Like the NFL, game odds are published early in the week and are subject to the usual market pressures. It's not unusual for college football point spreads to fluctuate 3 points or more over the course of the week, so selecting bets, and pulling the trigger early can make a difference in your long-run profitability if you're correctly anticipating a trend toward the better team.

Margin of victory

College football is similar to the NFL in terms of key final game margin numbers. In Figure 11-1, you see some familiar features: 3 and 7 are popular final margins, making up one-sixth of all college football game outcomes.

REMEMBER

Your football point spread betting should take into account the fact that one final margin is far more likely than its neighboring margin. Say you've handicapped a game and you've found a point spread you want to bet. Now with that in mind, it's time to do a little analysis on the betting market and see how you can select the most advantageous odds.

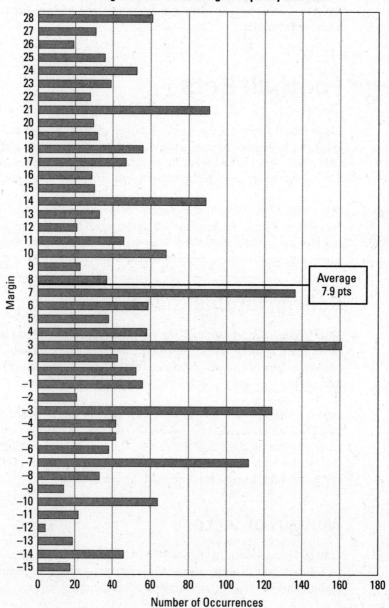

FIGURE 11-1: College football home margin frequency.

TIP

What exactly do I mean "select your odds"? You select your odds in two basic ways:

>> You might find different odds at a different bookmaker. The odds you see on offer from book to book are going to be similar, but often enough with slight differences. Whether you live in a state with in-person sports books, or if you have multiple accounts with offshore books, you're going to want shop around.

>> Your favorite sportsbook will often let you buy (or sell) half-points on your point spread at the time you place your bet. They'll list their base point spread for a game at –110 (the standard 11/10 bet), but you'll have the option of trading it in for a different set of odds should you prefer. If you buy a half point, you'll receive more advantageous odds than –110, and if you sell a half-point you'll receive worse odds than –110. It's never a bad idea to assess the relative advantage of buying or selling a half point.

Let's say you've assessed a game and have decided you like the road underdog at +2½ points. Your favorite bookmaker is offering this point spread at standard –2½ –110 odds. Just to break it down, here are the possible outcomes on your –3 point spread bet:

>> The road team wins, or the home team wins by only 1 or 2 points; you win.

>> The home team wins by 3 or more; you lose.

When you step to the window to place your bet, you find the odds have changed to +2 at +110 odds. Should you still bet on the road team with the new odds? Let's consider the new array of possible outcomes:

>> The road team wins, or the home team wins by 1; you win.

>> The home team wins by exactly 2; your bet pushes.

>> The home wins by 3 or more; you lose.

Here's where your knowledge of the historical averages come into play. Two-point victories are so rare that it shouldn't bother you too much to surrender that half point in exchange for a better payoff.

College football totals

Football's goofy scoring patterns mean your total betting should be informed by key numbers, just like point spread bets. But these numbers aren't identical to the

NFL's key totals. Because college football scores are higher, and because the kickers aren't quite as reliable, the key numbers for your totals betting hit at different places.

Figure 11-2 shows the most important key numbers for totals. Due to the size of the data set, I left out the extremes on either end of the scale, but these numbers should cover about 95 percent of every college football total you will ever encounter.

REMEMBER

The total points scored in a college football game are more likely to end up on key totals due to the scoring patterns inherent in the sport. And knowing what the most likely total scores are can positively inform your bets. For example, if you decide to bet over a 45 point total, and it moves up to 46 before you can make the bet, it's not a huge deal, because 46 is such an unlikely final total score. On the other hand, if you like a total bet on under 55½ and the line drops to 55 before you can make the bet, that drop is more significant because of the relative likelihood of a 55-point game occurring compared to a 56-point game. If you bet under 55, you've transformed an uncomfortably large slice of the possible outcomes to being a push rather than a win.

Using push frequency to select the best odds

If you look at a database of college football games, you can see that a home victory of exactly 3 happens about 4.7 percent of the time. But in the denominator, we've included every single game in college football history, regardless of the circumstances. It stands to reason that (if the oddsmakers are good at their jobs, and they are), a game lined at –3 is far more likely to end up in a 3 point victory than a game lined at, say, –28, right? It turns out that when the point spread is exactly –3, the game ends with a 3-point home victory 7.3 percent of the time.

This calculation, where we determine how common a specific outcome results in a bet neither winning nor losing is called a *push frequency.* If you want to be an advantage handicapper, you need to understand how to shop for the best odds, and you can't do that without understanding how to use push frequency to calculate the relative advantage different odds.

For a given betting number (point spread or total actually), the push frequency is the number of times a bet ends up in a push divided by the total population of games.

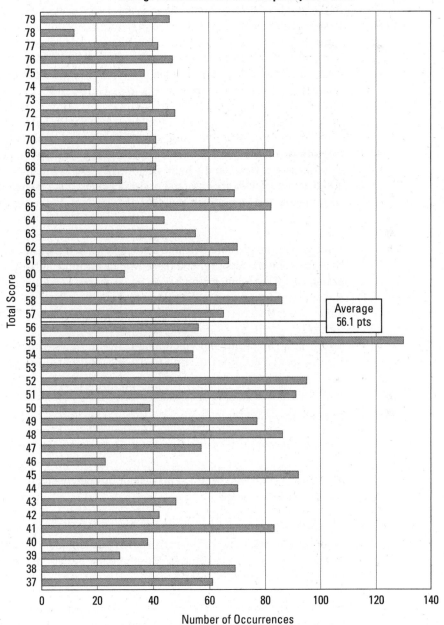

FIGURE 11-2:
College football
total score
frequency.

WARNING

In the words of Robert Plant, "If you can clarify, please do." Yes, that definition lacked some precision. But choosing a denominator for push frequency is a subjective exercise. I showed above the overall push frequency (the number of 3-point home wins divided by the total number of games played at any spread) and the exact push frequency (the number of 3-point home wins divided by the total number of games lined at exactly −3).

Which one is correct? There's a popular compromise listed in Stanford Wong's book, *Sharp Sports Betting*, where your denominator is all games lined within a touchdown of the point spread in question. So for games at −3, you include 7 points above (to +4) and 7 points below (to −10). From 2009 to present, I found 3,080 games in this category, and of those games, 205 resulted in a 3-point home win, making the Wong push frequency 6.7 percent. We'll use that number going forward.

Let's look at the possible outcome of this game, setting aside our initial handicap that put us on the favorite. You'll see why in a minute. Make the assumption that either side of the point spread has an equal chance of winning. Now plop the push frequency of 6.7 percent in the middle and you'll see that the remaining chance of either side is 46.7 percent. (46.7% of a win + 46.7% of a loss + 6.7% push = 100%.)

To fill in a composite expected value using those assumptions, let's say we're talking about a bet of $11 to win $10. The possible outcomes are these:

» The home team wins by 4 or more; you win. $10 × .467 = +$4.67

» The home team wins by exactly 3; you push. $0 × 6.7% = 0

» Home team loses (or wins by only 1 or 2); you lose. −$11 × .467 = −$5.14

That means if we know nothing else about this bet, we'd put the expected value at $4.67 − $5.15 = −$0.48.

So how does that help us? Well, if you shop around and find a spread that's half a point off at different odds, you can use that push frequency number to help determine where the betting value is. Say there's a bet at another bookmaker listed at −2½ at −120 odds. Is the additional half point worth the more expensive odds?

With the new point spread, we know a 3-point win now results in a spread *win* rather than a *push like before.* So let's recalculate our outcome tree as follows:

» The home team wins by 4 or more; you win. $10 × 46.7% = +$4.67

» The home team wins by exactly 3; now it's a win! $10 × 6.7% = +$0.67

» Home team loses, or wins by 1 or 2; you lose. −$12 × 46.7% = −$5.60

Notice how we adjusted the amount bet in the third bullet. When the odds are −120, we have to bet $12 to win $10. I like to say the payment odds are less advantageous, but the *cross-section* for our win improves because a 3-point result is now a win rather than a push.

TIP

In other words, our odds of winning the bet (46.7 percent) have improved by exactly the push frequency. That's a fancy way of saying that if we assume the historical distribution of college football margins, the probability goes up that a random score will result in a win for us.

(I borrowed "cross-section" from nuclear physics, where an atom's cross-section refers to the probability that a neutron will contact it and interact with it. There are probably better analogies, but I give you this little gift so that if you happen to be discussing sports betting among a group of nuclear physicists, they will nod their heads knowingly, and you will feel nothing less than triumphant.)

Where were we? Okay, so combine the values for each possible outcome in the latest outcome tree and you get an EV of $4.67 + $0.67 − $5.60 = −$0.26.

Wait a second. There's still a negative expected value. Why would we bet this?

REMEMBER

The premise of this bet is that your handicap of the game led you to decide that it makes sense to bet on the favorite at −3. But because we saw a bet at −2½ −120 and a bet at −3 −110, we need a way to figure out which one is a +EV play. Is it better to take a lower payout in exchange for a slice of bets pushing rather than winning? Or is it better to have the bet win more often but require a bigger risk at −120.

Hopefully you can see how the large push frequency made the lower spread worth the −120 odds. All things being equal, if the push frequency had been only 1 percent (rather than 6.7 percent), it wouldn't have been a +EV play to bet −2½ −120 rather than −3 −110. And you'll also notice how your selection of which type of push frequency you use can affect the results as well. If you had used the overall push frequency of 4.7 percent, it gives the move from −3 to −2½ less impact because the winning cross-section of the bet is 2 full percentage points lower than if you used the Wong push frequency.

TIP

This basic approach to analyzing odds can be applied to any point spread or total bets. Your analysis should show you that one or the other options is better. It might even lead you to conclude that betting on opposite sides of a bet with two different point spreads. (For example, a bet on Team A −3 −102 as well as a bet on Team B +3½ +110 would land often enough on one bet winning and another bet pushing to make the total expected value positive.)

Multiples: Parlays and teasers in college football

While most parlay odds are standard across the NFL and college football, you'll often see sports books offer slightly better payout odds for college football teasers due to the fact that each point you add to a college football score is slightly less meaningful than a point in an NFL game.

Table 11-3 shows what you can expect for college football parlay odds.

TABLE 11-3

College Football Parlay Odds

Teams	6 Points
2	+260
3	+600
4	+1,100
5	+2,200
6	+4,000
7	+7,500
8	+14,000

And Table 11-4 presents a common set of college football teaser odds.

TABLE 11-4

Common College Football Teaser Odds

Teams	6 Points	6½ Points	7 Points
2	–110	–120	–130
3	+180	+160	+140
4	+280	+350	+180
5	+450	+400	+350
6	+700	+600	+500
7	+900	+800	+700
8	+1,200	+1,000	+900

The above tables represent odds on multiple bets assuming those bets are straight 11/10 bets. You are welcome to include the primary point spread and total bets in your multi-way bet, but if one or more is offered at something other than –110, it can affect your odds. It should go without saying that teaser and parlay odds vary from book to book. My main online account starts two-way teasers at –120, and they are consistently 10 percent worse (or so) than the odds listed above.

Parlay and teaser rules, on the other hand, are close to universal. If any one of your selections lose, the whole bet is a loss. If there's a push on one leg of your selections, that bet is ignored and your bet is treated as if it were made with one fewer leg. For example, if you place a $10 4-way 6-point college football teaser bet at +280 odds, and three of your picks win, and the final bet pushes, your bet is a winner but you're paid off at +180 (odds for a 3-way teaser).

The same goes for parlays. The only difference is when you've made a 2-way bet. If one leg from your 2-way parlay pushes and the other wins, your parlay bet wins and is paid off as if it's a straight bet (paying –110 or whatever the odds were). A teaser with one win and one push is treated as a push and your wager is refunded.

NFL, college football, and basketball have different odds for each pairing of size (number of teams) and points added. You can parlay any bet across any sport. But what happens if you want to mix sports in a single teaser? The usual treatment by a sports book is to accept the bet but give you the payout odds from whichever sport pays the shortest odds. So where an NFL 6-point teaser with two teams pays –120 and the same college football teaser pays –110, if you add one selection from each sport, your teaser will only pay –120.

You can't mix your points-added within a teaser bet. For a football teaser, you'll need to pick the points-added as either 6, 6½, or 7 point teasers, and it will apply to all football teams in your bet. When your teaser includes a basketball team, you'll be forced to take the "matching" point added number in hoops, which are 4, 5, or 6 points.

Teaser and parlay bets are not the same as teaser cards, or parlay cards that are often made available in brick-and-mortar sports books. The concepts of the bet are the same, but the rules and odds are almost always different.

Thinking about teaser and parlay odds

We know that break-even winning percentage for a standard –110 bet is 52.38 percent. When you tease two teams (that is, place them in a single teaser of, say, 6 points), you get a positive handicap of 6 points in your favor. That means, if you teased an over bet where the total on Iowa versus USC is 47½, the 6 points in your direction means the two teams are only required to get over 41½ points for the over bet to win. If you had bet under Iowa/USC in a teaser leg, your under would win provided the total score was less than 52½.

Getting 6 points for free is great, but teaser rules disadvantage the player by requiring both plays to win and by paying out −110 for the entire bet. That means your expectations of winning each bet (with 6 points added to each in your favor) better be 72.37 percent or more.

REMEMBER

You calculate the probability of multiple independent events all happening by multiplying the individual probability of each event together. The chance of drawing the ace of spades from a pack of playing cards is 1/52, or 1.9 percent. But the chances of drawing an ace of spades *and* rolling a 1 on a single die is 1/52 times 1/6, or 1.9 percent times 16.7 percent, making 0.3 percent.

We know the break-even percentage for a −110 bet is 52.38. Since a two-way college football teaser pays off at −110, and both legs of a teaser have to win for it to pay off, the break-even percentage for our teaser is 52.38 percent. So by the rules of probability, we need both legs' win probability to be able to be multiplied together and equal at least 52.38 percent. In a basic way, that means we require the individual win probability of each leg to be the square root of .5238, answering the question, "What times itself equals .5238?"

And the answer is .7237. When you bet a two-way teaser, make sure that you estimate the probability of each leg at 72.37 percent or more, or it's not worth it. (Of course, the probabilities of the two events don't have to be exactly even. If you estimate the probability of one leg at 90 percent and the probability of the other at 60 percent, the combined probability is 54 percent, which makes that teaser a +EV play.)

So evaluating a teaser leg is as simple as asking the question: Does the points added for this point spread or total boost my winning percentage to 72.37 percent? Think about it this way: If you picked two random games for your teaser that you know nothing about, beating the spread is a coin flip. We know that getting 6 points to your advantage in a spread or total raises your chances of winning the bet, so do 6 points elevate your chances of winning from a 50 percent coin flip to 72.37 percent? Are those 6 points worth 22.37 percent (from 50 percent to 72.37 percent)?

In the NFL, it's sometimes possible to use your 6-point teaser to move your effective spread across several key numbers that represent a big share of the outcomes. For example, if you teased a team +2, the cross-section of your winning bet moves up to +8, moving the 3, 6, and 7 outcomes from the losing column to the winning column. There's no such beast in college football. Because college football scores are higher and more dispersed, there's no automatic point spread that moves you from 50 percent to 72.37 percent winning percentage.

Offseason Evaluation and Betting

With college football players only having four years of eligibility, teams roll players in and out that outside analysts have precious little information about. So when the summer rolls around and it's time to evaluate which preseason and early season bets deserve your attention, there are only a handful of variables available:

>> **The team's record last year.** It's self-explanatory that more wins is better, but teams that close the year on a roll, or with a big bowl win, are often thought of as better than teams with a similar record but who lost games toward the end of the season.

>> **The team's recruiting success.** It's the college football version of the draft, where college football team rosters get refreshed with the influx of freshmen (and transfers). Scouting services grade and rank every recruit, and there is even a mythical recruiting class ranking that is of questionable value to college football bettors. Writer Talal Elmasry did an analysis a few years ago that about 9 out of 10 national champions have a four-year average recruiting class ranking in the top 10.

>> **The mythical returning starter data.** First off, how many of the 11 starters on each side of the ball are back from last year's team? And second, what positions are returning? The conventional wisdom holds that more returning starters, especially in key positions like quarterback, means more experience and cohesion for the team in question.

Other factors come into play when it comes to team expectations and rankings. Is the coaching staff stable from one year to the next? Did any shooting stars emerge at the spring practices? And of course, does the school's brand and history warrant additional attention from prognosticators?

That returning starters thing

Because college players burst onto the scene then exit a few short years later when their eligibility is up, it can sometimes feel like the turnover is too much, making it hard to evaluate teams with lots of turnover. That's why analysts got very focused on counting up returning starters. What else is there?

But I am less sanguine about the value of returning starters for bettors. Here are the objections I have collected over the years:

>> Is a returning starter *always* better than a new player? Of course not. Kyler Murray wasn't a returning starter a few years ago at Oklahoma, and he had an insanely successful season.

>> To the previous point, what if there are a bunch of returning starters and the teams was terrible last year? We don't want some starters to return!

>> Who counts as a starter? If I was a backup last year and then started the last game of the season, do I count as a returning starter? How many games would I have had to start last year to count as a returning starter?

>> No really, who counts as a returning starter? If I started last year at left guard and I'm switching this year to right tackle, a position I've never played before, am I a returning starter or not?

>> No, I'm seriously asking, who counts as a returning starter? I started two seasons ago and then got hurt in preseason practice and sat out last year. I haven't played in a live game in 18 months. Am I a returning starter?

There are even more reasons to doubt this number: Many teams rotate positions regularly (like defensive ends) to keep them fresh. Do all four guys count as returning starters? What about a "starting" strong-side linebacker who only plays 25 percent of the snaps because his team's base defense is the nickel. Is he a returning starter?

Alternatives to returning starters

When you think about it, the returning starters metric is meant to measure both experience and the cohesion of a college football team. Many handicappers and analysts have also had their moments of doubt about this metric and have come up with other ways to draw conclusions about a team:

>> **Returning letters:** The legendary handicapper Marc Lawrence, who publishes a college football yearbook in the summer with reams of team-by-team data, has an elegant way of looking a the experience question. Instead of trying to muck through the subtleties of who should count as a starter and who shouldn't, his staff counts up returning lettermen and divides them into position groups, like offensive and defensive linemen. The idea here is a team with 11 returning lettermen on the offensive line, but only 2 of them were officially "starters" last year, is going to be deeper and more cohesive than a team with only 5 returning lettermen, but 3 of them were starters.

>> **Returning production:** Like college basketball, some handicappers make use of returning production numbers. For the offense, add up last year's final productivity stats (passing, rushing, and receiving yards and touchdowns) and then check this year's projected rosters to see which players are returning and what share of last year's production they represent. This methodology doesn't concern itself with who was on the field for the first snap; it's all about what they did with it. For offensive linemen, you can use number of snaps played, and for defensive players you can look at stats like tackles, assists, and — if you want — turnovers and sacks.

BET on hope as a strategy?

Here's a system derived from one discussed by handicapping legend Mark Simons. Simons suggested experienced teams coming off a high-leverage season should outplay expectations in the early season. Here's the setup:

In a college football FBS game

Where it's being played in August or September AND

Where one team has 7 or more returning starters on each side of the ball AND

Where that team has at least 14 upperclassmen starting AND

Where that team's quarterback has thrown at least 50 college passes AND

Where that team won at least 4 games last season AND

Where that team is an underdog AND

Where teams are close to meeting the starter requirements, consider other focusing factors from last season, like a disappointing ending to a good season or a surprise ending to a mediocre season

BET the underdog's point spread.

Simons creates his list of experienced teams in the summer and uses it to determine preseason plays. He says that his 2018 list delivered more than 60 percent ATS wins in September.

WARNING

I've spent many hours looking for profitable systems related to returning starters. When facts are so scarce prior to the season starting, it only makes sense that we focus on it as a fundamental factor in evaluating teams. Maybe I lack imagination, maybe I'm just unlucky, or maybe it's a metric that's already heavily factored into the market, but I have never found a regular, repeatable returning-starters trend. Mark Simons's approach makes sense as an exercise in fundamental analysis, just not as an automatic betting system. When I ran the 2019 numbers, it didn't rise above profitability.

Summer betting

In late May, it's common for a few of the biggest sports book consortiums to release a few "games of the year" where they pick out several dozen of the highest profile games on the upcoming schedule of the biggest nonconference games in the upcoming season and list waaaaaay in advance of the season. In betting parlance these games are called openers. Then in June, the Golden Nugget offers odds on over 200 of the most prominent college football games. In addition, over the course of the summer, sports books will start offering over/under bets on season win totals for college football teams. No doubt this trend will continue with the proliferation of legal betting.

REMEMBER

Betting in the early season and preseason is less about systems and angles and more about fundamental analysis of teams.

>> You're not trying to crown the champion or select an All-American team. Your job is to figure out who the public has either overrated or underrated.

>> Ignore preseason polls if at all possible; polls and rankings anchor how you assess teams without adding objective value.

>> The public often keeps memorable bowl games in mind from the previous season. If a team suffered a public humiliation, they might be underrated in the early season.

>> Like any sport with a point spread, some college coaches appear to monitor the spread, and they will make game choices knowing they'll hear it from boosters if they fail to cover the spread.

>> The players are kids. They change. Don't cement your perceptions into place about how good or bad an athlete is based on a game you watched a year ago. Kids get great coaching as they get more comfortable in the game, and of course they mature between ages 18 and 22 like all of us did (well, like some of us did).

Why don't you just meet me in the middle?

TIP

If you are willing to monitor sports books like Golden Nugget, CG Technologies, and Fan Duel sports books, you'll have an opportunity to put your preseason assessments to the test by betting these sneak-preview bets. These games are offered at lower limits, but if you notice early enough, the odds can be so different as to create arbitrage opportunities. For example, in the 2019 season, Fan Duel-based sports books opened Oklahoma as 15½ point favorites in their September matchup against Houston. If you were in Nevada at the Golden Nugget, you would have seen Oklahoma open at −27½.

In rare situations like that where odds diverge so widely, astute bettors have an opportunity to place a *middle* bet. When you middle a game like Oklahoma and Houston, you're betting Houston +27½ at Golden Nugget and betting Oklahoma −15½ at Fan Duel. Here are the possible outcomes if you had placed those two $110 bets:

>> Oklahoma wins by 28 or more: Houston bet loses, OU bet wins. Net: −$10

>> OU loses or wins by 15 or less: Houston bet wins, OU bet loses. Net −$10

>> OU wins by anywhere between 16 and 28 points: both bets win. Net +$200

So you're effectively risking $10 for the chance to win $200! To be clear, middle opportunities with such a wide win cross-section are very rare, and the two bookmakers likely moved those point spreads towards each other in a hurry. But there are opportunities out there if you look hard enough.

Placing very low-risk or even no-risk bets due to differences in bookmaker odds is known as *arbitrage* betting. Arbitrage is a concept borrowed from the world of finance and refers to trading in a way that takes advantage of different price conditions across different markets to make money.

There are software packages available to bettors that will let you monitor odds changes across dozens of online betting venues up to the second. There's even some software that will identify and spot arb opportunities for you, calculate the odds, and recommend underlying bet sizes.

WARNING

Beware that for many online bookmakers, arbitrage betting violates the terms and conditions of your account. As ridiculous as it might sound, many bookmakers include a "for entertainment only" clause that gives them the right to limit or close your account if you are suspected of executing any kind of professional (read "winning") betting strategies.

Regular Season Betting

College football has a more varied schedule than the NFL. You've probably caught the occasional Tuesday or Friday night game — not days of the week you'd call "action packed" in the NFL. Nevertheless, a similar rest day regime prevails with some common rest days and rest differentials.

Essential statistics for betting

The best college football betting analysts I know usually have a pet statistic or two, and their analysis of those stats is mixed in with some kind of secret process. I am fortunate enough to have been let in on some of it though. Here are a few observations:

>> Sharp bettors' go-to football statistic is yards-per-play on offense and yards-per-play on defense. As a starting point for any power rating, lots of pros look at the differential between the two stats.

>> When looking at recent game history, don't focus on final score. Sure, winning and losing is important, but more important to the bettor is a team's ability to be in a position to win, and for that I've had several people recommend tracking scores at the end of the 3rd quarter. That exercise helps you filter out a lot of running up the score and can give you an indication of teams that are competitive through the game and are maybe one lucky break away from being able to pull an upset.

>> Football Outsiders' Bill Connelly has written about "five factors" of college football (which will remind some of Ken Pomeroy's "four factors" in college basketball) as the best way to boil down a team's potential. Using that as a base, here's where your attention should be focused in terms of stats: efficiency (getting required yards for down and distance combinations), ability to create (and prevent) explosive plays, winning the field position battle (that is, starting offensive drives closer to the end zone than your opponent), and converting red zone drives into points.

>> Certain stats like sacks and pancake blocks are like biceps: they're beach muscles only and aren't exceptionally useful. Why is a sack so much more celebrated than a simple tackle for a loss?

Rest

Table 11-5 gives you a look at how rest days affect some common stats.

TABLE 11-5 **The Effects of Rest Days**

Rest Days	Share of Total	Home Avg Points	Away Avg Points
4	2.0%	31.1	24.3
5	5.4%	29.5	27.4
6	72.2%	31.6	24.6
7	4.8%	32.4	23.6

Rest Days	Share of Total	Home Avg Points	Away Avg Points
8	2.9%	33.3	23.6
9	0.9%	28.6	28.1
10	0.4%	29.2	23.2
11	0.9%	28.4	27.6
12	0.6%	31.3	27.3
13	8.9%	30.7	24.9

Your eyes should be drawn to six days of rest, by far the most common setup in college football, where teams play Saturdays and rest and practice for six days.

BET rested roadie

There are many systems that rely on rest as a variable in the winning formula. This one looks at the rest differential between the two teams rather than the absolute number of days, and uses the premise that the betting market likes big home underdogs, and big road favorites are already unappreciated by the betting market. Here's the setup:

> For a FBS college football regular season game
>
> The road team is equally rested as the home team or is *better* rested by 1 to 4 days AND
>
> The road team is a double-digit favorite
>
> **BET** on the road team's point spread.

This scenario is in the running for my favorite college football system because it exhibits so many outstanding qualities. In the last 10 complete seasons of data plus most of the 2019 season, you get a 58 percent winning percentage. There are 50+ opportunities per season, and the 10+ year ATS record is 465–340 (Z-score of 4.37). It's been profitable in 9 of the last 11 seasons, and it performs throughout each week of the season. It's simple and has clean endpoints. The best part is that it shows continuity around the edges. In other words, there's no sudden drop-off; high single-digit favorites go a little over 50 percent.

But wait, there's more! There's another big category of equal-or-better-rested road teams that are profitable as well: single-digit underdogs. Replace the final condition of the previous system with this:

> The road team is a single-digit underdog or the game is a pick'em

This system happens a ton. In the last 10+ years, the spread record is 811–649, which is 55.5 percent (Z-score of 4.21) and in that span it's been over 50 percent ever year (although not over 52.38 percent every year).

When you encounter a long-term system that shows you a consistent advantage with a high number of instances per year, there are usually ways to tighten it up using the database of your choice. I call this process *winnowing your system*. Winnowing your system is about adding conditions that remove coin-flip chaff while preserving as much of your system's excess wins as possible. (In this case, there are 162 more wins than losses.)

WARNING

Mind your balance! While you want to add conditions to remove chaff, it's possible to add too many. I talked about the dangers of p-hacking, where you use a scalpel to carve an intricate (and nonsensical) set of conditions that preserve your excess wins but lose touch with the original rationale. If you have to add more than three or four new conditions, you've probably gone too far.

TIP

Keep systems simple; see if there are simple conditions that move your system in the right direction. For example, maybe it works best early in the season, for high total games, or when the home team lost its previous game. Consider it your homework assignment.

Running up the score

It has been argued that the college overtime rules are inherently unfair because the team that gets the ball *second* in overtime have a 54 percent chance of winning. The idea is that once the first team completes their possession, the second team knows whether they can win the game by kicking a field goal or scoring a touchdown, so the choices they make — like going for it on fourth down — are more attuned to winning the game. (I'm skeptical of this assertion. Someday I'd like to check the data on this 54 percent stat.)

TIP

The home team wins 53.3 percent of college overtime games, and the point-spread favorite wins nearly 59 percent of overtime games. Statistician Kevin Rudy looked at what happens when a team ties the score with less than 30 seconds to go in the 4th quarter to send the game into overtime. Does their last-second miracle spark momentum? The result indicates a let-down effect: only 41 percent of the teams that snatched an OT game from the jaws of defeat went on to permanently escape those jaws.

To give you an idea on how to college football scores are spread out, the average spread is −8.2, and 90 percent of the spreads are between −37 and up to +16. Ninety percent of spread bets land between about 20 points from the spread, either way. The average total is 55.8, with 90 percent of totals ranging from 44½ up to 69.

Very nice! It turns out that the 90 percent of over/under margins fall within 20 points either way as well.

Quarter scoring trends

You can bet quarters and halves in college football games. As you would expect based on NFL patterns, history shows that college football starts slowly in the 1st and 3rd quarter and picks up steam in the 2nd and 4th.

According to Table 11-6, the 2nd quarter by far sees the most points scored.

TABLE 11-6   ## Scoring by Quarter

Year	1st Qtr Home Score	2nd Qtr Home Score	3rd Qtr Home Score	4th Qtr Home Score
2009	11.74	15.71	11.51	13.27
2010	12.4	16.21	12.45	13.02
2011	12.38	15.97	12.64	13.42
2012	12.94	16.4	12.94	13.3
2013	13.51	16.48	13.25	13.51
2014	13.32	16.34	12.66	13.6
2015	13.09	17.04	13.07	13.6
2016	13.66	16.62	13.27	13.94
2017	12.81	16.52	12.6	13.53
2018	13.05	16.98	13.15	13.9
2019	12.76	16.47	12.47	13.64

BET tie goes to the under

Here's a halftime betting system that takes advantage of a behavioral quirk:

> For regular season FBS college football games
>
> Where the home team is an underdog AND
>
> The game total is 48 or more AND

The game is tied at halftime AND

Both teams scored at least once in the 2nd quarter

BET under 2nd half total.

The idea is that games with some offense tend to slow down ever so slightly if the teams go into halftime knowing that the third quarter is a (quote-unquote) brand new ballgame. This system hit around 60 percent in 2019.

Runnin' and gunnin'

While NFL has gone to a more pass-heavy offense, the college game has remained a little more steady. Table 11-7 gives you a breakdown of the running stats.

TABLE 11-7 **Rushing versus Passing**

Season	Average Offensive Plays	Rushes per Game	Passes per Game
2009	67.86	37.58	30.29
2010	67.92	37.45	30.47
2011	70.71	39.16	31.55
2012	71.65	39.37	32.28
2013	72.07	40.25	31.82
2014	72.53	40.34	32.19
2015	71.46	40.42	31.04
2016	71.95	40.66	31.29
2017	69.88	39.08	30.8
2018	70.61	39.69	30.92
2019	70.02	39.38	30.65

Pace has picked up while the ratios have been steady. It's possible that the spread-offense wave already passed over the college football game and more recently penetrated the NFL.

BET you shall not pass

Here's a betting system that deals with play selection:

> In an FBS college football game
>
> Where one team is favored by a touchdown or more AND
>
> The favorite won their last game AND
>
> The favorite threw 15 or fewer passes in their last game
>
> **BET** the favorite's point spread.

Run-heavy teams are rare these days, and it's especially hard for teams to prepare against feisty option teams like the service academies. This system seems to be getting stronger by the year: Seven straight years of wins and a salty 19–3 in 2019 (129 wins and 88 losses overall; 59.4 percent and a Z-score of 2.58).

Turnovers

It is common knowledge that turnover margin has a close correlation with margin of victory. If you turn the ball over more than your opponent, you will lose way more often than you win.

But as important as turnovers are when we look backwards, they're nearly impossible to use as a tool when we look forward. The correlation between a team's turnover stats from one year to the next is small, bordering on insignificant. And if bettors can't accurately predict a factor in a game, it's hard to put it to use in a sports bet.

Looking backward at turnovers can still be informative though, and here's an example. By making a chart that shows home team net turnovers and incremental points per net turnover, we reveal that with 0 net turnovers, the home team scores about 2½ points more.

From there, the first turnover is worth about 6 points off the home field advantage, and then there's a disparity. The home college football team seems to contain the damage of a negative turnover slate, losing only 4½ and 3 points for the 2nd and 3rd negative net turnover.

But go the other way and you find that if the home team gets the turnovers, they net 7 points and 4½ points. It's all summed up in Table 11-8.

TABLE 11-8

Turnovers and Scoring

Home Turnover Differential	Avg Home Margin	Margin Points per Net Turnover
–8	21.33	–2.67
–7	38.67	–5.52
–6	25	–4.17
–5	25.06	–5.01
–4	22.13	–5.53
–3	19.05	–6.35
–2	14.68	–7.34
–1	8.24	–8.24
0	2.47	
1	–4.45	–4.45
2	–11.41	–5.71
3	–16.19	–5.40
4	–19.01	–4.75
5	–22.59	–4.52
6	–24.65	–4.11
7	–32.86	–4.69
8	–12.5	–1.56
Average Final Margin Points per Net Turnover	–5.001	–1.56

TIP

Studies have been done to try to predict when turnovers occur, and while there's not much to go on, one lesson that comes from college football is that defense defines turnovers, not offense.

First, predicting how much your team will give the ball away based on quarterback experience, offensive style, or backward-looking statistics is a lost cause. Feeding these variables into a super computer reveals nothing.

On the other hand, Football Outsiders has done some work that says the better and more efficient a defense is can be predictive of future turnovers. Their stats can be arcane, but the underlying approach is that fewer points per drive is better (duh), and it's even better if it's accomplished against good teams (double-duh).

Betting the Post Season

Conference championship games have been a source of controversy in the playoff era because there have been instances where having an early loss and therefore avoiding a tough conference championship game potentially works to a team's advantage when it comes to qualifying for the playoff.

At least every major conference is now holding a championship game, which wasn't always the case. In essence, the playoff hunt has become a matter of winning your conference and not being in the weakest of the five conferences.

What follows are some interesting topics around betting postseason college football games.

Revenge is overrated

Conference championships have increased the frequency of teams facing off for a second time in a single season, something that almost never happened in the past. This phenomenon raises the question: Does this unusual scenario present any obvious psychological advantage for one team or the other? The conventional wisdom says "It's hard to beat a team twice in the same season." That and $4.50 will buy you a cheese Danish at Starbucks.

The truth about rematches is that there's not a lot of data to draw conclusions. In the 50 or so games I looked at (mostly conferences and a few bowls), the straight-up and spread results don't show any systematic advantage for or against the team seeking vengeance.

TIP

The one glimmer of interesting data in in-season revenge games is that the total result in the second game matches that of the first game about 60 percent of the time. If the first game was an under, bet the under in the second game. If the first game went over, bet the over in the rematch. But the evidence is flimsy at best. In a few years, there may be enough historical data on rematches to create a bettable system.

Postseason motivation

Nothing stings a team worse than just missing the four-team playoff. And before the playoff there was the BCS and the big post-New Year's Bowls. There's no tried-and-true setup that can quantify motivation, but there's a few markers you can watch for:

» Did a team get upset in their conference championship game? Or if they were underdogs, did they hang tough in the game only to lose late, or lose in overtime?

» Did a team have their path to a big-time bowl cut off by a loss to an inferior opponent?

» Did a team with hopes of the playoff end up in a New Years week bowl?

» Did a team with hopes of a New Year's week bowl end up in a lower-tier bowl? A team who had their sights on the Sugar Bowl isn't going to be motivated to win a game in the Sweet 'N Low Bowl.

» On the other side of the coin, bet on teams who see the bowl game — regardless of tier — as a chance at redemption after a disappointing season.

» What's the coaching situation? It can be hard to predict the impact of lame-duck coaches with new jobs waiting for them after the game. One theory says bet against the team if it's a lateral move, but bet on the team if the coach is making a big move up in class. Sports betting analyst Kenny White (@KWhiteyVegas) has advised to bet on any one-last-hurrah situations where the coach is retiring.

» Then there are coaches still on the hotseat during bowl season. Sometimes a bowl win can tip the balance for a coach that means the difference between being on the sidelines next year versus being in a breadline next year. If that coach is well liked, look for his players to show up and outperform.

» Finally, brush up on your geography. When bowls draft teams, they do so looking to fill the stadium up, so it's often the case that one of the participating teams plays their home games much closer to the bowl site than the other team. Remember, college football is a sport driven by emotion, and noisy crowds can fire teams up.

Saving yourself

One other note is the recent trend for draft-eligible seniors to sit out from their team's bowl game, especially if there's no championship at stake. The rationale is simple: If a player knows he's going to the NFL, a final bowl game is not a good enough reason to risk a major injury. It used to be something only prima donna players would dare do, but dozens of players do it every year now, including some prominent talent.

Examples of teams losing top talent in the last game of the year abound. In 2018, West Virginia starting quarterback Will Grier sat out the Camping World Bowl along with fellow prospect Yodny Cajuste, and the result was the 16-point favorite Mountaineers getting crushed by Syracuse. Michigan's Rashan Gary and teammate Karan Higdon sat out the Peach Bowl, and the favored Wolverines got a 4 touchdown tune-up by Florida.

REMEMBER

Before you bet on a bowl game, you'll want to look deeper than the injury list. Make sure you understand who the healthy scratches are and how well equipped the coach is to replace them, or to build a scheme without them. Timing is also important. If a player becomes unavailable at the last minute, it's going to be more disruptive than it would be for a team that has multiple weeks to prepare.

More College Football Systems

College football is subject to similar rhythms and patterns as professional football, and you won't have to look very hard to find systems that pay. I've compiled some of my favorites that have given consistent performance over the last several seasons.

BET under the home back to back

The college football season is a grind, and by the time October rolls around, teams value long stretches at home. Consider this setup:

> In a college football FBS regular season
>
> Where the game is being played in week 7 or later AND
>
> The home team was home in their last game AND
>
> The away team was home in their last game AND
>
> The home team lost their lost game AND
>
> Both teams are operating on less than a week of rest AND
>
> The home team's last game total went under by at least 5 points
>
> **BET** under the game total.

Sure, it's a little busy, but it makes sense to me. October is the dog days of college football, where you're banged up and tired, but you've got miles to go before you sleep. From that starting point, we have a team leaving the friendly confines of their home campus while the home team has been chilling at home for a week or two. In the last decade, this is a system that's gone 24 over and 70 under (74 percent wins on the under, for a Z-score of 4.64). This system is especially ripe in October.

BET far to go

Thursday game systems don't offer a big sample size, but even with limited data, there are some clear trends forming. For starters, it appears that four days of rest has a severe equalizing effect on teams with disparate talent. Look at this setup:

> For FBS regular season games
>
> Where the game is played on a Thursday AND
>
> Both teams are on exactly 4 days of rest
>
> **BET** on the underdog's point spread.

Simple setup, and the result is 70–45 ATS (61 percent, Z-score is a middling 2.26). Hey, it's Thursday night; what else have you got to do?

BET over the hype

This is an example of letting the public's imagination get out ahead of itself and taking advantage by going the opposite way. Check out this setup:

> In a college football FBS game
>
> Where one team scored 10 points or fewer in their previous game AND
>
> That same team scored 7 points or fewer the game before that AND
>
> That same team scored 6 points or fewer the game before that
>
> **BET** over the total.

Yes, it looks dreary attempting to bet over when a team's offense has shown itself to be so pathetic, but the over is 25–8 in these situations. That's a respectable Z-score of 2.79. I don't offer it as a surefire path to victory lane and riches; it's more about the underlying lesson that following the public is not profitable in the long run.

REMEMBER

The squarest bettors will go by their impressions of two teams and do zero research before placing a bet. The next class of slightly less square but still quite rectangular bettors will spend a few seconds looking at recent history: How did they do last week? Who did they beat or lose to? How many points did they score? With that small spoonful of information, they will draw their conclusion and place their bets. You can imagine someone looking at our team in this scenario with their eyes bulging as they think, "This team can't score at all. How in the world will the game possibly go over?"

But so many people see the same information and stop there, that the under will inevitably get lots of attention bet, depressing the total so much that a simple reversion to the mean by the team will mean an easy over.

Having said that . . .

BET kick 'em when they're down

Here's a situation involving a sequence of low scores, where it appears that the market isn't quite digesting how bad a team is. The setup:

In a College Football FBS game

The home team's previous game was away from home AND

The home team scored 10 points or less in their previous game AND

The home team scored 9 points or less two games ago AND

The road team is a single-digit favorite or an underdog, or the game is a pick'em

BET the away team's point spread.

This just might be a case where bettors are looking for a bounce back at home, but none is forthcoming. This one has a record of 137–81 going back 4 decades (Z-score of 3.73) and has only shown 5 losing seasons out of 40.

BET with the hype just this once

Now we find another situation where we're looking at a team's recent performance. This time, however, we're looking for teams on an offensive roll:

In a college football FBS game

Where the home team scored 50 or more points in their last game AND

The home team scored 40 or more points two games ago AND

The home team scored 40 or more points three games ago AND

The home team is favored by 20 or more points

BET on the home team's point spread AND/OR

BET the home team as a leg to a teaser or parlay.

It seems impossible that this team would have escaped the notice of the betting public, and yet, since 2008, this system is 38–13 (nearly 75 percent, Z-score of 3.36). The most effective point spreads for this approach over the long run has been to find point spreads where the home team is favored in the 20s, but in the last ten years, it's barely mattered.

What's going on here? I have two theories:

>> The betting public thinks football is football and therefore they apply NFL heuristics to college football. College games mean higher scores and bigger blowouts. A spread in the 20s in the NFL are as rare as a fat coyote, so there is natural square gravitation toward vicenarian underdogs.

>> Teams play to impress the playoff committee now. Where winning margins have almost no impact on the NFL postseason, style points matter in getting picked for a more lucrative bowl game, or for the playoff itself. So college coaches have more of an excuse to run up the score when they badly outmatch an opponent.

BET over the early season mismatch

Here's one for good measure that takes advantage of mismatches we see in non-conference play in the first few weeks of the season. When the favorite team's point spread is a huge portion of the total, the oddsmakers are telling you they aren't expecting much from the underdog:

In a college football game where the favorite is an FBS team

Where it's week 1, 2, or 3 of the regular season AND

The game total is 55 points or less AND

The spread is at least 60 percent of the total (ignoring the sign)

BET over the game total!

An example might help here. On September 7, 2019, the Wisconsin Badgers played host to the Central Michigan Chippewas for an early season warm-up. The point spread was a not-very-welcoming −35 and the total was 53.

REMEMBER

The oddsmaker implies a certain final score when he offers a spread and total on a game in any sport. To see for yourself, first throw away the minus sign and assign the point spread points to the favorite. Then assign equal points to each team until the total score equals the oddsmaker's total. For the Wisconsin/CMU game, give Wisconsin 35 and then split the remaining 18 points (since 35 + 18 = 53) evenly to make 44−9. That final score hits both the point spread and total exactly. While the final game score isn't likely to land there exactly, that's the oddsmaker's projection of the most likely result among many possibilities.

In this particular day, Wisconsin won 61−0. The betting public regularly underestimates the total points scored in these games, either by assuming the favorite will let off the gas, or perhaps figuring there's no way the little schools will score at all. But in ten years of history, games fitting these conditions are 91−47 in favor of the over (65.9 percent, Z-score of 3.66). This system works pretty well for totals above 55 too. But 55 has shown consistent winning results over the last decade, including an 8−2 run in 2019.

Chapter **12**

Betting to Win on NBA Basketball

No sport has change in the last several years more than the NBA, and the ripple effects can be felt throughout the betting markets. Pro hoops has undergone a genuine offensive revolution, and it's changed how rosters are constructed, how coaches manage lineups, and most of all, what tactics are used by the teams on the court. Gone are the days of relying on a Shaquille O'Neal or an Hakeem Olajuwon as targets in the paint for layups and five-foot jumpers. Gone are the days when the 3-point shot was best left to the long-range specialists.

Thanks to analytics, or maybe thanks to Steph Curry, who showed the rest of us the way, teams began realizing in the mid–2010s that the expected value of a hard-to-make, contested 2-point jump shot was lower than an inevitably less-contested 3-pointer. And when teams started putting a premium on 3s over 2s, the results were clear: They scored a lot more points.

And that trend has spread like a virus. Three-point attempts in the 2018–2019 season were more than double what they were in the 2011–2012 season. And the mid-range jump shot is slowly but surely going the way of the dodo bird, having fallen from 31 percent of the league's total attempts to less than 15 percent last season.

One side effect of this shift of focus is more transition basketball, played at a faster pace. The fastest run-and-gun team in the league is getting at least 10 more possessions per game than the fastest teams of the mid-2000s.

Betting the Offensive Explosion

Okay, what does more scoring have to do with betting on the NBA? Betting markets can't see the future. Oddsmakers and bettors can only speculate about how scoring patterns will change over time, whether they are driven by the never-ending evolution of strategy and gameplay, or from rules changes. Anyone who can see the future a little more clearly than the average bettor can turn that clarity to their advantage. For example, if you were paying close attention, you would have noticed the quantum leap in NBA pace and 3-point attempts over the last few years, and you just might have turned that into cash money.

Table 12-1 demonstrates that the betting markets continually raising the totals on the highest scoring games but the overs kept piling up. In other words, the game had evolved, but the betting markets had not.

TABLE 12-1   **NBA Regular Season Totals of 225 or Higher**

Season	Average Total (All Games)	Over (Total>225)	Under (Total>225)	Over%
2015–16	204.8	14	6	70%
2016–17	210.6	54	37	59.1%
2017–18	212.4	57	38	60%
2018–19	221.8	257	218	54.1%
TOTAL		382	299	56.1%

The oddsmakers' statistical models (and the betting public's mental models) lagged behind the game being played on the court. Blind betting the over in high-total games would have given you 346 wins and 278 losses if you had started on day 1 of the 2016–2017 season. Many gamblers would kill for a 55 percent winning percentage, especially one where the setup is so easy to identify.

WARNING

Good times never last, do they? The market has just about evened out for these high total games. In the first half of the 2019–2020 season, games totaled 225 or higher are down to about 53 percent overs, barely keeping your head above water. But it looks like there's still value in extreme totals: Games with a 230 total or higher have hit nearly 60 percent overs so far this season.

And the new offense-dominated game has had other corollary effects as well, like the number of big blowouts. The 2018–2019 season saw a record 56 regular season games where a team won by 30 points or more. Faster-paced games means more possessions, so the better teams will pull that much farther away from their opponent in the span of 48 minutes. If it's a lasting trend, it begs the question: Do today's spreads account for the possibility of bigger game margins?

There's good evidence that they don't. Table 12-2 lists the spread record for regular season home favorites of 12 points or more.

TABLE 12-2

Records of Home Favorites of 12 Points or More

Period	Spread Win	Spread Loss	Win%
2014–2018	274	206	57.1%
2009–2013	179	207	46.4%

This system (it's so simple that I'm not sure it deserves the "system" moniker) has been an absolute hammer of late, going a ridiculous 60–26 against the spread in the 2018–2019 season (that's 69.8 percent, for a Z-score of 3.38).

WARNING

Although I find the system I described above eye popping, and I think there is a rationale for it working after 2013 and not before, some aspects of it do indeed give me a case of the heebie jeebies. For starters, 12-point favorites is an arbitrary break point. Why would a system like this be effective for a team laying 12 points but not a team laying 11 or 10 points? I could understand if it worked at 10 points but not at 9, because athletes, coaches, and bettors likely have a minor psychological breakpoint around double-digit wins. But this system doesn't merely flatten out at –11½ and smaller favorite lines; it completely reverses polarity, going 121–170 against the spread over the same time period for small double-digit favorites. When I see big flip-flops like that, it makes me think my "system" is an illusion. Nevertheless, so far in the 2019–2020 season, it's off to a roaring 27–14 start.

One and a Half Curses

Speaking of possible illusions that I will probably bet on anyway, the above system reminds me of the infamous curse of being favored by 1½ points in the NBA.

If you profile every point spread over the last ten years, you'll find the betting results for each spread hover very close to 50 percent in terms of ATS wins and losses, with a single statistical outlier: 1½ points. When home teams open up as 1½ point favorites, they not only lose against the spread at a surprising rate, but they lose outright as well.

Normally, you'd expect a team's straight-up winning percentage to increase roughly increase in proportion with the point spread. A 10-point favorite wins 85 percent of the time; a 5-point favorite wins 61 percent of the time; and a 2-point favorite wins about 54 percent of the time. But for some reason, the bottom falls out of home 1½-point favorites: They lose more often than they win! And it's not even close, winning straight up a miserable 43 percent of the time. Not surprisingly, betting against them has been a huge point spread winner. In fact, if you bet on road underdogs getting exactly a point and a half over the last decade, your bets would have gone 169–108 (61 percent for a Z-score of 3.6).

Every instinct in my body tells me this is a phantom trend, an illusion, the simple by-product of randomness. If you look at ATS results across 40 different home point spreads, of course there will be an outlier or two. But still, I wonder if perhaps there's a weakness in the most common NBA models used by oddsmakers that results in a 1½-point spread for inferior home teams. Or maybe there's something off with their calculation of home-court advantage. This so-called system works across every month of the regular season, in high total games and low, with teams that are well rested or not. And early into the 2019–2020 season, it's a frosty 11–2 against the spread.

And yet it doesn't work in the playoffs. It doesn't work for −1½ road favorites. And it doesn't work for home 1- or 2-point favorites. That tells me it's just got to be bunk.

WARNING

Even if it's true that this is some magic point spread, it doesn't mean it will be easy to profit from it. This strange record is based on the NBA opening line, which often gets pounced on by sharp players. So you'll have to be on your toes if you want to get in on the anti-point-and-a-half "miracle" system, because the longer you wait, the greater the chance the odds will change. And second, there is no single "official" set of odds. This isn't the stock market after all. What appears as a 1½-point favorite at one book could easily be a 2-point favorite at others.

The NBA Betting Market

The NBA's share of Americans' betting dollar has been on the rise, and in the last several years, basketball has grown at a faster pace than football. Some say it's related to the offensive explosion; others say it's related to the NBA's new friendly relationship with sports books around the world.

To give you an idea of the size, Nevada casinos took in over $320 million in NBA playoff bets in June 2018 alone, followed closely by New Jersey's $270 million. About 20 percent of that total was bet on the 7 games of the NBA Final. In case you're wondering if the sports books have an interest in which teams advance in the playoffs, how far each best-of-7 series goes, and how closely matched the teams are, the prior year's Warriors-Cavaliers final that Golden State won 4 games to 1 generated a little over half the sports book handle.

Preseason betting

What? You didn't realize the NBA played preseason games? Alas it's true. If you've been wondering what that missing element in your life is, it's obviously the two weeks leading up to the NBA's regular season tip-off in late October.

Preseason schedules get announced in the summer, and most teams schedule five games, some home and some away. But teams also mix in gimmick games, like an exhibition in a non-NBA city, or a game against a foreign professional team.

WARNING

Sure, the United States and Canada are the basketball capitals of the universe. But don't be fooled; it's not a given that an NBA squad will wipe the floor with a team in the top division from Spain or Israel. The foreign team is likely to hold the edge in motivation, and the NBA team's starters are there to work out kinks and then head to the bench. You've been waiting for months for the NBA to start back up again, and lo and behold, there's a spread listed on that Bucks vs. Adelaide 36ers game. Do yourself a favor and pass on it.

There are lessons to be gleaned from the preseason that might help you in early season betting. With only five games on the docket, the preseason isn't going to tell you who's going to win the championship, but if you pay close attention, you can track offensive style, shot selection, and especially pace. In an October 2019 article, Zach Kram of *The Ringer* pointed out that the preseason's 3-point shot attempt rate and pace numbers have historically been excellent predictors of the regular season.

TIP

To be certain, the oddsmakers are paying close attention to the NBA preseason, but if you monitor the preseason stats and roster moves, you'll be a step ahead of most square NBA bettors, firmly affixed to their image of the previous season. Early season NBA betting is rife with opportunities, and the betting public is like the proverbial general who's always preparing to win the last war rather than the next war. Put your preseason lessons to work for you in October and November before the rest of the betting public catches up. Here are some themes you can focus on in the preseason:

>> For teams where lineups are largely unchanged, are there improvements in offensive or defensive efficiency?

>> For teams who've acquired a big name in free agency, is he contributing to an overall improvement in team efficiency? Or is he just displacing shots from teammates?

>> For teams with marquee rookies, how much time are they getting? NBA.com has an excellent sortable statistics where you can track which teams are relying on rookie minutes over veteran minutes.

>> For teams with new coaches, have they made wholesale changes to the scheme compared to last year? Look at pace and shot selection.

Preseason betting is available at nearly every sports betting venue, online or brick-and-mortar. With the higher variability, bookmakers keep betting limits lower, and naturally, that means less betting volume. As you know by now, less liquidity in the betting market means lines don't adjust as quickly (or as correctly) as they will in the regular season.

TIP

Unlike the NFL preseason, I've never found much systematic value in any kind of technical analysis of NBA preseason. Where I have seen some ability to profit during preseason is with some basic fundamental analysis in the form of monitoring injury reports, listening to coaches' statements, team press releases, and player interviews. Simply knowing a player's status, whether he's going to be minute-limited on the night, or the team's approach to playing time, I've been able to pounce on a few in-game opportunities per preseason. If a team jumps out to a 15-point lead midway through the 2nd quarter, but you know the plan is to sit the veteran with the gimpy ankle who has accounted for 40 percent of the team's points, there's a good chance to find a bargain by live-wagering the opposition. There's not an easy formula for this approach, but if you're a fan of the game and you're going to be monitoring the action anyway, it's not a bad idea to be ready when a narrative unfolds early in the game that you know is illusory.

Postseason betting

Starting in March, teams start mathematically clinching playoff births, and then in mid-April, the regular season ends and the top 8 teams from each conference go to the NBA Playoffs, comprised of a seeded fixed-bracket tournament where the #1 seed plays the #8 seed; the #2 plays the #7 and so on. The NBA uses the 2-2-1-1-1 home/away format (as in Team A hosts games 1, 2, 5, and 7, and Team B hosts the others), although the NBA has been known to experiment with that structure. Home-court advantage goes to the team with the better record, and historically, the team with home-court advantage has won about three-quarters of playoff series. The playoffs consist of 15 series, and the NBA Finals wrap up in mid-June.

Defenses clamp down in the postseason. While home offenses tend to score about the same as they do in the regular season, the stats show it's harder for road teams to match their normal output. As a result, overall scoring is usually a little lower in the NBA playoffs. Table 12-3 provides a few years of data.

TABLE 12-3 **Regular Season versus Postseason Scoring**

Year	Total Points/Game — Regular Season	Total Points/Game — Playoffs
2014–2015	205	199
2015–2016	211	212
2016–2017	212	208
2017–2018	222	215

Fans and square bettors get obsessed by a team' seeding in the postseason, which is determined by their full body of work from the regular season. But sharp bettors focus in on how teams are playing the weeks and months leading up to the playoffs.

Table 12-4 shows the spread and total performance of teams by round and seed for the last decade.

TABLE 12-4 **Spread and Total Performance by Round and Seed**

	Seed Pairing	Against the Spread Wins and Losses	Over and Under
First Round	1 vs 8	52-52	46-57
	2 vs 7	61-41	47-55
	3 vs 6	63-53	54-62
	4 vs 5	50-63	52-60
Second Round	1 vs 4	21-17	19-18
	1 vs 5	31-24	30-24
	2 vs 3	49-41	49-39
	2 vs 6	8-8	7-9
	3 vs 7	4-0	4-0
	4 vs 8	7-7	8-6
Conference Championship	1 vs 2	25-35	29-30
	1 vs 3	12-12	12-12
	2 vs 4	8-12	9-11
	2 vs 5	3-1	2-1
	3 vs 4	3-2	3-2

BET on #2 Live Crew

If you're looking for a blind betting strategy in the NBA playoffs, look no further than the #2 seed.

> In an NBA playoff game in rounds 1 through 3
>
> Where #2 conference seed is at home OR
>
> The #2 conference seed is a road favorite
>
> **BET** on the #2 seed's point spread.

This might be the simplest system in the book, and the only explanation I can give is that at playoff time, square gamblers flock to the marquee teams. So while the #1 seeds get all the attention, the #2 seeds are taking care of business. They went 12–8 in the 2018–2019 season (when the #2 seeds were the Nuggets and the future-champion Raptors), and are now 132–82 over the last ten years (61.7 percent for a Z-score of 3.35). Many of these wins are the #2 seed beating the #7 seed in the first round, but there's a healthy dose of winners in round 2 and round 3 as well, and there are even circumstances where it works if the #2 seed is playing on the road.

This system will dry up one day, perhaps the minute this book hits the shelves, but it's been churning out postseason winners since the Y2k bug was a concern for your IT guy. Hopefully it still has legs when you read this.

Common NBA Bets

NBA betting looks a lot like NFL betting in that bettors can bet on sides via moneylines and point spreads, and they can bet on totals. In fact, odds notation in the NBA is identical to football odds.

Sides

Betting on a point spread in the NBA means placing a –110 (or close to that) bet and either getting extra points against the final game margin (if you bet an underdog) or losing points against the game margin (if you bet the favorite). Point spreads are denominated in half points, but unlike the NFL, which has the possibility of tie games, there are no NBA point spreads of exactly ½ points.

NBA games typically open for betting the night before or the morning of the game. Spread movement can seem quite dramatic if you're used to football point spreads, with the line moving as much as 4 or 5 points prior to tip-off.

While there aren't major key point spread numbers in the NBA, the structure of the game has an impact on how final game margins are distributed. As a basketball fan, of course, you know that in a non-blowout, the trailing team will be fouling the leading team. The hope is to quickly trade possessions where the team on top gets something less than 2 points from imperfect free-throw shooting, and the team trying to catch up gets 2 or 3 points at a time.

This game plan has a peculiar impact on final margins: a 1-point victory is as rare as a 17-point victory. Again, if you're merely 1 point down, you'll continue to send the opposition to the line. As a result, the NBA margins of the last decade look like what's shown in Table 12-5.

TABLE 12-5

NBA Margins of Victory

Margin of Victory	Number of Games	Percentage of Total
1 point	557	4.1%
2 points	715	5.3%
3 points	756	5.6%
4 points	762	5.6%
5 points	919	6.8%
6 points	841	6.2%
7 points	946	7%
8 points	865	6.3%
9 points	759	5.5%
10 points	678	5%
>10 points	5770	42%

As the final margin increases past 10 points, the number of games gets smaller as you might suspect. Only 13 percent of NBA point spreads extend past 10 points, even though 42 percent of game margins land beyond 10 points. That's a testament to the runaway nature of basketball games. When you put your opponent on the free throw line at the end of the game, if he converts his freebies and you don't convert your chances, a closely contested game for 46.5 minutes can look like a blowout victory.

If you want to know how efficient the side market is, consider that 40 percent of NBA regular season games end on a final score that's within a single possession of flipping the point spread result. Fully 70 percent of games end within two possessions of the spread.

The top of the key

Football teams score in blocks of 3, 6, 1, and occasionally, 2 points, which makes certain scores and margins of victory more likely than others that you'll need to consider when you bet spreads or totals. You might think that's not the case with basketball because points get scored in more granular packets of 2s, 3s, and 1s. It turns out there is a weak but well understood inflection point in basketball games at 7 points. Seven is a popular margin because, so the theory goes at least, when the margin is three possessions, the trailing team is more likely to accept its fate, stop fouling, and let the winner dribble out the clock.

TIP

Key numbers are critically important when betting on football games. And they're basically forgotten in basketball. But the 7-point inflection point is worth paying attention to if you're considering betting a team and the spread moves from −6.5 to −7, or worse, from −7 to −7.5.

NBA moneyline

If you want to bet on a team without the leveling effects of a spread, you can do so with a standard moneyline bet. NBA moneylines work like any other moneyline: Winning margin is unimportant as long as you bet on the winning side.

NBA moneylines, like all moneylines, correspond roughly to the point spread. Table 12-6 shows point spreads and their correlated moneylines.

Bookmakers vary moneylines a surprising amount, and I always urge you to shop around to find the very best odds if you've settled on an NBA pick. Every moneyline corresponds to a break-even win rate that you have to meet or exceed if you expect to make money betting. Shopping around and betting on an underdog with a +195 moneyline instead of a +191 moneyline shaves a few whiskers off your break-even win rate, and repeating that discipline over hundreds and thousands of bets can mean the difference between winning and losing.

REMEMBER

It's natural for the distance between the favorite moneyline and the underdog moneyline to increase along with the magnitude of the mismatch. That doesn't necessarily mean the bookmaker is charging you more in vigorish than a pick'em game, where each side is a −110 bet.

TABLE 12-6 Point Spreads and Moneylines

Favorite Spread	Favorite ML	Underdog Spread	Underdog ML
–11.5	–750	+11.5	+525
–11	–700	+11	+500
–10.5	–620	+10.5	+480
–10	–550	+10	+430
–9.5	–500	+9.5	+410
–9	–450	+9	+380
–8.5	–400	+8.5	+330
–8	–350	+8	+290
–7.5	–310	+7.5	+260
–7	–290	+6	+245
–6.5	–270	+6.5	+230
–6	–240	+6	+205
–5.5	–220	+5.5	+190
–5	–205	+5	+175
–4.5	–190	+4.5	+165
–4	–180	+4	+155
–3.5	–170	+3.5	+145
–3	–150	+3	+130
–2.5	–140	+2.5	+120
–2	–130	+2	+115
–1.5	–122	+1.5	+110
–1	–116	+1	+106
–.5	–112	+.5	+100
Pick'em	–110		

Totals

NBA totals are played just like you would expect. Like point spreads, they are denominated in half points. Combine the scores at the end of the game, and if the total is more than your under bet, you win. If it's less than your over bet, you win. Scoring done in overtime periods counts like any other point scored in the game.

TIP

If you're wondering whether overtime affects teams, as a rule of thumb, I hesitate before betting on a team that won in overtime in their previous game. To be specific, I follow this setup:

> In a regular season NBA game
>
> The game is being played in October, November, or December AND
>
> The home team has won their last game in overtime AND
>
> The home team is favored by 3 or less, or is an underdog
>
> **BET** the point spread of the road team.

This humble little system comes up once or twice a month, and over 20 years has gone 64.7 percent against the spread (55–30, with a Z-score of 2.6). It's not going to make you rich, but it's a good one to keep in your pocket.

Characterizing NBA totals bets isn't easy in this day and age as the offensive production keeps climbing higher and higher. If you just look at the 2018–2019 season and the first half of the 2019–2020 season, totals average about 220.5, with 90 percent of games falling between 209 and 230.

Early season herding

A research team led by Dr. Richard A. Borghesi concluded that the early season NBA totals market takes a few weeks to get its bearings. Specifically, the researchers concluded that there's betting value available by simply following the herd on downward-trending totals. In the first two weeks of the season, betting under any total that has dropped at least a half point from the opening number yielded nearly 57 percent wins in the 20 years of data they looked at.

That paper was written in 2007, and I mention it here for a few reasons:

> » It's a good reminder that betting markets behave differently over the course of the season. Oddsmakers and bettors aren't unchanging robots. Opportunities may appear in one part of the season that are unavailable in other parts of the season, particularly for marathon sports like baseball and basketball.

>> In spite of my low expectations, a quick check of the last few seasons showed that this approach still yields profits. In the 2019–2020 season, betting these unders won 24 times and lost 16 times.

Quarters and halves

NBA offers pregame betting on the 1st quarter and 1st half spreads and totals, and at halftime you can make bets on the 3rd quarter and the 2nd half. Some bookmakers will allow you to bet each of the quarters ahead of the game too. Table 12-7 lists what the stats look like across the quarters.

TABLE 12-7 ### NBA Quarter Stats

Quarter by Quarter	Average Total Points	Cumulative Home Margin	Cumulative Favorite Margin
1st Quarter	55.85	.7	1.93
2nd Quarter	56.12	1.66	3.71
3rd Quarter	55.3	2.1	5.12
4th Quarter	54.22	2.7	6.26

Handicapping factors in NBA

There are only a few fundamentals that I track in today's NBA of high-powered offenses, but you could do worse than spend your time getting to know the factors in the following sections.

Pace

In the old days, you might have looked at point per game or point allowed per game, but today, you want to measure offenses first and foremost by *pace*. Pace is a metric that shows the average number of possessions a team gets per game, so pace is simply how many possessions a team gets in a game, but its true significance is shorthand for a team's offensive style. The betting market follows pace values carefully: The higher the pace, the more chances a team gets at scoring, and vice versa. In the 2019–2020 season, the Milwaukee Bucks in the East and the Houston Rockets in the West are the epitome of the modern 48-minutes-of-action, offensive-focused game, with over 105 possessions per game on average. On the other end are the (relatively) methodical Denver Nuggets and Sacramento Kings, who have a pace number in the upper 90s.

Efficiency measures

Efficiency measures the number of points relative to pace. Specifically, offensive efficiency projects the points scored per 100 possessions. Efficiency is an elegant amalgam of turnovers, rebounds, and field goal and free throw shooting percentages mixed together into a single number that represents the offensive expectation per trip down the floor.

From offensive efficiency, it's a simple hop, skip, and jump to projecting the final score of a game by predicting the total number of possessions per game and adjusting the efficiency accordingly. For example, if the Dallas Mavericks' offensive efficiency is 113 and they get 100 possessions in a game, that would lead you to believe they'll score 113 points. If you project they'll get 105 points per game, you just multiply 113×1.05 and you get 119 points.

Of course, there's more to it than just offensive efficiency. Team defensive efficiency does exactly what you'd expect, averaging out a team's opponent's points scored per possession. The question is this: If Team A's offensive efficiency is 113 and their opponent's defensive efficiency is 97, which one prevails?

Rest days

Unlike Major League Baseball, NBA teams in the regular season play single-game series, and over half the time they play with a single day's rest in between games. Table 12-8 gives the breakdown for teams divided between home games and away situations.

TABLE 12-8   **Rest Days Home and Away**

Days of Rest	As Home Team	Home PPG	As Away Team	Away PPG
0	11.5%	109.3	20.3%	106.5
1	64.2%	110.2	57.4%	108
2	18.3%	110.2	18.1%	108.2
3	4%	111.1	2.7%	106.7
4+	2%	112.1	1.5%	111.9

The idea here is to show you the proportion of games played by rest days. First, notice that in most cases, teams are playing after a single off day, whether home or away. Second, I find it interesting that the NBA is willing to schedule more back-to-back road games than back-to-back home games. The NBA has gotten feedback from teams to reduce the back-to-back frequency on the regular season schedule, and the NBA has responded, so there are fewer than ever on the schedule in the 2019–2020 season.

In terms of points scored, remember that because the offensive landscape is changing so rapidly, these numbers are directional more than absolute. Road teams playing on no rest average a point and a half less than they would with a day or two of rest.

TIP

As much hype as the dreaded back-to-back NBA games get, the oddsmakers appear to account for any performance changes. I was unable to find any profitable system that targets back-to-back situations for either spread bets or total bets. I have seen theories that teams in an early season back-to-back is a good spread bet because oddsmakers tilt the spread toward bettors who tend to be overly sensitive to back-to-back setups. But the numbers I've seen aren't convincing.

Having said that (I tend to use that phrase a lot) . . .

There is some evidence that the same bettor overreaction on back-to-back games has made the over an attractive betting target. Betting over a high total (225 or more) on a road team on no rest has resulted in a 61 percent win rate in the last five years. I am skeptical about whether that result has anything to do with the back-to-back and is simply an artifact of the aforementioned scoring glut.

Travel

Opinions abound on the impact of travel on an NBA team. The NBA schedulers have teams hopping around the country, with the most common home and road stretches being one and two games. The NBA teams do have rare longer home stretches, but the schedulers do their best to break up long road stretches with single home games.

The NBA has teams crisscrossing four of the continent's time zones, and most experts agree that travel throws off your routine and affects sleep, which results in higher stress hormone levels and lower testosterone levels, and goodness knows those guys need their testosterone. Ultimately, that plays out on the basketball court with lower mental acuity, slower reaction times, and worse muscle performance. The question for bettors is this: Does travel create an angle worth betting on?

Table 12-9 give you some basic stats for teams crossing two time zones.

This table is showing you how team performance varies when they play away games within their time zone and two time zones over. The main theme is less about the absolute point totals and more about the way there's more scoring variation when you cross two time zones.

TABLE 12-9 **Points per Game for Traveling Teams**

Month	Eastern Teams Playing in the East (ppg)	Eastern Teams Playing in the West (ppg)	Western Teams Playing in the West (ppg)	Western Teams Playing in the East (ppg)
October	215.3	217.9	231.2	218.5
November	216.4	214.5	217.1	218.8
December	214.2	211.7	229.3	209.9
January	214.2	219	224.8	221.8
February	219	219.4	230.1	223.4
March	215.7	219.4	217.4	223.4
April	216.5	223.3	218	232

WARNING

I'm mixing data sets in my tables. This table shows points scored across the 2017–2018 and 2018–2019 seasons. I wanted to reflect the growing point production in the league, but I wanted enough data to get a good broad sample of teams.

BET west bound and down

In spite of the scoring explosion in the NBA, there's a notable travel-based system worth mentioning. Here's the setup:

> For a game played in the NBA regular season
>
> The road team is an Eastern time zone team AND
>
> The road team is playing at least their second game away from home AND
>
> The home team is a Pacific time zone team
>
> **BET** under the total.

Starting with the the pivotal 2014 season, this system has gone under 163 times and over 108 times. That's a little over 60 percent with a solid Z-score of 3.3. There's no doubt in my mind this system could be refined further.

Home-court advantage

Professional basketball teams get better results in their own barn, just like you'd expect. Factors include fan support (or lack of fan hostility on the road), the comforts of and routine of home, and, for the conspiracy theorists, there's a widely accepted assertion that the zebras give home teams the benefit of the doubt when it comes to toss-up foul calls. And there's even some data to back it up: Home teams get 5 percent fewer foul calls than road teams.

You could certainly ascribe some unique advantages to certain NBA teams. The nightlife of New York and New Orleans could mean greater possibilities for distracting young men of means. The Celtics and Magic both play on courts with parquet floors, rumored to have subtle variations and dead spots.

TIP

The important thing to understand about home-court advantage is that it exists, but it deserves more of your attention than simply peanut-buttering a few points across every team. Home-court advantage is a combination of factors and it varies widely from team to team. Think about it: With only 5 guys on the floor at any one time, having one or two players who are particularly susceptible to hostile crowds or unusually sensitive to sleep deprivation can have a material and hard-to-predict impact on overall team play.

If you know the distribution of a team's home and away performances in terms of offensive and defensive efficiency, you're on you're way to quantifying their home-court advantage.

Bad altitude

The Nuggets (5,191 feet) and Jazz (4,265 feet) play home games at considerable altitude. (Bar bet opportunity: The next highest NBA arena belongs to, drumroll, the Oklahoma City Thunder at 1,200 feet.) Table 12-10 lists points per game differential for teams when they play in a non-mountainous elevation and when they play in Denver or Salt Lake City.

TABLE 12-10 **The Elevation and PPG**

Team	Road PPG (Anywhere but Denver or Salt Lake City)	Road PPG in Denver or Salt Lake City	Altitude Delta
Bucks	112.05	113	+.95
Bulls	105.01	99.25	-5.76
Cavaliers	106.63	103.75	-2.88
Celtics ·	106.89	104.4	-2.49
Clippers	111.22	103.86	-7.36
Grizzlies	101.13	94.67	-6.46
Hawks	106.52	107.8	+1.28
Heat	104.94	87.6	-17.34
Hornets	106.97	102.5	-4.47
Kings	105.35	101	-4.35

(continued)

TABLE 12-10 *(continued)*

Team	Road PPG (Anywhere but Denver or Salt Lake City)	Road PPG in Denver or Salt Lake City	Altitude Delta
Knicks	102.26	110	+7.74
Lakers	112.39	98.14	–14.25
Magic	104.38	91.75	–12.63
Mavericks	106.14	100.78	–5.36
Nets	109.64	104.5	–5.14
Pacers	105.95	108.5	+2.55
Pelicans	113.01	113.38	+0.37
Pistons	104.05	94.5	–9.55
Raptors	112.01	107.5	–4.51
Rockets	111.65	108.62	–3.03
Sixers	110.08	106	–4.08
Spurs	106.31	101.25	–5.06
Suns	107.41	98.1	–9.31
Thunder	110.73	102	–8.73
Timberwolves	110.46	104.56	–5.9
Trailblazers	108.97	101.75	–7.22
Warriors	115.05	109.89	–5.16
Wizards	109.57	100.2	–9.37

What's clear is that the vast majority of teams score fewer points than normal in the two mountain arenas. It's not so clear whether we can attribute that difference to the altitude or simply the fact that the Nuggets and Jazz simply operate at a slower-than-average pace relative to other NBA teams.

NBA Systems and Angles

WARNING

Yes, this same warning is going into as many chapters of this book as my editor will allow. There is no such thing as a winning system that is both well known, simple, and permanent. When systems and angles get publicized, they lose their efficacy. Think about it: As winning systems get more and more well known, that side starts attracting lopsided action from bettors. And what do bookies do when there's outsized action on one side of the bet? They make that side of the bet more expensive. Eventually, the winning edge from that system dwindles to nothing. That's the betting market working toward equilibrium.

Having said that, I'm a believer that if you take a disciplined approach to bankroll management, bet-sizing, odds-shopping, and handicapping, there are ways to exploit predictable behavioral patterns in teams, coaches, bettors, and oddsmakers.

Regular season

Betting against the public is almost always a good move. When the square bettors drive the odds one direction, they often push the bet into territory where it's profitable to bet the other side. The following system is one that takes advantage of this tendency in the regular season.

BET the struggling offense

You should always take note when teams have outlier performances. It means either they're likely to react in a predictable way, or the betting market is likely to react in a predictable way that you can take advantage of. Here's a setup for a team that can't make a shot to save their lives in the 1st half of a game:

> It's a regular season NBA game
>
> The road team was favored in its previous game by more than 7 AND
>
> The total in the road team's previous game was more than 218 AND
>
> The road team scored less than 47 points in the 1st half of their previous game
>
> **BET** the road team's point spread.

What's going on here? We're wagering that the betting market will overreact to a poor shooting night from a team expected to win and score a decent amount of points in their last game. In over five years, this system has hit at 63.8 percent (83–47, for a Z-score a little above 3).

There are doubtless dozens of ways to take advantage of betting markets overreacting to teams having uncharacteristic nights, or defying expectations in some extreme way. Other factors I've taken advantage of for this approach are things like over/under margin (how much the final combined score exceeds, or falls below, the total), the ATS margin, and fundamental factors like field goal percentage.

BET under the middle of the road

There's some evidence in 2019 that the oddsmakers still aren't quite sure what to do with matchups that point to low overall total points scored. It's as if there's an anti-gravity machine on all totals, whether the teams involved warrant them or not.

Here's a setup I've been betting that will no doubt dry up eventually, but it's been productive for a few years and continues during the season of this writing:

> It's a regular season NBA game
>
> The game total is between 200 and 215 AND
>
> The home team is either an underdog or a single-digit favorite AND
>
> The home team's previous result was a loss or a non-blowout win (less than 18) AND
>
> The home team is equally or better rested than the road team
>
> **BET** under the total.

This is a system that hits at a 57 percent clip, but it's worth mentioning because the frequency is impressive. Through December of 2019, it's produced 48 winners and 34 losers. It came up over 200 times in the 2018–2019 season, and twice that number the season before. Restrict this bet to the first half of the season and the results go well above 61 percent, with 251 wins and 160 losses. (That Z-score is 4.5, by the way.)

Carpe diem because I don't think an imbalance like this can possibly last very long in the betting market.

Postseason

A note to bettors in the postseason: It's a different beast. You have teams playing each other in series, and the win-or-go-home aspect of it means there's much less concern for managing player loads.

BET the mythical winning zig-zag method

One of the most well known NBA postseason betting strategies is known colloquially as the zig-zag method. Here's the question we need to answer: Is the method mythical? Or is the winning mythical?

The setup is straightforward: When a team loses in the playoffs, they beat the spread in the following game. The underlying premise is one (or maybe all) of these factors: Betting markets overreact to a single playoff loss; a losing team derives extra motivation; or the winning team relaxes.

Taken by itself, that setup produces a winning percentage barely above 50 percent over the last decade and a half, but with a few refinements, we can do better. There are many possibilities for slicing this data: I've seen handicappers do it by round, by seed, by magnitude of loss, and many other twists. Here are a few popular ones that I've seen:

>> Betting on a team that lost as a favorite in the first two rounds of the playoffs produced a 90–71 spread record (56 percent), but that Z-score is only 1.42, which is not too impressive.

>> Betting on a team that lost as an underdog and is now a home favorite produces a 73–47 spread record.

>> Betting on playoff seeds #1 to #4 playing a home game after a playoff loss in the first three round has produced an impressive looking 226–169 record since 2001, which has a decent 2.8 Z-score. But this system may be an example of one that's too popular for its own good, as it's gone a little flat in the last several seasons and has even produced a couple of real stinker years of late, including going 8–17 ATS in 2016.

However, there is a slice of the data in the above scenario that appears to still do well. It turns out that if you restrict your betting to big favorites, there are fewer opportunities but the zig-zag effect has been steadily positive for two decades. Here's the full setup:

The game is in the first three rounds of the playoffs

The favorite lost their last game AND

That team opens as more than a 9-point favorite

BET on the favorite.

This simple flavor of the zig-zag system only comes up a handful of times per playoff season, but it's gone 30–10 over the last 15 years (75 percent for a Z-score of 3.00).

BET the first round zig-zig system

In the last three decades of NBA playoffs, there's been exactly one instance of a team seeded lower than #3 winning the championship. (If you're curious, it was the 1995 Houston Rockets, who also happened to be the defending champions.)

Expanding on that fact, let's assert that the NBA playoffs feature an upper crust of six truly trophy-worthy teams combined with ten inevitable also-rans. And yet, there seems to be something about the playoffs that causes bettors to project a mental flattening of talent levels. It's as if they say, "Well, that team is in the playoffs, they *must* be worthy."

That attitude (combined with overconfidence in the aforementioned zig-zag system) leads to a playoff betting system that I call the *zig-zig*, where teams who get pummeled in a first round game doesn't have some hidden reserve of performance they can turn to in their next game. In fact, they've shown us their true colors in their loss, and it's time to fade them. Here's the setup:

> The game is in the first round of the playoffs
>
> It's game 2 or later of the series AND
>
> The team seeded #4 through #8 lost the previous game by double-digits
>
> **BET** against them in their next game.

In the last ten years, betting on a double-digit winner has produced a 93–62 ATS record (for a Z-score of 2.4). The 60 percent winning percentage of this system goes up if you limit it to bigger blowouts. There are other restrictions you can place on this system to produce a higher winning percentage, but with fewer opportunities:

>> Require a bigger blowout in the previous game (for example, 15 points or more instead of 10 points or more).

>> Pass on Game 2, which doesn't exhibit this effect consistently.

>> Only bet in situations where the teams are changing venues: Bet against the home team if they got blown out on the road, and bet against road teams if they got blown out at home.

Chapter **13**

Betting to Win on College Basketball

The NCAA might as well spell itself AACN given how backwards the organization is. The governing body of collegiate athletics has been dragged kicking and screaming into the legalized sports betting era. They're now lobbying individual states to keep college sports off the betting menus, sometimes succeeding.

But residents and visitors to Nevada have been betting on college hoops for decades, along with multitudes who bet offshore or with unofficial bookies. With all that wagering, incidents of point shaving and game fixing have been few and far between. (It can't possibly taint college hoops any worse than the scandals born of crooked recruiting, which appear like clockwork every year.)

The popularity of the NCAA tournament combined with the new betting explosion means lots more eyeballs on TVs, which means more revenues for colleges. That's good news considering declining attendance at the games themselves and growing program costs. At the end of the day, gambling will be a boon for college athletics. Some day, the NCAA will follow the lead of the professional leagues and embrace the gaming industry rather than maintaining an outdated, adversarial stance toward it.

What makes college basketball great is the vast expanse of competition. Unlike college football, where there are really only a few dozen teams who have a legitimate hope of winning a national championship, in college basketball things are settled on the court. Three-hundred fifty colleges of all shapes and sizes compete in Division I for the same national championship, awarded each spring at the conclusion of the NCAA tournament.

College basketball is attractive to bettors for a number of reasons. All those teams made up of volatile teenagers create matchups that are hard to predict. If you're a student of the game or a follower of a handful of teams or an obscure conference, you stand a good chance of having a better feel for an upcoming game than the oddsmaker does.

But it's not easy. The wide variety in the schools and players lead to mismatches in speed, athletic ability, coaching prowess, and wacky disparities in home crowds and home-court advantages. When UMass Lowell plays against Duke, you're looking at a handful of guys who look pretty good at the local pickup game versus a future NBA lineup. But does that make them 20 points worse than Duke? Or 30 points? If you know the answer, you can turn it into a winning bet.

And then there's the postseason, one of the most popular events for bettors in all of sports. It starts with the chaotic chain of events resulting from conference tournaments, whose champions automatically fill slots in the NCAA Tournament. If that champion happens to be an out-of-nowhere underdog, it means they're taking a slot in the tournament that's suddenly unavailable to a more worthy school. Then the tournament itself gets underway, and the great single-elimination filtering begins. Six wins in a row leads to glory.

The Basics of College Basketball

College basketball games are played to much lower scores than their professional counterparts, to the tune of about 80 points, and that happens due to several structural differences in the game:

>> The games are only 40 minutes long (as opposed to 48 in the NBA).

>> College basketball's shot clock is longer, so offenses can pass it around longer before having to take a shot, and teams can take an extra two seconds to advance the ball past half court.

>> Although fouling out in college basketball is proportionally the same as the NBA (5 fouls in 40 minutes versus 6 fouls in 48 minutes), college basketball teams go through a period of shooting 1-and-1 free throws, which doesn't exist in the NBA.

Interestingly enough, the 3-point shooting revolution that has overtaken the NBA has not invaded college basketball to the same extent, even though the 3-point arc is closer. A recent study by Todd W. Schneider showed that college players shoot consistently worse from distance than NBA players, so it's not surprising that college coaches create offenses with the assumption that the optimal shooting distance is from midrange and in.

WARNING

Prior to the 2019 season, the college basketball 3-point line was moved back to 22 feet, 1¾ inches. The NCAA's stated goal was to match the international distance, but it's no secret that nudging the 3-point distance more than a foot deeper makes it less likely that college basketball will evolve into a run-and-lob league like the NBA has become. Early results show that 3-point attempts are slightly down over the previous year, as is scoring (for better or worse).

Size of market

College basketball during the regular season is a distant second to the NBA regular season in terms of betting market size, but all that changes once the postseason begins. Bettors descend on betting windows in droves to bet on tournament games and props. Most estimates suggest that around $10 billion total is wagered on the NCAA Tournament alone, but that number includes millions of bracket contests. At least $300 million is wagered legally at U.S. casinos per year.

The efficiency of the NCAA basketball betting market

No betting market can top the NFL in terms of efficiency, and it's no surprise that there are no major structural biases in the college basketball betting market that are big enough to be profitable (that is, that rise to the level of statistical significance to cover the vig). Studies have shown that big favorites and "public" schools are indeed over-bet if you take a wide lens of the market, but the advantage is only a point above average.

Long-term regular season results show the oddsmakers do an excellent overall job in setting the point spread. Home favorites beat the spread about 51 percent of the time, and road favorites beat the spread almost exactly 50 percent of the time.

The College Basketball Betting Cycle

College hoops has become a year-round sport for bettors and enthusiasts who bet the season from October through the tournament in April, follow the recruiting and summer workout news, and start betting futures as they're released in the late summer.

Preseason

College basketball preseason polls are announced in the late summer and early fall, at which point many bookmakers began releasing conference champion and national champion futures bets, as well as futures for whether a given team will make it to the NCAA tournament or not.

The regular season

The regular nonconference season of play starts for teams in early November. Big schools often schedule warm-up games for non-Division 1 opponents, which are usually such mismatches that oddsmakers don't even assign odds.

During nonconference play, the bigger the program, the more nonconference games they'll play at home. It's not unusual for a top flight program like Michigan to play 8 games at home, 2 or 3 on a neutral site, and 1 marquee away game.

Postseason

Conference play typically lasts from the beginning of December through the beginning of March, when conference tournaments begin to crown the conference tourney champ (which is different from the conference champ, who finishes atop their conference standings prior to the conference tournament).

It's all in aid of being one of the top 64 teams in the country to join the 4 week-long NCAA tournament, a 63-game single elimination tournament hosted at dozens of sites around the country and concludes with the national championship.

Betting on Games

During the regular season, college basketball lines are posted by sports books no later than the morning of the games. For weekend games with early starts, the lines are available the night before at most books.

The standard pregame betting options include full game and 1st Half point spreads, totals, and moneylines, as well as full game total bets for each team's total points. Most offshore bookmakers offer alternate point spread and totals betting. For games with more public interest, you'll find prop bets available on individual player stats, provided it's allowed in the jurisdiction you happen to be betting from.

Table 13-1 provides some descriptive statistics and odds for the most recent handful of college basketball seasons.

TABLE 13-1   ## Total Points and Margins in Recent Seasons

Season	Avg Total Pts	Avg Total	Avg Home Margin	Avg Home Spread
2015	145.2	143.9	7.3	−4.9
2016	146.1	145.2	7.1	−5
2017	146.8	145.2	8.2	−5.1
2018	144.7	143.9	7.7	−5.5
2019	141.7	141.0	8.2*	−7.5*

Partial data for 2019, representing the first half of the regular season. You can see how the biggest mismatches usually occur in the nonconference games of November and December.

Full game spread

In Table 13-1, you can see that the average point spread is a little over 5 points in favor of the home team. About two-thirds of all games feature a home favorite, and the remaining games feature a home underdog (plus a few dozen games per year that go off as a pick'em). Ninety percent of all regular season spreads fall between the home team favored by 22 and the road team favored by 8.

Table 13-2 shows several years of results for home and road favorites.

TABLE 13-2   ## Results for Home and Road Favorites

	Win & Cover	%	Win & Don't Cover		Lose Outright	
Home Fave	5,666	51%	2960	26%	2,534	23%
Away Fave	2,052	50%	673	16%	1,376	34%

TIP

Athletes and teams are creatures of habit. When I pick games, I'm often interested in outlier games — that is, games with unusual circumstances, or uncommon combinations of outward characteristics, like extremely high totals and spreads, or teams off of a win or loss that stands out statistically in some way. When there are unusual circumstances, habits get broken, something the market might not price into the spread and total. It's also true that unusual situations often bring about predictable reactions from the teams themselves that can be bet on, and if not the athletes, then the oddsmakers and betting public are subject to reacting in a way that a perceptive bettor can take advantage of.

For example, favorites expect to win. After all, they win over two-thirds of the time. So when a favorite doesn't just lose, but loses in humiliating fashion, is there a notable reaction from the team or betting market that we can take advantage of?

BET follow the humiliation

Good teams rarely have two terrible shooting nights in a row, but the betting public often sees the recent shellacking at a reason to downgrade that team's offensive abilities, and they're often wrong:

> For a regular season game
>
> The favored team's last game was a 20 point (or more) loss AND
>
> The favored team's last game was on the road AND
>
> The favored team has had at least 2 days off
>
> **BET** over the total.

While college teams may not be aware of game odds, a 20-point loss is something everyone notices: fans, boosters, starters, backups, assistant coaches, girlfriends, not to mention your average bettor. You didn't just lose by double-digits; you got thrashed. But as bettors are giving last rites, the teams themselves are likely to put maximum effort into erasing the humiliation, and with a few days to stew on it, their shot selection will be better, their passes crisper, and you can expect a better offensive performance.

Over a five-year run, this system hits over 57 percent of the time (260-192), whether the favorite is at home or on the road. As always, there are probably many opportunities for refinement. (Does the location of the game matter? Does the opponent's most recent result matter? There's money to be made for those who find out.)

Home-court advantage and the spread

Home-court advantage is a major factor in college hoops, with lots of analysis over the years going into quantifying which schools get the biggest built-in boost from playing at home, with estimates ranging from nearly nothing to as much as 6 or more points.

REMEMBER

You can rest assured the oddsmakers pay attention to the big schools' home-court advantages and build them into the line. But when it comes to the small schools, they're probably assigned a basic 2- or 3-point edge at home.

The inimitable Ken Pomeroy has a simple and elegant model where he takes a team's past 60 games of home and away performance and then adds in other variables like elevation, steals, and perhaps most importantly, fouls. The result is a prediction of future scoring advantage, which ranges from around 5 points to as low as 2 points.

An interesting research idea would be to measure how much team experience and cohesion factors into home-court advantage. It's possible that a senior-laden team has the ability to overcome distractions of a boisterous road crowd.

Betting against the public

Look at the guys around you at your local casino. They place bets with surprisingly little information, long on gut, short on feel, and with a minimal understanding of betting markets. For all intents and purposes, those average Joes make the spread what it is by betting teams well beyond their true value.

The bookie takes and pays your bets, but what you're really trying to do is outsmart those square bettors. The idea of betting against the public isn't just throwaway advice: To win money betting on sports, you have to find inaccurate public perceptions and bet against them. The premise of this system assumes the public flocks to big conferences and inflates point spreads from those schools.

BET the underappreciated team

For this to work scenario, look at big conference games where one team is receiving much less action than the opponent.

> In a game involving participants from the ACC, Big East, Big Ten, Big 12, Pac-12, or SEC
>
> For mid-range total games (128 to 144) AND
>
> One side has gotten less than 25 percent of the point spread bet tickets
>
> **BET** on that team's point spread.

This has been a slow but steady system, with a 55 percent ATS winning percentage over the last five years. Check out Appendix A for some free sources of betting market metadata like which team is getting all the attention from the small-ticket bettors.

Full game total

College basketball full game totals are centered around 144 points or so. Odds-makers in general are right on the money with setting totals, as you can see in Table 13-3.

TABLE 13-3   ## College Basketball Totals

	Over	%	Under	%
Home Fave	5,577	51%	5,649	49%
Away Fave	2,065	50%	2,070	50%

About 90 percent of all college basketball totals fall between 130 and 159. So while you can't expect oddsmakers to misprice totals very often, there are plenty of opportunities out there if you look for the right scenarios. Sometimes it means targeting the extreme totals, and sometimes it's about odd situations that lead teams to materially score (or allow!) much more or less than everyone expected.

The great under

Betting the under when a team is off a great shooting night seems counterintuitive, but it's a great example of how bettors can win by being contrarian.

When statisticians talk about reversion to the mean, they're talking about things like field goal percentage on a basketball team, where a college squad settles around an average shooting percentage but occasionally has a great night. The more unusual the result is, the more likely it is not to be repeated. But here's the thing: Oddsmakers and bettors connect dots. Their algorithms and eyeballs tend to see what happened last game as the best possible indicator of what's going to happen next game.

BET overshot

Teams on a monster shooting binge have trouble repeating it, and you can take advantage of that as a bettor.

In a regular season college basketball game

The road team is off of fewer than six days of rest AND

The road team shot 56 percent or better from the field in their previous outing AND

The game total is 145 or higher

BET under the total.

This is one of the steadiest concepts in college basketball betting because it's so difficult for teams to replicate outstanding shooting performances. Starting in 2014, this system is 207 overs and 270 unders (56 percent for a Z-score of 2.84). This system is a slow, steady drip, with lots of opportunities each season. Just remember that you're going to win six games for every five you lose, and that's enough to grow your bankroll and be a successful sports bettor. Astute readers should look for ways to tighten up this trend to raise the success rate with only minimal sacrifices to the frequency of the opportunity. For example, what happens if both teams are coming off of big shooting nights?

WARNING

In the last chapter, I explored the paradigm shift that's taken place in the NBA, where scoring has gone way up. For followers of long-term trends like this one, I urge you to be on guard for structural changes in college basketball that might cause the average shooting percentage to change over time in a way that would make you reconsider whether 55 percent shooting from the field represents enough of an aberration to use as a betting precursor.

Theoretical game score

When you're looking at a total and a point spread in a basketball game, you can calculate the oddsmaker's best guess at a final score in the exact same manner I discussed in the football chapters. After all, the point spreads and totals are not accidents; oddsmakers set them with a particular game score in mind. You can easily project the oddsmaker's final score using the odds:

1. Subtract the point spread from the total.

2. Divide the result by 2, and assign that number to both teams as the base score.

3. Add the point spread to the favorite's score.

So if the total is 141, and Rutgers is favored by 11 over Penn, Take 11 from 141 to make 130, split those points up between the two teams to make Rutgers 65 – Penn 65. Finally, add the spread points to the favorite, making the final theoretical game score Rutgers 76 – Penn 65.

You'll also find that these scores are what the oddsmakers use for betting over/under the team point totals.

Wagering on the 1st and 2nd half

College basketball is played in two 20-minute halves. During halftime, there's a 15-minute break for the players. A few minutes after the start of halftime, most sports books will offer 2nd half wagers on point spreads and moneylines.

1st and 2nd half systems

I've had success in college basketball playing derivative bets. In 2019, I put my winning normalized winning percentage at just under 55 percent, with about 60 percent of my bets being either 1st half or 2nd half wagers — sometimes spread bets but more often totals.

REMEMBER

As I will say on every page, systems and angles come and go. The best ones might last a decade or more, but there are precious few with immortality, and if you know of one, you'd be wise not to say anything. Publishing a system in a book weakens it because there will be more price pressure on the bets I'm recommending, which will eventually lower the ROI to 0 percent.

WARNING

There's money to be made in 2nd half betting, but you often have very little time to process the information and place a bet during the 15-minute halftime. On a busy college basketball Saturday or perhaps a Wednesday night, there's more going on than you can reasonably keep up with.

First-half totals are set at about 47 percent of the full-game total, which matches the broad trend in college basketball scoring. Table 13-4 provides a comparison of 1st half and 2nd half scoring:

TABLE 13-4   **Comparison of 1st Half and 2nd Half Scoring**

Scoring Relationship	Home Team Points	Away Team Points	Combined Team Points
Games Where 1st Half Score <= 2nd Half Score	3,685	2,492	2,949
Games Where 2nd Half Score > 1st Half Score	5,955	6,401	6,691

Table 13-4 shows data for the 2017, 2018, and 2019 seasons that ended in regulation time, and includes regular season and tournament play. The conclusion? Maybe it's a drop-off of defensive intensity late in the game, or maybe it just takes time for college players to find their shot. Either way, teams score more in the 2nd half than the 1st.

2nd half totals

During the 15 minute intermission, the oddsmaker will issue a new spread and total that applies to the 2nd half alone. Here are some characteristics of the 2nd half total:

» On average, the 2nd half total is 53 percent of the original game total.

» 2nd half totals are tightly clustered around the average. At the extremes, about 10 percent of 2nd half totals are set at 51 percent of the game total or less, and 10 percent are set at more than 54 percent of the game total or more.

» The 2nd half total is closely correlated to the amount of scoring in the 1st half and the size of the lead.

TIP

Even when there's been tons more (or less) scoring than expected in the 1st half, adding up the 1st half total and the 2nd half total is usually within a point or two of the original game total. This gives you an insight into how oddsmakers come up with their totals in the first place. It's all about applying a rate-of-success to the number of scoring opportunities, like this:

Team Score = Number of Scoring Opportunities × Average Points Scored Per Opportunity

This basic approach works for nearly any sport. For basketball and football, a scoring opportunity is better known as a possession. How do the oddsmakers know how many possessions a team will get in a game? They don't know exactly, but they can project a team's average pace and constrain it against the length of a game to come up with a decent guess of how many possessions a team will get. If a college basketball team expects to have 100 possessions in a game and historically scores .63 points per possession, 63 points is a decent starting point if you're trying to figure their score in the next game.

BET under the runaway

When there's a big disparity between the two teams' scores at the end of the 1st half, there is a strong under tendency:

For a regular season college basketball game

The home team is down by 11 or more OR

The home team is down by 16 where the game spread was between –3 and +3 OR

The home team is leading by 22 or more OR

BET under the 2nd half total.

I only have a few years of historical data for these three scenarios, but the 2nd half under has been a winner in nearly 60 percent of these games. The theory is that big point discrepancies mean one team or the other takes their foot off the gas in the 2nd half, or perhaps their good luck in the 1st half runs dry in the 2nd.

Extreme total games

It's clear that oddsmakers aren't sure how to handle games where teams have averaged lots of points and are therefore projected to score lots of points. That makes the totals of such games vulnerable to exploitation.

BET 2nd half under of points fests

A regular system over the last five years or so has been to watch for extremely high total games where the home team is favored. Here is a setup to watch for:

> The home team is favored by 8 or more AND
>
> The game total is 160 or more
>
> **BET** under the 2nd half total.

The overall over/under margin since 2014 is 56 percent, but a much more stable trend is to pounce on extreme total games at halftimes. By formula, oddsmakers tend to make the 2nd half totals 12 to 15 percent higher than the 1st half totals, but in these extreme total games, the teams have not been able to keep up.

WARNING

There are no ties in college basketball. When they're tied at the end of regulation, teams play 5-minute overtimes until somebody wins. If you place a 2nd half wager, any points scored in the overtime periods are in play for your bet. For example, if you make a 2nd half bet on N.C. State −4 against Duke, and in the 2nd half the Wolfpack outscores the Blue Devils by 9, your bet is a winner if the game ends in regulation. If that 9-point 2nd half advantage results in a tie though, you can take comfort in having handicapped the 2nd half correctly, but your bet isn't decided yet. If Duke outscores N.C. State 10−2 in the 2nd half, your bet's a loser. To assess the results of a 2nd half wager, add all the 2nd half points together with all the overtime points.

Overtime games

Oddsmakers have to include chances of the game going to overtime when they set 1st and 2nd half odds. College basketball games go to overtime about 6 percent of the time. When they do, you can count on an average of 25 points being added. To get a little more precision, overtime means an additional 17 percent of the initial points will be added to the total score. If you're an under bettor watching your bet evaporate in overtime, there's nothing more frustrating. If you're an over bettor and you didn't quite get there in regulation, bully for you.

BET on an early season OT loser

There are no obvious approaches to betting a team following an overtime game; you can't blind bet the OT winner or loser. But there is evidence of some niche systems that show promise:

> The home team's last game went to overtime AND
>
> The home team's last game was a loss AND
>
> The game is being played in November or December
>
> **BET** under the total.

Since 2016, this system has gone 24–53 over/under (Z-score of 3.08). The scenario doesn't come up all that often, but when it does, it's a solid play.

Buying points (or not)

While it makes sense to buy points to improve your point spread to nudge a football point spread onto (or off of) a key number, no such advantage exists in basketball. There are no key numbers in basketball, so there's not much evidence that says an extra point is makes it worth it.

Having said that, let me give you the exact opposite advice. In the system that follows, a point could make a big difference.

BET top 25ers

This is a long-term system where there's a long-term spread advantage to betting on ranked teams against unranked teams, particularly early in the season.

> A team is ranked in the AP Top 25 AND
>
> The opponent is NOT in the AP Top 25 AND
>
> The game is a regular season game (that is, not a postseason tournament)
>
> **BET** the ranked team's point spread.

Table 13-5 shows a breakdown of this system by month. On the left is a summary of the against-the-spread record, and on the right is the record on the total, with data covering the years 2015 through 2018.

TABLE 13-5   **ATS Wins and Losses by Month**

Month	ATSW	ATSL	Within +/−1	Win %	OV	UN	Under %
Nov	295	215	41	58%	218	290	57%
Dec	231	179	41	56%	185	224	55%
Jan	405	350	68	54%	404	351	46%
Feb	352	321	66	52%	312	368	54%
March	89	70	12	56%	67	92	58%
ALL	1,372	1,135	228	55%	1,186	1,325	52.8%

I'm trying show how the college basketball season's betting opportunities can evolve and also demonstrate the relative value of buying a point on the spread due to the high percentage of games where the margin is within a point either way of the spread. I also show the over/under results because those look compelling as well.

Even if you take this betting strategy at face value, it's shows remarkable stability in that it works for all the obvious data slices. It holds up regardless of whether the ranked team is home or away. It works in high total games and low total games. It works whether the ranked team is away or home. It works in high total games or low total games. It works with large spreads or small spreads. And it works on high-ranked teams, or teams on the cusp.

There are doubtless many ways to tighten this system. For example, I saw one handicapper suggest that the real value is playing only AP Top 15 teams in November only.

A good research opportunity might be to see if this works beyond the AP Top 25. Pomeroy and Sagarin rank teams all the way down to #353. Is there something magical about the AP ranking that makes this work? Or is it just about good teams in general playing slightly less good teams?

The one inconsistency is time. At first glance, the effect appears to fade as the season goes on, which may give us a clue as to what's happening. Here's what I think is at play:

>> The talent disparity in college basketball is enormous, and the biggest mismatches happen in the early season before conference play begins.

>> There's so much turnover at the top level of college basketball teams these days that it's just incredibly hard to judge how good teams will be from year to year.

This system provides a stark reminder of how dangerous and costly it is to follow advice of analysts and bettors who don't provide backing data. I've read multiple sources online who claim the exact opposite of this system is profitable. Without naming names, his claim was to bet on unranked home favorites versus ranked teams. They say it's one that "many bettors swear by." Color me skeptical, because when I run the numbers, it's a losing proposition from every angle I could find.

(Maybe that's what makes the above system profitable in the long run. If betting unranked favorites against ranked teams is the conventional wisdom, that counts for a lot of square bettors pushing the odds in the direction of this system, making the ranked teams cheaper to back.)

BET unranked dancers

No matter how I sliced or twisted the data, I could not find a similar regular season scenario where a bettor would want to bet on an unranked team versus a ranked team. But when I dug into the postseason, I came up with this rare but convincing trend:

In the NCAA tournament

A team is unranked in the AP poll AND

That team's opponent is ranked in the AP poll (#1 through #25) AND

The unranked team is favored

BET on the point spread of the ranked team.

Hold on to your head, Fred. This system produced a 36–6 record against the spread over the last five years. That's an 85 percent record against the spread. And the higher the point spread, the greater the chances of a winning bet. Unfortunately, it doesn't come around very often, and there were no examples of this setup happening in 2018 at all.

Even if you take the tournament condition out of this system, it still favors the ranked team against the spread to the tune of 53.5 percent. That's enough of a winning percentage to make a profit (assuming it keeps up), but just barely. Either way, those gamblers who believe and peddle the idea that unranked home favorites are worth a bet need to keep guessing, or better yet, rethink their approach so that it includes some real data.

NCAA Basketball Teasers

If you want to combine college basketball bets together with an additional margin on your point spread or total, you can bet a *teaser*. A teaser means you agree that a combination of bets have to all win for the bet to pay off, and in return you get anywhere from 4 to 6 points in your favor on either the spread or the total.

For example, if you like Texas +3 against Baylor, and you like Texas Tech −11 against TCU, you can make a 4-point teaser bet that moves the spreads on each bet 4 points in your favor on each bet. In this case, your bets will be evaluated as Texas +7 and Texas Tech −7. If you win both bets, your teaser pays off. If you lose either bet, your teaser bet loses.

You can place a teaser bet that involves anywhere from 2 to 10 teams, and you can select an advantage of anywhere from 4 points up to 7 points. (At some sports books, you can make teaser bets of up to 10 points.) You can include any mix of point spread bets and over/under bets, and the point value you select will be added to each one of your bets in whatever way that favors you.

Table 13-6 describes standard payoffs for teaser bets. Odds may vary with any particular sports book:

TABLE 13-6 **Standard Payoffs for Basketball Teaser Bets**

Points	2-way	3-way	4-way	5-way	6-way	7-way	8-way	9-way	10-way
4	+117	+200	+335	+525	+805	+1,200	+1,775	+2,600	+3,800
4.5	+103	+190	+315	+490	+745	+1,100	+1,600	+2,400	+3,500
5	−110	+165	+265	+410	+610	+890	+1,275	+1,825	+2,600
5.5	−120	+150	+240	+365	+550	+800	+1,100	+1,550	+2,150
6	−150	+120	+185	+370	+380	+530	+725	+975	+1,325
6.5	−180	+100	+153	+220	+300	+405	+540	+715	+935
7	−210	−110	+136	+195	+265	+355	+465	+610	+800

As you can see from this table, your payout grows as you add more teams to your teaser bet, which makes sense because you need them all to win. And the more points you select for you teaser bet will reduce your bet incrementally.

For example, if you want to place a 5-way teaser, at 5.5 points, you'll bet $100 to win $365. You'll need 5 independent selections: any combination of point spread bets and over/under bets. The book will give you a 5.5-point advantage on each bet. Favorites will be favored by 5.5 points fewer than listed; underdogs will get an additional 5.5 points added to their point spread. If you include an under bet in the teaser, the total points you have to land under gets 5.5 points added to it. And if you bet an over, the total point number you have to exceed is 5.5 points less than that published total.

REMEMBER

The payout odds at different sports books is not a standard chiseled into stone. If you have multiple outs, you will notice that the odds offered for teasers of different bet numbers and points will vary considerably. And that's the key: When the payout odds are higher, you can afford to win your bets at a lower rate and still break even.

College Basketball Angles

All kinds of fantastic statistics are available to you to describe something that happened in the past, particularly if you slice your data by a certain team or conference. I've learned over the years to be skeptical of team-specific trends (also known as *angles*) because the are often simply descriptive without being predictive.

TIP

When someone approaches you with a betting strategy, system, or angle, or asserts that one approach is always profitable, your first instinct should be to back-test it against a set of real historical spread and total data. If it passes the historical test, you might be on to something.

DON'T BET the slider

The seductive nature of systems and angles knows no bounds, and you would be wise to learn how to look for them. I just read advice from a handicapper who told me that I should bet against a certain team on Saturday because they are 0–9 ATS in their last 9 games.

Sounds like a rough situation. Losing 9 games against the number is an interesting stat, but is it predictive? After all, 0–9 ATS is simply looking at the past when what we really want to know is whether that team is likely to lose its tenth spread matchup in a row.

Fortunately, with the various data tools available online, we can find examples of other teams in exactly the same situation.

Care to take a guess at how teams generally behave after an 0–9 run against the number? In the last five years, I came up with 36 examples of teams in this exact situation. If history was any guide, you might suspect these 36 sad-sacks went 5–31 in their 10th game, or 10–26, or something equally horrendous.

Try the opposite: Teams on an 0–9 spread skid are 20–16 against the spread.

That's the perfect example of why I avoid team-specific angles. While I believe oddsmakers, bettors, and teams react to certain general scenarios involving wins and losses, rest, margins, and odds, I don't attach that same predictable behavior to single teams.

Think about what Mr. 0–9 was suggesting. He's saying that this team has failed to meet expectations 9 times in a row, so there must be something unusual about that team that it can't beat the spread, and there must be something about them that makes the oddsmakers and public unable to catch up with how bad they are. Both premises beg belief.

The only way to prove that this team is worth betting against is if you can show me that oddsmakers, bettors, and teams have a tendency to react in a certain way when situations like this arise. And the interaction of the oddsmaker, betting public, and the team conspire in such a way that the spread isn't set low enough on the tenth game. To prove that assertion, you'll have to show me other scenarios where the same thing has happened regardless of the names on the jerseys.

TIP

Incidentally, if you're looking for insight on how a college basketball team does after *winning* 9 games in a row against the spread, you're out of luck. The results are equally inconclusive as for a team losing 9 against the spread.

BET spread streakers

Something good came from that last scenario at least. I looked for ways to exploit spread streaks and found that there is some evidence that bettors and oddsmakers tend to overreact if a team starts trending toward ever larger spread wins.

> A team beat the spread in its last game by more than 15 points AND
>
> A team beat the spread in the game before that by more than 10 points AND
>
> A team beat the spread in the three games before that
>
> **BET** the point spread against the team on an ATS roll.

This system of betting against the betting market's overreaction has gone a respectable 50–28 (64 percent, Z-score of 2.38) in the last five years. And I feel certain that there are more profitable situations to be found around streaking teams.

BET over conference surprises

Some of us think conference tournaments are even better than the NCAA Tournament because the outcome is so deliciously convoluted. Teams that sneak past the first round tend to really bring it in the second round. Check out this setup:

During a conference post-season tournament

It's a second-round game or later AND

The underdog in the game was an underdog in their last game and won that game AND

The underdog won their previous game after more than 5 days of rest

BET over the total.

In most cases this system operates in the second round of a conference tournament. When there's a rolling underdog, betting the over has gone 27–10 (73 percent and a Z-score of 2.63).

Betting the NCAA Tournament

Of the $5 billion legally bet on sports in 2018 in Nevada, nearly 10 percent of that was wagered on the NCAA Tournament, also known as the Big Dance. The 63-game tournament (not counting the play-in games) every March and April following conference tournaments is a focal point for bettors because of the concentration of games and the win-or-go-home motivation for each team. And in the later weeks of the tournament, you can count on fascinating matchups between the top teams in the country, plus one or two Cinderellas. (Cinderelli? Cinderellae?)

If you've never paid attention or you need a refresher, here are the basics of the tournament:

>> A conference committee selects 64-ish teams, some by virtue of winning their conference, some for at-large slots based on their regular season performance.

>> The committee assigns the 64 teams into 4 regional tournaments; each region has 16 teams seeded #1 through #16.

>> The single-elimination tournament commences with each #1 seed playing the #16 seed, the #2 seed playing the #15 seed, and so on, through the #8 seed playing the #9 seed.

>> The first two rounds of the tournament are played in the first weekend (actually Thursday through Sunday); the second two rounds play the second weekend; and the national semifinal and final games are played the third weekend.

Seed-by-seed results

Many people have made extensive study of the matchups that occur in the NCAA Tournament. In this section, I'll share a few insights.

The mythical #1 versus #16 matchup

Nobody thought it could ever happen, but in 2017, it finally did. After four decades of tournament play with 16 seeds per region, no #16 seed had ever beaten a #1 in the first round of the tournament, but the Retrievers of UMBC (that's Maryland Baltimore County if you're keeping track) knocked off top seed and AP #1 University of Virginia. They didn't just beat them; they beat them by 20! And just to add insult to injury for the venerated Virginians, UMBC went on to lose in the next round to Kansas State

TIP

There's not a ton of data available, but big underdogs don't typically fare well after they win in the NCAA tournament. If your team wins as an underdog of more than 10 points, they're 3–9 ATS the following game, or 28–43 if you consider all postseason basketball.

Seed anchoring

Bettors and bracket pickers should stock up on liquid paper before the tournament and blot out the seed numbers next to each team before they assess the games. Seeds represent the worst kind of *anchoring* effect for anyone trying to pick winners in the NCAA Tournament.

Anchoring is a well known cognitive bias where a bit of prominent preexisting information acts as a starting point for your judgment. While the tournament committee slots teams in to seeds in the order they believe represents the quality of the teams, the actual difference of these teams can be quite hard to measure. Nevertheless, it's surprisingly hard to pull the trigger and pick a #11 seed to beat a #6 seed, even though it happens more often than you might think.

How often? Table 13-7 shows the straight-up historical results for the first-round tournament matchups.

Keep these proportions in mind as you think about tournament games, either for your bracket or for moneyline betting. Your bracket should contain at least two #9 seeds advancing and at least one #10, one #11, and one #12.

When it comes to picking how far a team will advance, consider the historical best of each seed, shown in Table 13-8.

It's possible the sample size isn't big enough, or perhaps there's something especially hard about the matchups a #5 seed faces.

TABLE 13-7

NCAA Tournament Results

Seed Matchup	Straight-up Win/Loss Record
#1 vs #16	139–1 (Sorry, Virginia)
#2 vs #15	132–8
#3 vs #14	119–21
#4 vs #13	111–28
#5 vs #12	107–53
#6 vs #11	102–58
#7 vs #10	99–65
#8 vs #9	84–80

Data courtesy of mcubed.net

TABLE 13-8

The Best Finishes for Each Seed

Seed	Best Finish in Tournament History
#16	Round of 32 (once)
#15	Sweet 16 (once)
#14	Sweet 16 (2 times)
#13	Sweet 16 (6 times)
#12	Elite Eight (once)
#11	Final Four (4 times)
#10	Final Four (once)
#9	Final Four (2 times)
#8	National Champion (once)
#7	National Champion (once)
#6	National Champion (2 times)
#5	Final Game (3 times)
#4	National Champion (once)
#3	National Champion (5 times)
#2	National Champion (7 times)
#1	National Champion (24 times)

Spread records

Understanding how one seed beats another is interesting for bracket pickers, but what about for bettors? Is there a seed-based advantage in the tournament for bettors?

The round-by-round historical records against the spread don't show much in the way of advantage for a bettor who wants to blind bet on one seed versus another. The biggest extreme is the #7 seed, which has a spread advantage in the mid 50s, with hardly enough sample size for any meaningful conclusions. You're going to have to dig deeper to find patterns and systems to bet on in the NCAA Tournament.

BET tourney twofer against and under big tourney faves

Teams appear to do just enough to move forward in postseason play, but they appear to not care much for defense or covering the spread. When the oddsmaker has hung a big number in the teens around the favorite during tournament play, it probably indicates a team that's a sure thing to make the NCAA field. With no pressure to impress the committee, big point spreads aren't easy to overcome.

>   For games in a conference tournament or the NCAA tournament AND
>
>   A team is favored –15 or greater AND
>
>   The total is moderate (144 or less) AND
>
>   The team is playing its second game in a row on a neutral court
>
>   **BET** on the over AND bet the underdog against the spread.

Again, there's not a ton of data to work with, but games in this situation have gone over 15 times and under 4 times, with the underdog covering the spread 14 out of the 19 times.

Chapter **14**

Betting to Win on Major League Baseball

B aseball was a statistician and probability expert's sport early on and, after horse racing, was what popularized gambling. In the first half of the 20th century, they say the outfield stands of Yankee Stadium and Wrigley Field had more bookmakers than they had actual fans.

And after the advent of Sabremetrics, analytics, and the *Moneyball* age of baseball, the level of technical sophistication and data-driven decision making available to the bettors has become truly staggering. Add in the fact that Rotisserie Baseball was around long before fantasy football ever became a thing, so there is an entire community of number-crunching, player-performance-predicting pseudo-analysts out there completely separate from bettors like you. That's good news because they also theorize, crunch numbers, and write at a prodigious rate. So you don't just have raw baseball data at your disposal, sliced a hundred different ways, but you also have genuine scholarship available to you online — well thought-out argumentation with genuine statistical rigor.

What's more, betting on baseball is fun. As a baseball fan, I admit, I only follow when the Texas Rangers have a chance at breaking my heart in the playoffs. But as a baseball bettor, I follow many teams closely; I watch highlights and even (if I'm feeling frisky) an entire inning of a game. Yes, I know, I'm a true fanatic.

The Basics of Major League Baseball

As I stated early on, I'm not here to teach you the rules of the game. And the beauty of betting on sports is that sometimes you don't even have to know the rules! But just so you know the basics, here's a refresher on how America's pastime is set up:

>> Major League Baseball is made up of 30 teams, divided into two 15-team sub-leagues, further subdivided into three divisions.

>> Teams play 162 games in the regular season, with a schedule that's heavy in their own division, less heavy in the other divisions of their sub-league, and with a smattering of interleague play mixed in.

>> A team plays roughly six games per week, and they face their opposition in series of 2 to 5 games at a time to cut down on travel.

>> The three divisional winners of a sub-league play the winner of a play-in game . . . er, sorry . . . it's technically the first round of the playoffs. The wildcard play-in game is a do-or-die between the two non-division winners with the best record.

>> There are four divisional series in the playoffs where teams have to win 3 of 5 to advance. Then each sub-league holds a best-4-out-of-7 championship series, followed by World Series, another best-4-of-7 between the two sub-league winners.

Baseball offers some advantages to the bettor in that it's a stat heavy sport — the original stat-centric sport. And with 162 games in the season, there's a lot of time to figure out the "character" of a team.

Unlike football, there are no "key numbers" in baseball. Runs are more or less smoothly distributed around the mean. That factor, plus the fact that there's no point spread to consider in baseball, means the oddsmakers can adjust odds on games in a straightforward way: If the betting on a −180 favorite ticks up just a bit, the oddsmaker can adjust the moneyline to −181.

Several academic studies have shown that the baseball market is nearly as efficient as the NBA and NFL markets.

REMEMBER

Market efficiency means that there are no major areas where the odds systematically differ from the outcome. That comes about because bettors and oddsmakers move quickly to close up any mismatches where the bookmaker's odds don't accurately reflect the best-known probabilities. If a team or a pitcher is mispriced, bettors are plentiful and astute, and oddsmakers are reactive enough to make adjustments and close the gap.

But saying that baseball has an efficient market does not mean you can't make money betting on it. Continue, dear reader.

Baseball Bets and Odds

The standard listing for baseball bets (shown in Figure 14-1) shows a handful of key pieces of data:

>> **Time/Date:** When the first pitch is schedule for each game.

>> **Rotation numbers:** The unique identifier for each side of a baseball bet.

>> **Teams and starters:** The away team is always listed on top, and the home team is always listed on the bottom, with projected starters (and sometimes whether they are right- or left-handed).

>> **Opening odds:** This is optional, but bookmakers sometimes show the opening moneyline and total. You can't bet on those numbers anymore, but it can give you a feel for where the betting markets are leaning when you compare the opening numbers with the current odds.

>> **Current moneyline/total:** At a minimum, a baseball odds listing should show the moneyline odds for the favorite (with a negative 3-digit number), and the game total (which will be somewhere between 5 and 15).

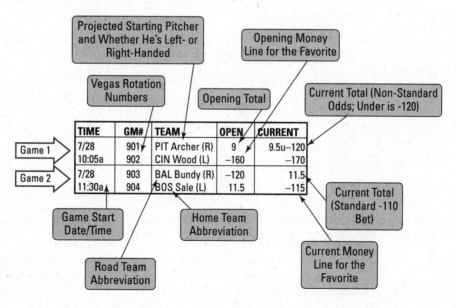

FIGURE 14-1: Baseball odds notation and explanation

The baseball moneyline

By now you're familiar with the moneyline. A moneyline bet is a bet on a team to win the game. It doesn't matter by how much; it doesn't matter if it's in 9 innings or 19 innings.

REMEMBER

To split the betting action between teams of differing quality, oddsmakers have two choices:

>> They can handicap one team by including a point spread. Betting on either side will be close to an even-money 11/10 bet, but the final score is adjusted by a certain number of points to determine the winner of the bet.

>> The alternative is the moneyline, where the final score of the game indicates the winner, with no point or run adjustments, but the payout schedules are different depending on whether you bet on the favorite or the underdog.

There are different explanations for why baseball doesn't operate with a point spread. One theory is that margin of victory in a baseball game has less to do with the quality difference between the two teams. Another is that overall variability of the game makes it more difficult to attach a spread to. Historians point out that after horse racing, baseball is the original bettors' sport, and by the time the point spread was invented in the 1940s, there was enough accumulated knowledge and tradition in offering odds on baseball bets that the points spread simply wasn't necessary.

Either way, a moneyline is a moneyline. Baseball moneylines are no different from any other moneyline: You need the team you bet on to win the game if you want your bet to pay off.

Moneyline encoding

The moneyline of a baseball game comes with several key pieces of information. Let's consider a baseball game where the home team is listed at −110 and the road team is listed at +100:

>> The home team is a slight favorite. The break-even winning percentage for a bet placed at −110 odds, as you know by now, is 52.4 percent. (To calculate breakeven rate on a negative [favorite] moneyline, divide the line by itself less 100 (−110/−210).

>> The break-even percentage on the underdog (+100) is 50 percent.

>> The bookmaker's vigorish, or theoretical hold, is about 2.3 percent. A moneyline by itself does not tell you how much vig is being charged by the bookmaker; you need both the favorite and the underdog moneylines to determine what the vig is.

There are no ties in baseball (except in the occasional All-Star game). Your moneyline bet is on the final result of the game, including extra innings (if they are necessary).

Win-loss record perils

If you're a moneyline bettor in baseball, you can't judge your success by looking at your win/loss percentage. If you bet on every baseball team with a −170 moneyline in the 2019 season, you would have won 62 percent of your bets! That sounds like a lot of winning, right? Let's do a quick calculation to see if you would have broken even:

Since we're looking at bets in the past, we know the actual winning percentage of the bets (62 percent). What we're interested in is the break-even winning percentage of bets at a −170 moneyline. If those 2019 bets won at a higher rate than the break-even winning percentage, it means they would have been profitable. If the actual winning percentage is below the break-even rate, they would have lost money.

For a favorite, the break-even winning percentage is the moneyline (−170) over itself minus 100 (−270). Here's the calculation:

−170/−270 = 62.9 percent

So you have to win 62.9 percent of −170 bets to make a profit. That should make sense to you since every time you lose a −170 bet, you're losing $170 (or $17 or $1.70), and every time you win that bet, you only win $100 (or $10 or $1, respectively). Winning less than 62.9 percent means you're losing money, and that's just what would have happened in 2019 had you bet on every single −170 favorite. It might feel strange to win 62 percent of your bets and lose money, but since 62 is less than 62.9, that sad fate is what would have befallen you.

The flip side of that is that if you're an underdog bettor, it feels strange to win less than 50 percent of your games and be profitable, but that's what happens sometimes. In 2018, if you had bet on the Marlins every time they were +250 or greater underdogs, you would have won 2 and lost 5. But because those occasional payoffs are worth so much more, that 2–5 record would have also netted you a +14.3 percent ROI.

Point spread bettors can generally tally up wins and losses and judge whether they've been successful or not. And the point spread gives you an explicit message, "The betting market thinks Team A is 6 points better than Team B."

REMEMBER

There are no such signposts when you're a moneyline bettor. When wins and losses become less meaningful, you are forced to think in terms of win probability, ROI, and returns. But don't be afraid: With a little experience, you'll learn to calculate in your head. When you see a moneyline on a baseball game, you'll be able to do a quick mental calculation on the implied odds and decide whether they match your expectation on the outcome.

Total runs bet

Bookmakers offer the typical total bet on baseball, and it works just as you'd expect. The oddsmaker sets a number of total combined runs in the game. Bet the over and you'll need the teams to score more than the total. Bet the under and you'll need the pitching to dominate to the point that the total scored runs is less than the total.

Bookmakers offer baseball totals as straight 11/10 bets with −110 odds on either the over or under. And as you might expect, baseball totals are offered in increments of ½ runs.

As with football and basketball, any extra game play is included in your total bet. In other words, extra innings count toward your total. If you've bet under 8.5 and the 9th inning finishes at 4−4, you've got a losing ticket, because the game will continue until one team tops the other.

Run line bet

Since oddsmakers don't offer a point spread in baseball, there's no such thing as a standard 11/10 side bet with −110 odds. But Major League Baseball obviously has teams with wide quality differences, and sports books realized long ago that some bettors don't find extreme moneylines appealing. Favorite bettors don't get enough payoff to make it worth it, and underdog bettors start to feel like they've bet a longshot prop, where the payouts are handsome but rare.

The result was the run line. The run line is like a hybrid between a point spread and a moneyline, and it operates according to these rules:

>> A favorite run line bet means a −1.5 handicap is applied to the final score.

>> A favorite run line bet is offered at odds equivalent to a moneyline bet on the favorite *plus* about 80 to 110 points.

>> An underdog run line bet means a +1.5 handicap is applied to the final score.

>> An underdog run line bet is offered at odds equivalent to an underdog moneyline bet *minus* about 80 to 110 points.

REMEMBER

When oddsmakers tweak your chance of winning, they make an equivalent adjustment in the payout schedule to maintain the same level of risk and return. Spotting the underdog a run and a half means that run line bet is more likely to win, but, as you would expect, the bet pays less in the event of a win. And it works in reverse for the run line favorite. These adjustments allow the bookmaker to maintain a level of profitability while offering bets that appeal to bettors' different tastes and appetites.

As always, examples pave the path to comprehension. Table 14-1 shows a pair of games with the moneyline odds listed alongside the run line odds:

TABLE 14-1

MLB Games with Moneyline and Run Line Odds

Team	Pitcher	Moneyline	Run Line
Miami Marlins	P Lopez -R	+170	+1.5 -130
Philadelphia Phillies	V Velazquez -R	-185	-1.5 +110
Atlanta Braves	D Keuchel -L	-105	+1.5 -210
New York Mets	M Stroman -R	-105	-1.5 +185

The Phillies are favored in the first game, as evidenced by the lower moneyline. If you bet the Phillies run line, you take on a −1.5 handicap for the game's final score, but in exchange, your payout schedule improves from −185 to +110. If you bet $1 at −185 odds, you profit 54 cents. With the run line bet, your $1 bet makes a $1.10 profit. In this case, the odds shifted 95 cents in your favor from −185 to +110.

If you like the Marlins run line bet, you'll get +1.5 runs added to your final score, but you lose a full dollar on your odds, from +170 to −130.

The second game is illustrative because the teams are listed as even in terms of moneyline. But the oddsmaker always picks one team to be the run line favorite and one team to be the run line underdog.

REMEMBER

Bookmakers take a variety of approaches on baseball odds. Some offer low-vig betting where the theoretical hold is as small as 5 cents. (For example, a moneyline favorite is listed at −105, and a moneyline underdog is listed at +100.) Some bookmakers offer noticeably better odds on favorites at the expense of underdogs, and others, vice versa. While the run line handicap is always 1.5 runs, the odds differential — that is, how much the moneyline odds increase or decrease for the run line — can vary as well.

The lesson is that regardless of your baseball bet, you should (appropriately) have at least 3 outs! That is, make sure you have betting options so that you can get the best odds possible on your bet.

The moneyline favorite always gets a –1.5 run line handicap, and the moneyline underdog always gets a +1.5 run line handicap. In cases where the moneyline odds are completely even, the bookmaker picks one side to be the favorite.

If you're curious about how often the run line comes into play, here's the breakdown of the 2019 season:

>> Favorites won 1,489 games and lost 918.

>> Of those 1,489 games, favorites won 376 by just 1 run, so the moneyline favorite bet won, but the run line bet would have lost.

And 2019 is in line with historical averages. Assuming you pick a winning favorite, they'll win by exactly one run about a quarter of the time.

Baseball's "ACTION" condition

Because starting pitchers are so central to the outcome of a baseball game, most side bets (money line, run line, and 5 inning line) are conditional. Look at the moneyline and total odds for this game:

Time	Gm#	Team	Pitcher	M/L
24-Jul	909	Houston Astros	J Verlander - R	–240
5:35 PM	910	Tampa Bay Rays	D Castillo - R	210

The default moneyline bet on the Astros/Rays game is called a *listed starters* bet. That means your bet is conditional on the starting pitchers listed with the bet actually starting the game. To be specific, a bet on the Astros is only valid if both Justin Verlander and Diego Castillo start the game. Technically, oddsmakers consider it a start as long as the listed pitcher takes the mound and throws at least one pitch.

When you make a baseball bet, you'll see specific language on your betting ticket or on your online betting receipt that states both starters have to play for the bet to have action. If either pitcher fails to start, the bet is called *no action*. No action means your bet is effectively cancelled. Bettors at live bookmakers should take their ticket back to the counter, and their bet gets returned. If you bet online, your wager will be returned to your account automatically. There is no juice or fee charged on a no action bet; it's treated like any other push.

In addition to listed starter bets, many bookmakers offer the option of placing an *action wager* on baseball. If you choose an action bet, your money is on that bet, regardless of any changes to the starting pitching. But there's a catch: The bookmaker reserves the right to change the odds if there's a pitching change.

In the example above, if you had checked the "action" box when you made your bet on the Rays, you'd accept that should Verlander and Castillo both start, your moneyline odds would be set at +210. And that makes sense, as anyone who saw Verlander play in 2019 knows he was a hard man to break, so if the Rays were to do it, you'd get rewarded for your Tampa faith.

Now consider the scenario where Verlander pulls a hammy in warmups and the Astros turn to an untested rookie to start the game. The chances of Tampa winning just went way up. Bookmakers aren't willing to accept that kind of risk in baseball, so there's no way they'll pay you +210 on a fourth-rate starter subbing in for Verlander.

If you had taken a standard bet, Verlander's absence would cancel your bet. But if you took an action bet, your payout schedule changes to reflect how the betting market would otherwise feel about this pitching change. An action bet means you're still in on the Rays, but the bookmaker gets a chance to reset the odds and payout schedule for the ticket you hold.

There are very few circumstances where advantage bettors would consider placing an action wager as a +EV play. Action wagers are for fans of a team, or for people watching a big game on TV, who don't care all that much about who's on the mound or what the odds are. There is money to be made betting baseball, but not through action wagering.

There are virtually no other circumstances where you don't get paid the odds stated on your betting ticket in sports betting. Bookmakers protect themselves from big swings in win probability for a given team by either halting betting altogether on a game with a big injury question mark or *circling the game.*

It's slightly out of fashion these days, but when a bookmaker offers a circled game, it means there is incomplete information on injuries or playing status of one or more key players. A circled game means you can still bet on it, but at reduced limits.

9 divided by 2 = 5 inning lines

There's no such thing as halftime in baseball. Sure, the middle of the 5th inning is halfway through the game, unless it isn't, when the home team is winning and doesn't bat in the bottom of the 9th.

Most bookmakers now offer their version of a halftime line on baseball games called the *5-inning line*. As you might expect, the 5-inning total is around half of the game total. The moneyline usually lands very close to the game moneyline as well. The run line has a slight difference: Instead of a standard −1.5/+1.5 handicap, the 5-inning run line is −.5/+.5, but like its full-game cousin, the 5-inning run line is a derivative of the moneyline. All 5-inning bets resolve once the home team has made 3 outs in its half of the 5th inning.

The average innings pitched per start is around 5.5, so as you would expect, the 5-inning moneyline is a much more pure reflection of the two starting pitchers than the game moneyline. It's very rare for a starter to pitch a complete game, so game moneylines have to account for bullpen and closer quality in addition to the starter.

TIP

Baseball's 5-inning results are tightly correlated with the full-game results. The 5-inning leader goes onto to win the full game 7 times out of 8. For total bets, games flip-flop a little more often; a 5-inning under ending with a full game over (and vice versa) happens 1 game out of 6.

Like other derivative bets, bettors might find some opportunity in monitoring full-game odds against 5-innings odds for situations where one reacts to news and another doesn't. For example, if word comes out before the game that one of the team's big sluggers is a scratch for the game, you might see the game total drop by a full run as bettors flock to the under in light of the diminished offensive firepower. In theory, that same loss of offensive firepower would be felt in the first 5 innings as well, so the 5-inning total should dip by a half-run just like the full-game total did. But often that's not the case.

But because full-game odds get more attention from bettor than 5-inning odds, the latter is often less responsive to market forces, even though the two results are highly correlated (see preceding paragraph). If the market correctly downgrades the full-game total by a run, the 5-inning total should shrink by a half run. But often it doesn't. That's a classic +EV opportunity for a 5-inning under.

It's something akin to the market getting new information that causes a certain stock to rise. If the market has determined that company is suddenly more valuable than they thought previously, then the preferred stock, call options, and other associated derivative investments should go up too. So if the betting market thinks there will be fewer runs scored, all bets based on run scoring should reflect that new valuation.

Other common baseball bets

Beyond the "big 3 bets" (moneyline, run line, and total) and their derivatives, most online casinos offer a smorgasbord of prop bets, but the most common are as follows:

Team scoring total

Bettors can wager over or under a team reaching a certain score:

Rockies at Rangers — Team Run Total

Rockies	4.5
Rangers	5.5 over –120 under +100

In this example, there are 4 possible bets on offer. The Rockies team total is 4.5, and a bet on either the over or under has implied –110 odds. If the Rockies score 5 or more, your over bet wins and the Under bet loses. If the Rockies score 4 or less, the under wins and the over loses. That result happens regardless of the Rangers score, and regardless of whether the Rockies win or lose. All that matters for this bet is how many runs the Rockies score at the end of the game.

The Rangers' team total works the same way. In this example, the bookmaker is trying to balance action toward the under 5.5 side of the bet by making the over bet slightly more expensive relative to the under. As you know by now, if the action gets too lopsided on the over, the bookmaker might increase the Rangers' team total to 6.

TIP

Team total bets are good alternatives to betting sides (moneyline and run lines) or overall game totals when you have a good feel for one side of the pitcher vs. batter matchup, but not the other.

Will there be a score in the 1st?

This is a binary yes/no bet with moneyline-type odds, given like this:

Rockies at Rangers — Will either team score in the 1st inning?

YES	–140
NO	+115

The bet is decided as you might expect. If you bet "NO" and the 1st inning goes in the books with the score 0–0, you win. Any other score and your bet wins, regardless of who scored, and how much they scored.

Odds for this bet are based on the quality of the leadoff hitters and early-game pitching tendencies for the starters. Some great starters (Yu Darvish comes to mind) are prone to give up runs early and then settle in.

Some notes on 1st-inning scoring to help you bet:

>> If you're wondering, there's a run scored in the 1st about 52 percent of the time overall, so odds for each side will hover close to even, with occasional forays into 2-to-1 territory for games predicted to be shootouts. The top teams in terms of 1st-inning scoring percentage are normally between 35 percent to 40 percent by the end of the year.

>> 1st-inning scoring is largely a function of overall runs scored, but you'll see cases where bad offensive teams appear at the top of the 1st-inning scoring percentage rankings; they have a knack for scoring early even though they don't score as much late. Teams with productive hitters batting first, second, and third sometimes lack quality throughout their lineup, so are more likely to be at the top of the rankings in terms of 1st-inning runs without owning other offensive categories. The reverse can also be true where high-output teams fail to score in the 1st.

>> When betting on the 1st inning, consider the manager's approach as well. Some like to scratch out runs one at a time instead of waiting for a big rally. If a manager likes to bunt, steal, hit-and-run, you'll see a higher percentage of runs scored in the early innings when the top OBP (on-base percentage) guys bat.

>> 1st-inning run-scoring consistency is largely predictable during the season. For the handful of seasons I analyzed in the late 2010s, the leading teams in 1st-inning scoring 8 weeks into the season were still near the top of the list by the end of the season. For example, in 2019, 8 of the top 10 1st-inning scoring teams at the halfway mark ended the year in the top 10. The starting pitchers are a different story, though. The starting pitchers leading the league in 1st inning runs allowed are much less likely to be on the list in the second half of the season.

>> Further analysis needed: There's an opportunity for bettors if they can identify those teams that have lost their 1st inning punch. In 2019, the Dodgers and the Mariners were scoring in the 1st inning regularly at the halfway mark, but they fell of greatly and landed out of the top 10 in 1st-inning scoring percentage by the end of the year. If you could identify the factor or factors that led to the drop-off, you could get out ahead of the market and bet "NO" on runs scored in the 1st at advantageous odds.

BETTING ODDITIES: ROBIN VENTURA'S GRAND SLAM SINGLE

Baseball rules require baserunners to legally circle the bases and step on home plate in order for the run to count. Bettors learned this lesson in a big way in October 1999 at the end of Game 5 of the National League Championship game.

The total closed at 7.5, and under betters thought they were in pretty good shape when the game went to extra innings tied up 2 to 2. History shows a 2–2 game will land on under 7.5 about 90 percent of the time.

In the 15th inning, with the game still tied, the Mets started putting runners on base, something both over and under bettors had an interest in. Over bettors needed a grand slam to take advantage of the baseball rule that says that a home run in the bottom frame of extra innings means all runs, including the batter's run, count toward the final score. For any other hit, the game ends as soon as the first runner legally touches home. (By the way, this means the game can't end on an inside-the-park grand slam unless the home team is down by exactly 3 runs.)

And sure enough, over bettors were thrilled as the Mets loaded the bases for Robin Ventura. It was the nightmare scenario after 15 innings of waiting. Ventura promptly sent the ball into the stands, making history as the first batter to ever hit a walk-off grand slam in the postseason. Or was he?

As under bettors were tearing up their tickets and over bettors were jumping for joy, something unusual happened. Ventura was mobbed on the base path by his team-mates. There's a rule in baseball that the runner can't be touched or assisted by his own team in any way, although it's often ignored for high-fives on the third-base line near home plate. But in this case, as the three base runners each touched home, Ventura got completely waylaid. After a minute or two, the umpires declared the game over since Ventura had "surrendered" his run around the bases.

The result? Without Ventura's touching home, it wasn't a home run — even though the ball went into the stands. Without the home run, the game ended when the runner on third touched home. And so the game officially ended as a 3–2 Mets win, with under bettors cashing their miracle ticket, and over bettors left dazed and confused.

The Ventura grand-slam single isn't even the only one in baseball history. In at least two other situations a home run with 3 baserunners did not lead to 4 runs going up on the board. Baseball has quirky rules that can bite bettors sometimes. Consider that in certain situations, games that get postponed prior to being made "official" in the 5th inning

(continued)

(continued)

can be restarted completely, wiping out the stats accumulated before the delay. That's why you can't collect on certain bets (like the prop that either team will score at least one run in the 1st inning) until after the game is complete and in the books.

The lesson for bettors is this: After 150 years, there are some quirks built into baseball rules. What makes a home run is the batter touching home, not the ball going over the fence. Don't celebrate your wins or mourn your losses until the game is well and truly over.

Baseball Scoring Patterns

Baseball, like any sport, has "eras" where scoring happens in multi-year and decade-long trends. As always, if you're looking for historical context in the statistics, be wary. New ballparks, rules changes, scheduling changes, league directives for umpires to call plays a certain way. All of these factors can lead to a given year not being comparable with another.

Runs per game

Take a look at Table 14-2 and you'll see the recent evolution of scoring in both the first five innings and for full games. Improved strength training and a trend toward shrinking ballparks have led to a steady increase in scoring over the decades. The late 1990s — also known as the steroid era — saw a flurry of offense peaking in 2000 when teams averaged 5.1 runs per game. The 2010s saw a brief return to normalcy as runs per game averages hovered between 4 and 4.5. Over the last 5 years or so, the total runs scored after 5 innings averages about 5.2 runs, and the average 9-inning score is just under 9 runs. In 2019, teams were closing in on 10 runs per game, setting all-time records for home runs in the process (and strikeouts too, just for good measure).

Runs per inning

As you might expect, with an average game score around 9 total runs, baseball games average about 1 combined run per inning, with the runs evenly distributed across the innings, with a few exceptions. The 8th inning sees about a 20 percent dip in scoring, and since the home team occasionally doesn't bat at all in the 9th inning, scoring in that frame is way down. The only other irregularity is the 2nd inning, where nearly every team has a noticeable dip in run production. Perhaps this is due to starting pitchers settling in and getting past their 1st inning jitters plus the advantage of facing lesser hitters in the middle or bottom of the order.

TABLE 14-2

Major League Baseball's Recent Scoring History

Average Runs Scored by Season	First Five Innings		Full Game		
	Avg Home Team Runs	Avg Road Team Runs	Avg Home Team Runs	Avg Road Team Runs	Total Runs Scored per Game
2009	2.82	2.47	4.73	4.49	9.22
2010	2.68	2.32	4.52	4.25	8.77
2011	2.5	2.38	4.3	4.27	8.57
2012	2.68	2.36	4.41	4.24	8.65
2013	2.5	2.32	4.19	4.14	8.33
2014	2.41	2.19	4.1	4.02	8.12
2015	2.58	2.29	4.34	4.15	8.49
2016	2.73	2.4	4.53	4.42	8.95
2017	2.82	2.56	4.75	4.54	9.29
2018	2.63	2.37	4.52	4.37	8.89
2019	2.84	2.61	4.82	4.83	9.65

Assessing hot and cold streaks

The hot hand question as it concerns baseball hitters is a well-studied phenomenon. Bettors evaluating an upcoming game might be tempted to look for teams with hot bats. But no matter how you look at it, it's difficult to prove that a recent offensive tear make a player more likely to get a hit in his next at-bat. Many analysts have made a strong statistical case that in any random distribution of unlikely events (like hits over the course of a season full of at-bats), you'll see clustered events. They're randomly distributed events cleverly disguised as streaks.

And if the hot hand isn't random? Another possibility is that a player getting a hit versus not getting a hit is the result of minute changes in batter concentration, recent preparation and habit development, park effects, health and wellness factors, and even confidence in certain situations. But as baseball stats guru Bill James stated in a 2013 blog post, while those things are technically "knowable," they are not visible to an external viewer, and because the fluctuation in those factors results in the fluctuation of output, it has the same effect as randomness.

Starting Pitching and MLB Odds

Starting pitchers are the most dominant factor in any baseball game's outcome, and oddsmakers rely heavily on their recent performance to set the odds of any game.

WARNING

Look beyond traditional statistics. Let me say that a different way: Don't just look beyond them; don't look at traditional statistics at all. You're not trying to figure out who's going to win the Cy Young this year. You're looking for pitchers who give their team a better chance at winning than the oddsmakers give them credit for. Wins, losses, and ERA are garbage when it comes to picking winners.

Consider these statistics instead when you look at pitchers:

>> **WHIP:** This stat, walks and hits per inning pitched, is becoming more commonplace and very useful. It's like the more familiar ERA in that it's normalized (ERA over 9 innings, WHIP over 1 inning), but it's walks and hits. The downside of WHIP? It doesn't give pitchers credit for being able to escape from jams in the form of reduced runs allowed.

>> **FIP:** You can figure out that IP means "per inning pitched," and FIP is known colloquially as Fielding Independent Pitching. This stat normalizes stats based on fielders' range in the infield and outfield.

>> **Strikeouts and walks:** In some form, these stats are favored by baseball prognosticators. Some say strikeouts per inning minus walks per nine innings is all you need to know about a pitcher's ability to get outs.

BET on rest

The only time teams get more than a day off is during the All-Star break in the second week of July. Nevertheless, there are opportunities to bet on teams that are more rested than their opponents. Consider this setup:

For regular season MLB games

When the home team has more rest than the visitor AND

The game total is 9 or more

BET over the total.

It's not life changing, but the result is 145–105 over/under in the last decade. That's a 58 percent system for you to study, use, and refine.

Home/away splits

Major League Baseball has one of the smaller home field advantages in all the major sports. But small doesn't mean nonexistent, as there are lots of reasons it helps to play at home:

>> Home baseball games mean continuity, less travel, and players living at home.

>> Fielders have a chance to get more familiar with the contours of the foul areas, outfield barriers, and in some cases the weather conditions.

>> Your hitters and pitchers can get comfortable with the lights, shadows, and the critical site line between home plate and the pitcher's mound.

>> Over the long run, a team's general manager can build a team to match the ballpark. For stadiums with a shortened right field, you can stack up lefty power hitters. For smaller ballparks in general, you can trade away your fly-ball pitchers for ground-ball pitchers.

And of course, if you're the Houston Astros, you can plant bugs in the opposing team's clubhouse and fine-tune the closed-circuit camera system for stealing signs! (Sorry, Astros fans. That was in the past, right? We can all have a good laugh about it now. Right, Dodgers fans?)

Just so you know the premise is true, Table 14-3 shows some data from recent seasons. It's a small sample, but looking further back shows roughly the same advantage for the home team.

TABLE 14-3   **MLB Home Field Advantage**

Regular Season	Home Team Win %	Home Favorite Win %	Home Underdog Win %
2016	53%	59%	42%
2017	54%	60%	43%
2018	52.7%	60%	40%
2019	53%	62%	38%

If we knew nothing else about two major league teams facing each other, we would install the home team as a −112 favorite. That moneyline equates to a shade over 53 percent in terms of break-even winning percentage.

Betting on home field advantage is tricky in baseball. Teams that start off playing well at home don't always finish well at home. For example, in comparing home winning percentages of 2019 teams between the first and second halves of the season shows that 4 of the top 5 home field performers were languishing in the middle of the pack before the All-Star Break.

The Park Factor

Perhaps the most unusual aspect of baseball is the fact that the field of play varies from park to park. Sure, the pitcher's mound and bases are all positioned identically, but step beyond the infield, or outside the foul lines, and the resemblance quickly stops.

It seems crazy, but the field of play is different in every Major League park. The most noticeable are the outfield dimensions, where the distance from home plate to the foul poles and straight-away center can vary. Very few parks are symmetrical; most have nooks and crannies that befuddle fielders with their odd caroms. Most unusually, when the Houston Astros built Minute Maid Park (then called Enron Field), it included a small berm in center field with a flagpole in the field of play. It's almost as if teams relish the irregularities they can introduce into their fields.

There's more. There are no rules about the height of the outfield barriers, giving rise to the 37-foot-high green monster in Fenway Park, which is opposite a right-field wall so low that the fielders can use it to vault into the stands to catch would-be home runs. In fact, only nine parks have an outfield barrier with a consistent height all the way around.

Park factor statistics

The combined effect of outfield dimensions and quirks, along with foul territory, weather, and sight lines, make for a combined effect that some sources of Major League Baseball data call the *Park Factor*.

Park Factor gives you a single stat that quantifies the effect of the park's peculiarities on the game. The higher the Park Factor, the better it is for the offense. The lower the Park Factor, the better it is for the pitcher.

Coors Field is consistently in the top of the Park Factor list, possibly because of Denver's altitude, but also because, maybe counterintuitively, when the designers set the outfield walls back to counter the altitude effects, they created more space in the outfield for extra-base hits as well.

WARNING

Baseball fans, analysts, fantasy nerds, and bettors alike put a lot of stock in statistics, both hitting and pitching. But consider that aggregate stats of a player or a team are largely dependent on the field they play on. Countless studies have been done to the tune of "If Josh Donaldson played his home games at ABC ballpark instead of XYZ ballpark, he would have had a very different season."

The changing configuration of parks from year to year means comparing statistics is fraught with peril. When the San Francisco Giants moved from Candlestick Park to AT&T Park, they lost 33 percent of their foul territory. That has the same impact on pitchers as moving the fences in because it reduces the number of fly ball outs that can be caught outside the foul lines.

Park Factor research opportunities

Baseball's wide variety of parks means that there's abundant data on how players and teams perform at different venues. But not nearly enough of this research has connected ballpark information with betting outcomes. Are certain fields more likely to produce overs and unders in general? Do some fields create impossible shadows if the game starts at a certain time of day during a specific month? How much is home field worth in each stadium in terms of moneyline odds, and does the oddsmaker and betting market properly account for it? Baseball is waiting for you to unpack these mysteries and many others. Speaking of weather . . .

Weather

Out of 30 teams, only six have home parks with retractable (or permanent) roofs, with the Texas Rangers mercifully scheduled to add a seventh in 2020. But with so many games played outside, a careful baseball bettor should keep an eye on the weather and understand how it impacts the game. Everyone accepts the premise that when the wind is "blowing out," more home runs are likely, but there's more to weather than just wind, and there's more to baseball than just home runs.

Let me tell you about wind

It is commonly understood that higher wind velocities equate to more runs scored. Research has shown that calm days produce the lowest average runs, and every mile per hour of wind increases scoring by .1 run. The wind starts to have a big impact when it really starts gusting.

TIP

Bettors monitor the wind and hammer over wagers when the wind is blowing strong at any outdoor ballpark. There are a couple good opportunities for the astute bettor to profit from the wind if you're willing to put the work in:

» **Bettor enthusiasm for wind-driven unders is not the same as it is for overs.** Look for games where the wind is blowing squarely in and take the under. There's a good research opportunity if you're willing to dive deeper into the data and determine if certain parks have stronger wind effects than others.

» **Wind changes over time.** The direction and velocity of the wind eight hours prior to the first pitch is often quite different from what it is mid-game. Look for situations where the wind vector changes substantially within a few hours of game time. Not only does it give the betting public less time to grind down the total odds, but if the change is dramatic enough, it also means the total might be skewed in precisely the wrong direction at game time, making for an easy over or under bet.

You are my density

The distance a ball travels is inversely related to air density, which is why fly balls carry at Coors Field in Denver. Fewer air molecules to bump up against means less drag. The *International Journal of Sports Science and Engineering* (IJSSE) put out a fascinating paper in 2009 about how air density changes the flight of a baseball. Their approach lends itself to creating an air density rating that you can apply to any game.

The Simplified Air Density Estimator

Start with the assumption that the game is played in "average" atmospheric conditions, so your Simplified Air Density Estimator (let's call it the SADE — I'll let you make your own "diamond life" joke) starts at 0 and is adjusted as follows:

» **Altitude:** For every 500 feet of altitude above 2,600 feet, add 2 points. For each 500 feet below 2,600 feet, subtract 2 points.

» **Temperature:** For every 5 degrees above 85 degrees Fahrenheit, subtract a point. For every 5 degrees below 85, add a point.

» **Relative humidity:** If humidity is below 25 percent, add a point. If humidity is above 75 percent, add a point.

» **Barometric pressure:** If the barometer reads less than 29.5mm Hg, subtract a point. If the barometer reads more than 30.3mm Hg, add a point.

Combine the factors together to get your air density effect. For example, a game played at Chase field in Phoenix (~1,000 feet elevation) in the midst of a high-pressure system with 100-degrees temperatures, 30.5mm barometric pressure, and 0 percent humidity would be calculated as:

Gametime SADE = –6 for altitude, –3 for temperature, +1 for humidity, + 1 for air pressure

Add them up and you get –7, so we would say that the atmospheric conditions of the game have caused air density to be 7-percent lower than average.

So what if air density is 7-percent lower than average? What does that mean? The IJSSE paper estimated a variation as high as 15 percent in terms of distance a home run ball would travel if you executed identical hits in two locations with extreme air density differences. At the extremes, your SADE is 15 on a hot day at Coors Field and –15 on a cold dry day in a stadium near sea level.

As a part of your game handicap, check the weather and calculate the SADE to see how much air density will play a factor in the game.

WARNING

While altitude has the biggest effect on air density, there's not that much variation in ballpark elevations throughout the majors. After Coors Field, no ballpark sits higher than 2,600 feet. Most of the rest cluster at the low end of the range between 1,000 feet and sea level. Based on the SADE calculations, temperature becomes the largest determinant of air density for any yard outside of Colorado.

Air density and pitching

The effectiveness of a pitcher's arsenal of pitchers is dependent on his ability to vary speeds and locations along with the movement of his pitches, the apparent rise of a fastball, the drop of a curveball, or the slice of a slider.

TIP

Air density has differing effects on different pitches. Lower air density means more velocity on a fastball. Extreme levels of SADE can alter a fastball by 4 to 5 mph. So a fastball pitcher in a low-density environment will have thin air on his side when he dials up the heat. But lower density means less air to bite against the seams, which means less movement on the pitches.

Other weather effects

According to researchers at University of Nevada-Reno, player behavior changes with weather as well. For example, several offensive statistics go up with temperature, including runs, batting average, home runs, and slugging. The same study found that hitters walk less in warmer weather compared to cooler weather, which may have to do with a pitcher's reduced ability to grip the ball in the cold.

Betting against the Public

Baseball bettors tend to get enamored of teams on a roll. As pitchers get hot, and especially as the teams themselves start to roll, their odds get slightly longer than they're worth. And the inverse is true as well: Teams who have hit rough waters look worse in the eyes of the average bettor than they really are.

REMEMBER

Game odds are a function of the oddsmaker and the bettors. The oddsmaker estimates a team's chances of winning and sets the odds accordingly, with some adjustments for predictions of the public's perception and perhaps an adjustment for park and weather effects. But then the odds are released into the wild. If bettors wager heavily on the favorite, their odds quickly get longer, and if bettors heavily bet the underdog, the odds go the other way.

Team streaks

Teams on win streaks tend to attract unearned attention from bettors. Remember the lesson of coin flips from Chapter 6: Just because a coin has come up heads 5 times in a row, it doesn't suddenly become more (or less!) likely to hit heads on the 6th flip. Sure, baseball teams aren't coins. The trials aren't independent because teams can get down on themselves or feel that they have a certain level of momentum.

But there's also a psychological effect at work on the betting side. If you bet against a team on a 10-game winning streak and lose, you'll feel like the guy that does a faceplant into the plate glass window, thinking it's a door. So it's not just a matter of bettors flocking to the streaking team; it's also a matter of the normal attention you would expect the other side of the bet to receive starts to attenuate as the streak goes on. Add it all up, and you have potential for profit.

TIP

Bet against home teams on a moderate roll. History has shown a steady trend of +EV betting is available if you're willing to bet against a home team on a winning streak. After 4 wins, the public seems to take note of the hot team and the over-betting begins.

Run line and moneyline bets against the streaky club have shown a positive ROI in the neighborhood of 5 to 10 percent. And there are several ways to make it more lucrative, such as finding the streaky team that's a rare home underdog. This might happen if they're up against the road team's ace starter, for example.

BET the win streak ends here

You should do your own exploration, but here's the setup you're looking for:

> During the MLB regular season
>
> The home team has won their last 4 games AND
>
> The home team last lost 5 games ago
>
> **BET** the visitor's moneyline or the visitor's run line.

A home team on exactly a 4-game win streak has offered contrarian bettors an overall 7 percent ROI on both the moneyline and run line bets. And the good news is that this scenario comes up about 100 times per year during the MLB regular season. In the data I looked at, if you blind bet this system, you would have made money in 8 of the last 10 years.

PROGRESSIVE BETTING

You've probably heard of the Martingale or similar betting strategy where you bet 1 chip, and if you lose, you bet 2 chips. If you lose again, you bet 4 chips, and so on. In theory, you're eventually going to win, so as long as you increase your subsequent bets by enough, you're guaranteed to win. It might work in very short-term situations, but because casinos and bookmakers have betting limits, you quickly run out of real estate to increase your bet.

The fact that baseball teams on win streaks are often over-bet makes it tempting to apply some sort of progressive multi-game betting strategy to the situation. For example, if you bet against the 4-in-a-row team and they win, you could double your bet and try betting against the same team again. In this scenario, your initial bet would lose a little over half the time. (Remember, you were betting on the underdog, so it's okay to have a sub-50 percent winning percentage.) If you followed up that loss with a double-bet against that same streaking team, you'd end up with a positive ROI, even though it would be especially painful to lose two in a row.

In general, I don't recommend progressive betting, but I have encountered handicappers and pickers who swear by multi-game betting systems like this. I suggest these precautions:

- Have a clear exit strategy; no open-ended systems. If your plan is to make increasing bets against a streaking team, set a maximum number of losses (how about 2?), at which point, you bail out.

- Make sure that the betting limits of your bookmaker are high enough relative to your bet amount so that you can easily increase your bet as needed.

The trend works on a 5-game win streak as well. If the home team has won exactly 5 games in a row, betting their opponent blindly would have yielded you 11 percent on the visitor's moneyline and 6 percent on the run line.

More streak betting

What about a 6-game winning streak and higher? Here, the numbers aren't so clear because the sample size dips to the point where the effect becomes harder to measure and more volatile. Betting against the home team on a 7-game streak was a money loser in 2019, but it only happened 6 times, so it's hard to say if the system loses its potency or if there simply aren't enough instances to take a good measurement.

It's possible that what we're seeing is that bettors overvalue a team on a win streak by a certain standard amount, whether it's a 4-game streak or a 10-game streak. But the team themselves doesn't gain any kind of momentum edge until the win streak has gotten close to double digits. At that point, they really do have an edge in terms of confidence that raises their chances of winning beyond what the betting public sees. It's possible, but I wouldn't blame you for being skeptical of that rationale.

What about the other way? Do baseball bettors undervalue teams on a losing streak the same way they overvalue teams on a winning streak? The short answer is no. Unlike betting against teams on a win streak, betting for teams on a losing streak has not been lucrative. And it makes some sense when you consider the basic behavior of bettors: They bet *for* teams rather than *against* teams. Even though both insights are potentially profitable, bettors pay much closer attention to winning streaks than losing streaks, so the former get overvalued while the latter remain undistorted by the market.

MLB Systems and Angles

Major League Baseball sees big fluctuations in offensive production, and the most recent season, 2019, is the poster child for this phenomenon. In the years 2005 through 2018, there were 2 games with a total north of 13, and in 2019, there were 20! Some of my favorite systems and angles to explore are ones revolving around "extreme" odds, like very high or very low totals, or extreme disparities in the moneyline. But when the game can change so dramatically from year to year, it can be difficult to demonstrate a system's effectiveness over a long period of time (one of the characteristics of a high-quality system).

Betting against home favorites in extremely high total games (13 or more runs) was profitable in 2019. The underdogs won 11 games straight up and lost 5 for an ROI over 50 percent. That's not a big enough sample size to reliably determine if we've got a winning system or not, and ideally, we'd like to look backwards and see if this system was profitable in previous years. Unfortunately, there just aren't enough games totaled at 13 or greater to supply us the history we need.

BET under extreme totals!

While the 2019 season saw the virtual disappearance of games totaled 7 or lower, they aren't extinct, merely endangered. Betting markets appear to find it difficult to bet that a game will land on 7 or fewer runs when the league average is closing in on 10 runs! You can profit from the market's inability to imagine a game without much offense. Here's the setup:

> In the Major League Baseball regular season
>
> If a home team is an underdog AND
>
> The game total is 7 or less
>
> **BET** under the total.

Over the last decade, this system has produced a 55 percent record and an ROI of 5.6 percent. This system would have put you in the black nine of the last ten years. In high-scoring seasons, the opportunities are less abundant, but baseball changes from year to year, so by the time you read this, the high-flying home-run hitting offenses of 2019 might just be a distant memory, and you'll have opportunities to bet under the 7-run total in droves.

TIP

The success at betting under extremely low totals is an indicator that there is a certain gravitational pull in the betting markets, almost certainly created by bettors' preconceived notions about what a reasonable outcome is. The reality is that when two aces face each other, with great bullpens behind them, 4–0 and 3–1 games are relatively common . . . but gamblers have reflexive discomfort betting under extremely low totals.

Having said that, the number of games with totals at or below 7 has been steadily shrinking as run production has gone up.

WARNING

Make the total bet at −110 odds. When the under is bet heavily, the odds will change before the total itself will move from 7.5 to 7. For example, if bettors are pounding the under 7.5 at −110, it will move to 7.5 −115, then 7.5 −120, and 7.5 −125 before moving to 7 −110. And as the odds move from −110 toward −125, the break-even win percentage increases. You have to win 55 percent of your bets to be profitable on −125 odds.

BET big favorites!

Although studies have shown that heavy favorites and home teams tend to get undue attention from bettors, the results of the last decade of baseball unequivocally show that there's money to be made betting with the favorite rather than the opposite.

If we assume home favorites get over-bet, the same is not true of road favorites. Here's a simple setup you can watch for:

In the Major League Baseball regular season

If a team is favored by –201 or more (i.e., a more negative number) AND

That team is on the road

BET the road team's moneyline.

It's simple but profitable: A bettor who started following this strategy in 2009 would have seen a 12.3 percent ROI since then with only two down years. Table 14-4 give you the data.

TABLE 14-4   ## Betting Big Favorites

Year	W/L Record	ROI
2009	13–1	+35.4%
2010	15–7	–1.4%
2011	6–9	–41.5%
2012	9–0	+45.5%
2013	9–1	+29.6%
2014	5–1	+20.3%
2015	12–4	+7.3%
2016	29–9	+9.7%
2017	38–11	+9.4%
2018	65–14	+17.1%
2019	87–20	+13.9%
Total	288–77	+12.3%

A few things to think about with these systems:

- >> The data I collected comes from a combination of sportsdatabase.com and my own homegrown baseball database. My data suggests heavy favorites are three times as likely to get more expensive than less expensive (which is an indicator that favorites naturally get more attention from bettors, or possibly that this is a publicly known system). That is, a game listed at –220 is much more likely to go off at –230 than –210. That means betting early is important for this system.

- >> These 365 games have an average line of –241, or a 70 percent break-even rate. The 78.9 percent win rate of this system is more than enough for profitability, but you can see where shopping for the best odds matters.

- >> I'm listing ROI rather than a flat profit number because clearly the amount of money a bettor makes is dependent on how much is risked. I don't flinch at showing the very negative returns from 2011 because there were so few betting opportunities. If you were using some form of Kelly bet-sizing or flat-betting, you wouldn't have lost much of your bankroll on this strategy.

- >> We can conclude that the game has been changing in recent years. Particularly, the prevalence of high road favorites has gone through the roof, indicating that perhaps Major League Baseball has a parity problem. In 2014, there were only 6 betting opportunities out of 2,430 regular season games, and in 2019, there were over 100.

- >> Data suggests that betting on the road run line favorite is slightly more profitable, and I've even gotten this recommendation from people within the bookmaking industry.

WARNING

As with any system, this one could dry up tomorrow, or it could continue for another decade. If more people know about it, more people bet it. If more people bet it, the prices on big favorites go higher. As big favorites get more expensive, the break-even percentage goes up.

The good news is, like any long-standing, simple, broad system, this one is begging for an astute bettor to dig in and refine it. Maybe the win percentage gets better if you avoid high-total games or exclude big public teams like the Yankees and Cardinals.

BET pitcher's duel losers!

In the spirit of betting against public sentiment, consider the premise that there is nothing more pathetic in modern baseball than a team that loses 1–0. Your batters are so ineffective that they can't produce a single lousy run for your poor, overworked, overachieving pitcher.

Keep your eyes peeled for situations where good teams are on the wrong end of a 1–0 shutout. It appears to have a motivating effect on the next game's batters:

In the Major League Baseball regular season

If a team lost by a score of 1–0 in their last game AND

The losing team is favored in their upcoming game

BET on the favorite team's moneyline.

In the last decade, this situation has come up about 10 to 15 times per season and has produced a +11 percent ROI. It works at home and on the road, but the very best situation seems to be when a team loses 1–0 in their final series game against an opponent. These teams effectively take their frustration out on their new opponent, building a 56–25 record, for a +18 percent ROI.

4
Mastering the Craft

IN THIS PART . . .

Get some graduate-level wisdom on how we process information. Understand the psychological phenomena that drive gamblers, analysts, and fans to see things that aren't there, to create narratives that aren't true, and to develop bankroll-draining habits.

Learn why Excel is the ideal tool for the average gambler, and get a head start on building helper spreadsheets to track bets, calculate betting metrics, and sift through data.

Chapter 15

You versus You

I believe it is *extremely* difficult to make a living betting on sports. But that is not the same thing as saying that bettors can't make a long-run profit. Wagering enough to live on, and winning at a 55 to 60 percent clip will get the attention of bookmakers. And once you're profiled, it becomes very difficult to stay in the game at levels that allow you to quit your day job.

So who wins money betting on sports? Let's break it down. Cohort studies show that after a year, 80 to 90 percent of new accounts on an online sports betting site have less money than when they started. Normalized to a $100 deposit, about 50 percent have lost their stake, and about 40 percent are in a long tail of people who have lost anywhere from a few dollars to most of their stake.

I have also read multiple studies that have shown how few people with online accounts win over months and years. Just looking at fully regulated online against-the-spread contests will give you ample evidence that it's hard to win over the long term.

The difference between winning and losing is seemingly innocuous moments of discipline that I too often was unwilling to display. That makes me think that it's perfectly reasonable to transform 49 percent losing bettors into a 53 percent winning bettors by attaching some rigor to their process, and to ask them to work diligently on maximizing their returns.

Normal people who want to get good betting on sports need to know where to start. Many of the battles you face in this pursuit will be against yourself. This chapter is all about ways that you can get to know the human mind (geez, I hope you, dear reader, have a human mind and not anything else) and leverage that knowledge in your career as an athletic prognosticator. And I'll also talk about the many ways that bettors torpedo themselves.

Who Actually Wins at Sports Betting?

So how do you get to be one of the elect, one of the chosen few? I've talked about this subject in early chapters, but here's a brief perspective of who's up and why:

>> They're folks who adopt a handicapping strategy, and they stick to it.

>> They settle on a bankroll management strategy and a bet-sizing strategy, and they stick to it. If there's a bet that they can't quantify as plus EV, they pass on it.

>> They accept the random nature of sporting events and understand that sometimes wise game pickers lose, and unwise game pickers win.

>> They understand the nature of betting markets. For bettors of the biggest sports, there are few "structural" inefficiencies in the marketplace, so, there's no silver bullet that leads to riches.

>> They have multiple outs, and they are willing to take the time to find the very best odds before they place a bet.

Conventional wisdom suggests that they certainly aren't normal folk. The story is always about a numbers genius, the kind of guy who sees equations floating in the air, synthesizing the data in a montage moment. Even if those people do exist, they make their money betting on stock market algorithms if they make it at all. The common notion that people don't win by gambling doesn't paint the real picture. Normal people can win betting on sports.

Sure, they need more than just a cursory knowledge of the game, or the league. They need a solid way of making predictions too. They need a deep knowledge of the game and the league and its rules and the players involved. They need a starting bankroll. They need to be willing to lose and improve. They need to be able to go up against themselves and ask the sort of deep rational questions that build good models and good predictions.

You've probably heard about the gambling success stories. You might have also heard that the really good gamblers get blackballed. Get good enough at sports betting and you might find yourself with nowhere to bet. To be sure bookmakers will place limits on advantage bettors — those with a high winning percentage. But if you make the right kind of small bets, spread out enough to avoid notice, you *can* win long term without catching the eye of the people who want to stop you.

Decision-Making and Judgment

You want to be a good bettor. Good bettors make good decisions. They make good decisions about probabilities. You're here reading this book, so hopefully you aren't too scared of numbers and probabilities and statistics and all the technical stuff that goes into being a good bettor. It turns out that some very smart people have written some very dense books about formal probability and decision making. They've also written some great books about how bad people tend to be at it.

But you don't have time right now to sink your teeth into Daniel Kahneman's Nobel Prize-winning *Thinking, Fast and Slow.* You've got power ratings to build and games to watch. While you're at it, learn a little about the ways that people, you included, make judgements on the fly, and in the face of evidence.

In fact, knowing where your gut feelings may be very wrong could save you from making some very bad decisions in the future.

Heuristics

Do you bet with your gut? No, not the gut that was built up beer by beer, but your "inner gut," where you have an instinct about a team or a player and what he might do in tomorrow's game.

Before you put your money where your small intestine is, let's talk about it. What is a gut feeling, anyways? Psychologists like to bandy about the word *heuristics.*

Heuristics are the back-of-the-napkin, seat-of-the-pants rules-of-thumb that you lean on to make rapid decisions, without stopping to carry the one. You do this all the time, every single day. You might even be able to describe the rule you've decided to follow (like a beginning chess player who thinks it's best "never move a piece twice in the first ten moves"). There's often a grain of truth, or deeper meaning, in a rule, or it wouldn't catch on. In politics people often mention the "kind of guy I'd like to grab a beer with" heuristic. That makes sense because people prefer politicians they can relate to on a personal level.

Over the course of millennia, humans have developed many built-in heuristics. These subconscious rules-of-thumb guide our behavior in ways we might be totally unaware of.

Though this list is by no means exhaustive, in the following sections, I've tried to list some of the most common biases due to heuristics that come up when we talk about gambling (and human psychology in general). Instead of getting bogged down in the complexities of the heuristics, I've opted simply to describe the biases themselves.

Insensitivity to predictability

Placing a wager will always require you to make prediction about future events. Maybe it's a bet on the over or under; maybe it's a judgement about the final score or the performance of a backup QB.

Are these things actually predictable? Yes, but not as much as you think.

Humans are not only naturally optimistic about their internal crystal ball, but they tend to assess future events as being far more predictable than they really are.

To borrow and only slightly bastardize a statistics concept, analysts calculate a correlation coefficient when they build models to predict an outcome based on historical data. The correlation coefficient is a value between 0 and 1 that represents the proportion of an outcome that can be explained by the historical data. If the number is 1, there's a 100 percent correlation, and if it's 0, you might as well be comparing two sets of unrelated random numbers.

If we port that concept over to our ability to predict the future, you could imagine the outcome of an event, like the number of points a team will score in an upcoming game, is dependent on two families of factors:

» Observable variables, like the ones I talk about throughout this book: historical performance, days of rest, strength and speed of the team and opposition, quality of the coaches, and many more

» Random events and processes, or events that are determined by factors outside the ability of observers to understand and measure

If a baseball player hits a bat off a tee, the ball will obviously not land in the same spot in the field every time. Tiny variations in the hitter's concentration, how muscles fatigue and fire, and even random gusts of wind can affect the trajectory of the ball. You might say that 60 percent of that event is predictable based on the batter's strength and skill, but 40 percent of it is based on elements of performance that we can't see or understand — to all intents and purposes, random. Research tells us that we overestimate the predictable component of a future event and therefore underestimate the random component.

If you accept that a game score is 20 percent predictable and 80 percent random, the result is that there will be great variation in the results. Teams and players will regularly defy expectations and prediction. But as a sports bettor, if you're able to grasp the predictable components correctly, your predictions will be right in the long run.

Information cannot inoculate you from randomness

When we make predictions, we grab information that's available to us, and we label it (mentally) as a contributor to a future outcome. That's natural, and that's how all predictions work. But if you accept there is a cap on the predictability of events, you'll realize that stacking up data does not shield you from the effects of randomness. In fact, compiling lots of information can give the illusion that events are more predictable than they are.

Even if you watched every Washington Nationals game during the regular season and compiled detailed stats on every single player, there's still a limit to how well you can predict the result of the next game. That's not to say there are no good bets to make, but my point is to caution you from believing you're in more control than you actually have.

The illusion of validity

On November 19 of the 2018 NFL season, the Rams and the Chiefs played a record-breaking offensive game. Because that game was so remarkable, it had a certain stickiness in the mind of bettors, who couldn't shake the idea that Chiefs and Rams would score 50 points every week.

It's another common problem: conflating some statistic or measurement with over-all probability. It turns out that high-scoring-ness fails when trying to predict who will win the conference finals. It turns out that, among the myriad of statistics available for all kinds of sports, none are able of giving great predictions when used alone and very few are even useful when trying to predict games in a general way. By falling in love with a certain statistic or past event, you'll begin to believe that it is a good way of predicting outcomes, even if it isn't. When you are wrong (or even when you are right), the reasons for that outcome slip down the memory hole.

Keep a journal about why you picked games the way you did and how they turned out. On reflection, you might find that you've misattributed wins and losses to statistics that at the time seemed important but in retrospect did not matter at all.

Read about how other sports bettors assess games and also how they assess themselves. Sports betting is a never-ending quest to find the most predictive metrics and factors.

Thin-slicing

Humans are built to make instant judgments and predictions. If you read *Blink: The Power of Thinking without Thinking,* you'll remember how Malcom Gladwell describes experts (and non-experts sometimes) who can take in a tiny amount of information and make an assessment. The classic example is the art expert who has an immediate instinct that a painting is a forgery but is unable to explain why.

Gladwell calls this phenomenon "thin-slicing," and the power lies in our tendency not to question our initial judgments. Dovetailing with this, Daniel Kahneman writes at length about two distinct mental processes humans use to make judgments and predictions: the thin-slice version that produces quick judgments and a slower, more conscious and deliberate process where we embellish and sometimes adjust that initial conclusion.

The problem is, we often put that second process to work in simply finding ways to rationalize and support the conclusion of the first process. No matter how slap-dash the blink-fast conclusion is, our rational mind by default looks for ways to justify the decision we have already made. Sports watchers and bettors are particularly prone to this self-deception. "There's no way the Eagles, led by a backup QB, can beat the Patriots." Without digging any deeper into the meat of the question, we decide that backup quarterbacks are worse than starting quarterbacks, and so we decide that the Patriots will win. If you had bet on that Super Bowl, you would have lost good money.

Misunderstanding regression to the mean

When you see an outlier in the data, you should not expect the outlier to persist through future data, but rather, that future measurement will look more like the previous mean measurements. This is the essence of analyses based on *regression to the mean.*

To put it simpler: Extreme performances are most often followed by totally normal performances, not by more extreme performances. Maybe you'd expect that if a team is hot (and in this chapter, I cover the hot-hands fallacy too), they will stay hot.

But if Luka Doncic drops 50 points on Tuesday night, the most likely outcome on Wednesday night is that Luka will score fewer points.

People misunderstand this concept in a couple common ways. The most obvious misunderstanding occurs when people do not expect the regression. This is the line of thinking where one exceptional game should lead to another. The other way people misunderstand regression is by expecting it but coming up with bad reasoning to explain it.

TIP

Regression to the mean is a powerful concept in sports betting because there is great temptation for bettors to put too much emphasis on performances that are both extreme and recent.

Let's talk about a game that results in a big spread surprise: Maybe a slight favorite beats the spread by 30 points, or a big underdog gets an outright win. How do you account for the surprise? One explanation is that we had misjudged these teams: We overrated the loser and underrated the winner. But a second explanation is that it was simple luck. We know that much of the outcome of games is due to random variation, so in fact, there was no major misassessment of the two teams.

But we also know that people (gamblers in particular) are always looking for a sign. They are hungry for information, and they are susceptible to dramatic recent events. So the betting market, as a whole, will revise their assessment of each team. Bettors who don't understand how teams regress to the mean will tend to overreact to events like this. And an overreaction from the betting market means an opportunity for the astute bettor. Many of the systems and trends contained in this book take advantage of overreactions in the betting market.

More Cognitive Biases

In this section, I will outline a few more of the most common biases that afflict sports bettors. These biases have less to do with the formal work of recent psychologists, but they are nonetheless vital to understanding your own thinking process and how to improve.

The Gambler's Fallacy

The Gamblers Fallacy says that independent random events are "due" to go one way or another. The classic example comes from the roulette wheel. You've been sitting at the table for half an hour, and you've seen black come up ten times in a row. You're smart and you know about probability. You know that the chances of getting 11 black spins in a row are around 0.00269 percent. You think this means there is now a 99.998 percent chance that the next spin will come up red. You thought wrong! The odds of each individual spin stay the same: For a color bet in roulette, the odds are a little less than 50-50 for each spin. It's easy to see how this way of thinking can be extended to sports betting.

You might think that after 10 bad bets in a row, you are due for a win. You have to win sometime, right? The same can be said of your favorite team, (the Cardinals can't lose that many in a row, can they?) or really of any events that seem to go together in a sequence. So long as the events — the games, the bets, whatever they are — are *independent*, the outcome of one event does not affect the probability of the next.

Untangling events from each other in this way is tricky. How independent are games in the same season? Games in a series? Certainly, a lot of punditry is devoted to explaining sports in terms of the athletes' mental states. That would make it seem like individual games are connected. Maybe a devastating loss throws off a star player's next game. Then again, maybe it just hardens his resolve to come back and win the following night. The fact that this sort of narrative analysis produces conflicting predictions is reason enough to completely discount it.

You should treat games as independent events until proven otherwise. Of course, players remember what happened last week, and it can affect them this week. And there are certainly opportunities out there to bet on multi-game performances. But if you can't put math behind it, you should never place a bet just because some team is due for a win.

Confirmation bias

The King of All Biases commands you to kneel!

It's time to talk about possibly the most important bias of all. When you're making a case for betting one side of a game or another, your brain switches into *confirmation bias* mode, where you draw a conclusion and then filter incoming data differently depending on whether it supports the case you're making or not.

Confirmation bias is your inner lawyer talking, where one half of your brain tries to find evidence that supports the other half's conclusions. Do you think you're a good judge of character? Of course you do. Everybody does. Why? Because you give privileged positioning to memories when you had an instinct that somebody was a creep and it turned out to be true. What you conveniently forget is all the times when you misjudged someone.

It's okay. We all do it. It's a survival tactic. But sports betting is a truth machine. You can't afford to bend facts to support a previously made conclusion. Reality will always intervene in the form of lost bets.

TIP

Here are a few tactics you can consider to help stave off confirmation bias.

» **Tactic 1:** Argue both sides. Make an effort to build a case against the side you picked. Are you about to bet on the over? Spend a few minutes looking for evidence that the team is about to get shut out.

» **Tactic 2:** Try your rationale out on other people who know what you're talking about. See if you can convince them. Better yet, talk to people who disagree with you and see what they say. You might find their real arguments more convincing than what you had imagined.

» **Tactic 3:** Read sports writers who have different takes than you. Someone who writes about sports for a living may well disagree with your take. Understanding their arguments and how they conflict with your own may help you think about your own views better.

» **Tactic 4:** Use technical handicapping or situational handicapping, which lends itself to establishing certain rules, systems, and angles. Then bet based on the analysis, eliminating your own biases entirely in favor of concrete rules and data.

» **Tactic 5:** Keep good, honest records. Don't fudge point spreads in the past to make your record look better than it was. By looking back and realizing how often you're wrong, you'll realize the utter necessity of not getting attached to one side of an argument or another.

Recency bias

When you over-weight the most recent data points, you are falling victim to *recency bias*. If the Oregon Ducks played a flawless game last Saturday, how does that affect your judgment of them? Is that game a better representation of their future capabilities than the three prior games when they lost by an average of 24 points?

In sports, we know teams and players evolve over the course of a season. But while you want to leave room for adjusting your assessment, you want to always remember that the last game doesn't represent a single "truth" about a team. Maybe it does matter more, but how much? Make sure you are considering new information as it comes in, but also make sure that you don't forget the older information when evaluating a team's chances.

Availability bias

Availability bias highlights a problem with human memory in general. We are, as a rule, more likely to favor and use information that's readily accessible, or what stands out in our memory.

But what stands out isn't always representative of the truth. The Dallas Mavericks choked away the 2006 NBA Championship, which was a painful and vivid memory for me. So when they made their playoff run in 2011, I dismissed their chances too easily. Sure enough, the choke I watched in 2006 wasn't representative of the team on the court in 2011 that got its revenge on the Miami Heat. Recognize memorable outliers (and enjoy the great games), but keep track of all the data so that you can make informed decisions.

Familiarity bias

You're a big soccer fan and you support your team every chance you get. You are likely to overestimate the quality of your favorite team for a couple reasons. You want them to be good, so you have a confirmation bias. But also, you have watched more of their games than have any other team's. This is the *familiarity bias.* Because you know more about the team, you are more likely to have strong, over-confident opinions about that team's performance in upcoming events.

Peas and carrots

These biases are all about things that go together: peanut butter and jelly, grilling and game day, advanced ape-brains and faulty reasoning.

Post hoc ergo propter hoc

Here we have perhaps one of the most famous, and most Latin, of the classical logical fallacies. It means "after this therefore because of this." One thing happens, say the Crimson Tide QB hurts his shoulder, and then another thing happens, like maybe Ohio State beats Clemson the next week. There is probably no causal connection between the two, even though they happened one after the other. People indulge in this fallacy more often when the two events seem like they should be connected. Take care when figuring out causation, as there are often many factors at play, and just because one event happens before another does not necessarily mean that the first event caused the second.

Illusory correlation

This bias is related to the preceding one. We have overactive imaginations when it comes to the frequency of the co-occurrence of events. When people utter the words "no hitter," sure enough, the next inning, the no-hitter gets broken up. It's a jinx, right?

Come on, people. It's natural to say "no hitter" when a pitcher doesn't give up a hit in the first six innings. But no-nos are rare! It's relatively much more likely for a pitcher to give up a hit in the last three innings than it is for him to complete the no-hitter. But saying it didn't cause it! Don't overestimate the correlation between a rare event and its associated precursors.

The Gambler's Fallacy's evil twin: The Hot Hand

There have been scores of studies on whether the Hot Hand is real or not. That is, can a player temporarily raise the baseline probability of making a shot, or hitting a putt, or kicking a long field goal?

It has been incredibly difficult to mathematically prove that the Hot Hand exists. A famous study from 1985 declared the Hot Hand Fallacy was a real thing, and that runs of improved shooter accuracy are illusory. These performance streaks fit well within the expected range of outcomes. A 40 percent lifetime 3-point shooter will inevitably have games where he makes an insane number of treys in a row, and he will inevitably have games where his hand is ice cold.

TIP

Now, allow me to do an about-face. Recent studies have suggested that the one area where a version of the Hot Hand might exist is in basketball free-throws. A player who hits a free throw has an elevated likelihood of making the next free throw in a way that's slightly outside the expected statistical results. The lesson for bettors should stand, though: Assume the hot hand is nothing more than coincidence.

The Momentum Fallacy

Momentum is malarkey. Teams have momentum! Right up to the point when they don't. When the Cowboys faced the Packers in the 2017 playoffs, the Cowboys came roaring back from a big deficit. It felt like they were unstoppable. Dak Prescott couldn't miss! They were rolling!

Until they didn't, and their magnificent comeback resulted in a narrow loss.

Consider also the dramatic Patriots-Falcons Super Bowl that year. After falling behind 28–3, we heard all about how the Patriots had reacquired momentum and were using it to spark a huge comeback and win the game.

So what is momentum again? The concept is obviously a close cousin to the Hot Hand, just at a team level. I wanted to mention it because I find momentum an especially insidious concept. It's a narrative pushed by pundits who are more interested in building a dramatic story than they are giving out useful information. The problem with momentum is that it is useless to bettors because it only describes the past. That's the Momentum Fallacy. The Cowboys and the Patriots both had momentum on their side in the 2017 postseason, but the games' outcomes were equally unpredictable.

The Fundamental Sports Betting Attribution Error (FSBAE)

(Okay, I made this up.) You're sitting pretty because you made a bet that paid off big time. Your instinct will be to attribute this win to some good quality about yourself and your prediction. You are likely to think that you are just good at predicting basketball, say. But you could have won your bet for a whole host of reasons that had nothing to do with the reasons you came up with for making the bet in the first place.

In the same vein, when you lose a bet, you can just chalk it up to chance or the fact that predicting sports is a tough business and it just won't go your way all the time. But you must consider the attribution error. You may well have lost the bet because your reasoning had flaws. But the FSBAE says that you won't be able to see it that way so easily. Make sure that you are always checking for this faulty pattern in your own thinking. Awareness could save you a whole lot of money.

REMEMBER

It's possible to be completely wrong and win, and to be completely right and lose. If you bet on the Chiefs because you think Pat Mahomes is "due for a big game" and then he has a big game, it doesn't mean you were proven correct. Perhaps he played a mediocre game, but the other team's defense played far below their ability.

Chapter 16

The Sports Bettors' Essential Excel Toolkit

I n my younger and more vulnerable years, before I made the leap to computers, I used to look for historical betting trends with nothing more than a pencil, a notebook, and a sports magazine that listed past scores and spread results. I'd spend hours tracking everything by hand, and if I was lucky, I'd be able to make use of a calculator.

Fortunately, things have changed. Actually, they changed 25 years ago, but I'm still celebrating the advent of modern spreadsheet software, and so should you.

Even if you're a shoot-from-the-hip fundamentals gambler who laughs in the face of "analytics," you're going to want to become friends with your local spreadsheet software. Spreadsheets allow you to logically arrange, manipulate, explore, and visualize data. And if you invest just a little bit of time, you can use Excel to load and transform data as well as simulate games, size bets, track schedules, spot hedging opportunities, and more.

TIP

Call me old fashioned, but I'm a long-time user of Excel on Windows. I would have switched over to using Excel on a Mac long ago, but the current version of Excel for Mac lacks a feature I've found I can't live without: VBA (Visual Basic for Applications). While it's not an absolute necessity for everyone, I lean on it extensively for scripting advanced functionality into my sports betting-related workbooks.

The grapevine (my editor) informs me that if you're willing to get the no-longer-supported Excel 2011 for Mac, it comes with VBA. Whatever your platform, I strongly recommend VBA.

In this chapter, I'll spend most of my time on putting Excel's formulas to work for you, most of which have good analogs in other spreadsheet tools and on other platforms.

Excel Stuff Even Non-Bettors Should Know

I'm going to make some assumptions that you at least know the basics of Excel:

>> Create and name worksheets.

>> Reference a cell in a formula by its row and column address.

>> Know the difference between a formula cell and a text cell.

>> Paste formulas across a range of cells.

>> Set and use the basic cell formats (like "date" or "number").

If you aren't comfortable with these concepts, or if you just want to build that muscle, allow me to recommend one of many outstanding editions of *Excel For Dummies* by the incomparable Dr. Greg Harvey.

Reference types

When your formula takes a value from another cell, it's called a reference, and there are several ways to do it depending on your needs.

Relative references

If you reference another cell in your formula, Excel makes it easy to reuse that formula across many cells. When you copy and paste a formula, Excel adjusts any references automatically so that the cell performs the same role as it did before to the surrounding cell. Figure 16-1 gives you a simple example.

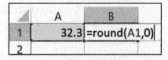

FIGURE 16-1:
Pasting a relative
reference.

As soon as you hit enter, the formula in cell B1 will take the value in cell A1 and round it from 32.3 to 32. Another way of thinking about it is that the formula in B1 takes the value from the cell to B1's immediate left and rounds it.

If you copy the contents of B1 to any other cell, Excel assumes you want the new cell to do exactly what B1 did, which is to round up the cell to its immediate left. That's why it's called a *relative reference:* The formula references change relative to where the cell is in your worksheet.

For example, if you copy and paste from B1 to C2, Excel automatically updates the reference in the formula from A1 to B2 (which is the cell to the immediate left of C2). The formula in C2 will say "=round(B2,0)" without you having to intervene. Whether you're copying and pasting or dragging formulas across multiple cells using the fill handle at the lower-right of your selection, the references will update for each new cell.

Absolute references

Sometimes you need your formula references to not change when you cut and paste. In Excel, that's called an *absolute reference,* and you can force that action by adding the $ character before the row and/or column address of your original formula.

In Figure 16-2, the formula in C6 is multiplying the value in column B by a number in cell C1. Because I have a list of players and I want everybody's rushing yards to be modified by the same number, I made the reference to the cell in C6 an absolute reference.

	A	B	C
1	Yardage Modifier:		9.35%
2			
3	Player	Raw Yds	Net Yds
4	Kamara	102	111.54
5	Murray	92	100.60
6	Smith	88	=B6*(1+$C$1)

FIGURE 16-2: Pasting an absolute reference.

REMEMBER

When it comes to evaluating a formula or calculation, relative references are no different from absolute references. It only matters when you copy and paste the cell that contains the reference. In the above example, if the formula in C4 had started with a relative reference to C1 like "=B4*(1+C1)" it would have calculated correctly in that cell. But when the formula got pasted to C5 and C6, it wouldn't work anymore.

Partial absolute references

You may run across situations where you want to copy formulas across cells so that the row number is locked but not the column number, or vice versa. This is most common when you build complex tables and you want a reference a single value across multiple columns, but you need that or a single value in a column across multiple rows.

Excel lets you do this by putting the $ character in front of only the row, or only the column. In Figure 16-3, I'm taking the value in column A and using it as a key to look up multiple stat columns in a table called "TeamStatsTable." If I drag this formula down from B2 to B3, and beyond, the reference will change from $A2 to $A3 and beyond with each new row. But the $ character in front of the reference lets me drag that formula across columns to the right, and the column piece of the reference will remain locked on A.

	A	B	C
1	Team	2pt Baskets	2pt Attempts
2	Texas Tech	=VLOOKUP($A2,TeamStatsTable,2)	
3	Boston College		
4	Duke		
5	North Carolina		

FIGURE 16-3: Pasting a partially absolute reference.

TIP

One of the most beautiful shortcuts you'll ever meet lets you cycle through absolute and relative references You can cycle through cell reference types in Windows with the F4. On a Mac, the shortcut is ⌘-T. What makes it great is that it doesn't force you to select the whole reference: Just put your mouse on any part of the reference and click F4 and watch it cycle . . . and smile.

Naming cells and ranges

You might have noticed in the last example I pointed a formula at a table called TeamStatsTable.

You can make your formulas clearer in Excel by using *named cells and ranges*. This feature gives the user the ability to label a cell or multiple cells in a meaningful way. It makes complicated formulas clearer and gives you a shortcut when you want to reference cells in subsequent formulas.

The name of the game is readability. In the first example of this chapter, I referred to a cell as a yardage modifier in cell C1 that I referenced repeatedly in the subsequent table. There are several ways to name cells, but the easiest is to use the name box, the wide dialog box at the top of Figure 16-4 that says "C1."

	A	B	C
1	Yardage Modifier:		9.35%
2			
3	Player	Raw Yds	Net Yds
4	Kamara	102	111.54
5	Murray	92	100.60
6	Smith	88	96.23

C1

FIGURE 16-4:
Using named ranges.

The name box always shows you the address of the cell you have selected, or if there's a name associated with it, it shows you the name. To add or change the name of a cell you've clicked on, just go into the name box, type it in, and click Enter.

Going forward you can use that name in future formulas, and Excel will treat it as any other absolute reference. If you have Excel configured to give you context tips as you type, it will show you the names you've created when you type the first few letters.

WARNING

If you've referenced the newly named cell in existing formulas in your worksheet as a plain old address (like C1), Excel will not replace those addresses with the new name. It will update your formulas only if you change the name or remove the name as a reference to the cell.

Label a table

You can also use this functionality to give a nickname to multiple cells or an entire table of data. This makes reading your formulas much easier, and you can reference that table just like you would a table that you referred to only by its address range (for example, $A$1:$D$28) data.

TIP

Excel keeps track of all your named ranges and cells with Name Manager (CTRL+F3). There are some advanced functions available in Name Manager that you might find useful; you can alter the scope of the name, so that the reference is only available in a single worksheet versus the entire workbook. You can also alter the formula of a named range. This comes in handy when you've added or deleted rows from a table and you need to adjust the name definition to include the change. I use the Name Manager so much that I added it to my shortcut Ribbon via File→Options→Customize Ribbon.

Absolute pasting

Excel treats named ranges as absolute references, so copying and pasting a formula that contains a reference to a named range or cell means it will be unchanged in its destination cell. If you are trying to copy a range of cells that you have not named, you will have to change the formula to have absolute references either by using F4 to cycle through the different kinds of absolute references or by manually entering the dollar signs as needed.

Find values in a table with VLookup

Excel has a number of functions that let you use a value as a key to unlocking data in another table. The most common function is Vlookup, where the V stands for, uh, veal parmesan? It probably stands for "vertical" since there is a corresponding function called HLookup (in case you're the kind of weirdo who keeps their data organized in rows instead of columns).

Let's start with a simple VLookup use case. You have a table with team stats in one worksheet, and you want to reference specific stats from that table somewhere else. Figure 16-5 shows the data table.

	A	B
1	TEAM	POINTS
2	Arizona	23.5
3	Atlanta	28.5
4	Baltimore	19.3
5	Cleveland	18.9
6	Denver	24.2

FIGURE 16-5: Using the basic VLookup command.

And on another part of the worksheet, you want to be able to type the name of the team in and have it return the points listed in the table associated with that team. In Figure 16-6, you want to type a team name into cell G1 and have the points appear in cell G2.

F	G
Team Name:	Atlanta
Points:	28.5

FIGURE 16-6: Using vlookup with a named range.

Looking up values in a table is what VLOOKUP is built for, so here's the VLOOKUP syntax and a description of each parameter:

=VLOOKUP(value, table, column, range_lookup)

Let's go through the formula one piece at a time:

>> The *value* is the key that Excel will use to figure out which row you're trying to reference. For our example, the key is going to be what we type into cell G1. In the world of databases, it is essential that every row of data is uniquely identifiable in some way, and that unique identifier for a row is called the primary key. We'll shorten the formal term here and just call it the key, but the meaning is the same. When you build a table of team data, for example, you don't want to list the same team on multiple rows of the same table unless there's another meaningful way to divide the table up. (For example, on rare occasions you'd want to have a table that had data split into "team seasons" and so might have Ravens2019 and Ravens2020 key values.)

>> The *table* refers to the range of cells that make up the table, or the name of the table if you gave it one. I didn't give this table a special name, so we'd just use $A$2:$B$6. There are ways to get the column headers involved, but for now, I'd just advise you to make the table reference start with the first data row and go to the last data row.

>> With the first two parameters, Excel will be able to find which row of data you want to consider, so now it needs to know the column of the exact field you're looking for. Assume column #1 is the team names, so column #2 contains the points. You can reference any column number you like, no matter how wide your table is.

>> The optional *range_lookup* value is an optional TRUE (or 1) or FALSE (or 0) switch that tells Excel what kind of matching you expect for the key value. If you set this to TRUE, Excel does an approximate match between your key value and the key column, and it will return the closest match it can find. If you set it to FALSE, you're ordering Excel to do an exact match only. Anything other than an exact match means you'll get an error (#N/A) back.

For our example, we'd set the formula in cell G2:

=VLOOKUP(H1,B1:D6,2,FALSE)

A few important notes:

>> Vlookup can only refer to columns to the right of the key column, so the key needs to always live in the left-most column of your table.

» Provided you set the range_lookup flag to FALSE, your list does not have to be alphabetized.

» The key value matching process is not case-sensitive. If you enter "atlanta" instead of "Atlanta" Excel figures out what you mean.

When I have done troubleshooting for friends using VLOOKUP, about 90 percent of all problems trace back to them failing to use FALSE in the range_lookup parameter. It's the smart play. If you enter nothing, Excel sets it to TRUE, and the results can be very confusing if your list isn't perfectly alphabetized and de-duped.

How about a multi-column example?

Let's say you have a table of NBA player stats like the one in Figure 16-7. Your first column (B) contains player names, so it will be the key to the rest of the stats. You select cells B2:E6 and give the table the catchy name "AverageStats2017.2018."

	A	B	C	D	E
1		Player	Avg Points	Avg Assts	Avg Minutes
2		Steph Curry	26.4	6.1	32
3		Lebron James	27.5	9.1	36.9
4		Kevin Durant	26.4	5.4	34.2
5		Damian Lillard	26.9	6.6	36.6
6		James Harden	30.4	8.8	35.4

FIGURE 16-7: Referring to a multi-column table.

The key to the table is player name in the left-most column, so any formula that needs to retrieve data from this table will need to use a key that appears in this list. If you want to look up Curry's average assists, you count the number of columns after the key column and use that in the "column" field, resulting in:

=VLOOKUP("Steph Curry", AverageStats2017.2018, 2, FALSE)

Conditional love: Using IF statements

Excel's IF formulas are like little switches where you describe a condition and two possible formulas. Excel evaluates the condition, and if it's true gives you the result of the first formula, and if it's false gives you the result of the second formula.

It looks like this:

=IF(condition, true_output, false_output)

Excel's IF statement condition is — like other TRUE/FALSE values — known as a *Boolean variable*. That means it evaluates to either being TRUE or FALSE. If a Boolean formula is not TRUE, it is by definition FALSE; there is no in-between. Look up Boolean logic if you're interested in learning how to use some advanced logic to determine the value of a Boolean statement.

For our purposes, we're going to stick with basic operators, like greater than (>), less than (<), equals (do I really have to show it?), and not equals (<>) in addition to some logical operators masquerading as Excel functions like OR, AND, and NOT. A simple example is using Excel for translating American odds into decimal odds, where the formula is slightly different depending on whether we're looking at a favorite or not. So if you wanted to create a little calculator in Excel, you'd have to create two formulas or take advantage of an IF function, as shown in Figure 16-8.

Here's the favorite formula in cell C2: =1-100/$B$2

Here's the underdog formula in cell C3: =1+$B$3/100

And here's the combined formula in cell C5: =IF(B5<0,1-100/B5,1+B5/100)

When we enter American odds into B5, Excel will respond with decimal odds in C5.

	A	B	C
1		American	Decimal
2	Fave Only	-110	1.91
3	Dog Only	139	2.39
4			
5	Either!	-190	1.53

FIGURE 16-8: Checking conditions with an IF statement.

REMEMBER

How do we decide if American odds represent a favorite or an underdog? As you know from earlier in the book, favorites are always listed with negative odds, and underdog odds are always positive.

So in the combined formula in C5, Excel first evaluates the condition: Is the value in B5 a negative number? If so, it executes the first formula stub and ignores the second. If it determines the condition is false (B5 is a positive number), it executes the second formula stub and ignores the first.

He says in parentheses: Nested IF statements

You can do very powerful things by putting IF statements inside the formula stubs of other IF statements. This is known as a *nested* IF statement, or a *nested conditional.* It's akin to a decision tree where the branches are followed according to how each condition evaluates. Here's a basic map of two nested IF statements.

=IF(condition1, IF(condition2, true_output2, false_output2), false_output1)

When the condition1 evaluates to TRUE, Excel evaluates the formula that starts after the first comma (even if the formula contains another IF statement). If condition1 evaluates to FALSE, it skips that content and evaluates the formula after the second comma. Once condition1 has proven true, Excel treats the second IF statement as a self-contained formula, evaluating condition2 for truth or not and proceeding accordingly.

An odds example of nested IFs

We know that American odds are valid for favorites at −101 and less. And an even-money bet is listed at +100, with underdogs' odds going up from there. That means the numbers −100 up through +99 are not valid American odds. We could use nested IF statements to do an error check in the example above.

We can alter the formula in C5 to take the following structure (in plain language):

=IF(Are the odds in B5 valid American odds? (If so, are we looking at fave odds or dog odds? [Then calculate accordingly.]) If the odds weren't valid to begin with, return an error message back to the user.)

So to make sure we have valid odds, we need to check that the value is either 100 or higher, or −101 or lower. This is a perfect spot for Excel's OR function that lets you list comma-separated Boolean conditions and then return TRUE if any or all conditions evaluate to TRUE. So inserting our "valid odds" condition into the skeleton formula results in:

=IF(OR(B5<=-101,B5>=100) (If valid, are we looking at fave odds or dog odds? Then calculate accordingly.) If the odds weren't valid to begin with, return an error message back to the user.)

For the next step, we already created this code with our first IF statement. Remember the combined IF from the previous example? Just plug it in! That makes:

=IF(OR(B5<=-101,B5>=100),IF(B5<0,1-100/B5,1+B5/100) (If the odds weren't valid to begin with, return an error message back to the user.)

Now it's just a simple matter of adding an error message:

=IF(OR(B5<=-101,B5>=100),IF(B5<0,1-100/B5,1+B5/100), "American Odds Must Be Either -101 or less OR +100 or more")

WARNING

You are free to nest as many IF statements as you can handle. Excel doesn't mind your nesting instinct, but just be prepared for a parenthesis hurricane. Excel does its level best to help you along with color-matched parentheses and context-sensitive help, but nested IF statements can get harry. Trouble-shooting one is like trying to bull's-eye a womp rat. Some friendly advice: Create a skeleton of your nested IF statement first with all the commas and parentheses in place along with dummy return values and conditions. Then build each individual IF statement out in a separate cell to make sure each piece is working properly. Once you've got the pieces right, plug them all into the skeleton statement.

Eliminating errors with IfError

You'll find a few common error messages crop up frequently when using Excel. If you're using VLookup, we talked about how #N/A comes back if Excel can't match the key you provide it. You'll also see the #VALUE or NAME?error when you're trying to do math on something that doesn't want math done on it (like text).

Seeing error messages from Excel is not bad per se, but it can clutter up the screen in some instances. For example, if you're transforming a list of data but you know some fields don't conform, it's often better to leave them blank rather than showing the big ugly error message.

Wrapping your statement in an IfError is a quick and easy way to deal with statements that sometimes result in data you want and other times result in errors. Here's the format:

    =IfError(value, value_if_error)

What it means to Excel is this: Please execute the formula inside the "value" parameter. If it returns one of those ugly error messages, show what's in the "message" parameter.

Here's a quick example where I've downloaded hundreds of rows of raw baseball data that represents a list of teams each week that had three or more wins. In Figure 16-9, because my spreadsheet uses the team nickname instead of the city abbreviation, I need to do some data processing to translate one to the other.

The problem is that if I apply a simple VLOOKUP, it will throw an error if it sees a value in column A that's not a city abbreviation, and every few rows is a piece of non-team data.

The formula in cell B7 attempts to run the VLOOKUP to my translation table called tblTEAMS, and if I send it a bad key value, Excel will jump to my value_if_error parameter, which is just a blank cell (entered as "").

	A	B	C	D	E
1	**Team**	**Lookup Name**			
2	ARI	Diamondbacks			
3	COL	Rockies			
4	TEX	Rangers			
5	Week 3				
6	NYY				
7	BOS	=iferror(vlookup(A7,tblTEAMS,2,FALSE),"")			
8	MIA				

FIGURE 16-9: Using IfError to sniff out bad data.

Essential Gambler's Formulas

Every sports bettor needs to have a handful of formulas at his fingertips. I've made it easy for you by giving you the exact Excel syntax.

Translating moneyline odds into break-even win percentage

Remember that every moneyline implies a winning percentage that if you can match in the long term, you'll break even as a bettor. Betting on a +200 underdog means you profit $2 if you win your bet, and you lose $1 if you lose your bet. If you placed an infinite sequence of +200 bets, you'd need to win at least one of every two to break even. Any less than that and you'll eventually go broke.

For an underdog moneyline to break-even win probability

Where A1 contains the moneyline odds (like +140)

```
=1-A1/(A1+100)
```

When this gets evaluated with our example number, you get the following:

= 1-(140)/(140+100) = 1-(140)/(240) = 1-0.58 = 0.42 = 42%

I've rounded away the repeating decimal just for the sake of clarity.

For a favorite moneyline to break-even win probability

Where A1 contains the moneyline odds (like −210)

```
=ABS(A1)/(ABS(A1)+100)
```

This gets evaluated like so:

$$= ABS(-210)/(ABS(-210)+100) = (210)/(210 + 100) = (210)/(310) = 0.68 = 68\%$$

TIP

ABS is the Excel version of "absolute value," which is a fancy way of saying negative numbers are treated as positive, and positive numbers are positive.

Combined into a single conditional formula, you get this:

=IF(A1>0,1-ABS(A1)/(ABS(A1)+100),ABS(A1)/(ABS(A1)+100))

REMEMBER

A moneyline of 0 corresponds to an even win probability, or 50 percent.

Win probability into an equivalent moneyline

Here A1 is the cell that contains your break-even winning percentage. These formulas use percentage in a decimal form, meaning that 50% is written as .5.

REMEMBER

Negative moneylines correspond to win percentages greater than 50 percent and positive moneylines to win percentages less than 50 percent.

If your win probability is less than 50 percent, here's how you get the break-even moneyline:

=100*(1-A1)/A1

So say you have a break-even winning percentage of 45 percent. Using this formula, the calculation looks like:

$$= 100*(1-.45))/(0.45) = 100*(0.55)/(0.45) = .55/.45 = +122$$

In other words, if you find a prop bet that you think has a 45 percent chance of winning, you need to be getting +122 or better odds in order to make it a bet worth making. If you're getting more than +122, it's a +EV play.

Greater than 50% chance to equivalent moneyline

If your win probability is greater than 50 percent, use this formula for a break-even moneyline:

=-100*A1/(1-A1)

Suppose that our break even winning percentage is 55 percent. Using this formula, we get the following:

$$= -100*(0.55)/(1-(0.55)) = -100*(0.55)/(0.45) = -122$$

In the two example calculations, we see that a win probability of 45 percent corresponds to a moneyline of +122, and a win probability of 55 percent corresponds to a moneyline of −122. This makes sense because both 55 percent and 45 percent are both the same probabilistic distance away from the coin-flip odds of 50 percent; they just go in different directions.

We can use a simple IF statement to put these calculations together in Excel:

$$=IF(A1 > 0.5, -100*A1/(1-A1), 100*(1-A1)/A1))$$

This statement first checks to see if the win probability is greater than 50 percent. If so, we use the favorite formula. If not, we use the underdog formula. Keep in mind that a 50 percent chance exactly translates into a fair moneyline of +100.

Tracking win%

If you're analyzing a system, or if you're simply looking at your own win loss record in betting, your winning percentage is simply the number of wins over your total number of bets:

$$=A1/(A1+A2)$$

Where A1 contains your wins and A2 contains your losses.

Normalized winning percentage

If all you do is bet −110 games, you can look at your wins and losses and make sure you're winning at least 52.38 percent to cover the vig. The reality is that nobody bets exclusively at −110 odds. Baseball side bettors rarely bet any games at −110, and even if all you do is bet football and basketball point spreads and totals, you'll have bets at −110, +105, −115, +101, and so on.

With a mix of odds, you can't judge your win loss record the same way as a pure −110 bettor. While you could just judge your success by the amount you've won or lost, I find it's helpful to maintain a normalized win loss record as well.

There are several approaches to doing this. Figure 16-10 shows a simplified bet tracker with data from baseball bets in rows 2 through 6. Column B shows the listed odds, column C shows the amount wagered for each bet, and column D shows the betting result.

	A	B	C	D
1	**Bet**	**Odds**	**Risked**	**Profit/Loss**
2	Tigers	-110	$110	$100
3	Braves	+200	$100	$200
4	A's	-150	$150	-$150
5	Rangers	-200	$200	-$200
6	A's Over	-115	$115	$100
7	**Net Profit / Loss**			$50
8	**Gross Winnings**			$400
9	**Total Risked**		$675	
10	**ROI**			7.4%
11	**Normalized Winning%**			59.3%

FIGURE 16-10: Tracking win percentage for bets other than –100 moneyline odds.

You can derive several key performance metrics from this tracker:

Formula in D7 is simply the sum of column D.

Formula in D8 is a conditional sum of column D's positive entries (=sumif(D2:D6,">0").

Formula in C9 is the sum of column C (total amount risked).

Formula in D10 is D7/C9.

Formula in D11 is winnings over risked D8/C9.

Discounting wins

Another technique I sometimes use to normalize my bet data is simply discounting my wins and losses by the amount of the odds, which allows me to compare wins and losses in a more meaningful way.

For example, if I lose a +300 long-shot bet, but I win three –110 bets, is it fair to say I'm 3–1 on the day? In absolute terms, yes, I won three bets and lost one bet. My bankroll balance is what it is. But if I'm trying to judge my ability to pick winners, I don't think counting a +300 bet as a full loss is a fair reflection of my abilities.

So instead of counting that +300 bet as a full loss, I'll reduce it according to the break-even percentage. For this tracker, column E is doing most of the work with an IF statement:

=IF(D2="W",0.5238/C2,C2/-0.5238)

As you can see in Figure 16-11, if the bet result is a win, the result gets altered by taking the break-even winning percentage over the implied winning percentage of the bet. And if it's a loss, the formula is flipped. The result is a value in column E that gives me more credit for winning a long-shot bet, less pain for losing a long-shot bet, less credit for winning a heavy favorite bet, and more pain for losing on a heavy favorite.

	A	B	C	D	E
1	Bet	Moneyline	Implied Win%	Bet Result	Normalized Result
2	Dodgers	200	33.33%	W	1.57
3	Marlins	-110	52.38%	L	-1.00
4	Angels Under	220	31.25%	W	1.68
5	D'Backs	-220	68.75%	W	0.76
6	Astros Run in 1st	200	33.33%	W	1.57
7	Cubs Over	140	41.67%	L	-0.80
8	Rays	-110	52.38%	L	-1.00
9	Mariners Over	-110	52.38%	L	-1.00
10	Padres Run in 1st	-110	52.38%	W	1.00
11			Wins	5	6.58
12			Losses	4	3.80
13			Win%	55.6%	63.4%

FIGURE 16-11: Column E gives you normalized results.

In this tracking sheet, I've won 5 bets and lost 4, for a nominal winning percentage of 55.55. But because my mix of bets has included winning some long-shot bets, my normalized winning percentage is 63.4 based on 6.6 normalized wins and 3.8 normalized losses. I find this metric particularly useful when I do regular betting on moneylines or on game prop bets and I want to track how well I'm able to pick winners and losers (independent of my betting dollars).

REMEMBER

There's no GAAP accounting board that's going to be reviewing your performance metrics. There are lots of ways to do it, and there are a million sports bettors on social media preparing a message to tell me there's a flaw in my system. They're not wrong. But performance metrics have to work for you. And if it's not abundantly clear by now, the bottom line is the bottom line when it comes to betting. Winning percentage is great and performance metrics are fun, but your bankroll ultimately tells the tale. Is it growing or is it shrinking? Are you losing at a rate you can afford? Are you depositing more than you planned to in your online accounts?

Kelly Criterion formula

As I discussed in Chapter 5, Kelly Criterion is a formula for making an individual bet in proportion with your bankroll and your expected winning percentage. Here are the Excel instructions for creating a little worksheet like the one in Figure 16–12 that will help you determine the recommended Kelly bet size:

1. You enter your estimated win probability in cell D1.

2. You enter the available moneyline odds in cell D2.

3. The formula is D3 is the two conversion formulas combined into a conditional statement:

   =IF(D2<0,1-100/D2,1+D2/100)

4. You enter your current bankroll in D4. The formula in D5 is where Kelly does the magic:

   =(D1*D3-1)/(D3-1)

   The result is the proportion of your bankroll recommended by the Kelly Criterion.

5. You enter the Kelly adjustment into D6.

   Kelly can be murder during a bad losing streak, so sports bettors often reduce the Kelly recommendation by this fraction. In this example, the Kelly recommended bet size will be multiplied by .5, or cut in half.

	A	B	C	D
1	Probability of Bet Win			0.55
2	Moneyline			-110
3	Decimal Odds			1.91
4	Bankroll			$ 1,000.00
5	Raw Bet Amount			0.055
6	Kelly Adjustment			0.5
7	Recommended Bet Amount			$ 27.50

FIGURE 16-12: Calculating bet amounts with the Kelly formula.

The output of this worksheet is the recommended bet size amount listed in D7. The formula is simply =D6*D5*D4, which multiplies your bankroll times the Kelly recommended bet proportion, multiplied by the adjustment factor you put into D6.

The Gambler's Z

For a binary variable like overs/unders or heads/tails, we assume that if the result of each trial is totally random, in the long run, the tendency will be to get

50 percent of each value. When our actual result strays from 50 percent, we need a way to determine if what we're seeing is due to normal variation, or if there may be a reason to believe the coin we're flipping isn't perfectly fair. But making this determination is a function of both how far we are away from 50 percent and how big our sample size is.

That's what makes the Gambler's Z so valuable: It rolls up sample size and the resulting percentages and spits out a single number. The bigger the number, the less likely it is that the results you see could be due to normal variations.

If you have your number of wins in cell A1 and losses in cell A2, here's what you'd plug into come up with the Gambler's Z:

=(A1-0.5*(A1+A2))-0.5)/SQRT((A1+A2)*0.5*0.5)

There's a simpler version that produces roughly the same result:

=(A1-A2)/SQRT(A1+A2)

5

The Part of Tens

IN THIS PART . . .

Read a concise list of what not to do as a bettor. Let others make mistakes so you don't have to.

Check out the books I've found extremely helpful in developing my own understanding of the world of sports betting.

Chapter 17

Ten Betting Mistakes You Should Avoid

There are more pitfalls in sports betting than an Indiana Jones movie. Don't make the mistake of grabbing the medallion before you check to see if it's room temperature.

In this chapter, I'll discuss ten tactics, ideas, and concepts that you'd be wise to avoid. Some may be obvious to you; some counterintuitive. Some of these ideas might even be directly contradicted in other books about sports betting. That's okay with me, because in a marketplace where most bettors lose, contrarianism makes a lot of sense.

Chasing the Late-Night Slumpbuster

There will be days when it feels like every single bad call goes against you. A bad bounce starts your day with a loss, then before you know it you're 0–2 and then 0–3, and by late afternoon, you're 0–5, 7.5 units in the hole.

Don't panic. Your losing streak doesn't mean you're a bad person. It doesn't mean you've done something wrong. But what it *really* doesn't mean is that you're "due" for some good luck, or a win. There is no "due" in sports betting, there is only "do" or "do not" (*Star Wars* joke). In this case, if you think you're *due*, you should *do not*.

Professional bettors win 56 or 57 percent of their bets. As a profitable hobbyist, your goal should be to win 54 percent. At those percentages, mathematics dictates there will be agonizing periods of failure.

On those days where the breaks are beating the boys and you can't even remember what it feels like to have a bad call go your way, treat the last game of the day like a poison apple — a temptation to be avoided. If you didn't plan to place a big bet on the late game, don't make one up on the fly. Take your losses, lick your wounds, get some sleep, and start working on tomorrow.

Spinning Your Records

I talked early in the book about the importance of tracking your performance. At the very least, you should be maintaining a record of the bets you've made and the running total of money won or lost. One degree better would be to track some description of the rationale or handicapping methodologies that led you to each bet so you can start to do more of what works and start to do less of what doesn't. Most important of all, you want to stay within the financial limits that you've set for yourself.

At some point, you'll be tempted to retrospectively adjust the odds in your favor. If you know what's good for you, you'll stay away from self-deception and record the action honestly and accurately. The easiest fudge to make is when you place a bet, the *opening* line turns out to be a loser, while the *closing* line turns out to be a winner. Record the bets in the terms you get, not in the terms you want. If you're testing the results of a handicapping angle, pick a standard — either opening or closing odds — and be consistent. Honest, consistent record-keeping is the only way you'll improve.

Limiting Your Options

The vast majority of bettors wager on a game with a *side bet* — either a moneyline or point spread on one team. These bets get the bulk of the action with bookmakers because they follow the natural contours of our emotional connection with games. After all, sporting events are constructed to determine a winner and loser, and to predict a game means predicting a winner, right? Wrong. Don't restrict yourself to the most common bets when there are other ways to profit from your predictive talents.

You're in this to win money. If you just want to show that you're a super fan, go buy a foam finger. If you just want to prove you can predict the future, go buy a crystal ball and set up shop at the local carnival.

As you develop handicapping methods and familiarity with an athlete, a team, or a sport, you may find that winning, losing, and margin of victory are not the most predictable elements of a particular contest. If you discover an element of an upcoming game that's predictable regardless of who wins the game, dig deep into the menu of available bets until you find a way to bet it profitably.

REMEMBER

Professional bettors aren't just skilled prognosticators who can find a good angle on a game; they are also masters of the craft of finding ways *to get at it* (that is, to bet it advantageously).

Realism: It's Not Just for Pre-Raphaelite Artists

Professional bettors are thrilled if they can sniff a 60 percent winning percentage over the course of a year. Pros are successful if they win 56 percent of their bets over their career. Aficionados and hobbyists who keep their day jobs are in good shape if they're winning 53 to 54 percent of their bets, which allows them to eek out profit over the vig.

But here in the real world, there are very few professional bettors, not because it's hard to pick a few winners, but because it's hard to consistently pick winners, and it's really hard to maintain discipline and avoid bad lines and silly bets. (Or in my case, reinvesting my winnings in online slots games. I'm sure I'm just about to hit that progressive jackpot!)

Keep it real, chum. Your sports betting goal should be to have fun, learn the ins and outs of the marketplace, and if you're lucky, make enough money to buy yourself a steak dinner from time to time. Don't be disappointed if you aren't able to quite your day job, or if you have to reload your online account from time to time.

Thinking Yesterday's Game = Today's Game

There are two constants in sports betting:

>> There are always profitable systems, trends, angles, and handicapping techniques.

>> Profitable systems and angles shift over time.

When bettors notice a trend, they'll keep betting it until the bookmaker catches up and makes it unprofitable to do so. Not only does the marketplace evolve and fill in profitable holes, the sports themselves change. Consider the rise in NBA scoring after 2010, or the offensive-friendly rules changes in the NFL over the last several decades.

If you find a profitable system, ride it as long as you can. But don't be afraid to admit when the market has caught up. Every well runs dry eventually.

Passing on Passing

Good sports bettors take their cues from football's run/pass option. There are times in life when you need to you develop your run/pass option to *pass* on a bet, and there are times you need to *run* for your life.

I'll spare you the "only winning move is not to play" lecture. Sports betting is a hobby, and I urge you to partake in the fun to the extent you can do so in a healthy, fun way.

One of the worst habits of all is feeling you have to bet every game. Sports bettors can enhance their careers if they develop an instinct for identifying games where the winner is too close as well as the discipline to not bet those games.

TIP

Don't ever force yourself into a decision on a game. Set a time limit on your analysis, and once the clock runs out, if you don't have a clear picture of which side is the right bet, pass on it. If you just can't resist the temptation because it's Monday Night Football, or the Wimbledon Final (or another contest you really want action on), pick an interesting prop and place a tiny bet on it.

Paying for Picks

Touts will use every enticement to convince you that they have insider information on a team, or that they're connected with "whale" bettors, or that they have some kind of top secret analytics regimen. But when producing picks is essentially free, it tends to saturate the market with con artists.

Touts should be a hard pass, no matter how much they brag and no matter how deep your losing streak goes. And you'll have a happier, healthier, more satisfying and more profitable sports betting career.

Falling for the Five Star Fallacy

There will inevitably be bets you fall in love with, and the temptation will be there to jack up the amount of your bet in conjunction. Don't do it.

You'll see touts and social media characters talk about their betting range (1 to 5 units or the like), with the idea being you'd vary your bet amount with the "rating" they give to their picks. I am highly skeptical that anyone is able to differentiate the quality of their picks to such a granular level. Unless proven otherwise, keep your bets completely flat, or bet no more than 150 percent of your normal amount in only the rarest of instances.

At the very least, *prove* that you have different quality of handicaps before you actually start betting differently. It's easy enough to attach a quality rating to your picks in your bet-tracking spreadsheet. After 100 picks, if you start to notice your higher-rated bets win much more frequently, then you can consider varying your betting amounts and declaring those bets to be your "best bets." But until there's mathematical proof, it makes life easier to assume that all bets were created equal.

Listening to "Experts"

Remember the media's role in the sports betting world: Your favorite radio or podcast personality is in business to add listeners. The talking heads on the sports television show are there to get ratings. A megaphone does not an expert make.

That means their motivation is not the same as your motivation. When the loud-mouths undercount their losses or misrepresent a position, and it tempts you to make a losing bet, they'll never know the difference.

Treat "expert" handicapping and sports opinions the same way you would spam email in your inbox. In both cases, the purveyor can do it at almost zero cost. Making predictions about a player or a team or a league is as easy as flipping a coin and typing a few words. If you're following someone who doesn't keep track of his record to the same level you do, his or her opinion might not be worth your time.

Being Too Focused on Averages

The standby evidence for describing the quality of a team is the average. No matter how detailed or minute statistics get, at their heart, you'll find some kind of a mathematical average. While they are incredibly useful and in fact necessary, dependence on them is dangerous.

Just because averages are predictive does not make them descriptive. Take a look at the Carolina Panthers 2018 season (Table 17-1) to see how helpful an average would have been in predicting the offensive output from week to week.

TABLE 17-1 **Carolina Panthers 2018 Season**

Opponent	Points Scored	Avg Points Scored (So Far)	Difference
Dallas Cowboys	16	16.0	
Atlanta Falcons	24	20.0	8.00
Cincinnati Bengals	31	17.0	11.00
New York Giants	33	18.0	16.00
Washington Redskins	17	24.2	−1.00
Philadelphia Eagles	21	19.0	−3.20
Baltimore Ravens	36	25.4	17.00
Tampa Bay Buccaneers	42	20.0	16.57
Pittsburgh Steelers	21	26.8	1.00
Detroit Lions	19	21.0	−7.78

Opponent	Points Scored	Avg Points Scored (So Far)	Difference
Seattle Seahawks	27	26.1	6.00
Tampa Bay Buccaneers	17	22.0	–9.09
Cleveland Browns	20	24.9	–2.00
New Orleans Saints	9	23.0	–15.92
Atlanta Falcons	10	22.9	–13.00
New Orleans Saints	33	24.0	10.13

In case you're not following what's going on here, the middle numeric column is their average points scored up to that point in the season. So at the time they faced the Baltimore Ravens in their 7th game of the season, they were averaging 20 points per game, and that day they scored 42.

In the rightmost column, you can see how close the average was to predicting their points scored for a given week. In brief: not very close at all. In fact, using their average points would have gotten you within a touchdown of their actual score just 5 times out of 16 games!

WARNING

Averages are just numbers to help you describe a team's performance so far. They give no context; they don't tell you about special factors in a given day; they rarely take the opposition into account. Averages tell a part of a story about a team, but hardly the whole story. Beware the handicapping "expert" who is over-reliant on a simple average in his predictions. It's just the truth; I'm not trying to be mean (math joke).

Chapter **18**

10 (or so) Books You Should Devour to Make Yourself a Better Sports Bettor

A few of the books in this chapter have something to do with sports, and a few have to do with betting. But most of these books teach a larger lesson, which is the importance of thinking independently, rationally, and with a sound mathematic foundation.

The Signal and the Noise by Nate Silver

Election forecaster and NBA fan Nate Silver's seminal 2015 book capped his rise to prominence that began with the 2008 general election, cementing his status as America's top celebrity prognosticator and poll whisperer. The book brings to life a plethora of engaging real-world forecasting examples covering elections, sports, poker, epidemiology, climate science, and more. For each example, there's a discussion of where the forecasters succeeded, where they went off the rails, and why. Did they misunderstand the underlying processes at work? Did they miss the true causal relationships? Did they mistake the signal for the noise?

Maybe best of all, it's a primer on both the power of data-driven forecasting as well as and its limits. Sometimes systems are simply too complex for us to model with numbers, but that shouldn't stop us from trying.

SuperForecasting by Philip E. Tetlock and Dan Gardner

This book draws its lessons from a cadre of professional forecasters and teams involved in predicting events in business and politics. Lessons emerge after several years that any good sports bettor can put to good use that cover both scientific and psychological factors in why forecasting is so hard to do, what mistakes are most commonly made, and why we have such a hard time communicating and understanding the actual meaning of predictions.

Bettors will recognize one of the biggest challenges to assessing the value of forecasting, sometimes known as the *wrong side of maybe* fallacy, where an event with a 50 percent likelihood of occurring doesn't occur. Because of the human tendency toward discontinuous reasoning, the failure to occur gives the illusion that the forecast was somehow inaccurate. Does this sound familiar, bettors?

Confidence by Tomas Chamorro-Premuzic

This book dives into the question of why some people are more successful than others, professionally and personally. And one of the many conclusions is that success comes about through hard work much more than dreaming big, believing in yourself, and faking it till you make it. To delve into the world of bettors, bookies, and sports fans is a trip through bravado, showmanship, swagger, ego, and . . . confidence. But this book will train you not to be fooled by any of it. The best people in any field display a quiet competence and demonstrate hard work leading to expertise. And they do honest assessments of their mistakes in order to get better.

Superbookie by Art Manteris

Art Manteris belongs on the Mount Rushmore of American sports betting, having run the sports book at the Las Vegas Hilton for many years. Although written a few decades ago, *Superbookie* is full of anecdotes and wisdom about the business side of booking bets that still resonate today. The stories take place in a slightly more parochial setting: the days before the internet, the offshore casino explosion, and of course the 2018 legalization craze across the states.

The long-anticipated *SuperBookie 2* came out in 2019, written by Manteris and coauthor David Purdum. In the sequel, the authors continue the Las Vegas stories through the rise of the internet and into the modern age of extreme competition.

Failure by Stuart Firestein

The subtitle of the book is "Why Science Is So Successful" because in essence, it's a 250-page valentine to the scientific method, which we have to thank, one way or another, for almost every improvement in our lives over the last 500 years. The scientific method means welcoming with open arms doubt, uncertainty, ignorance, and failure into whatever you're doing. I found this book so useful because it's a reminder that one hallmark of success is the willingness to learn from and then move past failures. It's a test of dedication and a test of how passionate you are to improve and master something like sports betting.

Scorecasting by Tobias Moskowitz

Scorecasting dips into that territory and challenges how sports fans, media, and other observers construct narratives around teams, games, and seasons. But thankfully it's not myth-busting for its own sake; bettors will not only find the specific examples useful in their own handicapping arsenal, but the examples also provide a great template for sound statistical reasoning. The book takes on the conventional wisdom from many different sports, validates it sometimes, and dispels it other times. We learn that players and coaches are not robots; they are like everyone else: prone to mistakes, bias, and unevenness, and motivated by a mix of incentives.

How to Lie with Statistics by Darrell Huff

Sure, this book a little dated. But what was true in 1954 is true today, and that is that statistics are tools that are as useful as they are dangerous. They lead us to truth as often as they lead us nowhere. Don't worry. This is not a statistics text book. You will not learn any methods of statistical inference, and there will be no homework assignments. What you will get is a classic look at how statistics are used to bend narratives in ways they shouldn't be bent. This is clearly a key source of motivation for the phrase "lies, damn lies, and statistics."

Sharper by Poker Joe

The literature on sports betting has swung from bubble-gum "anyone can beat the spread!" books, devoid of much in the way of actionable content, to a new generation of books with an undertone of "you can't possibly think you can succeed doing this." *Sharper* is definitely in the latter category, with a series of essays that dive deep on topics related to the business of booking bets, the way professional bettors operate and think, deep discussions of sports betting metrics and approaches, and lots of applied math and Excel.

While Poker Joe (probably not his real name) doesn't dedicate many pages to handicapping specific sports, the few he does are worth the price of admission. He's trying to arm you with a realistic understanding of the betting markets, and part of that reality is that being a professional sports bettor isn't as simple as reading box scores for an hour, circling a few games, and popping some beers on the couch to watch the winners come in. It's a grind, and Sharper will make that point over and over in between the solid-gold lessons it provides.

The Big Short by Michael Lewis

Don't skip the book just because you've seen the movie. *The Big Short* is the story of the 2008 subprime mortgage crisis from the perspective of financial professionals inside the big banks. A handful of unlikely heroes recognized structural weaknesses in the real estate securities market that had been papered over inch by inch during the real estate boom of the 2000s. Sports bettors will realize immediately that it's easy to get hypnotized by complexity in such a complicated interconnected marketplace. But underneath it all are facts and data that can't be denied. It's a stunning story of the triumph of courage, independent thinking, and empiricism. In sports betting, you'll often hear that it's a closed system: All the angles have long been flushed out, and all the rules of thumb are well vetted and market-proven. Don't believe it.

The Black Swan by Nassim Taleb

This is a book about reality and chance, risk and opportunity. One of Taleb's basic themes is that the world is full of, if not built on, highly improbable events that defy prediction. Sports bettors will recognize a lot in this book. I wasn't able to get through the many black swan examples without building analogies to sports events in my head: the wild endings, unlikely bounces, and who–would–have–predicted–it outcomes. Bettors rely on data and patterns, and this book should give you pause when you hear claims that those patterns have been well defined when perhaps they aren't knowable in the first place. Just ask the turkey who gets fed lovingly by the devoted farmer for a year, right up until the day before Thanksgiving.

Moby Dick by Herman Melville

If I were king of the world, I would make everybody read and write a book report on this book by Herman Melville. What does *Moby Dick* have to do with sports betting? Well . . . nothing really. But of course when we read it, we get to see the joys of being along for the ride in life and the power of curiosity and faith in the people around you, who, like you, are riding their own personal Pequod on a vast ocean. In the book, Ishmael gains an encyclopedic level of knowledge about a profession he previously knew little about, and he bears witness to the dark side of obsession, how it leads to blindness, emptiness, and destruction. What fan of the Cleveland Browns won't relate to that?

6 Appendixes

Appendix A
The Best Online Resources for Sports Bettors

Some bettors are fine sending money to their bookmaker, placing bets, watching games, and calling it a day. If you aspire to be more than a seat-of-the-pants handicapper or casual participant, you're going to want to take advantage of the extensive information sources and services available to you on the internet. In this appendix. I point you to some of the best and most useful online resources I've leaned on over the years. With a few notable exceptions, everything listed below is free of charge.

One last thing. Follow me on Twitter at @swainscheps. I'm going to be updating this list, and I'd like to hear from you about what internet resources you've found to be the most useful to your sports betting activities.

Sports Betting Databases and Data Sources

>> **KillerSports.com** and **SportsDatabase.com** have to be listed first as the home of SDQL, the free sports betting database that lets you build complex queries in order to dig into the oceans of historical data they store for all sports.

>> **Covers.com** and **PreGame.com** are similar free web communities that both offer some historical sports betting data. Their real attraction is the live odds and betting metadata that lets you see how game odds are evolving, what the most popular and heavily trafficked wagers are, and much more.

>> **Oddshark.com** has a simple, free NFL database that lets you create some simple queries on basic factors like home/away, favorite/dog, month, bye, and so forth. It's another site that let's you track pregame odds movement.

>> **Teamrankings.com** has situational trends for teams in major sports and summary data of spread records for baseball and football.

>> **Sportsbookreview.com** is a great site for comparing near-live odds across multiple betting venues. This site has been critical to my own sports betting successes because they're one of the only free sources I know of that has historical quarter and halftime odds.

>> **DonBest.com** is the eponymous fee-based live odds software that is ubiquitous among professional bettors who use it to line grind and pounce on oddsmaker mistakes. But aside from that, the site houses an extensive set of free historical odds data.

>> **rotogrinders.com** is a multisport resource with field conditions and weather data for baseball and football. You can pay extra to get additional meteorological data points.

Bet Tracking Apps

>> **Actionnetwork.com** has the most popular live odds and bet tracking app these days, but that's likely to change as this book ages. When you start to bet more than a game or two per week, it's nice to have a way to store all your picks in a single place and get alerts (should you choose) when your games hit certain milestones.

>> **Betsperts** is another bet tracker like Action Network, and it has made some inroads with the betting community in America through an aggressive marketing campaign. Its app is more usable than Action Network's, but the community isn't as big. Stay tuned to this brewing battle royal.

NFL and College Football

>> **sportsoddshistory.com** has a valuable historical database of preseason futures odds, including NFL team win totals, odds to make the playoffs, to win the Super Bowl, and so on. If you're looking to bet on NFL futures, check this site out first.

>> **footballoutsiders.com** is an indispensable site if you're in the market to create a power rating for NFL teams. These guys have been looking at football from their own angle for decades, and they've develop a ton of advanced stats that you can incorporate into any analysis you choose.

>> **Pro-football-reference.com** is the *Encyclopedia Britannica* of NFL football, with sortable and searchable team and player data. Unfortunately, the site does not include gambling information among the historical data.

>> **Walterfootball.com** might look a little limited at first, but there's some interesting historical system data that you can peruse for both NFL and college football setups.

NBA Basketball

>> The website **nbastuffer.com** has a good mix of statistics, data visualizations, and discussions on advanced analytics for professional basketball. It's built more for the NBA fan than the NBA bettor, but there's a ton of valuable content here.

>> Basketball has a good reference site too called **basketball-reference.com** that has a panoply of scores and stats for the NBA, up-to-date, accurate, and simply laid out.

NCAA Basketball

» I corresponded with Matt Mark of **mcubed.net,** a site that offers a nice array of current stats and historical data across all major sports, and a few minor ones. (Check out his Bowling data!) I am listing it here because I got great utility out of his NCAA basketball postseason analysis.

» Ken Pomeroy is the original college basketball stat guru, and for a very reasonable fee you can access a vast array of college hoops data, from team stats to player stats. **Kenpom.com** is an easily navigated, one-stop shop for all your needs, with one glaring exception: He does not track betting data.

Major League Baseball

» **baseballhq.com** has an excellent starting pitching predictor.

» **dailybaseballdata.com** has real time weather for all major league baseball parks.

» **baseball-reference.com** is the Major and Minor (and college) League baseball version of pro-football-reference.com. It's a sleek source of every stat you could want to look at, going back the entire history of major league baseball (well, at least until the Wilson administration). Like its NFL cousin, there is no gambling data here.

Best Gambling Podcasts

» R. J. Bell is the founder of pregame.com, and while he's been a sometimes divisive figure in the world of sports betting, his **Dream Preview** podcast during football season is of the highest quality if you're looking to learn how experts and advantage bettors think about games.

» The **Deep Dive** is another regular in my rotation podcast I've found worth listening to for both week-to-week analysis of upcoming games (across all sports) as well as a general attack on general sports betting topics, from the mental game, to handicapping tools, to the business of bookmaking.

» **GambleOn** is a nice, concise regular listen that discusses the latest on state-by-state legalization of sports betting, sports book business results, plus a modicum of sports betting advice.

>> If you're interested in diving into the world of sports analytics, check out the cleverly titled **Covering the Spread** featuring Stanford PhD Ed Feng, whose thought process on sports betting checks all my boxes (which I'm certain he'll be over-the-moon to discover if he reads this).

>> Jeff Ma and rising sports betting personality Rufus Peabody host **Bet the Process,** which is another solid analytics podcast with a heavy focus on football. These guys have a ton of wisdom to share on approaching sports betting as a marketplace where betting value is king.

Best Twitter Follows

Here are a handful of Twitter profiles I follow. They are either sharp, efficient game pickers or have sports betting wisdom to share. And I'll add that a few of them were helpful with this book:

>> @sharpsandman

>> @PooyanGhaziani

>> @NJCappo

>> @locks_igor

>> @NFLTotals

>> @NCdoubleA

>> @InsiderHustle

>> @RJ_Picks

>> @MoneyonTennis

>> @RinseyJones

>> @bartlett157

Appendix B

Online Sports Book Comparison

When it comes to online sports books, remember the words of Robert Plant, "Never let 'em tell you that they're all the same."

Truer words have never been put to a lilting tune. If you're lucky enough to live in Nevada, New Jersey, or any state with more free-wheeling laws that allow for diversity in brick-and-mortar bookmaking establishments, you've got choices when it's time to place your bet. Even then, isn't it easier to place a bet from the convenience of your phone or laptop? What follows is a table listing some of the most popular sports books serving U.S. customers, along with first-hand commentary on how they do in each of several important areas.

The five online bookmakers in the following table are some of the more prominent, but you'll find dozens of them if you look online. Appendix A has my list of free online resources, and that includes several sites that offer more comprehensive information on how bookmakers stack up. A few words of caution: If you're taking online advice on who the best internet bookmaking companies are, make sure you're reading current information, and make sure the site doing the recommending demonstrates relative independence.

If you don't mind me breaking my arm to pat myself on the back, I confess that I considered, then decided against, contacting the marketing teams of various online bookmakers to see if they wanted to create a special affiliate discount or bonus code for readers of this book. For one thing, this book is likely to be on shelves for several years, and it's not clear how well those codes age. For another thing, I need more convincing that sign-up and reload bonuses are actually beneficial to bettors in the long run. And most important, I want my voice to be independent and not compromised by temptation of getting paid .000001 cents for every new customer I refer to this bookmaker or that.

I'd like to hear your experiences with these bookmakers as well. Follow me on Twitter at @swainscheps.

Activity	Bovada	5Dimes	BetOnline	Heritage Sports	Intertops
Moving Money					
Signing Up	No special restrictions or information necessary. Easy two-factor verification.	No special restrictions or information necessary. Requires a phone consultation.	No special restrictions or information necessary.	Sign-up was extremely difficult with credit card. BitCoin recommended.	Sign-up was extremely difficult with credit card. BitCoin recommended.
Methods of deposit	All major credit cards. Bitcoin. Bitcoin deposits are heavily incentivized with bonuses.	VISA, BitCoin, money order.	All major credit cards, BitCoin, money order.	All major credit cards, BitCoin, money order.	All major credit cards, BitCoin, money order.
Methods of withdrawal	Instant withdrawal with BitCoin. Check by courier (usually received within three weeks). Faster check delivery available for a substantial fee.	BitCoin free. Cashier's check, money order, wire available for a fee.	BitCoin free. Cashier's check, money order, wire available for a fee.	BitCoin free. Cashier's check, money order, wire available for a fee.	BitCoin free. Cashier's check, money order, wire available for a fee.
Deposit and withdrawal limits	Minimum deposit starts at $10; minimum withdrawal starts at $100 (BTC, check).	Minimum deposit starts at $25; minimum withdrawal starts at $25 (BTC), $40 (check).	Minimum deposit starts at $20; minimum withdrawal starts at $20 (BTC), $500 (check).	Minimum deposit starts at $17; minimum withdrawal starts at $100 (BTC), $500 (check).	Minimum deposit starts at $20; minimum withdrawal starts at $100 (BTC), $125 (check).
Customer service	24/7 phone support	24/7 phone support	24/7 phone support, online, chat	Business hours phone support only.	24/7 phone and online support
Location restrictions	None	None	NJ restricted	None	None

Activity	Bovada	5Dimes	BetOnline	Heritage Sports	Intertops
Betting and Odds					
Sportsbook	The sportsbook is catered to the casual bettor. Wagering is uncomplicated and easy to understand by beginner bettors. Very good coverage of major and fringe sports. Leagues covered across the world.	5Dimes is a well-regarded sportsbook, with a modern extensive selection of sports and leagues. Reduced juice system makes it a go-to site for professional bettors.	The simple interface lends itself well to a sportsbook geared to the casual bettor. Odds format can be changed with a single mouse click.	Heritage Sports is known for its wide selection of promos, excellent customer service, and reduced juice lines.	One of the earliest online sportsbooks. Caters to a slightly outdated, simple experience. Has a fair amount of line options and lots of bonuses, but live betting is being redesigned.
Casino and racebook	Yes. Wide selection of casino games. Known for good poker play.	Yes. Wide selection of casino games. Live dealers.	Casino was under repair.	Could not log into casino.	Yes. Wide selection of casino games.
Lines, betting options within event, exotics, props	The juice isn't the lowest. Dual lines are used. Lines on popular teams tend to be shaded. Moderate amount of alternate lines, props, and futures. Futures are usually somewhat limited and late to post.	Well known for its variety of exotics. Focused on bettors that know what type of wager they want. Reduced juice, lines as low as –101.	No reduced juice. Exotics limited to parlays and futures.	Reduced juice program is available. –108 odds on NFL/NBA. Largest selection of exotics among sites reviewed.	Stands apart with the widest selection of prop bets.
How early lines are posted	Not early on posting lines. Usually waits till lines are established elsewhere.	Lines are available overnight.	Lines are available overnight.	Lines are available overnight.	Overnight lines mostly available by 10 p.m.
In-game betting	In-game betting is selection is robust but usually clunky. Locked and changing lines can make it difficult to submit a live bet.	Extensive in-game betting with an interface that allows you to search by line.	In-game betting is available.	In-game betting is available.	Live betting site under development.

Activity	Bovada	5Dimes	BetOnline	Heritage Sports	Intertops
Bonus types	Standard bonuses apply. Welcome, loyalty, and refer-a-friend. Bonuses heavily prefer BitCoin.	New account and reload bonuses. A variety of special casino bonuses. Bonuses disable reduced juice.	New account and reload bonuses.	New account, sports cash back, and reduced juice program.	New account, reload, and cash back bonus. Some interesting parlay bonuses.
Betting limits	Most wagers start at $1; moneylines and totals cap at $2,500.	$.50 to $5,000 for major sports.	$1 to $25,000 (NFL)! Most leagues are capped at $5,000.	$2 to $2,000 for major sports.	$1 to maximum changes daily.

Index

Symbols

= (equals), 381
> (greater than), 381
< (less than), 381
<> (not equals), 381

A

absolute pasting, 378
absolute references, 375
accountability, of private bookmakers, 80
ace Rothstein-esque, as a sports bettor
    type, 21
achieving balance, 94–95
action
  baseball, 338–339
  defined, 94
action wager, 339
Actionnetwork.com (website), 410
The Action Network app, 95
addiction, 30–32
advantage bettors, 17
Aikman, Troy, 248–249
air density
  Major League Baseball and, 350–351
  pitching and, 351
Alabama, 26
allocating bets, 116–117
alternate point spreads, 63
altitude
  as an NBA Basketball handicapping
    factor, 303–304
  in SADE, 350

analysis
  fundamental
    benefits of, 168–169
    challenges of, 166–171
    downsides of, 169–171
    home-field advantage, 168
  technical
    about, 187–188
    analytics, 188–189
    angles, 192–193, 194–195, 201–202
    benefits of data-driven analysis,
      195–196
    complexity of, 199–201
    de-randomizing historical data, 191–192
    downsides of, 197–199
    modeling, 189–191
    p-hacking, 199–201
    systems, 192–194, 201–202
    trend-spotting tools, 202–205
analytics, 188–189
AND function, 381
Ang, Richard (author)
  Betting on Horse Racing For Dummies, 67
angles
  betting, 192–193, 194–195, 201–202
  college basketball, 325–327
  Major League Baseball, 354–358
  NBA Basketball, 304–308
  NFL Football, 250–252
apps
  bet tracking, 410–411
  casino, 79

West Virginia, 27

WHIP, 346

win probability, 89

wind

  Major League Baseball, 349–350

  NFL Football and, 250

win-loss record/percentage

  about, 139

  baseball and, 335–336

  as a measure of success, 126

winning, st sports betting, 12–14

winnowing your system, 274

wins, discounting, 387–388

The Wire Act (1961), 24

Wong, Stanford (author)

  Sharp Sports Betting, 262

Wyoming, 27

Z

Zalinsky, Taylor, 160

zero point spread, 54

Zimmerman, Andy, 160

Z-test, 160

About the Author

Swain Scheps lives in Oregon with his wife Nancy, twins Otto and Libby, and a misanthropic dog named Pootie. His professional life has been dominated by technology, with positions at several Fortune 500 companies leading application development teams along with various management roles in data & analytics supporting advanced reporting, data warehousing, data visualization, artificial intelligence, and machine learning solutions.

That technology work has dovetailed perfectly with his three decades of sports betting activities. That side of his life began in college, where he was a clueless bettor at the University of Texas. He quickly realized the value of collecting mountains of historical data and built a custom NFL database and game simulator from scratch using a programming language too outdated and embarrassing to name here. In the pre-internet era of the early 1990s, where information was at a premium, he and two friends started a company to sell historical betting data and systems to gamblers and, well, anyone who would buy them.

The company didn't make it, but the sports betting candle never flickered. He wrote on sports betting topics, lobbied Congress to loosen restrictions on internet betting, developed more sports betting-related applications and databases, and built a network of contacts in the industry. In 2008, he published a book connected to his daytime profession, *Business Intelligence For Dummies.* That book marked the beginning of a decade-long drive to convince the publisher that sports betting was a topic that deserved its own *For Dummies* book! With an assist from the Supreme Court in 2018, that effort finally paid off with the book you are now holding in your hands. Please follow Swain on Twitter at @swainscheps.

Dedication

To Otto Lange Scheps and Elizabeth Mary Scheps.

Acknowledgments

I got a ton of direct help with this book, starting with my research assistant Genna Hughes who wisely ran away to New Mexico for love. I blame/credit my friend and colleague Cale Garrett for reigniting my long simmering interest in sports betting several years ago, and I thank him for his diligent work on this book reviewing online bookmakers. I was lucky enough to stumble across erstwhile bartender/writer Sean Sweeney, who did great work compiling and composing the bulk of the "The Sports Bettors' Essential Excel Toolkit" and "You versus You" chapters with precious little input from the author. Sean, if you're reading this and I still owe you money, you know where to find me.

I must thank many people who were generous with their time, energy, and/or resources. My wife and kids patiently let me remove myself to the basement for much of the fall of 2019 and put up with my stress eating and injured digits. In terms of people I'm *not* related to, number one on the "thank you" list is the legendary Tony Miller of The Golden Nugget sports book in Las Vegas, who didn't hesitate when I asked him for a few minutes of time to discuss my upcoming book project. If only more people were like Tony, the world would be a better place. Second on the list is the equally legendary Norm Hitzges of Dallas/Fort Worth radio fame, who took the time to write the foreword without batting an eye or demanding my bona fides. I also appreciated the correspondence with various friends of friends, including Thad Haines via his sister Kristen. Speaking of Night Ranger, I had a ton of help from Twitter friends, including the great @sharpsandman, who made himself and his professional perspective available to me; the inimitable @locks_igor wrote the hockey chapter that never was but was a regular source of encouragement. Andy Molitor provided general advice, insight, and inspiration, as did @rinseyjones, @bartlett157, @betonjimmy, @RJPicks, and @NFL_Totals. @findersecond gave some great tips on identifying Twitter scammers. Finally, although I never was able to track him down, I owe a debt of gratitude to Joe Meyer and the creators and contributors to SDQL. So much of the research for this book was backed up with SDQL that it terrifies me to think where I'd be without it.

The only thing worse than writing a book must be waiting on an author to write a book, and for that I tip the cap to Lindsay Lefevere at Wiley, and my editor Tim Gallan, who refrained from issuing a missing persons report while waiting on chapters from me. As always, Matt Wagner at Freshbooks was a patient go-between. Finally, I must thank authors Kevin Blackwood and Alan Simon, who each gave me a chance many years ago, and the late Marion "Turk" Turner, whom I met on the plane returning from my honeymoon. Mr. Turner and the story of his ship, the USS *Perch* (SS-176), inspired me to start writing professionally — somewhere over Nevada appropriately enough — back in September of 2003.

Publisher's Acknowledgments

Executive Editor: Lindsay Sandman Lefevere

Project Editor: Tim Gallan

Proofreader: Debbye Butler

Production Editor: Siddique Shaik

Cover Image: © Brian P Gielczyk/Shutterstock

Leverage the power

Dummies is the global leader in the reference category and one of the most trusted and highly regarded brands in the world. No longer just focused on books, customers now have access to the dummies content they need in the format they want. Together we'll craft a solution that engages your customers, stands out from the competition, and helps you meet your goals.

Advertising & Sponsorships

Connect with an engaged audience on a powerful multimedia site, and position your message alongside expert how-to content. Dummies.com is a one-stop shop for free, online information and know-how curated by a team of experts.

- Targeted ads
- Video
- Email Marketing
- Microsites
- Sweepstakes sponsorship

20 **MILLION**
PAGE VIEWS
EVERY SINGLE MONTH

15
MILLION
UNIQUE
VISITORS PER MONTH

43%
OF ALL VISITORS
ACCESS THE SITE
VIA THEIR MOBILE DEVICES

700,000 NEWSLETTER
SUBSCRIPTION
TO THE INBOXES OF
300,000 UNIQUE INDIVIDUALS
EVERY WEEK

PERSONAL ENRICHMENT

Staying Sharp

9781119187790
USA $26.00
CAN $31.99
UK £19.99

Facebook

9781119179030
USA $21.99
CAN $25.99
UK £16.99

Guitar

9781119293354
USA $24.99
CAN $29.99
UK £17.99

Investing

9781119293347
USA $22.99
CAN $27.99
UK £16.99

Beekeeping

9781119310068
USA $22.99
CAN $27.99
UK £16.99

Digital Photography

9781119235606
USA $24.99
CAN $29.99
UK £17.99

Meditation

9781119251163
USA $24.99
CAN $29.99
UK £17.99

Pregnancy

9781119235491
USA $26.99
CAN $31.99
UK £19.99

Samsung Galaxy S7

9781119279952
USA $24.99
CAN $29.99
UK £17.99

iPhone

9781119283133
USA $24.99
CAN $29.99
UK £17.99

Crocheting

9781119287117
USA $24.99
CAN $29.99
UK £16.99

Nutrition

9781119130246
USA $22.99
CAN $27.99
UK £16.99

PROFESSIONAL DEVELOPMENT

Windows 10

9781119311041
USA $24.99
CAN $29.99
UK £17.99

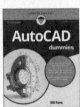

AutoCAD

9781119255796
USA $39.99
CAN $47.99
UK £27.99

Excel 2016

9781119293439
USA $26.99
CAN $31.99
UK £19.99

QuickBooks 2017

9781119281467
USA $26.99
CAN $31.99
UK £19.99

macOS Sierra

9781119280651
USA $29.99
CAN $35.99
UK £21.99

LinkedIn

9781119251132
USA $24.99
CAN $29.99
UK £17.99

Windows 10

9781119310563
USA $34.00
CAN $41.99
UK £24.99

SharePoint 2016

9781119181705
USA $29.99
CAN $35.99
UK £21.99

Fundamental Analysis

9781119263593
USA $26.99
CAN $31.99
UK £19.99

Networking

9781119257769
USA $29.99
CAN $35.99
UK £21.99

Office 2016

9781119293477
USA $26.99
CAN $31.99
UK £19.99

Office 365

9781119265313
USA $24.99
CAN $29.99
UK £17.99

Salesforce.com

9781119239314
USA $29.99
CAN $35.99
UK £21.99

Coding

9781119293323
USA $29.99
CAN $35.99
UK £21.99

dummies.com

dummies®
A Wiley Brand

Learning Made Easy

ACADEMIC

9781119293576
USA $19.99
CAN $23.99
UK £15.99

9781119293637
USA $19.99
CAN $23.99
UK £15.99

9781119293491
USA $19.99
CAN $23.99
UK £15.99

9781119293460
USA $19.99
CAN $23.99
UK £15.99

9781119293590
USA $19.99
CAN $23.99
UK £15.99

9781119215844
USA $26.99
CAN $31.99
UK £19.99

9781119293378
USA $22.99
CAN $27.99
UK £16.99

9781119293521
USA $19.99
CAN $23.99
UK £15.99

9781119239178
USA $18.99
CAN $22.99
UK £14.99

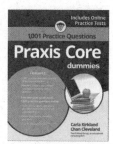

9781119263883
USA $26.99
CAN $31.99
UK £19.99

Available Everywhere Books Are Sold

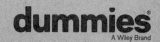

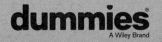